One of these is the author…

A LOVER
A FIGHTER
AND
A TUGBOAT RIDER

Steven Carl Stanga

ISBN: 978-1-57579-413-6

Library of Congress Control Number: 2009935114

For additional copies contact:
Steven Stanga
22061 471st St.
Brookings, SD 57006
agnats@itctel.com

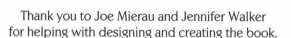

Thank you to Joe Mierau and Jennifer Walker
for helping with designing and creating the book.

Printed in the United States of America

PINE HILL PRESS
4000 West 57th Street
Sioux Falls, SD 57106

Good luck with the book, Steve!
If you actually get it finished, you will be defying the
Stanga tradition of NEVER finishing anything.

~ *Julianne Elaine Kolbeck*

ANCHORS AWEIGH, MATEY!

~ Steve Stanga

CONTENTS

FOREWORD

Unable to locate even a single one of my former shipmates and partners in crime who are mentioned in these pages – let alone all of them – and thereby seek written permission to use their real names, I have very grudgingly elected to use aliases for all the characters in this book. So while the names have been changed to minimize any potential charges of libel and slander, dear reader, please keep in mind that they do represent real people, and that this is a work of non-fiction in all other regards.

After graduation from high school, my days and nights were spent slaving over a hot grill at the Town House café, and holed up in my small apartment which I enjoyed for a dollar a day. I didn't know what I wanted to do with my life. I was becoming increasingly bored with living day to day in South Dakota. The winter of 1966, with its never-ending back-to-back March blizzards, was next to unbearable for a lad with chronic *wanderlust.*

I was restless and had sand in my shoes, without even knowing what that meant. More than anything else, I wanted to travel and see the world, and knew that the military was one mechanism for accomplishing this. But I was torn between the Navy and the Army. In the end I felt that I would much rather ride than walk, so I joined the Navy. Besides, I had this thing for bell-bottom pants.

The technicalities seemed to take forever. Half a dozen of my former classmates from high school had a mind to join the Navy, too. Over the ensuing months we made several trips together from Mitchell to the induction center in Sioux Falls for testing and paperwork purposes, where we encountered hundreds of other eager young South Dakotans, both men and women, who were just entering the Navy as well.

I had a pilonidal cyst on the end of my tailbone which was doing its best to keep me out of the Navy. Why such a minor thing should be allowed to prevent me from serving my country was totally beyond me. I flunked four physical exams because of it.

But I kept coming back. Finally, on the fifth try, I had a new doctor examine me, and my cyst was overlooked. I kept my mouth shut and I was accepted as fit for military service at long last. I said goodbye to the girl next door and packed a light duffle bag. They shipped me out of South Dakota during the first week of October in 1967, right after my nineteenth birthday. What follows is the true account of those four strange years in the US Navy.

I.
BOOT CAMP

9 OCTOBER 1967 — 19 DECEMBER 1967

ARRIVAL

The whine of the engines decreased a degree in pitch, and the huge plane dropped even lower over the city. We had been flying over Los Angeles for the past fifteen minutes. It was impossible. No city on earth was that big. To a young man from a small town in South Dakota, my first jet flight was an incredible experience in itself. But to fly – in a powerful commercial jet of all things – over a town full of people for a quarter of an hour was almost unreal. The immensity of it!

And the multicolored city lights still stretched ahead as far as the eye could see, with no indication of them ever coming to an end. They were laid out in twinkling lines as straight and neat as a survey map. The houses were matchboxes, the cars and trucks were in one-sixteenth scale, the trees were perfect Japanese bonsai miniatures. And yes, the people below really did look like ants.

Finally, we approached the lights of the runway, and seconds later the wheels squealed their protest on the tarmac. We lurched forward in our seats as the engines suddenly reversed their thrust, and we went dashing towards the airport terminal.

The world was back in proper perspective by then. We taxied for what seemed an interminable length of time before the plane stopped and the "please fasten your seatbelt" sign went off. My ears still ached a little from the rapid descent, but that was largely ignored in the excitement of the moment.

We deplaned, each secretly grateful, I think, to be safely back on terra firma. We had been issued train tickets for the remainder of the trip, and it was all arranged for someone to transport our small group of recruits across town to the train depot, which they did as soon as we rounded up our luggage.

Fresh from the prairies of Dakota Territory, I was in culture shock at the frantic bedlam of southern California. This was certainly going to be some sort of adventure, I realized soberly.

The railway route to the south roughly paralleled the coast, and in the back of my mind I guess I was vaguely aware what important geographic feature of the earth lay directly west of me. But the area was so built up with uninterrupted civilization that I soon quite forgot about it. Eventually, the rails swung even closer to the coast, and it was inevitable that there would soon be a break in the landscape.

Gazing from my train window in a daze of jet lag and input overload, I barely noticed the trees begin to thin and then disappear altogether. The steady racketing of the rails was as good as a sleeping pill. But suddenly I was jolted into alertness. I found myself looking at something alien, something that stretched unbroken from the middle distance clear to the horizon, something that was not registering in my brain as logical. By god, nothing could be that immense! Why, it ran on forever! It took a few moments for it to dawn on me that I was seeing the awesome Pacific Ocean for the first time.

Still, it was disturbing that it looked somewhat familiar to me, although there was no good reason why it should have. True, I had been born in Long Beach and lived there until I was a one-year-old, and I suppose that it is conceivable my parents took me down to the beach a few times in those early months, but I had no conscious memory of those carefree times. None at all.

It's funny how dearly I would come to love that western ocean in all its many moods. Ironic, then, that after my Navy days had elapsed I should return voluntarily to live in the middle of the country, as far from salt water and tides as a person could possibly get. An example of poor planning at its finest.

It wasn't long before we pulled into the San Diego train station. A uniformed official of some sort told several of us from the train to report to Waiting Area B. There we met a larger group of guys, all just as lost and confused as the rest of us. Then we waited.

It was only the first of many long and obviously senseless waiting periods that we would endure in the next four years. Some guys slept in those spine-deforming plastic waiting-room chairs, some read paperbacks, some morosely clutched Styrofoam cups of acidic vending-machine coffee and chain-smoked… all seemed bored stiff. Many of us had been traveling most of the day already and were beside ourselves with fatigue, so the whole experience was seeming somewhat surreal.

Shortly after midnight, a drab gray bus pulled up outside the waiting area windows in front of us. It had two crossed anchors painted on it, above which was stenciled "US Navy." A ripple of anticipation flowed through Waiting Area B, and men began to stir. My breathing rate increased. This was what I had been waiting for...so many months.

A smartly-dressed and powerful Marine stepped off the bus and entered the waiting area. His hat was screwed down low over his eyes, and his mouth was set in a grim line behind a jaw chiseled straight from cold granite. The creases in his khaki shirt were knife-sharp, and he carried four rows of service ribbons over his heart. On his left sleeve were three inverted chevrons. The long expanse of un-wrinkled blue trouser, slashed by a blood-red stripe on the side, stretched down to black dress shoes so brilliantly spit-shined that you could see yourself in them. He looked like a recruiting poster for the US Marine Corps.

With the sound of a storm trooper hollering over a bullhorn, the Marine in-stantly commanded the attention of everyone within a four-block radius. Even the civilians in the airport concourse paused in mid-step to see what the hullabaloo was all about.

"Alright you turkeys, listen up! In just ten seconds I want you all outside on the sidewalk facing the bus! You will stand at attention in four rows! Not three! Not five! Four rows! Your gear will be at your feet directly in front of you! Your orders will be held in your left hand! I assume most of you turkeys know which is your left hand by now? There will be no talking! NOW, you turkeys, on the double! Move it! Move it! Move it!"

Those last three staccato commands were as effective as an electric cattle prod. I didn't know so many sleepy men could move so fast. We were quickly out-side in some sort of ragged formation, more or less as the sergeant had ordered. One guy in the front row was making a subtle remark to his closest buddy about the dubious lineage of the Marine when a well-aimed kick in the ass broke his chain of thought.

"I said 'no talking', you turkey!"

Already the transformation had begun. By some strange, atavistic quirk of na-ture, we had been changed from happy young men into moronic turkeys. It was to be the same throughout the next 48 months.

We were to be constantly reminded of our less-than-human status. We were not men. On the contrary, we were anything but men. We were turkeys, we were squirrels, we were mama's babies. And we were never to be so crass as to think otherwise.

Row by row, we were herded onto the bus like cattle doomed to the slaughterhouse. No one dared to break the stony silence again. The bus engine suddenly revved and we went careening through the cool California night air to god knows where.

What exactly was happening here? The Navy recruiter back home never said anything about all of this. The way he told it, it was all sunny beaches in foreign ports. Maybe the Marine took charge of the wrong group of men? We probably all look alike in civvies. Yeah, that must be it. But it was clearly a Navy bus. What had I gotten myself into? I was to ask myself that same desperate question repeatedly during the following 1,460 days. And the answer was always the same: there was no answer.

It was thus that I arrived at Navy boot camp on October 9, 1967.

Steve Stanga B617389
SR, Company 581
RTC, USNTC
San Diego, California
92133

October 12, 1967

Dear Family,

We have been given a half hour to write home. It's the longest rest period we've gotten since we arrived. Very warm here. You should see our Heinie haircuts! It only took them about ninety seconds to cut each guy's hair. The barber sheared my head so fast that he clipped off a mole on my scalp – then you should have seen the blood run down my neck! Thought we were going to have to call a corpsman.

Reveille is at 0430 (4:30 AM). The BOOD comes into the room while we're still sleeping, flicks on all the lights at once, kicks a metal garbage can down the full length of the barracks – all the while yelling obscenities at us. Can you imagine what it's like to wake up like this every morning?

We eat breakfast clear across the camp just thirty minutes later. I don't think I'll ever forget standing in formation in the dark out on the foggy parade grounds, half asleep, smelling the cold sea air, waiting for our turn to eat inside the warm galley.

The first two days of boot camp were spent getting us supplied and breaking our spirits, I think. We're called every name in the book, and when we aren't marching we're standing at attention hard as a rock and straight as an arrow. But our company commander is a pleasant man named B. Bollinger, a Machinist's Mate Chief. He has a good sense of humor and is not at all like the drill sergeants that you see in the movies.

Dinner is at 1300 (1:00 PM) and supper is at 1600 (4:00 PM), only three hours later. We're kept away from the water fountains and I guess we're getting used to it. Anyway, it really cuts down on the trips to the head! We can hit the sack at 2100 (9:00 PM) – if we're good. We shower and shave at night, and then take turns switching off every two hours all night long for security watch.

Practically all of our civilian stuff was confiscated right away, and that which wasn't, and couldn't be sent home, had to be "donated." We lost a lot of valuable stuff this way – like mouthwash, after-shave lotion, and all our girlie pictures in our wallets. Phooey.

There are eight Filipinos, three Negroes, and one Mexican in our company of sixty men. We have all gotten physicals, X rays, skin tests, eye tests…and blisters. But I am having fun, believe it or not! And fun is the best thing to have.

Time is up. We've got to go march around some more. I'll write again when we get another break. Love your son.

October 13, 1967 — 2045

Dear Family,

The days really fly by when everything you do is different each day. Our feet have passed the point of numbness now, so we are shaping up at last. We would much rather march than just stand at attention with our knees locked, and parade rest is even worse on the feet.

Surprisingly, the chow is pretty good, considering that it doesn't seem to be seasoned at all. Rumor has it that they put saltpeter in it. How do you tell? I've noticed that we haven't had the same food twice yet either. Quite the variety.

Some of the guys who disliked the Navy right off the bat on the first day have eventually changed their minds, while the others only get more ticked off with each passing day. A few guys absolutely hate boot camp. Correct me if I'm wrong, but didn't these guys *volunteer* for the Navy? We're well aware that a WAVE training center is on the other side of our base, just overflowing with girls, and the adjoining US Marine Corps Recruit Depot is immediately northeast of us – chock-full of jarheads.

I caught a glimpse of the ocean and a large ship in the distance this afternoon when the fog lifted. You can see tall skyscrapers southward in the haze, which is downtown San Diego. Big jets fly overhead all day but not at night, thank goodness.

For the time being you'll have to be satisfied with these short notes, as we are so very rushed. Oh yeah – I'm supposed to tell you that if there is ever an emergency at home, you are to contact the Red Cross if I am needed right away, and they'll know how to reach me wherever I am. Okay bye.

Taps now.

October 14, 1967 – 1910

Dear Family,

We finally figured out that the quicker we shaped up and got in step, the less we would get yelled at, and the more time we'd have for smoke breaks and grab assin'. For good conduct, we got a radio in the barracks and we really appreciate it. It is our only link to the outside world.

Each evening we scrub up all of our own clothes on a big cement table outdoors with stiff bristle brushes and undiluted Whisk detergent. Then we hang them up to dry until the following evening. We are given no clothespins, no, that would be too easy. All clothes are hung on the clothesline spaced exactly three fingers apart, tied with little bits of string in nothing but uniform square knots. The fly of our skivvie shorts must face north towards the Marine base to conform with the camp slogan: "Piss on the Marines." By way of returning the favor, the recruits over in the Marine boot camp hang up their skivvies with the ass end towards us, y'know, as in "Shit on the Navy." This is called cooperation. A stranger would never guess that the Marine Corp was a vital department of the Navy.

We have a regular Gomer Pyle in our company who is constantly out of step with the rest of us, like he was just strolling around his house or something. If the company commander yells, "Right turn!" this poor sap will inevitably turn left and collide with half a dozen other guys and make a shambles out of the whole formation. He is a very small Jewish boy named Federman, quite likeable actually, but certain guys in the company seem to find great delight in making his life a living hell. However, I do not take pleasure in the misery of others, and try to be his friend, and tutor him when he needs it.

At R&O there is a sign above the door which reads, "Welcome aboard, you are now men of the United States Navy, the tradition of the service demands your utmost effort, give it cheerfully and willingly." But us guys can read between the lines; already we know the sign actually reads, "Abandon all hope ye who enter here!"

Chow today was the best ever! We get steak and ice cream every other day. A sign in the mess hall urges us to "Take all you want but eat all you take." I could sure use a good old-fashioned Pepsi-Cola right now, though. All we get to drink is milk and watered-down bug juice (Kool-Aid).

The Filipinos in our company are really a bunch of cards, but they sure can march great – they've had military training back home since high school. It is through some kind of special arrangement with our government that they are able to serve in our Navy instead of their own military services. My mate in the bunk below me is a shy, twenty-year-old Filipino named Virgil Manibusan, and we get along just fine. The oldest man in the whole company is a thirty-year-old Filipino; that is really old compared to the rest of us kids! Nearby sleeps another Filipino, Giorgio Dalogdog (which means "thunder" in Filipino), who coincidentally snores so terrible that he keeps many of us awake half the night. What's a fella to do?

It seems like most of the men in the company have a southern drawl (that is, "y'all," for example). Here is a breakdown of the men in Recruit Company 581:

Missouri	11
Texas	10
Kansas	9
Philippines	8
South Dakota	4
Nebraska	4
Georgia	4
Wisconsin	3
North Carolina	1
Oregon	1
Iowa	1
California	1
Tennessee	1
Oklahoma	1
Virginia	1
Total	60 men

Right now we are trying to memorize our Eleven General Orders and learn our chain-of-command officers here on the base. That's a real pain in the butt. But I'm still having fun yet, and am getting sort of tan in the bargain!

It has long been the custom in boot camp to designate the littlest guy in the company as the guidon bearer. That is to say, he would get to carry the company flag bearing our unit number, 581. Furthermore, he would march in the single most important position of the formation – the extreme right forward spot – from which every rank and file of the entire company would dress and align itself smartly as we did infantry drill or marched from place to place. It was a huge responsibility and honor.

There wasn't any scarcity of short guys in our company. Most of us hailed from the Midwest, and it seemed to be filled to overflowing with pocket-sized men, myself included. One of the more compact guys was our Jewish recruit, Federman. But as he already held the undisputed position of company "Gomer," the honor of guidon bearer naturally fell to our tiniest Filipino, Balubal Savid.

Balubal, or "Bali" as we called him because his real name sounded like somebody was choking to death, was a good-natured little Filipino, always ready with a humorous observation on any situation. He said his name meant "cashew" in Tagalog, and that seemed to suit him right down to the ground. He didn't have a chip on his shoulder, like so many sawed-off guys seem to have. On the contrary, he was a good egg.

At some point during every recruit's stretch of boot camp, they have to spend a few days over at the base swimming pool for swim instruction. It was a curious thing to observe the inability to swim of most sailors. And taken as a race, I particularly found it odd that all of the Filipinos didn't know how to swim either. Here was a nation of islanders, completely surrounded by ocean on all sides, and yet it was a rare Filipino who could actually brag he could swim.

I was not impressed with the quality of swim instruction that we received from the Navy. But this was probably due to the constraints of time and so many men to push through boot camp. The only requirement needed to pass the swim class was to be able to swim a complete circuit of the large indoor pool without once resting or hanging onto the edge. I could do this easily, as I had several strokes I knew to propel me eventually from point A to point B. But would these same pathetic self-improvised strokes save me at sea? Not likely.

There were lifeguards standing all around the perimeter of the pool, holding long sticks which they could reach to any man in the pool should he get into difficulty. But they were very clear when they instructed us about the sticks.

"Just grab hold of the stick if it approaches you, and hold on while the lifeguard pulls you to the edge. Do not attempt to climb the stick like a monkey, as the lifeguards will then *give* you the stick!"

But people never listened. Time after time, I saw a man get into trouble in deep water and start to panic; the lifeguard would extend the stick to the man – who would then immediately try to scramble up the length of the stick to safety and practically jerk the lifeguard over the edge in the process; the lifeguard would simply release the stick at this point and the man would sink back to the bottom of the pool with a puzzled look on his face; then they had to offer him another stick. You swallow enough chlorinated water and you eventually learn to follow directions.

While they had us a captive audience at the pool, they also gave us our aban-don ship class. We learned the proper way to enter the water from a sinking ship, and what to do if burning oil was present on the water's surface, etc. I thought it was extremely cool that we could take off our white duck trousers, tie knots in the bottom of the legs (all while treading water), whip them over our heads to fill the pantaloons with air – and the navy trousers made a perfectly good life preserver! They were more than buoyant enough to support a man in the water. The air would be held inside the wet trousers for a long time! And if the air leaked out somewhat, all that was needed was to swing them through the air again to fill them up. It was pretty darn neat.

November 4, 1967

Dear Family,

I'd write more if I had the time, but we're really kept on the ball here. We had our 3-1 Infantry Evaluation today, and our company got second place! We also got another haircut today, as it was getting totally out of hand: almost one-fourth-inch long! Mercy sakes.

Tomorrow we have more Abandon Ship Drilling, which I am looking forward to. They have a landlocked scale-model of a destroyer escort (the *USS Recruit,* TDE-1) built right on the base, which has been train-ing Navy recruits here at San Diego NTC for nigh onto 19 years.

It's starting to cool down to 70 degrees Fahrenheit dur-

The TDE-1 landlocked training ship at bootcamp.

ing the day now, so it is just right for being outside. Nobody has tried to go AWOL from our company yet, although several have gone over the fence from other companies. That's a biiiig mistake.

Oddly enough, I found that I love to march in formation! I would have done well in the Army. Marching is a very comfortable stride for covering long distances and going through our paces out on the grinder. I march on the far left side of the company, so everybody in my rank follows my lead and keeps in step with me. I keep in step with the guy directly in front of me. That would be a fella from Kansas name of Bob Alma. Seen from the rear he has a perfectly girlish figure, and I was shocked on many occasions to find myself watching his swinging hips with interest as we marched! That's what boot camp will do to a guy, ha ha!

We were taught a cute little jodie to sing as we marched along, which is sung to the tune of "The Twelve Days of Christmas":

> "On the first day of training, the Navy gave to me:
> 12 hours leave
> 11 general órders
> 10 minutes to eat
> 9 physical drills
> 8 little hankies
> 7 heavy drumbeats
> 6 pair of stockings
> 5 golden demerits
> 4 white hats
> 3 skivvie shorts
> 2 boondockers
> and an adjutant that wasn't worth a shit — *Sir!*"

I think boot camp is A-okay…even a bit fun at times. But I am in the minority to be sure. I'm starting to get a lot of mail from home now, and somebody always gets a package of goodies that he has to share with the whole company. So that helps. Write soon.

One of the more universally hated guys we had to deal with in boot camp was our adjutant, a sort of auxiliary helper to our company commander. He was a little rat bastard Hawaiian punk, name of Kane. I don't know if that was his first name or his last name, or a close relative to the original Adam. But we all agreed that we would like to catch him outside the front gate when this was all over with, and show him our gratitude.

He threw his weight around, all 110 pounds of it, like he was bantam king of the hill, and was a continuous thorn in our sides, harassing us without end about mickey mouse crap. One day during inspection out on the grinder, he didn't like the looks of my shined shoes. So he mashed his own size eights down on top of my foot, grinding back and forth with gusto right on my toe, and completely ruined any possibility of putting a decent shine on my shoes ever again. I had to purchase a new pair of shoes out of my own pocket, rather than fail inspections indefinitely from then on.

At first we thought he was a petty officer or something, so we would kow-tow to him all the time. But we eventually learned that he was nothing more than a fresh graduate of boot camp himself who was held back to help process a few new recruit companies. In other words, he outranked us about as much as a sol-dier ant outranks a worker ant. When we discovered this, we fumed at all of his past injustices, and he pretty much lost all effectiveness with us. One day he just didn't show up again, and we never did learn where he was transferred to. Good riddance. Boot camp life was much more pleasant after that.

November 8, 1967

Dear Family,

Seems like this month is going by even faster than last month, if that's possi-ble. It's 1915 right now, and we are going to hold our field day here in the barracks at 2000. We hold this every evening; it's a general cleaning period done usually before the next day's inspection.

I had a two-hour clothesline watch this morning from 0200 to 0400. Talk about catching your death of boredom! Guarding the clothesline in the middle of the night! Then to bed for a half hour – then rise and shine, swabbie! Luckily, tonight I have an "all night in" and will get to sleep straight through until morning.

Well, we started working in the galley today, and for eleven days we're going to have long, tough hours there. I have been assigned to the scullery department in the mess hall. Every company has to take their turn at KP while in boot camp.

Right now we are in Battalion Alpha. Matter of fact, we captured the battalion flag this week for superior marching. We should go over the bridge to Advanced Training on Monday to our new battalion: India.

Here's an amusing anecdote for you folks at home: One night I was shining my shoes just before taps, like we usually do, when a strange officer popped into the barracks. Somebody yelled, "Attention on deck!" and we all snapped to attention where we were standing. I was hoping I would remain invisible as he stalked up and down the long room, but he stopped to talk to me briefly anyway. Curse the luck! He stood there staring at my shirt pocket, which I began to suspect was probably unbuttoned. Sure enough, it was.

"How are our pockets supposed to be, recruit?" he growled.

"Buttoned, sir," I said, fearing execution in the morning.

"Don't you want that button anymore, boy?" he asked ominously.

"Oh yes, sir!" I assured him.

"Here you go then," he said, as he deftly pulled the button off my shirt and handed it to me. "Put it in your mouth."

I did as he directed. (I could tell the guys were enjoying this little scenario most tremendously.)

"What's your tenth General Order?" he snapped.

"'To salute all officers, and all colors and standards not cased', sir!" I repeated from memory, trying not to swallow the button.

"What's your seventh General Order?" he grilled me.

"'To talk to no one except in the line of duty', sir!" I rattled off automatically.

"What's your eleventh General Order?" he tried again to stump me.

"'To be especially watchful at night, and, during the time for challenging, to challenge all persons on or near my post, and to allow no one to pass without proper authority', SIR!" I said without hesitation.

"What's your name, son?" he asked in a more personable tone.

"Seaman Recruit Stanga, sir!"

"Carry on, Stanga," he said as he turned to leave, and then added, "You'd better get that pocket fixed."

"Yes, sir!" I barked. Throughout the next couple of days, the guys re-enacted this encounter for the amusement of those who had not been there. *sigh*

The next day Chief Bollinger came around and told me that some Lieutenant JG from headquarters wanted me to be the mailman for our company, because it had seemed to him that I was particularly squared away.

So that's how I became the mailman for Company 581. Being the mailman is rough work, though; that canvas sack full of letters and newspapers and packages gets to be over seventy pounds sometimes. I have to go clear across base to pick it up, then hump it back to the barracks. But the mail is very important to the men. Yesterday I, myself, got a mysterious letter with no return address on it. Upon opening it I read,

"Stanga, Go get the mail you asshole!

– The mail hogs of 581"

When I looked up from reading the letter, they were all laughing. What a bunch of jokers.

We have our biggest academic test tomorrow afternoon, so I suppose I'd better wrap this up and study a little more for it now. I try to write as often as I can and that's not very often, I know. But bear with me.

November 9, 1967

You remember the sign that the Navy recruiter had in his window, the one that enticed you to go in and sign up in the first place? You know, the one picturing a muscular sailor loading a torpedo that boasted, "Join the Navy and choose your own career!" That's pretty much a farce; they put you where they need you. Period. They can't allow everyone to pick whatever fancies him. Otherwise, the Navy would soon be overrun with scuba divers and Photographer's Mates and lookouts.

Halfway through basic training they take you over to Career Counseling and ask you what you want to be when you grow up. You get six choices of how you want to spend your four years of naval service. After they have informed you that all your preferred ratings are either full, or recently discontinued, or not applicable in your particular case, they continue with their next round of brainwashing.

"Did you have any electricity in high school?" the interviewer asks. (My transcripts are before him on the desk.)

"Yes, sir," I reply. "One year."

"And do you enjoy taking things apart, such as telephones and clocks and such?" he asks mechanically.

"Uh…yes," I answer cautiously, not knowing where the conversation is heading.

"Good," he says, as he writes in permanent ink on my records. "You're an Electrician's Mate."

And therein lies the truth of the Navy's placement of men.

Then there is always the "deadly shipmate" to deal with, a sailor's worse fear at sea: fire. When the time arrived for our fire-fighting class, they bused our entire company out to a piece of waste ground on the extreme edge of the training base, downwind from town. We sat through quite a spell of lectures before they actually lit the oil fires and filled the sky with nauseous black smoke.

Once we demonstrated that we could put out large open tanks of burning oil, they started another smoky fire inside a concrete training structure, and then sent us inside with hoses in small teams. The heat was intense, and I acquired a new respect for firemen. What a mess we made with water hoses and fire-extinguishers and mechanical foam! Some of us even had to toss away our oil-drenched dungarees afterwards and draw new ones from stores.

The day we were scheduled to go into the gas chamber was, how do you say, quite "interesting." As usual, we were given the lecture portion of the class first, and the proper use of the Mark V gas mask was demonstrated repeatedly by our able trainers. Finally, we were prepared to their satisfaction, and they had us don the masks and enter the gas chamber itself.

There was a gauzy haze of thin gas inside the room. And if you had put your gas mask on properly, your only sensation was a slight acrid smell and a faintly bitter taste in the back of your throat, and a cocky attitude that you did it right. We knew what was coming next, however, because they had told us beforehand: they had us remove our masks so we could see exactly what the full effect of the tear gas was like in reality.

Some guys started coughing and gagging immediately, while the remainder of us stood there quietly, wondering why the dumbasses weren't holding their breaths like the rest of us were. But the instructors were wise to this trick years ago, so they had us all start singing "Old MacDonald."

You can't hold your breath and sing at the same time, and soon we were all in distress, coughing and spitting up, our eyes streaming, bent over double and cursing, not being able to draw a decent breath whatsoever into our lungs. The gas was completely demobilizing; I had no idea! As they opened the exit and finally allowed us to escape the gas chamber one by one into the wonderful fresh air, a navy photographer was waiting just outside the door to happily snap each of our pictures for the boot camp yearbook. Smile pretty now!

Because of my familiarity with the guys, thanks to my postman job, I quickly made good friends with a lot of the boys. But my best friend during boot camp was without a doubt a black guy from Macon, Georgia, named Albert. He never wearied of hearing us cry out, "Hey, hey, Albert!" in our best Bill Cosby imitation. It was my very first experience dealing with a black, and I was his very first experience relating to somebody from South Dakota. I'm not sure what he saw in me, but I found the quiet, well-mannered southern guy absolutely hilarious. "So do you still have wooden sidewalks in South Dakota?" he asked. And laughter is the best medicine in a situation like boot camp.

November 10, 1967

Dear Gramma,

Yes, it's been one long and exciting month since I got into the Navy. Our first paychecks showed up yesterday – thirty-five dollars – which included a savings bond deduction. We had to pay twenty-five dollars for our Navy exchange coupon books, which we use to buy stuff at the base exchange. So that left me with a whopping ten dollars to blow! They don't sell candy or other junk food at the store; we get quite enough of that in the mail. (I delivered 17 boxes of homemade goodies from home to the guys the other day, and they must have weighed over eighty pounds altogether!)

Today, when we went to clean up our barracks on the Advanced Training side of the bridge, we were given Cokes, candy bars, and ice-cream sandwiches! That was a special treat! Besides that, we started wearing our white sailor hats today for the first time, and we were on top of the world! Up until now, we all had to wear our baggy blue ball caps. Now we feel like real sailors at last.

Thanks for the money and the postage stamps, Gramma! I'll put the stamps to good use right away, but the money will have to keep in my locker until we actually have a place to spend it.

Don't worry about me so much, I won't pick up any bad habits here; we've got a swell bunch of clean-cut guys in our company. All we're interested in now are girls and getting home soon for a leave.

We have to keep our windows in the barracks open all the time, and it's getting darn chilly now at night! Consequently, I have a terrible cold right now. But it'll pass. Still, it makes life miserable while I try to shake it off.

In answer to your question, a "yeoman" is the hardest working fellow in the whole company. He makes out watch lists, meal chits, walking chits, collects coupons for the barbershop, keeps track of the whereabouts of all persons at all times, constructs the POD, and usually keeps very late hours. In addition to my mailman duties, I am also assistant yeoman to this poor over-worked buddy of mine from Tennessee.

One nice thing about being the company mailman is that I got to know everybody in a hurry! Simply by delivering their letters twice a day I got to know their first and last names, and where they were from – something that I probably couldn't have accomplished on my own in the time span of boot camp. And they got to know me. The bad part of being their mailman is that if somebody doesn't get any mail that particular day, it's suddenly somehow MY fault! And there is always some chowderhead during mail call who thinks everybody else should hear *his* letter from home – while you are trying to read your own.

I'm having the family send me a couple of books. I'm about ready to go stir crazy for lack of something to read! I got disqualified for submarine service because I wear glasses; they don't take anybody with corrective lenses right now… one of their quirky little rules. Also, I've decided not to pursue the Bluejacket's Choir option (even though I did qualify for that), because it would mean leaving my present company and going to a new company of complete strangers. And I just don't want to do that. I've made too many good friends here.

I've got to say, we're given the most interesting classes here in boot camp, and most of them are aimed at making us better sailors and helping us survive disastrous situations. This week we had our all-important damage-control session, which was held on board the *USS Recruit* (TDE-1), that mock-up of a destroyer escort that I told you about earlier.

As usual, extensive classroom instruction preceded the actual baptism. They placed some of us inside a steel compartment aboard the *Recruit.* There was a huge "shell" hole in one bulkhead, which was to be our repair objective for that moment. They pointed out where all the damage-control equipment was stored, and closed the door behind us. Then they turned on the water.

It exploded through the hole with great pressure, and the icy coldness of it shocked us. In no time at all the level of the water started creeping up our legs, as we floundered about, trying to form repair teams, deciding which of the wooden plugs and tools we were going to employ to fix that particular problem. It was a real Chinese fire drill. Then they killed all the lights, simulating shipboard power failure.

Submersible battle lanterns were in the damage-control locker, thank goodness. The cold water rose up to our chests, and I began to sense the urgency of an actual shipboard emergency. And while the water level eventually rose nearly up to our chins, we got the hole plugged totally satisfactorily. Meanwhile, other teams from our company were supposed to be restoring electrical power, while others were assigned to pump the compartment clear of water. Just as it would be done aboard a real ship, with teamwork. All in all, an exciting day!

Well, we've got about 18 guys who failed tests recently, which I've got to help tutor before taps, so I'll sign off now.

November 21, 1967

Dear Gramma,

I got five letters in the mail today, plus a big ol' care package of goodies from Darlene Horst, one of the girls who used to work with me at the Town House Café. Wasn't that nice of her?! She's pretty cool.

Well, it started raining three days ago and it hasn't stopped since. We had to sit through church services outside in the rain, stand in line for chow in the rain, drill in the rain, go to classes in the rain, and whatever. Today it rained harder than I've ever seen it rain before in my life, and we got soaked to the skivvies in spite of our long Navy-issue raincoats. Luckily, we were confined to our barracks this afternoon to dry off…but that meant no afternoon mail call either. Who said it never rains in southern California?

A partial list of our mandatory activities during boot camp would read something like this: marching, mooring classes, boat etiquette, rifle range, calisthenics, fire fighting, inoculations, complete physical checkups, classification tests, television-based classes, first-aid lectures, ordnance and gunnery classes, seamanship, knot tying, tear gas chamber, swimming instructions, church services, KP, holding field days, and doing our own laundry; letter writing, if we can squeeze it in.

Today we had our highly important 5-1 (fifth week, first day) inspection, and we got a very respectable second place, which is pretty amazing considering the many companies represented here.

We had to put our petty officer badges on our dress white uniform the other day. It wasn't enough that we *earned* them — but then we had to buy them and sew them on ourselves as well. My badge was an eagle, below which was a square knot, below which was one stripe, signifying recruit mail petty officer, third-class. I must admit we look pretty sharp in our white jumpers, black neckerchiefs, and bell-bottom trousers! I'm going to have to show off a little when I get home.

Surprise, surprise! We just had an impromptu barracks inspection not two minutes ago, when some chief popped in on us, unexpected like. But we were squared away and got to continue with our letter writing, etc. Never a dull moment.

Happy Thanksgiving! I hope we get some sort of holiday routine around here, too. We might get to phone home this coming weekend, if we behave. We all hope so anyway! See you over Christmas, that's for sure. Bye for now.

II.
ELECTRICIAN'S MATE "A" SCHOOL

2 JANUARY 1968 — 14 JUNE 1968

GOING WEST WITH JENNY

The rigors of boot camp were finally concluded by December 19th, just in time for Christmas. Following boot camp, I had a two-week leave coming to me. I could not afford the ticket for a jet flight home, however. To save myself some money, I rode the train roundtrip from San Diego to Omaha, Nebraska, and back again. From Omaha I rode the bus up to Mitchell, South Dakota.

The lengthy trip was four days long – just one way! It did not bother me one bit that I was consuming half of my available leave time just riding the rails. The journey was the thing. I had never traveled much by train before, and I was seeing some spectacular scenery for the first time in my life. (As you recall, this was one of the primary reasons I joined the Navy in the first place.) Christmas with my family was lots of fun, and my buddies back home had tons of questions for me about Navy life. The return trip to the west coast was especially eventful as well.

The old train wasn't very crowded, as most people flew anymore. I had a double seat all to myself by the window. I couldn't afford a Pullman berth, but being in the Navy I had learned to sleep just about anywhere in any position.

The landscape flew by outside – rolling ranks of gray shelterbelts, houses with windows showing brief vignettes of families around the supper table under the butter-yellow lamplight, and the blanket of late-December snow glistening blue in the evening afterglow.

I was alone, but that kind of loneliness didn't bother me. A man who cannot stand to be by himself is a man who knows way down deep that he isn't good company; I read that somewhere. In spite of the winter weather outside, I felt safe and snug inside the train. The tracks stretched ahead, I presumed the engineer knew what he was doing, and I didn't have a thing to worry about for days on end, until the minute I was due to report back to my new duty station.

But I soon grew tired of watching the Missouri countryside slip by through my reflection in the window, and I looked around the compartment with renewed interest.

Across the aisle and a few rows ahead of me was a sleeping Marine, with his hat pulled down over his eyes. Maybe he was coming back from leave, too? I wondered if he had had a good time, and if some loved one was sorry to see him go. A couple of stocky old women sat sleeping directly across the aisle from me, leaning against each other, uncomfortably crammed into a multitude of misshapen coats and dresses, and breathing heavily in their cumbersome old-lady clothes.

At the far end of the car I stared at the back of a shapely blonde head and saw the curve of her cheek and her soft, shadowy face reflected in the dark window beside her. Was it just my imagination, or did she look lonesome, too? Maybe I could talk with her to help pass the time? But then again, she might prefer to be left alone. The last thing I wanted to be was a stereotypical pesky sailor. Anyway, it was worth a try; it would certainly make the time go faster for both of us, I would think.

With my white sailor hat in hand, I put on my healthiest smile and suddenly found myself standing beside her. Where had I found this uncommon bravery?

"Do you care if I sit down?"

With a polite smile she turned and nodded to me, then looked out the window again. The ball was in my field now, as they say, and I felt the pressure to keep the little scenario from failing miserably. Our reflection in the glass looked as if we were old traveling companions, and I improvised, "Nice-looking couple, aren't they?"

She couldn't help but laugh at that. I had broken the ice, so to speak.

"My name's Steve. What's yours?"

"Jenny," she said impossibly in a purring, perfumed whisper. It made her seem prettier somehow. A perfect name for a perfect vision.

"Do you go all the way?" I asked before I realized what I had said.

"W-what?!" she asked with mild alarm.

"How far are you going?" I recovered smoothly.

"Oh. Albuquerque," she answered friendly-like, and I was secretly glad in my heart that she had decided to trust me after all.

From there we drifted like old friends into personal topics of home, family, the Navy, the future…

That night, as luck would have it, and closely following old railroad tradition, we had a nine-hour layover in St. Joseph, Missouri, while our ancient locomotive received repairs of some sort. Still having a few bucks in my pocket left over from my 15-day mini-vacation at home, I took her downtown in a cab for supper and a movie. The movie we saw was "Thoroughly Modern Millie," starring Julie Andrews.

The next two days passed quickly and cheerfully enough, although the hours themselves were long and steeped in pleasant conversation. The nights were dark and intimate in the old-fashioned passenger car as we either slept contentedly side by side, or exchanged confidences in husky whispers, so as not to disturb the sleepers.

Jenny was a sweet 17-year-old girl, with much appealing charm in her natural simplicity and honesty. Meeting someone on a train is like opening a book to the middle; you don't know the beginning and you don't know the end. You know just enough to really get you interested. And I was totally smitten.

But all good things must come to an end sooner or later – most frequently all too soon. I viewed our westward progress across New Mexico with a growing sadness in my heart, because I knew what lay ahead in the journey. From pillar to post, from milk stop to milestone, my despondency grew inside as we neared her destination.

I've always loathed "goodbyes" with a passion. Sometimes it's easier to take leave of someone you've known all your life, than say "so long" to someone that you have just met…and ache to know better. I knew I would never see her again, and that was very hard for me to accept. It seemed so unfair somehow.

Saying goodbye to Jenny was not easy in the end, but we parted with a feeling of mutual goodwill in the air. We each kept a little bit of the other when she left the train that evening in Albuquerque. She made one last gesture of farewell, a gentle wave of her hand and a silent smile from the platform, before she rushed into her parent's waiting arms. They looked curiously after me as I stepped back onto the train.

The remainder of the trip to San Diego took on a persistent dreariness. I browsed through books, trying to forget her and not really wanting to, but the words blurred together on the page. The Rockies rose and slid away without much grandeur for me. I stared blankly out the window for miles and miles…and slept a lot.

FA Steve Stanga B617389
Basic Elec/Elec School
Division 6073, Class 05A3
SSC – NTC
San Diego, California
92133

February 6, 1968

Dear Gramma,

This afternoon is the perfect time to catch up on my letter-writing. I'm sitting in a civilian laundromat just off base, waiting for my clothes to wash. Quite a bigger load than I had anticipated. Sure wish we had someplace to iron them, too. I suppose there is, but I haven't found it yet. The thermometer in the window says 78 degrees Fahrenheit and the sun really feels good on my arms as I write this.

Well, this weekend a buddy and I went downtown San Diego and sat through nine different movies in a row, for the simple reason that we hated to go back to the base so early. It cost a total of $1.50! Next weekend we'll be on our way up to visit Disneyland. I'm going to look up a few addresses in Long Beach while I'm there, too, and see if I can find Los Cerritos Maternity Hospital, where I was born.

We attend Basic Electricity and Electronics night school, and then sleep all day in a barracks with darkened windows. I've never done anything like this before. I'm surprised we aren't all falling asleep in class by 1:30 in the morning! Do you know that we eat our breakfast at 9:30 at night? We're used to it by now, though.

School is going to be easier than I initially thought. Everything I learned in high school about electricity is quickly coming back to me. This gives me a slight advantage over most of the guys in my class who've never had any of that stuff before and don't know an amp from a volt. So far, I've passed all three tests in the high 90's. As an ex-school teacher, you can appreciate this.

I wonder who came on base this morning (while we were trying to sleep); they gave him a 21-gun salute. And that's normally reserved only for the President or a foreign dignitary. Sorry this letter is so short this time. I don't usually run out of things to say this soon.

February 8, 1968

Dear Gramma,

We've got an hour break for chow between classes, and I'm using it to get off a couple of letters. I thought for sure that it was going to rain today; I would have put money on it; but it didn't materialize after all. There was a terribly thick sea fog out last night. You'd never see such a pea-soup fog as that back in South Dakota.

We've got one Negro in our barracks who is always full of surprises. Last night he was eating live moths for a buck apiece! The guys were willing to pay the dollar just to see him do it. He's making lots of money, too. Just chews them right up! I guess a fella will do anything to earn money when he's flat broke.

Goodness but I'm tired tonight! I had a reveille watch (4:00 to 8:00 AM) the other morning and I still haven't caught up on my sleep. It's not easy to stay awake for four hours, just walking quietly up and down the barracks in the dark, especially when everybody else is sound asleep.

Matter of fact, once I sat down at the centerboard for a moment to rest my sore feet – and dozed off just like that! The roving patrol woke me up a few minutes later and told me to keep on my feet; he was a nice guy about it. I'll have to watch that stuff, or I'll get in serious trouble.

Sort of surprised to admit it myself, but I'm beginning to really enjoy electronics class. Our Negro instructor is most excellent! He's got a wonderful sense of humor, and our eight hours of school each night just seem to fly by. Electricity school here is five months long, but I'll be switching classes from time to time. (Thus, keep an eye on my mailing address, because it frequently changes. Be sure to use my most current one.)

When I got into my new barracks I was soon initiated. They threw me in the shower with all my clothes on, and later put itching powder in my sheets. But if you're not a "hard" sailor, you'll take it all in fun…and then help initiate the next poor slob!

Well, it's time to be getting back to class now. We get out of school on Washington's birthday, so that'll be great. Boy, I had a headache yesterday like I've never had before. And no aspirin! Otherwise, I've never felt better in my life since I got here. Maybe it's the pleasant southern California climate?

FA Steve Stanga B617389
EM/A School, Div. 6054
Class 6811, SSC – NTC
San Diego, California
92133

March 16, 1968

Dear Gramma,

Hi! I got your letter yesterday at the afternoon mail call; it was delayed because it had to be forwarded to my new address. Yes, I've moved again; I really get weary of that sometime. I moved into a different barracks and am now going to day-time classes. Thanks for the funny riddles you sent; my buddies thought they were pretty corny.

I was told that I'll get another leave in the middle of May when electrician school is completed. And after that, chances are fairly certain that I'm getting a ship! I can't begin to describe how anxious I am to finally go to sea. I have dreamed of little else for the past year.

In my leisure time, I've been hanging out at the base hobby center. I just recently mailed my homemade ceramic chess set to the folks where it should be safe – I hope it survives the trip, not to mention the riotous overcrowding at home. Have Mom show it to you when you come over; I'm really proud of it.

No, that wasn't me in that picture I sent you. It was a boy named Keefer from Kansas. We really do look just alike, don't we? They say that everybody has a twin somewhere in the world; who knew I would find mine in the same barracks? They call us "Big Brother" (me) and "Little Brother" (Keefer); he's a reasonably nice guy, but he claims he doesn't see any resemblance.

It was sunny and warm today, which it is nearly every day. Whitmore, a buddy of mine from San Antonio, and I were going to go to the beach, but we couldn't find each other. So I napped instead, had a light snack, wrote to the folks, took a few photos around this beautiful installation, went to the flick, and listened to records a while in the base library. Weekends can be quite boring sometimes when you can't hook up with any of your friends. Tomorrow, I'm going to slip into my dress blues and go out to Balboa Park to visit the San Diego Zoo for the whole day.

Well, we're done with Basic Electricity school now and we've already finished our first week in Electrician's Mate "A" school; twelve more weeks to go, but the time really flies. I still have an eighty average, but I will try to do better. I know I'm not putting everything I could into it. But the emphasis here is just to pass, not necessarily excel.

Right now I'm sitting here at the centerboard with my radio on, and it's only a half hour until taps. I should really go over to the mess hall and put a halfway decent meal under my belt, but it's such a long walk from here. Der Wienerschnitzel is much closer, just out the main gate and across the street.

I'm glad tomorrow is Sunday, because then we don't have to get up at 0600. I know I should go to church, but they only have Protestant services over the noon hour. That means I would have to skip dinner! And my stomach takes precedence over my soul any old day.

April 6, 1968

Dear Gramma,

My mail the last four days has been absolutely nil, and so I said to myself this morning that I just have to light a fire under those slack civilians back home.

I've got the duty this weekend and that means I won't be able to leave the base. It's just as well, because I'd only be spending money out in town that I should be saving for leave anyway.

I'm sitting here on the cement scrub-table outside the barracks with my blue Royal portable typewriter on my lap, so I should get a very large dose of that stuff that California is so famous for: sunshine. Actually, I spend most of my time indoors, either at the flick or reading at the base library, or writing letters in the barracks. But I figured it wouldn't look right if I came home on leave from southern California with hardly any tan to show for it, huh.

I've got two miserable midwatches this weekend. That means I go to bed at 10:00 PM, get two hours of sleep (if I'm lucky), stand four hours of watch, get two more hours of sleep, and get up for the day. Then I repeat this schedule the following evening. By the time Monday morning and school roll around I should be pretty well dead on my feet. Luckily, weekend duty only comes once every four weeks for us.

It sure was a terrible thing about Martin Luther King getting shot two days ago! Yesterday morning some white rednecks in class were talking real ugly about it and spouting off how happy they were that he got himself killed. Then they started talking about loading up their shotguns and going down to Memphis for a real nigger-shoot. That's about the time I lost my temper. Boy, did I ever cuss them up one side and down the other! I called them disgusting racists, and told them how sick they made me. I guess I had never been so furious in public before. Blah, blah, blah. But they only laughed at me, so I just clammed up. I was wasting my breath anyway on the likes of them.

My buddy, Whitmore, has joined one of those precision drill teams, so I don't see much of him anymore, since he practices all the time now. He sure looks sharp marching with his chrome-plated rifle and polished bayonet. Their stunts are pretty scary to watch, though, what with rifles twirling through the air and all.

As yet, I haven't heard anything about my application for EOD school. But these things take time. We are supposed to get our orders in a few weeks; I hope they won't be a big disappointment, because it's something I'll have to live with for a long time. I've heard of poor slobs who get orders to United States Naval Bases one after another, and never leave the States during their entire hitch. I'd like to get a ship off the east coast – most everybody does – that way I'll get travel pay to come home for leave. But we'll just have to wait and see.

School is gradually getting harder, and I find that I can't cut classes at all if I'm going to get any kind of a passing grade for the week. We've been troubleshooting direct-current controllers all this week and I've got them down pat. It's the written part of our tests that I always mess up. Circuits, circuits, circuits – I wish I'd never have to look another fuse box in the face!

Anybody who gets an electrical shock while working on a live 220-volt controller is automatically a member of the "220 Club." A certain degree of carelessness – or downright stupidity – will get you into the "440 Club" as well. Not surprisingly, I am a member in good standing of both clubs already. *sigh*

After my Electrician's Mate school, I will have a week of MPO school. EMs are the guys who show the movies to the men out in the fleet, so we have to know how to run all the different movie projectors; happily, that's part of our job. Fortunately, IC Electricians have to service them if they break down, not us.

April 13, 1968

Dear Gramma,

"Tempus fugit" (time flies). Easter already! It won't be too long before I'll be on my way home; and just a little while after that I hope to be on a ship heading somewhere out to sea. Looks like a promising future. We get our orders in just a few days now. Can you tell I think about it a lot?

It's a lazy Sunday afternoon here on base. The guys are out tanning on the patio and it's pretty quiet inside the barracks. Just the right opportunity for catching up on a few letters. Sorry about the sloppy penmanship, but it's much too early to get my typewriter out of the handbag locker (they are only open specific hours), and I plan to be downtown this evening, taking in a flick or two.

And speaking of movies, I really enjoyed myself yesterday! A friend and I took in three wonderful movies downtown: "Guess Who's Coming to Dinner" with Sidney Poitier was really a great show! (Any movie that can make me cry has got to be special.) "Planet of the Apes" with Charlton Heston had a surprise ending – too scary for comfort; the whole unusual movie was unnerving, but that is what made it good. "The Secret War of Harry Frigg" with Paul Newman was very funny. Newman is always a hit in my book. I don't think I've ever seen so many excellent movies back to back before. Movies are your best entertainment.

School is certainly getting difficult. I'll just have to bear down a little more and do less horsing around, I guess. I suppose it'll pay off in the long run. Electronics and I are trying to get along, but it's a love-hate relationship.

Did you hear about our dandy little earthquake recently? We felt it quite strong here in San Diego – powerful enough to bust some store windows and crack the sidewalks. I first felt it when I was going down the corridor to the head, and suddenly I lurched smack into the wall! That was very disorienting. I thought I was getting sick or something. The hall was moving right in front of my eyes, and I began to get quite dizzy. Then somebody yelled, "Earthquake!" I ran outside the barracks just like everyone else was doing all over the base. The quake only persisted about thirty seconds, I heard, but it was awfully exciting while it lasted. It makes a guy feel mighty small and useless when the whole earth heaves underneath you. This was my first earthquake.

I wonder if it would be alright with you if I moved my personal stuff to your house while I'm home on leave? You have such a big house and I wouldn't have to worry about mold, damp, heat, or little siblings getting into all my things. I'd feel a lot better while I'm away, knowing that it was all safe and sound up in your attic. What do you say?

April 15, 1968

Dear Family,

I thought it was just too nice of a weekend to rot here on base, so when Whitmore came over and said he had itchy feet, we went ashore. I can hardly believe that it has already gotten up to 89 degrees back home; it hasn't even been that hot out here yet!

Sunday was a wonderful day! After Whitmore went to Easter services, we took the bus downtown again. We saw four more movies – they're so darn cheap out here! "The Sons of Katie Elder" with John Wayne and Dean Martin was super good, naturally. And I really enjoyed seeing De Mille's "Samson and Delilah" (ca.

1949) again; it was every bit as good as when I first saw it about seven years ago. "Bonnie and Clyde" was very entertaining, but I don't like how they glamorize people like those two thugs and make them look like heroes. Then we saw "The Billion Dollar Brain" starring Michael Caine and headed back to the base. This morning came all too early.

The bullfights start in May down in Tijuana, and Whitmore would like to go see one, so we might go down there next month – in the daylight this time! We've been down there in the evening several times before, but the night life in Tijuana is undeniably grungy.

Today we started studying transistors in class. I stayed awake this time around and managed to understand it. It surprised me to find out that the things actually made sense. It almost sounds too easy. Maybe I'd better drop by Stupid Study tonight just in case; It wouldn't hurt to get in some extra tutoring before the big test.

I was doing a little bit of free-hanging on the bars in the head the other night after taps, when the night watch came strolling in. He saw me just hanging there in the dark and he almost had a heart attack. He thought somebody had actually hung himself in the toilet! It created quite a stir at the time, and at first I thought I was going to get into trouble. But it soon blew over.

Funny, but I've run out of things to say already. Guess I'm a little tired. I still have to write the rest of my correspondents, too. The BOOD is in the cube right now snooping around. He's a real lifer. He'll probably chew me out again for sitting on my bunk in my dungarees. Guess I'll wind this up right about here.

April 17, 1968

And now a few words about free-hanging....

HISTORY: Most athletic sports today have evolved from basic acts of survival, like running, jumping, throwing, and wrestling. But whatever happened to free-hanging? Only just recently is this ancient sport being revived.

OBJECT: To see how long a person can free-hang from a bar without touching the ground.

MECHANICS: Find a horizontal bar that will give you a comfortable overhand grip, which you have to jump slightly to reach. There are no regulations about the distance between your hands on the bar. Close your eyes and hang completely limp. There will be no regripping or wriggling.

RECORDS: The longest recorded free-hang is almost five minutes. (It's harder than you think!) Don't be discouraged if your first try is only a minute or so; even the champions had to practice to build up their endurance.

SENSATIONS: This feat should preferably be tried in a dark, quiet room for the best overall hallucinations. The arms, in their raised position, tend to constrict certain blood vessels in the neck supplying oxygen to the brain. Normally, visions only start to occur after two full minutes of free-hanging have elapsed. The room may seem to swim and rock around, while changing colors are sometimes visible behind your eyelids. One of the favorite sensations is acquired by waiting long enough to achieve the feeling of standing on your hands upside-down – instead of hanging from them! Free-hanging for an extended period of time is not even mildly harmful.

BUT BE WARNED: This sport can be habit-forming!

May 1, 1968

Dear Family,

May Day is a little bit different for me this year than last year. No May Day baskets and smooches from girls, that's for sure. I wonder how it went for you civilians? Thanks for your letter I got this morning. That makes one letter total I've received in seven consecutive mail calls. That's not too bad – considering I write 32 people!

Yesterday, the sun was pouring down and the birds were out singing in huge numbers. Today, it's been overcast all day and the officers at the school seemed in especially bad spirits. We'll see what tomorrow brings, I guess.

And now for the really big news: I got my orders last week and I'm just tickled to death! The word had come down one afternoon that the orders had been posted, so we all stampeded for the bulletin board and fought for a position to read the list. I finally saw my name near the bottom, after which was printed, "Subic Bay, P.I."

"What's a 'Subic Bay P.I.'?" I asked a buddy, having never heard of it.

"Subic Bay?!" blurted out another swabbie in total disbelief. "Stanga, you lucky shit! You're going to the Philippine Islands!"

And then they all pounded me on the shoulders and congratulated me most heartily, and told me how fortunate I was to draw such a good duty station right off the bat.

So, after a short leave at home, I'm flying to Subic Bay in the Philippines with a buddy of mine who got the same orders. We are supposed to be over there almost two years! Just think of all the fun I'll have down there; it's only sixty miles from the capitol, Manila; there's good skin diving, and on the weekends I can go inland to see the pretty countryside, meet the people, and learn the customs. Then there's all that stereo and camera equipment I can get so cheap. I'm half crazy with anticipation!

I should be home on the 25th of this month. I can't wait! It looks like I'm not going to get any travel pay, so I want you to send me some of my savings bonds to help buy my plane ticket. Several of my buddies back home are talking about enlisting in the Navy while I'm home so I can earn ten days of extra leave for that.

We had another surprise sea bag inspection this morning and I passed once again. This week in school is terribly easy; it would be a good time to bring up my grade point average. I've managed to get it up to 83, but it is supposed to be at least 87. I can't do more than try, I guess. With school rapidly coming to the finish line, we're awfully busy tying up loose ends. Those blasted jets from the San Diego airport fly overhead all day long. If we're in class, the jet engines make the pipes vibrate in the walls and the radiators knock and the windows rattle, but we try to ignore all the noise and study just the same.

I'm enclosing an aerial photo of the new radiomen barracks they just finished building. They were meant to be for us electricians, but we got gypped out of them at the last minute! While I was on a working party we had to put bunks, mattresses, chairs, desks, lamps, wastebaskets, rugs and ash trays in every single room! Then they gave the barracks to the incoming radiomen class. That really added insult to injury.

FA Steve Stanga B617389
EM/A School, Div. 6054
Class 6813, SSC – NTC
San Diego, California
92133

May 16, 1968

Dear Family,

Well, I've got some good news and some bad news. I have my plane ticket in hand at last. But instead of being home in a week like I had planned, I will be home three weeks from now – on account of I got my fool self set back in school two weeks!

Just because school was so nearly over with (it was our last week of instruction), and my leave was so darn close, I made the sad mistake of thinking I could just skate through as long as I had enough points to pass anyway. But apparently they're wise to guys like me.

So now I get to take the last two weeks all over again. At first I was so mad I could spit, but I'm back in good spirits now. I know that it was my own dang fault and that I've got to accept graciously what I cannot change. Anyway, I'll really try hard this time! I hope this doesn't alter any plans anybody has made at home. Sometimes time can be so irritating when you're waiting for it to pass.

The good news is now I get a thirty-day leave at home, instead of just two weeks, because I will be gone overseas for so long! That bit of news cheered me up considerably.

Last night, Ron and I walked out to Ocean Beach and explored along the coast. We found some mighty pretty sea caves and a few secluded stretches of beach. Then we sat in the sand and talked and just watched the sun go down. It can't be described on paper, and it probably wouldn't have come out on camera either. It's just something that you remember "up here." It was well worth the five-mile walk, though.

On the way back to base, then, we stopped and ate a good old-fashioned fried-chicken dinner at an antique shop of all places. We had hot biscuits, corn fritters with warm honey, spicy potato salad, delicious coleslaw, fresh milk, and real mashed potatoes and gravy. Sure made me homesick. And the atmosphere there was perfect: red-checkered oilcloths on the tables surrounded by hand-carved chairs under kerosene lamps hung low, coffee warming nearby on a blue and white enameled wood-burning stove, pale round pictures hung against dark oak-paneled walls, and delicate old china to eat from. We're definitely going back there again!

I've mailed most of my stuff home already, but still have more to box up. You'd think I was a pack rat the way my things accumulate! Sorry this is such a short letter, but taps is fixin' to go down any minute now. Bye.

May 26, 1968

Dear Gramma,

I'm holed-up here in the barracks. I'd be outside in the perfect 76-degree sunshine, but I'm sunburned across the shoulders already and am peeling real bad. I'm getting pretty darn good on my Hohner Chromatic "C" harmonica by now. The very first song I taught myself was "Sentimental Journey." I have a feeling my harmonica will keep me good company during long evenings at sea.

Here's a picture of me that I thought you might like: I'm working on a 440-volt switchboard over at the school. Out in the fleet, this same switchboard would provide power for the steering system if the main generator ever got "knocked off the line" (a polite term for men and machinery being blown to bits) by something such as, oh I don't know, a *torpedo*. Perish the thought.

Last night was a night to remember. I was lucky enough to go to the Bob Hope USO show in the San Diego stadium! We had terrific seats, too. I don't know when I've had such a good time or seen so many big stars in one place – never! We saw The Youth of America, Harpers Bizarre, Kay Stevens, the wife of the skipper of the *USS Pueblo,* Martha Raye, Raquel Welch, Les Brown and His Band of Renown, Honey Limited, and some others whose names I've already forgotten. Wow!

All the guys went wild over Raquel Welch, of course, but she wore a very disappointing ankle-length dress and didn't sing very well at all. To me, the highlight of the whole show was when Andy Williams sang "Danny Boy." I almost choked up.

At the end, five wounded Marines presented Bob Hope with the GI Joe Award and hailed him as "the most beloved American" while the whole stadium gave him a standing ovation. I believe Bob was actually at a loss for words for a moment there.

It was a four-hour show, but us servicemen sat in our seats from 4:30 in the afternoon until after midnight. And the poor boot-camp Marines and sailors had to sit Indian-style on the infield the whole time!

Boy, did we ever put on a show for the civilians there, too. Both Navy and Marine Corps bands took turns playing. As the Corps band started playing "The Marine's Hymn," the cheering of the Marines completely drowned it out. And when they played "Anchors Aweigh," a cold shiver of pride shot up my spine. Fifteen thousand sailors filled the stadium air with 15,000 white hats! That was something to see from our seats in the balcony! I'll never forget it.

Up above us floated the huge Goodyear blimp spelling out in lights, "Thanks… for…the…memories…Bob." There were 52,750 people attending, and they grossed over $200,000 – which goes towards a new USO building downtown. I had the time of my life last night! We'll be talking about this for weeks.

June 9, 1968, Sunday – 1900

It has been dreadfully overcast all day – dreadful for some people, but not for me. I guess it is on the verge of becoming chilly, for there is an unusually crisp breeze blowing over the base from the sea. In fact, the clouds filled the sky to such an extent that it was impossible to tell exactly where the sun was hanging today. But I'm thankful for any variation from the typical warm, sunny, Californian day which can get oh so monotonous after a while. I always was an avid fan of adversity in the weather.

I tried to persuade Ron to join me for chow, but I couldn't budge him from his rack, where the gloomy weather had driven him. I never did mind breaking bread all by myself, though. It's a very long walk back to the barracks from the mess hall – time enough, almost, to work up another appetite.

A few guys are writing letters at the centerboard in their skivvies, a few are amazingly fast asleep already, someone's in the shower singing Jimi Hendrix songs, and above it all is the strident din of six or seven transistor radios all playing on different stations. Ah, good times. Taps will sound at 2200 and that will be the end of my weekend – short and unexciting as it was.

June 10, 1968, Monday – 2100

Reveille went down at 0530, as usual. Hungry as I was, I skipped breakfast; that gave me over an hour to read a book before I had to report for a work detail. Even while working at the café back home, and it was nearing the end of the month, and I only had a buck or two left of my paycheck, I would often opt to skip a meal that day and buy a paperback book instead. As Mark Twain said: "Outside of a dog, a book is man's best friend; inside of a dog, it's too dark to read."

Some work detail! We spent maybe two hours the whole day just priming rust spots on some old bunks in the Beeper Barracks for radiomen. We were secured early at about 1330 and I came back to my own barracks. Home sweet home. Seems like they don't know what to do with all of us since school got out. Today was linen day, so I put clean sheets on my rack and then sat down to write a few letters. The cube was totally deserted; I could turn up my radio and enjoy my privacy for a change. Privacy is a pretty scarce commodity in the military.

About 1800, Ron and I took a municipal bus downtown to partake of several world-famous McCoy's hamburgers. It's always relaxing to stop in there for a delicious hamburger, a very good cup of coffee, listen to the nickelodeon, and eyeball the waitresses.

Of course, we had to stroll down Broadway and take in all the sights, too. As is our custom, we always stop in Movieland, an acre-sized arcade, and blow a couple of bucks in the shooting gallery.

You occasionally encounter a few panhandlers along Broadway, who mostly try to tap you for loose change. But this one old grizzled guy approached me and asked outright for a whole dollar! "I won't lie to you, man; I need a drink bad," he implored.

I humored him as I fished a dollar bill out of my jumper pocket that I just would have squandered anyway, "Okay, as long as you're not going to buy a sandwich or something else foolish." A dollar would buy him a whole bottle of Thunderbird wine.

The moon is unusually pretty and solemn tonight. It is hanging low in the sky over the eastern part of the city, huge and orange, with skyscrapers silhouetted against it. Rather chilly tonight, too, so I'll have to sleep in my socks again. Oh well, one day closer to the time when I get to go home for leave!

June 11, 1968, Tuesday – 2030

No living thing should have to get up at 0530 while it is still dark outside. I rolled over at that dreadful hour this morning, pried an eye open, crawled out of my rack and stood shivering on the cold floor, clinging to the bunk until I worked up enough consciousness to walk. What a way to start out every morning. I believe I went to chow; it's hard to remember what I do in my sleep.

While painting racks again today I spotted a copy of my hometown newspaper, *The Mitchell Daily Republic,* lying on the bedsprings of one cot. I questioned everybody I could find in that barracks, desperate to find another living soul from South Dakota, but nobody claimed it. In the end, I never did find out who it belonged to. A strange occurrence…

June 12, 1968, Wednesday – 1500

We're painting again today; this time it's the bulkheads of a head. We put paint rollers on the ends of long wooden handles to reach the overhead. That really stretched out our muscles and got them aching. We diligently gave the whole compartment two heavy coats of exciting white glossy paint, and were still finished by noon.

In the afternoon, I went over to Inoculation and got my oversea's shots with an air gun, one in each arm: plague and cholera. Now one arm is getting real red and sore, while the other one itches like the devil! They had my paperwork all screwed up over there, and had it recorded that I had already gotten my shots last month. For a fleeting moment I thought I might worm out of the shots altogether, but then I decided it would be more prudent to take my medicine rather than contract something dreadful down in the Philippines. So I 'fessed up and received the shots like a good boy.

I found out today that I'm going home for leave for sure on Friday. O frabjous day! Callooh! Callay!

Home on leave in dress whites.

III.
SUBIC BAY,
PHILIPPINES
15 JULY 1968 — 13 JANUARY 1970

July 13, 1968

For the last three days of my leave, I departed South Dakota early and traveled to Reverend B. Wiley's home in Fair Oaks, California, for a short visit. (He was my former preacher at the Mitchell Wesleyan Methodist Church before he up and moved out to the West Coast.)

Rev. Wiley was gracious enough to free up his schedule and show me all the sights in the area: Sacramento, the California Exposition, San Francisco, Alcatraz, Golden Gate Bridge, Golden Gate Park and the Japanese Tea Gardens, Candlestick Park, Nob Hill, Russian Hill, Telegraph Hill, Coit Tower, the Mark Hopkins Hotel, Grace Cathedral, Flood Mansion, the Palace of Fine Arts, and others.

We really did up the town! He and I had bird's-nest soup in Chinatown, stuffed shrimp at Fisherman's Wharf; toured the old clipper ship *Balclutha;* saw all the hippies and panhandlers and free clinics along Haight-Ashbury Streets; rode the cable car down Hyde Street; drove down Lombard Street (crookedest street in the world); and crossed the beautiful Bay Bridge for a brief visit to sunny, dumpy Oakland. He even let me drive home on the California freeway – at rush hour, no less – which is the last thing I ever want to do again in my life! Thanks to Mr. Wiley, my visit to the City-by-the-Bay was especially memorable. And he made sure that I got to where I needed to be to catch my plane out of the United States when it was time to go.

July 14, 1968

I left Travis AFB near Frisco at 1700 on a Saturday afternoon. We were riding an old "stretch-job" DC-8 airplane, converted to hold 220 passengers. I wasn't sure that I was entirely at ease riding in a plane which had had a portion of additional fuselage riveted into its mid-section by contractors who had put in the lowest bid. But I tried not to think about it, and just concentrate instead on the big adventure I was beginning. It took five long, tiring hours to fly over the Pacific Ocean to Honolulu, Hawaii.

We were allowed to stretch our legs and drop off a few postcards at the Honolulu International Airport. When I stepped off the plane I had two immediate sensations: first, the tropical heat hit me like somebody had smacked me with a hot pillow in the face and, secondly, the air seemed absolutely perfumed due to the exotic flowers growing everywhere. Inside the terminal, we were all given leis and a kiss on the cheek by cute local Hawaiian girls. There were also dispensers for all the free orange juice and pineapple juice that we could drink.

After a brief hour layover in Hawaii, we flew for another two hours on our DC-8 until we landed at Wake Island somewhere in the Pacific. We had crossed the International Date Line by then, so we got set ahead a full day – which made it suddenly Sunday.

Then we flew onward a couple more hours, only to touch down on Guam Island long enough to see the inside of a dinky terminal and use their head. Westward with the night once again, we flew for two or three more hours before landing at Clark AFB in the Philippines about midnight. I was exhausted. It seemed like I had been airborne forever!

THE PHILIPPINE NATIONAL ANTHEM
Music by Julian Felipe (1898)
Words by Jose Palma (1899)

"Land of the morning,
Child of the sun returning,
With fervour burning
Thee do our souls adore.

Land dear and holy,
Cradle of noble heroes,
Ne'er shall invaders
Trample thy sacred shore.

Ever within thy skies
And through thy clouds
And o'er thy hills and sea
Do we behold the radiance,
Feel the throb,
Of glorious liberty.

Thy banner, dear to all our hearts,
Its sun and stars alight,
O never shall its shining field
Be dimmed by tyrant's might.

Beautiful land of love, O land of light,
In thine embrace 'tis rapture to lie;
But it is glory ever, when thou art wronged
For us, thy sons, to suffer and die."

July 22, 1968

Dear Mr. and Mrs. Stanga,

It is with pleasure that I inform you that your son, Steven, recently reported to the Naval Station here for duty. My purpose in writing today is to tell you something about our Station. As a father myself, I know how interested parents are in the activities of their children.

The Naval Station is located at Subic Bay, Luzon, Republic of the Philippines. Subic Bay is a large, well-protected harbor on the west coast of Luzon facing the South China Sea. The city of Olongapo, with a population of 70,000 plus, is adjacent to the base, and the city of Manila is about a three-hour ride by car. The Filipino people are a happy and friendly people and their way of life is colorful and interesting.

The Naval Station is a part of the US Naval Base which is commanded by a Rear Admiral who coordinates and directs the activities of the different commands stationed here. Those commands include the SRF, the Naval Supply Depot, the Naval Air Station, the Naval Hospital, and several others. The overall mission of this Naval Base is to directly support the US Seventh Fleet in the Southeast Asia theatre. This is an important task in a troubled part of the world.

Republic of the Philippines.

The Naval Station also indirectly supports the Seventh Fleet. We provide complete harbor and port services such as tugs, pilots, dry-docks and various service craft. We operate a large dispensary and dental clinic. We provide extensive recreational facilities which include an unusually broad athletic program of indoor and outdoor sports, hobby shops, movies, boating, a library, and a travel agency. Clubs and restaurants are provided on the base for all personnel. We have a large shopping center with many types of stores as well.

In becoming a part of our organization, your son has assumed serious responsibilities. He is part of a military force which is all-powerful and all-important to the Free World. He has been properly trained to discharge his duties and I am confident that he will do a fine job. However, he may need our help from time to time to guide him. Unfortunately, young men nowadays rarely consult their superior officers when they need advice. If your son has a problem, he can consult his superior petty officers, his division officer, the chaplains, or me for advice and counsel at any time.

Please feel free to write me if you feel I can be of any service to you.

Sincerely yours,

G.B. Gunderson
Captain, US Navy
Commanding Officer

EMFA Steve Stanga B617389
US Naval Station, Subic Bay
Box 15, Service Craft
FPO, San Francisco
96651

July 28, 1968

Dear Gramma,

It was just like I figured; I wouldn't have enough time to write to everybody that I wanted to immediately. But, this being the weekend, I've got all day to try to reach some of the folks back home. I'm not going to get any letters way down here unless I start writing some, and circulate my new address.

We landed in the Philippines about midnight exactly two weeks ago, and had to wait in the Clark airport until 0600 before we could catch a bus going down to Subic Bay. There was no place to sleep, and we were a pretty miserable lot by the time morning rolled around. Jet lag was a teddy-bear picnic compared to what we were going through.

I'll never forget that bus ride as long as I live! It was a sixty-mile trip which took us two and a half hours because the narrow roads were so crowded with humanity and we had to pass slowly through so many small villages and over one-lane bridges. I could see all the houses up on poles along the rivers and smell the dirtiness of the towns. Old people squatted on their haunches beside the road, staring at us, and the young people waved to us from the backs of carabao (water buffalo) out in the rice paddies. Mountains here, jungle there – it was all very exciting!

Not long after I got on the bus I began to wonder if I was even going to survive the trip to Subic Bay. I'm telling you, the people drive like complete maniacs! There would be immediate oncoming trucks, and our Filipino driver would still pass the vehicle in front of him. Little brown people constantly dashed across the road in-between cars, while traffic never slowed a mile per hour. I thought death or dismemberment was imminent at every turn.

But I've been here two weeks already and I feel like it's only been half that time. I work in the Service Craft electric shop for now, repairing motors and generators, etc., while waiting for my permanent assignment. There's rumor that I might get a YW. "Easy," my buddy from boot camp and "A" school, who also got orders to Subic, is on a YO moored just a few yards from me, and he is already one very tired swabbie from working such long hours.

Already the petty officers here in the shop have tried to send me off to the Chief to request a "left-handed sky hook" or a can of "relative bearing grease," but I was not born yesterday, and I am wise to these pranks on the new guy.

A lot of different ships from all over the world pull in here to load and unload. On the base it's not uncommon to meet Aussies, Germans, Thai sailors, and Japanese. Ships from Vietnam come in to take on more ammunition and supplies, then pull out to hustle back to the war.

It's the middle of the rainy season now, so it rains almost every day and night. In August, it's supposed to rain without stopping for three or four *weeks* straight! Oh, I can't wait until then. We are expecting the first typhoon of the season pretty soon, too. One good thing about all this rain is that we sleep awfully well at night, as it is nice and cool in the barracks then.

They told me that I'll be serving 18 months here – unless I volunteer for Vietnam in the meantime (which is what I've been trying to do for some time now). All is well here, and I hope everything is fine at home, too. I had a swell time on my leave!

EMFA Steve Stanga B617389
US Naval Station, Subic Bay
Box 15, YG-52
FPO, San Francisco
96651

August 8, 1968

Dear Family,

Hi. I've got watch tonight for eight hours. Right now I'm sitting up in the pilot house, leaning back against the wheel, writing letters on my lap. It's just pouring rain outside, but it's real pleasant here inside. Pretty soon I'll have to go make my rounds, inspect motors, tighten up the mooring lines, check the bilge water, etc.

As you can see from my address, I am finally living on a boat like I always wanted! It's the YG-52, which is a self-propelled garbage lighter; 118 feet long, 389 tons empty, driven by an eight-cylinder direct-reversible Enterprise engine – rolling along at a mind-blowing seven knots. A sea turtle could swim circles around us.

I know it sounds sort of dirty and scroungy at first, but it's not. We never even come close to the garbage. We just pull up alongside the big ships in the harbor, and they dump their trash

The YG-52, yard garbage lighter, Subic Bay.

over their sterns into our garbage hoppers. Then we take it about 15 miles out to sea and dump it in the deep ocean, where it sinks. Garbage-boat duty is considered to be very good duty here in Service Craft, and some of the other boys were envious that the "new guy" got a YG right off the bat.

Here in the P.I., working down in a close space such as the engine room, I didn't realize that I could physically sweat so much! When I quit work today at 1600, my fingers were as wrinkled as if I had soaked them in water for hours. I am not kidding about this. Luckily, we get a shower every night, and the houseboy Gino keeps us in clean clothes every day. He is a fine Filipino lad who washes our clothes, shines our shoes, makes our bunks, and keeps the living quarters on the boat clean. We have a crew of eight and we each pay him four dollars every payday (every two weeks), which doesn't sound like very much to me, but he seems quite satisfied.

That reminds me, do you know how big our shower is on the boat? Only two and a half feet square; I measured it. Our toilet is only three feet square, and our galley is about as big as our tiny kitchen back home on Gamble Street – with the exception that eight of us eat in there! Pretty cozy.

But I'll have to admit that we sure don't eat very well here on this boat. My biggest complaint is the milk – of which there never seems to be any. (This hardly seems fair; all the other boats get fresh milk.) The only place we can get real ice cream is from the Filipino vendors on the streets of Olongapo City with their little pushcarts. The quality of our meat is very poor, too. And the galley seems to be overrun with bugs. We're accustomed now to seeing dozens of cockroaches scurry for cover every time we pull open the silverware drawer. Filthy things! And you can't eat any of the bread around here before first cutting off the blue, yellow, brown, gray, and green mold. What you usually have left over wouldn't suffice to make half an hors d'oeuvre. We're all used to much better fare back home, ain't no doubt, but since we're in the Navy we have to make allowances. Everything in this climate spoils so quickly.

Well, we have a new cook now at any rate. Our other one – a big, obese, obnoxious Negro – is sitting in the brig tonight. He was a lousy cook anyway, and had an even worse temperament. He would stand over the hot grill in the galley, dripping sweat off his face onto our scrambled eggs by way of seasoning, I guess. It seems that he has been holding back a lot of our food, like turkey and steak and fresh fruit – and milk! – and then selling it out in town so he could have some extra spending money. He got caught the other night taking a large load out through the main gate in his car. I say it serves him right. We'll see if this new cook treats the crew any better.

We are each allowed to buy only so many cartons of cigarettes per month. Some of the guys on the other boats want to use my cigarette ration card, since I don't use it at all. That way they can buy extra cigarettes to satisfy their own habit and even sell some out in town for a tidy profit. But I won't let them use my ration card, because if they get caught it'll be my ass, too. And I want a clean record when I get out of here.

…Just made my hourly rounds of the three YGs. They are nested. The outboard boat is the "duty boat" which goes out every day to work. The inboard boat, lying next to the pier, is the boat "in the yards," or OOC for minor repairs. We are in the middle of the nest this week, which means we are the "standby boat." We alternate regularly so that all three boats take their fair share of the duty, and each is given the proper preventative maintenance as well.

It is approaching sunset. Pretty soon it'll be dark enough for me to turn on all the standing lights, masthead lights, flood lights, etc. These are only some of the things that I had to repair after relieving the last electrician they had on board; he had left the boat in complete shambles.

Today I've been trying to get the crew's radio to work so we can all enjoy piped-in music in the berthing compartment. But the radio runs on AC power, and our boat is almost entirely DC power with the exception of one little AC motor-generator set down in the engine room. I'll see if I can get it hooked up tomorrow. Work, work, work.

We've got a big boat inspection coming up, and any electrical discrepancies will go down on my record, whether I'm responsible for causing them or not. The guys said that I won't have to worry a bit about my quarterly marks, however, because I am working all the time, and so often it's overtime. I hope they're right. I can't seriously be expected to get everything up and running by the end of the month that I inherited in defective condition.

Trivia about the Philippine Islands: The country is about the same size as Italy. It is comprised of over 7,100 islands. Nine-tenths of the islands are uninhabited, and three-fourths of them do not even have names. The island of Luzon, where you can find your poor son, is the largest one and makes up fully half of the country.

I learned a valuable lesson yesterday: I was walking around out in town with a buddy of mine, and like a rookie I had foolishly put some of my folding money in my shirt pocket – strictly for convenience sake, you understand. I don't think I had even gotten two blocks down the main drag when a Filipino kid *accidentally* bumped into me and then suddenly took off running down an alley. It took about ten seconds to dawn on me that he had just picked my pocket clean as a whistle, and left me twenty pesos poorer. So from now on I will be carrying my wallet in the front pocket of my jeans, like all the other guys do. Criminy!

While we were out of the harbor on a job last week they had a baby typhoon back here on base. It flipped cars and knocked down piers, not to mention all the fallen tree limbs and damaged boats. You know, I kinda thought it was particularly rough that day at sea, especially in our flat-bottomed garbage boat. The main deck has no lifelines to grab onto either. Standing up on the bow, we could hardly see the pilot house for all the driving rain. But I had never been in a storm at sea before, so I was sort of digging it.

We painted our whole boat yesterday from the weather deck down to the water line. I helped, too, even though it was a job strictly for the deckapes and I was not required. When we get her done she will be quite a good-looking boat – for a garbage scow, that is!

Tomorrow I have to go to an indoctrination lecture over on Mainside that I was supposed to go to last week, but wasn't told about, and consequently got chewed out for not being there in the first place. That's typical Navy procedure for you.

I guess the rain is letting up a bit now, as I can see the far side of the bay for the first time today. Time for me to make my rounds again. See yuh.

August 11, 1968

Dear Gramma,

It's a slow, overcast, sleepy Sunday afternoon and there seems an unusual amount of spare time for reading and letter-writing today. If you've written any more than two letters to me down here, then I guess they're still in transit. After all, I am over 9,000 miles from home! They'll eventually get to me, though; the Navy forwards everything, even junk mail.

Since there's only one billet for an electrician on board a garbage boat, they say that makes me the Chief Electrician. Okey dokey. All I know is that I've got a lot of electrical gear to look after. As you might imagine, outside of the diesel engine just about everything else is electrical nowadays. We eat and sleep and work right on board. The first day I got sort of seasick, but I've been okay from then on.

I didn't know a thing about the big earthquake in Manila until I picked up the newspaper a few days ago. But people here on the base felt it strong – even those on boats. I was asleep at the time, I guess. They

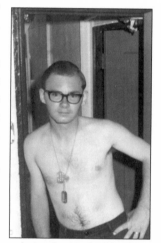

Just arrived in the islands.

were asking for volunteers to go to Manila and help search for bodies in the wreckage, and some of my buddies went. They said they found three bodies themselves. Not a pleasant chore, I'll bet. I had the duty, so couldn't go myself.

The chow is pretty good now, but once a week I still go over to the cafeteria on the other side of the bay, where I can get real milk with my meal. We still don't get any milk on our boat, and I was raised on the stuff.

In answer to your question, the rainy season is from July to November. The cool season is January and February, and the hot season is May and June; March and April are fairly pleasant. I'm really going to miss this first winter I'm away from home. Say hello to everyone in your part of the world for me.

September 3, 1968

Dear Gramma,

I thought I'd better let you know I hadn't broken my arm or something. Actually, I just got over five very sick days with flu, headaches and stomach cramps. Everybody on the boat got it eventually from the guys on the other boat. Heaven only knows where they caught it.

The last two days have been clear, hot and bright. But just prior to that we had two very stormy days when we were ordered not to leave the pier, even for our jobs. That's never happened before; I'll bet it was really wild out there! That's how we like it, though, the wilder the better. Kids down here (i.e., dependents of the officers) are just now starting their summer vacation from school.

We've been listening closely to the American convention coverage on the radio until it was all over with. Politics used to bore the heck out of me, but now I think it's all very complicated and exciting. Hubert Humphrey got the Democratic presidential nomination, I see; I wanted Eugene McCarthy to get it myself. Of course, South Dakota carried George McGovern as usual, but it was surprising how many votes he got from the other states, too!

The USS Long Beach (CGN-9), named after the place of my birth in California, y'know, pulled in here a couple of days ago. It's the first time I had seen her for real. Years ago as a child, I had a plastic Revell model of her, so I recognized the ship right off, even before I saw her name across the stern. You can't miss that square bridge anywhere. She's a nuclear-powered guided-missile heavy cruiser, and sure looks like she means business. I was surprised to learn how many thousands of shells she has fired into Vietnam thus far. I wouldn't want to be on the receiving end of her!

Olongapo City is getting on my nerves already, but it's just about the only place we have to unwind. Filipino jeepneys tear up and down the streets. Each jeepney is unique in that the owners try to outdo each other with outrageous decorations, religious statues, pinwheels, advertisements, gaudy paint, bronze horses, etc. You can ride a jeepney anywhere in Olongapo City for only ten centavos. You'd hardly think that would even pay for the gas. But they prosper by filling up the taxi with people for every trip.

I found out the reason why we don't have milk down here is because it's almost impossible in this heat to get fresh milk to us before it spoils. So they give us this repulsive sterilized stuff called "filled milk," which tastes something like baby formula, and you can hardly stand to drink it. I refuse to.

I'm currently the Scrabble champ of our boat, with only three defeats out of 13 games. But we can't play Scrabble all the time, so I'm having Mom send my Probe game down here, too. The board games keep us busy when we're stuck inside by all the rain.

Tomorrow night, singer Frankie Avalon is going to perform at a club here on the base. I'll be sure to catch him then, as I might never have another chance to see him live again.

OFFICIAL QUARTERLY MARKS
September 16, 1968
(Assigned to YG-52)

"Stanga is responsible for the operation, repair and maintenance of all electrical equipment on board the craft. He stands in-port security watches. Stanga is considered to be a capable and efficient electrician. He has not had a great deal of experience, but what he lacks he makes up for with initiative. His military behavior is exemplary and he obeys orders and regulations promptly and without complaint. Stanga's military appearance is well above the average, and he takes pride in his appearance. He contributes much to the morale of the crew and is a welcome addition to the Division."

September 21, 1968

Dear Gramma,

It's about 0100 in the morning here. You know I sure wouldn't be up at this ghastly hour if I didn't have the duty. Yes, I have the midwatch once again. I'd like a dollar for every midwatch I've stood in the Navy so far.

I guess it must be drawing to the end of the rainy season at last, as it hasn't so much as sprinkled in the last week. Already the grass has a slightly brown tinge to it, and it's getting to feel more and more like a South Dakota summer around here. It's hot already by 0600 in the morning.

US Naval Station,
Subic Bay, Philippines.

We are the standby boat this week, so we don't have to go out on jobs unless a garbage emergency arises. Instead, the day is spent trying to catch up on all the work details that can't be done while underway: painting, repair work, engine overhaul, etc. I usually try to carry my share of the load by helping out on deck, but the Chief told me that an electrician is not even supposed to do any deck work at all. So that puts an end to that, I guess. Sheesh. You'd think we were unionized or something.

I bought a used Algebra textbook, and in my spare time I'm trying to teach myself. I liked it in high school – I thought it was fun – but I didn't understand how it worked, and just barely passed it. Actually, this book makes it seem quite easy and logical. Besides, I don't want to learn a lot about one thing, I want to learn a little about a lot of things.

Smitty, of Auburn, California, one of my buddies here on the boat, got conked on the head the other day with a piece of sheet metal while we were tied up alongside a tender, receiving her trash. The wind caught the large flat piece of metal and sailed it right into his head. It barely broke the skin at the time, but he got a lump on his forehead the size of a goose egg. He's just lucky that he didn't catch a sharp metal corner in his skull.

This happened about a week ago. Since then, the lump has gone down, but his whole face is puffing up, his eyes are black and blue, and around his nose it looks like something is filling up underneath the skin. The corpsman says it's abscessed and will have to be lanced before it becomes a tumor. He's also lost partial hearing in one ear. Even this is enough for him to get a medical discharge from the Navy if he wants. But Smitty isn't interested in getting out. He's a tough nut to crack.

Here is a picture of myself and my struggling so-called moustache. I guess the guys liked it, too, as they ordered eight copies of the photo. Our engineman has one in his scrapbook alongside a picture of the Gerber Baby. Even I am surprised at the resemblance.

We're having a small revolution on board. It's against the "black power" co-

Aboard the YG-52.

alition here on our boat. I was never racially prejudiced before I got in the Navy, you know that, but these guys are really something else. Our craftmaster is Negro, so of course he's partial to the other three "brothers" on board. And the rules of the boat handed down only seem to apply to us poor white folk. So it would serve no purpose to take our concerns to him.

Meanwhile, the colored guys get away with murder. Everybody was given two hands; one to take what you need, and one to give to others what they haven't got. But these guys think both hands are for taking. They're regular freeloaders, and you never hear so much as a "thank you" out of them for anything. So us four white guys are seeing what we can do for a little fair play around here – by hook or by crook.

I think it's time next week to get my shot card updated; my last series of shots was clear back in boot camp. Oh well, it's better than getting sick, I guess. I had just gotten my fingers fairly healed up from electric fan blade cuts, and last night I burned a large hole in my left thumb when I got a bad electrical shock. Such is life as an electrician…

September 24, 1968

Just on a wild urge, four of us decided to spend the day down in Manila. We had to get up early this morning to catch our bus from Special Services. It was a very tiring four-hour trip, and it was awfully hot inside the crowded bus. We were sweaty and uncomfortable before we even got there.

We saw Manila Bay, the zoo, some famous statues, a couple of cool parks, and the American Embassy. It was good to see buildings over two stories tall once again. The people are a lot more friendly in Manila than Olongapo City, I noticed. Basically, we were on a fact-finding mission; we just wanted to find out what there was to see and do in Manila. That way, when we have a 72-hour liberty weekend sometime in the future, we will know exactly what we want to do down there, and won't waste half the weekend just wandering around looking for the action.

October 3, 1968

Dear Gramma,

Thanks ever so much for the five dollars! It seems you always know exactly what time of the week that I'm broke. Believe me, it's going to come in handy; at least I won't need to borrow before payday now.

Well, since I wrote last we rode the boat through Typhoon Elaine. It passed very close to Subic Bay, close enough to swamp the piers under water and send the big ships scurrying out of port. The wind was blowing so hard that the harbor was full of floating tree trunks and branches. It was kind of interesting.

Today was a glorious day, however, sunny and warm. We got underway first thing in the morning and went far out to sea to dump some old fuel oil. But on the way back we spent all afternoon relaxing at Grande Island (pronounced "Grandy"). A bunch of Negritos live and work on Grande Island; Negritos are very dark-skinned Filipino pygmies. They are numerically and physically among the smallest as well as among the least-known of all living human groups. I read that somewhere.

The colored guys went drinking together at the club there, while the rest of us went skin diving. It was my first time. I borrowed a pair of fins, a snorkel, a face mask, and a spear gun. We went into deep water where the pretty coral was. I never dreamed it was so beautiful down there! The colors of the fish are indescribable. Unbeknownst, I shot a blowfish, which puffed itself up to the size of a basketball; he had poisonous spines like a porcupine. I had never seen anything like it before. It took me thirty minutes to gingerly get the fish off my spearhead. It sure is a different world down there! We collected a lot of pretty seashells, too. Next weekend we're going back there, for sure.

Once again our food on the boat is bad as ever. I never griped about the chow in Dago because I never had reason to, but I'll gripe now. Our cook has the nerve to call them "square meals," too. Breakfast is the same every morning: bacon and eggs. That's all. Every single day! That can't be healthy. At dinner we crowd eleven guys around our dinky galley table for some greasy southern food. There is no supper offered.

Altogether, there are eleven guys on our garbage boat. I'm the youngest at age 20, and the oldest is nearly 22. So basically we're still a bunch of wet-nosed kids, I guess. (At least at heart we are.) We have three seamen, two enginemen, a troubleshooter, the craftmaster, a chief engineer, the cook, the houseboy, and the electrician – me. That makes four Negroes, two Filipinos, four white guys, and one South Dakotan.

I've been having all kinds of electrical trouble here on the boat lately. Gremlins everywhere. First, our scuttlebutt conked out; then the Red Devil blower in the after hold stopped working; and now the AC generator for the radio quit. What next? Maybe the boat will sink at the pier? No, we couldn't hope for that. But there are rumors that they're going to take two YGs off the line permanently. I'd hate to split up with my buddies, though.

A few days ago I finally got four sport shirts, two pair of trousers, a Probe game, my belt, and twenty packs of sunflower seeds in the mail from the folks. Woo hoo! Christmas come early! Sure was good to get into my old civilian clothes again. Made me feel just like a civilian when I hit the beach!

Well, I'll be honest with you. Now that I've been in the Navy a whole year already, there are still some times, not many, that I wish I was back in my apartment on Sanborn Street. It's not at all like I had expected it to be – more disappointments, more bureaucracy, if anything – but at least I'm getting to see the world. And that's the main reason I enlisted.

October 17, 1968

Dear Tootie,

Greetings, little sister! Goodness, it's been a long time since I wrote to you, but I've been studying for my big Fireman test a lot. And that's not a fireman like you're thinking of, but somebody who works in the engine room.

We've got another monkey on board now and her name is Alice. She is afraid of the horn on our boat. One of her arms is crippled, but she is still pretty spunky. This afternoon she drank half of my grape pop! Good grief!

We had a big water fight in the kitchen tonight. Nobody knows who started it. We threw water all over each other and made a big mess. Curtis poured a whole pitcher of water over Smitty's head. We mopped it up when the fight was over with, though. I heard somebody on the other boat say that we were all certified crazy. Could be.

We painted the deckplates orange down in the engine room today. We also painted the wheels and pipes different colors – like red, green, blue, yellow, and purple – depending on what they carry. Red stands for fire main or sea water, orange stands for oil, yellow for air, blue for fresh water, etc. This is called "color coding." We painted the walls bright white and the engines gray, and my switchboard shiny black. It sure looks pretty sharp now!

Are you getting ready for Halloween? Is it getting cold back home now? It's real hot down here. Just like summer all the time. We have to take cold showers just to cool off. Write soon, squirt?

EMFN Steve Stanga B617389
US Naval Station, Subic Bay
Box 15, YG-52
FPO, San Francisco
96651

October 22, 1968

Dear Gramma,

This is it. This is my last sheet of writing paper until payday. It's 0100 in the morning, and I have the midwatch, which is some prime letter-writing time. I should have planned ahead better, I guess.

Thank goodness we're getting out of the big Admiral's Inspection tomorrow! We have to go out into the harbor on a job. It's so much trouble to get our dress whites ready for inspection that we're always glad to avoid it…even if we do have to work instead.

The freshwater supply hose to the boat ruptured tonight and I had to run a fifty-foot hose to bypass the break. I really got soaked in the process, but it had to be done and there was no time for worrying whether I got wet or not. Just another hazard of being on watch all by myself. Heck, I'm wash-and-wear anyway.

I took the Fireman test last Tuesday and I was really worried if I could pass it or not, as it was pretty rough. But out of three guys, I was the only one who *did* pass it, so I suppose that all my studying paid off. Now I am advanced one pay grade and have three stripes on my uniform. And in February I can go up for third-class petty officer already! I had to pass the Fireman test before I can take the Electrician's Mate test.

The boys initiated me by lifting me high above their heads – and then throwing me over the side into the ocean! It sure is hard to swim with all your clothes and boots on! Then they threw me down into the bilges under the engine room. I was really a mess by then, but I was too happy to care. One of our enginemen made second-class petty officer today, also, so I got to help throw him over the side later. That was not an easy job, as he is one very husky guy from Flushing, New York!

November 12, 1968

Dear Gramma,

Many thanks for the money! There are a multitude of reasons why we're short of money all the time. We could be chiefs in the Navy and still not get paid enough.

Right now my average check is thirty-five dollars every two weeks. (I made twice that much back home at the café.) We have expenses down here. And everything by way of entertainment costs money: bowling, movies, riding horses, going to town, taxis, etc. We all have our own personal expenses back home, too: time payments, old debts, civilian life insurance, and others. I have a small savings bond taken out of my pay each month. I manage to squeak by every week, but just barely. At least I don't owe anybody down here like some of the other guys do. The only trouble with this rat race is that the rats are winning! My upcoming pay raise will help greatly, though.

I'm glad those politics are finally over with. It surprised me that Richard Nixon got elected. Even if I was old enough to vote, I probably wouldn't have anyway, as that wasn't even a good choice of candidates. Well, we'll see if Nixon can manage to straighten things out. Like it or not, he's now our new CINC.

A few days ago the ocean was covered with little jellyfishes as far as you could see. They were only as big as a twenty-five cent piece, and it was funny to watch them all wiggling through the water in unison. I've never seen anything like it before.

Smitty threw an old fire hose over the side while we were dumping garbage at sea today and it got all tangled up in our screw. I was down in the engine room at the time and I thought the engine was going to tear itself apart. We had to go underwater with diving masks and knives to cut the hose off the propeller. Never a dull moment around here!

The USS New Jersey (BB-62), a World War II battleship, pulled in here this weekend for minor repairs. The New Jersey was recommissioned just this year for a twenty-month tour of duty in the Vietnam war. Subic Bay is the largest ship-repair facility in the western Pacific. She'll probably get new 16-inch gun barrels while she's here, among other things.

I accidentally dropped my glasses over the side last night. Now they're at the bottom of the bay. Just plain carelessness on my part. It only takes twenty minutes to get a new pair made, and they're free, so I suppose I should try to get another pair made soon. I sure ain't much good without them otherwise.

Well, it looks like they're taking our garbage boat away from us during the first week of December and sending it to Vietnam. Then I suppose they'll split us up and put us all on different boats. There goes our tight crew and our swell liberty. We had it good for a while.

ABOARD THE GARBAGE BOAT

One night I was standing the security watch from midnight to 0400. Standing watch was pretty dull for the most part, especially in the middle of the night. Once every hour the watch had to make his rounds and check out the situation. The bilges down in the Hole were checked to see if the boat was leaking more than it normally did. If the water in the bilges was approaching the level of the deck-plates, then the bilges had to be pumped overboard into the harbor.

If any machinery on board was in operation, then electrical readings and lube-oil pressures and temperatures had to be taken and recorded in the sound-and-security log. Other duties of the watch were to see if the mooring lines were still secure (they had to be periodically loosened or tightened, depending on which way the tide was moving); shore-power cables and freshwater hoses had to be checked to see that they were kept clear from being pinched between the boat and pier. All this took about ten minutes; the rest of the hour I usually spent sitting on the fantail enjoying the balmy night air, either reading a good book or writing letters or making entries into my personal journal.

Fireman apprentice Gary Forrest, a skinny nervous hillbilly from the back-woods of South Carolina, had come back to the boat shortly after 0100. I could tell he was drunk by the way he sat on the pier and threw rocks at our boat, cursing the life that had brought him to be stationed on the YG-52 in the Philippines.

There is generally about three feet of space between the garbage boat and the pier to which it is secured. This made it necessary for anyone wanting to come aboard to jump rather nimbly from the pier to the gunwale of the boat. This is just what Forrest did, but alcohol-impairment misguided his depth perception and he landed short, falling in between the boat and the pier with a mighty splash. Not only was he in immediate danger of being crushed to death as the boat moved in and out against the pier, but he couldn't swim a stroke, and he was as drunk as a sailor could be.

Luckily, I heard Forrest yelling as he flailed about in the water, trying to climb up the sheer side of the boat. Taking a chance on getting crushed myself, I jumped over the side and grabbed hold of Forrest. He instantly tried to climb on top of me in a panic to get out of the terrifying black water, shoving my head underwater repeatedly, but I finally got him to settle down and quit struggling. I dragged him around to the other side of the boat where there were some handholds so we could climb back aboard.

Forrest thanked me over and over again for saving his life, before he finally got out of his wet clothes and went shakily to bed. He was suddenly sober, but trembling; his hands shook nervously the remainder of the time that I knew him. I stood there dripping all over the deck; my wallet was drenched through, and my only pair of leather boondockers were already beginning to shrink. I could see it was going to be one of those days.

During my four-hour watch I had consumed the better part of a pot of that terrible Navy coffee. You know the kind: made with recycled coffee grounds, a couple of whole eggs, shells and all, and a spoonful of salt. I didn't see any sense in crawling into my rack after I was relieved, as reveille was going down in less than two hours anyway, so I decided to stay up the rest of the night.

Around 0500 I noticed first light showing through the jungle trees up towards the Sky Club. This has always been my favorite time of the day. A strange, unexplainable wave of euphoria comes over me at dawn then, and I am at peace with the world. No reason for it really. An hour later I went down into the crew's berthing compartment and held reveille on them. After all, it was a work day, and there was lots of garbage to be scowed. Already the Stewburner was making his special S.O.S in the galley.

The Service Craft Division was bustling with activity by then, as hung-over crews were getting ready to begin their day's work on garbage boats, harbor tugs, pushboats, water tenders, and yard oilers. About 0730 I went down and lit off our main engine. By 0800 we were all ready to cast off. The deckapes threw the lines off the cleats on the pier and then hurriedly jumped back aboard. The craftmaster gave the first signal on the engine-order telegraph, and the garbage boat moved away stately from the pier.

Does the landlubber know the feeling of a good deck under his feet? Does he know the manly comradery of a tight crew? Does he know the thrill of the engine vibrating the entire boat as it strains to turn the massive shaft? Does he know the marvelous smell of diesel fumes in the early morning air? Does he know the exciting sound the screw makes thrashing away in the water? Does he know the pleasure of the breeze against his cheek, or the tang of the salt spray on his lips as the boat heads across open harbor? I doubt it.

Collecting garbage was an easy enough process. We simply maneuvered the garbage boat up alongside each ship anchored in the harbor, and let them throw their garbage down into our large open hoppers located on the forward half of the boat. We never had to touch the garbage once, unless we wanted to rescue something out of one of the hoppers, and then we used a boat hook anyway.

Duty on a garbage boat was known to be the best duty attainable in Service Craft, made even better by our inalienable salvage rights. Paperback books, *Playboy* magazines, dungarees, leather boots, etc. – these items and others could be traded to the Filipinos for beer.

The ultramodern *C.S. Neptun* lies at anchor in Subic Bay. The bright green cable-layer/repair ship remains ready to service more than 2,300 nautical miles of undersea telephone cables vital to the communications of the US Forces in Southeast Asia. It's been anchored here in the bay ever since I got here, and I haven't seen it get underway yet.

Nearby the *Neptun* is anchored a smaller Monrovian cable tender. Occasionally we had to stop and collect their garbage as well, and it was always an unpleasant job. I don't know what they were in the habit of eating on that boat, but their garbage was totally rancid and swimming with maggots every time we stopped. She had the most *mabaho* [stinky] garbage in the South China Sea!

After collecting the garbage, we steamed out of Subic Bay past the high rolling hills of Luzon. The craftmaster often let me take the wheel at this point, as there wasn't much of anything to run into out in the middle of the bay, other than some old rusty Victory ships swinging on their anchors. We steamed slowly past recreational Grande Island, sneaking under the silent Japanese gun emplacements hidden in the jungle there. Shortly afterwards we steamed past smaller Chiquita Island. Many times I had gone snorkeling with buddies off Chiquita Island, discovering brilliantly-colored marine life, seashells, and on several occasions – sharks!

Japanese guns on Grande Island, Subic Bay, Philippines.

We navigated the garbage boat about 15 miles out to sea, where we would dump the garbage. Up on the main deck were large wheels that took two of us to rotate. When turned, they winched open the huge hopper doors on the side of the boat, and the garbage literally slid out into the ocean. Anything that did not voluntarily exit the boat was propelled into the water by a blast from a strong-minded fire hose and long, persuasive bamboo poles.

We were usually followed by half a dozen Filipinos in their banca boats, their tiny trolling motors doing double time in the rough swells to keep up with us. They would try to save as much material as possible before it sank from sight, which it did rather rapidly; they pulled the debris to them with rakes and dragged it into their boats as fast as they could. Rarely did anything remain floating or was washed clear back into the harbor, with one exception – the beach on the seaward side of Chiquita Island was littered with hundreds of rubber shower shoes...flip-flops.

Once the garbage was dumped, we put our stern to the wind and headed back to Boton Valley. By then it was usually mid-afternoon, giving us plenty of time to get cleaned up and head out into Olongapo City for the rest of the day.

Our first stop was always at one of the many money-exchange booths right outside the main gate. As station sailors, we knew which booths consistently gave us the best exchange rate, so we could ignore the shrill yammering of all the Filipino touts on either side and forge ahead with confidence.

Our second stop was usually the American Legion Post, where we would sit out on the balcony overlooking Magsaysay Drive and put a few bourbons under our belts. Our third stop might be the Filipino restaurant across the street, where we would dine sumptuously on *lumpiya* [egg roll], *pansit* [noodle dishes], and shrimp-fried rice. The remainder of the evening could be spent barhopping, listening to rock bands, fighting off the peso-hungry bar hogs (they are especially excited when they get hold of a cherry-boy), visiting our honey-co if we had a regular girl, and slopping up ice-cold San Miguel beer. Life was good.

November 29, 1968

Dear Gramma,

Mabuhay [long live] is my Filipino greetings to you! I got your letter today – and thanks ever so much for the five dollars! You're too good to me. A couple of months ago I would have taken the money and run right out in town with the boys, but that's worn off now. I bought some Christmas cards and got a haircut instead. The postage stamps you sent were very timely, too; I've already used some tonight!

We had a wonderful Thanksgiving! The Stewburner surprised us and actually roasted a whole turkey. We also had mashed potatoes, gravy, biscuits, dressing, corn, salted nuts, cranberries, ice cream, and honest-to-god real cow's milk! It may not sound like anything out of the ordinary to you, but it was a royal feast to us! After dinner, four of us sat around and actually told the things we were thankful for. Sounds kind of corny now, though.

Well, they've stripped our poor YG-52 bare, boarded it up, welded the doors and portholes shut, and towed her off to Vietnam. Sure hated to see her go like that. We had a lot of good times on board. Now I'm temporarily assigned to a repair crew up at the main electric shop that sometimes even works at night. I'm sleeping in a barracks again (when I'm allowed to sleep, that is), and my buddies are separated and scattered all over the base. It's a change of pace, I guess, but I'm not especially enjoying it.

Our two favorite bands out in town quit and moved to Manila. Rats! Although there is usually a band to be found in every nightclub here, they were the two best bands in town in our estimation. We've been to a couple of evening softball games here and really enjoyed them. They remind me of the swell times I had at the Center ball field years ago, when I was farming with Swede and Lujeanne.

The Special Services Department here on the base is huge! They are in the business of recreation and employ experts in the field. They offer softball, bowling, golf, swimming, skin diving, pool, skeet shooting, ceramic shop, craft center, movies, trail riding, deep-sea fishing, tours, tennis, libraries, sailing, car rental, go-karts, musical band, dance lessons, little theater group, football, horseshoes, water skiing, volleyball, slot-car racing, photography darkrooms, handball, teen club, kennels, woodworking shop, model-airplane flying, jogging track, electronics lab, leather crafts, gymnasium, and much more. If we get bored with going out in town, there's always plenty to do right here on base, huh!

A couple of days ago a huge fire burned down the whole market out in Olongapo City, including some apartment buildings and a few nightclubs. Curtis and I were out in town at the time, and since we were Navy men trained in fire fighting, we got to fight on the front line with the hoses. We turned quite a few pigs, dogs, and chickens loose from houses so they wouldn't get burned up; We kicked in a few doors, got a lot of little cuts on corrugated tin, and pretty much ruined a good set of civvies. We left town at 0100 when the fire was under control. There was a blackout all over town at the time (they're always having those) and I heard that they suspect some candles started the fire. The very same market burned down last year, too.

Next week a Negro friend of mine has asked me to have dinner out in town. I was over at his house a few nights ago and his Filipina wife served me up some terrific chow! He has lived in the P.I. for several years, is married to a woman twice his age, and he can speak the native Tagalog (pronounced "tah-GAHL-oh") as good as a local. He just recently re-enlisted for another four years in the Navy so he could stay here longer.

NEWSPAPER CLIPPING

Taken from the *Subic Bay News*

"Faulty wiring sparks biggest Olongapo fire ever. It triggered a short circuit in the ceiling of Young's Bazaar, which caused the 10-million peso fire on the night of November 27th. In the spirit of *Bayanihan* [cooperation], sailors and Marines on liberty manned the hoses alongside Filipinos. There were as many looters as there were rescuers at times, and many of them were injured during their looting. This is the third major fire to hit the city in the last four months. A gloomy atmosphere pervaded as cleanup operations started on Thanksgiving morning. It razed two buildings and 34 residences, but there was no loss of life."

NEWSPAPER CLIPPING

Taken from the *Subic Bay News*

"During the month of November, 29 watches valued at $2,000 and 21 wallets valued at $1,000 were reported stolen from military personnel while going on liberty in Olongapo City. The standard operating procedure for liberty should always be the 'buddy system'. No one on liberty in Olongapo should be more than a few feet away from a buddy at all times."

December 6, 1968

The Air Force Veterinarian Corps is the only Air Force unit stationed in Subic Bay. You would expect them to be on some Air Force base taking care of dependent's cats and dogs. But their main job here is to inspect local and stateside produce used as food on the base, including milk, flour, *lumpiya* [egg roll], rice, fruits and vegetables. Of the 12 million pounds of produce that is used on the base, 114,000 pounds of food is purchased locally.

December 17, 1968

Dear Gramma,

I was so surprised to get your package this afternoon! I wasn't expecting it at all. The package got here in excellent shape, too; the cookies didn't turn hard inside the wax milk carton, so that was a good idea. They were really good, and the fellas all enjoyed them, too. The malted milk balls were okay until I took them out of the box, and then they started to melt, so we had to eat them fast! Thanks a lot, Gramma, the gingersnaps were really delicious. And we never get any chocolate down here because it can't survive the terrible heat. It was a real treat!

The family sent me a big package from home last week, too. They wanted me to wait until Christmas to open it, but I just couldn't hold out. I have no willpower! Weak as water. They sent me three jigsaw puzzles, a plastic-block game, a set of playing cards, a magnetic chess and checkers set, some great Avon soap on a rope, a big box of assorted hard nuts, and a favorite magazine of mine. Lot's of stuff to keep me occupied!

I'm still assigned to the electric shop, but most of the time I've been riding out on one of the tugboats to see if I can learn the electrical engineering plant on it. It's very hard; it must be like going to a technical college or something. It's much more complicated than the electrical system on the garbage boat, I know that for sure. But I'm trying my best; they can't ask for any more than that.

The funny thing is, the billet for electrician on the tugs requires a second-class petty officer, and I'm only a lousy fireman. Either somebody made a huge mistake up at the office, or else they think I'm a lot smarter than I really am. But I'm strong and healthy and not entirely half-witted, so I can probably handle it. I wish they would have left me on the YG where I knew what I was doing, though. The name of the tug is the *USS Mawkaw* (YTM-182); Navy tugs are named after Indian words and famous chiefs. *Mawkaw* was supposedly a Winnebago chief of sagacious repute.

I'm sure glad that tomorrow is payday because I'm desperately in need of some new dungarees. The heat and the sweat and the salt water – not to mention the oil, the paint, and the dirt – have completely ruined all of my boot camp issue, so that I cannot wear them around the base anymore unless I want to risk getting written up for being a slob by some eager-beaver officer. We're allotted six dollars per month in our paychecks for a clothing allowance, which most of the time hardly even covers the mending required.

I stand duty up here in the shipping office for now; that's why I suddenly have access to a typewriter. I sit here at the desk of the Service Craft warehouse and answer the phone all night long. Once an hour I go down to all the boats along the pier and make sure the bilges are halfway dry so they won't sink; check to see that the watches are all awake and on the job; and run messages. On the weekends I pick up the mail and packages and sort it out between all the boats. It's pretty easy work. I have the duty only once every five days now.

Once the rainy season sets in, it seems neverending, with the sun quickly becoming nothing more than a fond memory of light and warmth and all things dry. By necessity, life goes on as usual during the monsoon season – only then it also includes a daily umbrella and continual damp clothing. The relentless rain falling on the jungle vegetation that is everywhere in the Philippines creates a constant racket in the background that often makes conversation difficult.

It's my job to show the movies to the division men of Boton Valley each evening, which takes place outdoors behind the electrician's shop, under a huge canvas awning. (I always feel it is reminiscent of the drive-in theaters back in the States.) My motion-picture school finally came in good for something! During the wet season, I have to hook up an additional speaker to the sound system. And even then most of the dialogue is still inaudible, what with thousands of huge drops of monsoon water battering the awning; it is nonetheless a pleasant experience to watch the screen images show welcome reminders of home to the men, all to the accompaniment of rain on the roof.

I hung onto my chow pass after I was supposed to turn it in when I was transferred from the barracks to a boat, so now I can still eat at the main galley whenever I want…where I can have all the cold, fresh milk I desire. You see, there is a method to my madness. It's the little things that count.

I finished all my required courses for petty officer third-class. In January, I will take the Military Leadership test; and in February I take the petty officer test itself. The time in-between will largely be spent studying, for sure! A lot of benefits come when you make rate: you can put Cinderella liberty behind you and stay out until much later; your pay nearly doubles (there's an incentive right there!); you can throw your rank around (if you happen to be that kind of guy); and you might even get out of standing so much duty. It's certainly something to shoot for. But the test for Electrician's Mate is supposed to be one of the roughest; not everybody makes it the first time around.

They had another USO show at the station theater the other night. They have one just about every week. This was a good variety band from Hollywood, and I really enjoyed it. Singer Neil Sedaka will appear on base soon in Grande Island's Casa Grande Club.

I have access to a piano in the ballet studio on weekends when there's nobody dancing, and I usually go there to keep up with my playing. I certainly am rusty, but it gives me a lot of pleasure. Mom and Dad sent me a book of piano songs recently.

I got a letter from Bobby Anderson the other day. He is in the first couple weeks of Navy boot camp, and I think about him a lot. He said that after the first few days he could have murdered me for talking him into signing up, but now he's beginning to like it. Two more of my buddies, Al Larson and Doug Seiner, are going into the Navy in January on my encouragement; I hope I don't lose three good friends out of the deal! And later, another friend back home, Tom McNary, is going into the Coast Guard. It's two years shorter, otherwise it's exactly like the Navy. I really hesitated talking them into joining the service, because everybody is different, and I didn't know how they were going to handle it, or if they would enjoy it like I do.

A Negro friend of mine, who was on our old boat, invited several of us to a party at his residence out in town; it was his wife's birthday. She gave us all sorts of strange, delicious things to eat, of which I've already forgotten the names of. There was a sort of chow mein, sausages, sweet and sour pork, rice (of course), a taco/tamale mixture with fish and hamburger (!), a kind of egg custard, something like an egg salad with fruit in it, and homemade bread. As it turned out, my two white buddies didn't show up, so I was the only honky there with six Negroes and a couple of dozen Filipinos. But I had a great time!

Some of his in-laws were there from Manila, and he took me aside to explain who everybody was: his uncle-in-law – that fat, red-faced man with a limp – was supposedly the number one snatcher (kidnapper) in Manila about twenty years ago; that skinny man with the rat's-nest hair-do and the patch over one eye was his right-hand man; that woman with the fussy little girl on her lap is the mayor's sister (the Olongapo mayor is also a woman). I guess I was really in the company of "celebrities" (?), huh.

While we were at the party, we were serenaded by a motley gang of Filipino children with a ukulele and a fistful of sleigh bells who sang Christmas carols in Spanish. We gave them a few pesos when they were done.

Afterwards I got back through the main gate ten minutes late. The Marine sentry on guard duty just waved me on through anyway. I was lucky he was a tolerant guy; others have been thrown in the brig for breaking curfew by only five minutes!

Maligayang Pasko at Manigong Bagong Taon [Merry Christmas and Happy New Year]!

EMFN Steve Stanga B617389
US Naval Station, Subic Bay
Box 15, YTM-182
FPO, San Francisco
96651

January 14, 1969

Dear Family,

Boy, talk about a bunch of discontented guys! We just got the discouraging word: another towing job! They got us up at 0430 after two and a half glorious hours of sleep. They've been doing this to us about every two hours all night long. Why can't ships depart the harbor at a decent hour? And there isn't even any hot coffee on the stove – what *is* the Stewburner doing with his time?! Let's hear it again for morale! Yay! (And this is payday, too.)

As you can see by my address change, I am stationed onboard the tug full-time now! Besides moving other vessels in the harbor, our tug also shuttles around barges, cranes, and cargo floats.

Portions of the bay are presently being dredged deeper, and at least once a week we have to tow the filthy mud barges out to sea and dump them. This is a risky prospect at best, because when the trap doors underneath the barge are tripped open and the mud falls out the bottom, the barge is suddenly relieved of tons of dead weight and it leaps upward six feet or more. Sometimes you'd swear it was going to clear the water! So we have to make sure beforehand that all connecting lines between the tug and the barge have sufficient slack in them, and that everybody is standing well clear and hanging onto something firm.

When making up to another ship, we first have to get a mooring line over to them. This is accomplished by using a small-diameter heaving line with a monkey fist on the end of it. This is whirled around the head and suddenly flung while yelling, "Heads up!" We are all extremely accurate with placing the monkey fist on the other ship, and have never beaned a sailor on another vessel that I am aware of. Once they have the monkey

Aboard the YTM-182 tugboat,
Subic Bay, Philippines.

fist in their hands, they can haul in the heaving line and pull across a heavier line attached to it.

I took the Military Leadership test this morning. I thought it was pretty easy, but it's always the easy ones that foul a guy up. I'm still awaiting the results.

I've just been informed that I've been selected from the crew to design new built-in furniture for the galley and the berthing compartment. Why me?! All because somebody saw me sketching one day.

We've got another stupid Admiral's Inspection on Friday. Those people must think that all we've got to do around here is get those miserable whites ready for inspection. I'm sure that's all *they've* got to do.

NEW JERSEY ARRIVES IN WESPAC

"The battleship *USS New Jersey* (BB-62) recently arrived at the US Naval Base at Subic Bay to begin her tour of duty in the Far East. Her nine 16-inch guns, which can hurl a 2,700-pound projectile over twenty miles, give the enemy fearsome firepower to reckon with. At present the *USS New Jersey* is the only battleship in the world on active duty."

January 18, 1969

Dear Gramma,

Right now I'm supposed to be designing new furniture for the galley, but I've been working at it all morning and I'm just going to set it aside for a while and take a break and write a few letters instead. Maybe when I return to it later I'll have some fresh ideas. The chief engineer gave me the job after he saw the writing desk I built for the crew's compartment. But I don't really mind; it's kind of flattering. When I get the drawings completed, then some Filipino carpenters from the shop will come in here and knock the stuff together for us.

I passed my Military Leadership test four days ago; now I have just one more test in February to pass and then I'll be a third-class petty officer. And as they say, rank has its privileges.

Yesterday we had our big Admiral's Inspection over on Mainside. Our pickup had engine trouble along the way, so our whole crew was late in arriving. Here come the ten of us sneaking down the ranks while everybody else is popped to attention. (The division officer frowned at us a little bit.) I admit that I was fairly nervous about the inspection. I always am. I must have held my breath for five minutes and stood stiff as a cigar-store Indian as the fleet Admiral came slowly down the line and then looked me over from head to toe. And then he passed! And so had I. We only had one man faint from standing at attention so long.

Right now we are putting a tin can into dry dock. It seems they were following a bird farm over to Vietnam when the guys on the bird farm threw a log over the side. (Don't ask me what they were doing with a log; it was probably an old wooden beam or something similar.) It got caught in the tin can's screws and really messed it up. So our tug is putting it into the dry dock for repairs. Somebody's head will roll for that one.

The operation of a floating dry dock is pretty interesting and is simplicity itself. First of all, they pump the hollow walls of the dock full of water to sink it. Then they push the ship inside so that the keel will rest on pre-positioned concrete blocks. It is extremely important that the blocks conform to the structural members so that the ship is not damaged when its weight is no longer supported evenly by water. Navy divers assist in fine-tuning the ship's positioning. After that, all they have to do is pump the water back out of the walls to raise both the dry dock and the ship out of the water. *Voila!*

Ships sure look peculiar out of the water; normally you can't see but half the hull otherwise. We call the AFDM-5 floating dry dock "The Big Five," but actually it's only a medium-sized dry dock. We have several of the smaller ones here, too. Someday I'd like to see one of the really big ones!

They have built a brand-new Lutheran Service Center out in town. There is a snack bar, pool tables, a stereo and tape deck, typewriters, all kinds of books, even a piano and a ping-pong table! I think it's a pretty nice place to hang out, but none of my buddies would be caught dead there with me.

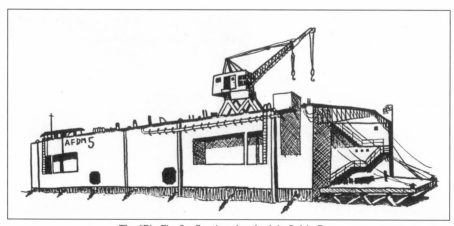

The "Big Five" a floating dry-dock in Subic Bay.

My girl back home, Suzie, sent me five dollars for New Years. I don't know what got into her; she's never done anything like that before. Maybe once a week I play the slot machines here on base. I never play more than a dollar, though, and I usually win. Other people get greedy when they win a few times, and end up losing all their money by stuffing it right back in the machine. They don't call them "one-armed bandits" for nothing. But I always quit when I'm ahead – even if it's just a dollar or two. The other night I finally hit the jackpot and won $12.50! I could hardly believe it. With the money I won I bought a diving mask, a snorkel, and a pair of fins so now I can go skin diving in style out at Grande Island tomorrow afternoon.

The guys keep complaining about the heat down here, but I don't mind it all that much. I guess if I can put up with South Dakota summers, I can put up with just about anything. The water is almost too warm for enjoyable swimming, though, and there is a lot of dust blowing around. It's cool and refreshing sailing out in the harbor, thank goodness.

A LETTER MEANS CARING

Taken from the *Subic Bay News*

"How many times have you seen the overseas 'mail call' where the postal clerk hands out letters until only a few dejected men stand by – those who didn't get one?

This isn't just a scenario from a movie. It happens quite often for various reasons. Mainly, it's because addresses have changed by constant moves, and the letters are somewhere in the pipeline.

However, let's reverse the situation. Family addresses back home seldom change. Yet, there are sometimes weeks and even months when they, too, become dejected waiting for letters from their servicemen.

Writing, between family members, is not always a matter of exchanging news, but of thoughtfulness and caring. Just a note to Mom and Dad, wife or sister, means that you care – merely by sending a few words.

Words from home bring a personal feeling of pleasure that only the reader understands. Remember, writing is a two-way street, and a letter means love and affection – whether you are 50 or 5,000 miles away. And, your letter brings you home – even for a moment or two."

January 23, 1969

Dear Gramma,

Here's hoping I have time to finish this letter before the movie marathon tonight. If not, then I'll finish it when I get back to the boat. Boy, I sure got a surprise yesterday. I got your Christmas card and enclosed five-dollar bill postmarked December 16th! A whole bunch of us guys got mail yesterday dated way before Christmas. I can see how this could happen with all the mail there must be around the holidays. A whole sackful must have gotten shoved aside for a while and totally forgotten about. And I bet you thought I was really a stinker for not having written and thanked you for the money, huh? Well, I'm thanking you now! I wonder if there's any more of our mail floating around somewhere.

Would you believe it rained today? Just a trace, though. And this is supposed to be the hot season. Anyway, it cooled things off for a little while at least. I don't care how much everybody complains about the weather back home either; I sure miss the snow and the blizzards. But I do enjoy getting outdoors each and every day down here. By way of getting some exercise for myself, I got out and walked ten miles the other day in two and a half hours.

On Sunday afternoon we went skin diving out at Chiquita Island, which you can wade to from Grande Island (as long as you wear tennis shoes to protect your feet from the coral). This is a much prettier area for diving, so we enjoyed ourselves thoroughly! There are so many canyons, cliffs, and underwater caves to explore, but this is where the open sea begins, so we have to keep an eye out for the occasional shark and moray eel. I'm pretty handy with a spear gun, though. Don't worry about ol' Steve.

The trouble is that we cut ourselves up so much on the sharp coral underwater, and on the barnacles adhered to the rocks. This really smarts in the salt water and the blood attracts undesirable marine life! But we got a good tan that day. One Filipino girl on the beach cut her hands so bad on the coral that I had to wrap them in my T-shirt before they took her back to the base dispensary. I've never seen anyone go into shock before.

WHAT IS A SAILOR?
Taken from the *Subic Bay News*

"Between the security of the first childhood and the insecurity of the second childhood, we find the fascinating group of humanity called Sailors! They come in assorted sizes, colors, and states of financial ruin.

They can be found anywhere: on ships, on leave, on the beach, at shore stations, at the flick, in their rack, in bars, in love, and always in debt. Girls love them, towns tolerate them, and the Government supports them.

A sailor is laziness with a deck of cards, bravery with a tattooed arm, and protector of the seas with a copy of *Playboy*. He has the speed of a turtle, the slyness of a sea lawyer, the sincerity of a chronic liar, the aspiration of a Casanova, the vocabulary of a wharf thug, and when he wants something it is usually connected with a liberty card or an overnight pass.

Some of his likes are beer, girls, sleep, women, liberty, more girls, and the opposite sex – just to name a few. He dislikes answering relative's letters, shaving, his whites, superior officers, the chow, standing watch, and getting up every morning.

No one else can cram into a jumper pocket a little black book, a pack of cigarettes, a lighter, a dozen pictures of his girl back home, a comb, a candy bar, and what's left of last week's paycheck. He likes to spend some of his money on beer and girls – in that order. The rest of it he spends foolishly.

A sailor is a magnificent creature in bell-bottom pants. You can back him out of your home but not out of your heart. You can scratch him off your mailing list but not off your mind. You might as well give up; he is your long-away-from-home lover, your unfortunate buddy in the service, and your one and only bundle of worry. But all your shattered dreams become insignificant when your sailor docks and he looks at you with those bloodshot eyes and says, 'Hiya, honey! It's good to be home!'"

February 8, 1969

Dear Gramma,

Glad to get your letter yesterday; mail's been few and far between these last couple of weeks. It's either feast or famine. It comes in batches – and then there's a long period of drought without any mail at all.

Weather-wise, we're having sort of queer weather at present. In the past three days we've had two torrential downpours! And this is the middle of the dry season! The average temperature during the day is about 90 degrees, and at night around 65 degrees. But while we're underway out in the harbor it gets pretty chilly, so we wear our work jackets in the early-morning and evening hours. You know, I'm glad I come from a state with four separate and distinct seasons, because continual sunshine and clement weather every day for months on end gets awfully boring!

Ships are of the female gender. The fast combat support ship, the *USS Camden* (AOE-2), latest thing in underway replenishment, is presently docked at Subic's POL piers. She just joined the fleet in 1968, and is a new type of ship: a combination oiler, ammunitions, and stores ship.

Hollywood is presently making a movie down here in Subic Bay. And there are all kinds of movie stars and important-looking people in sunglasses roaming around the base. The only three I've ever heard of before are actors Michael Caine and Cliff Robertson and Denholm Elliott. Producer/director Robert Aldrich and most of his staff arrived at Cubi Point Naval Air Station on Wednesday to begin filming the jungle scenes for "Too Late the Hero." Yesterday on the radio they were advertising for extras to act as British soldiers for ten dollars a day! This is a small fortune to us poor Navy swabs who only get paid a mere four dollars a day. But our division officer wouldn't let us off work.

I am taking a USAFI course now. It's a program where you can extend your education through a college-affiliated Navy correspondence course. If you do enough of them, you are credited with college credits and eventually a degree. The first course costs five dollars; but if you complete it satisfactorily then all the rest after that are free. I started with "Blueprint Drawing and Map Reading," to be followed by an algebra course. Heck, it'll be just like going back to school.

And then there were three… One of our tight little group, Moose Turner, has gone back to the States for leave, and then on to Vietnam. So that leaves just the three of us. Another buddy (my closest friend down here) leaves in ten days for the States, and then he goes to Vietnam, too. I'll sure hate to see Curtis go. Then there'll be only the two of us: Smitty and I. He leaves in ten months, which is not a particularly long time as fast as these days fly by. Just when you make a good buddy and get in tight with him, the Navy ships him out and surgically separates the both of you. Then you have to start all over again.

Want to hear something frightening? Sitting up on the bow yesterday we got to talking about this and that, as guys will do, and we found out some pretty scary things about ourselves. Out of a crew of 13 guys:

> None of us could say the Pledge of Allegiance correctly from beginning to end.
>
> Eight of us didn't know the name of our national anthem.
>
> Nobody knew all of the Ten Commandments.
>
> Only one guy knew the Lord's Prayer.
>
> And one chowderhead couldn't even remember the capitol of his home state of California!

We've been away from school so long we just start to forget things. But I'd sure feel dumb during an inspection if the Admiral suddenly asked me the name of our national anthem and I whipped out "The Stars and Stripes Forever, sir!" They'd probably lock me up for the rest of my unnatural days, and I wouldn't blame them a bit.

February 10, 1969

Dear Family,

It's 0200 in the morning and the only dummies awake are bats, burglars, and electricians. And to make matters worse, the cupboard is bare. No decent groceries in the galley at all. I've got the watch until 0400, so I guess I've got a couple of hours to kill yet.

Starting tonight, all military personnel are restricted to the base for an indefinite period of time. The Navy is laying off about 2,000 Filipinos who work on the base at SRF, and they are expecting trouble both on the base and out in town. The Riot Squad is on full alert. Funny thing is that half the sailors on the Riot Squad are Filipinos themselves! How will that work?

Did you know that singer Gary Lewis married a Filipino girl? Yes! I hear Boris Karloff died last week at age 81. And didn't I read somewhere that Irene Ryan died just recently, too? The other night out in town I saw a chap who looked exactly like actor Peter O'Toole! He had the same blonde-white hair, the same gaunt face, the same cold blue eyes, and the same maniacal half-smile. Hmmm, I wonder…

My harmonica playing is improving by leaps and bounds. The guys like to sit around on the fantail at night and listen to it while they look out over the harbor lights… and think about home, I imagine. I ran across a harmonica songbook over at the base library. It teaches you how to play the blues harp as well. They also had some novelties like playing the harmonica with a drinking glass over one end, and playing through your ears. But trying to learn how to play the harmonica from a book is next to useless.

Well, how's what's-his-name Nixon doing in the Presidency so far? About all the news we get lately are short headlines over the Armed Forces radio network between hillbilly songs and hilarious episodes of "ChickenMan." Nixon had a couple of speeches on the air, but I got up and left the compartment. There's just something about that guy that really goes against my grain. I can't put my finger on it. Is it true that he's going to abolish the draft? Well, all I'm interested in is the space race. I hope he doesn't mess with that. Let me know when we get a man on the moon, okay?

Would you believe I was talking to a guy from Liverpool, England, just this morning? He was on an Australian tin can that we were moving dead-plant. We were tied alongside them for about an hour and were talking across the rails to some of the fellows. I found out that you should never call them "Aussies," as this is derogatory to them! I always thought it was the affectionate generic nickname for anybody from Down Under. Like "Kiwis" are people from New Zealand, and "Canucks" are people from Canada. Oh well, you live and learn. Most of the rest of their guys come from around Melbourne and Sydney. They sure have sharp uniforms! (They think ours are sharp, too.) They wear a sort of fuzzy terrycloth T-shirt, shorts, a Donald Duck-type hat, and sandals. Sure does look comfortable!

Getting up every morning at 0500 – or even earlier – gets to be a real drag sometimes. At least on the garbage boat we could sleep in on Saturdays and Sundays. But here on the tug we haven't anything to look forward to. It's the same routine day in and day out: get up while it's still dark out and go to bed when it's dark again. There is one good thing about it, though; sunrises in the P.I. are something else, and are only outdone by the sunsets! I figure people miss a lot by not getting up with the sun.

The big ships are clumsy and helpless within the confines of a small bay. Thus, it is up to the tugs to herd them safely to the pier. It will take four to six tugs to manhandle a bird farm, where we would be tucked away under the huge, overhanging flight deck far above us. You cannot imagine how truly massive these carriers are, or why they should even float in the first place. Sometimes the rest of the tugs will be busy on other jobs across the harbor, and then it is up to us *alone* to move a bird farm.

Once we pulled the huge carrier *USS America* (CVA-66) away from the pier at Cubi Point with a single stern tow. Our husky nine-inch (circumference) nylon hawser was stretched incredibly tight as the tug strained to pull the carrier, until the hawser was no bigger than a heaving line – so taut that you could probably play a tune on it. During a stern tow, all hands are sent forward to the bow of the tug, so in case the line ever parted nobody would get crushed or snapped into two pieces by the recoiling nylon rope. Stranger things have happened.

In the past week I've read five books. I'd call that quite an accomplishment even for me, wouldn't you? Most everybody in Service Craft walks around with a paperback book in their hip pocket. I like to see people reading. It's important. Maybe some of the books they read wouldn't be approved by the Legion of Decency, but at least they're reading! And when you're reading, you can't help but assimilate something useful.

I don't think I told you that Johnny Cash was here a few weeks back. He put on his show at the China Seas Club and just about brought the house down. We got there a couple hours early, so we had really good seats. Once Mamie Van Doren was here and gone before we even knew anything about it! Grrrrr.

If I don't watch myself, I'm going to be just another statistic on the DOD's accident report. Electrician's Mate is a critical enough rate the way it is without me adding to it. I've never really been afraid of electricity, so maybe that's why I've grown careless around it. I almost got electrocuted yesterday – not once, but twice!

The first time, I was running armored cable behind the switchboard. Behind the switchboard are all kinds of live wires and switches, and I was being careful how I handled the clumsy cable, but I lifted it too high without first looking above me and jammed it right into some exposed resistors. Talk about sparks pouring down all over me! I thought it was the Fourth of July come early!

Later, I was down in the Hole really sweating it out. I had my shirt off, a rag twisted around my head to keep the burning sweat out of my eyes; my body was just running with water so that even my dungarees and skivvie shorts were sopping wet. Not a pretty picture.

I was hooking up some ventilation motors, and I had the power shut off so I could work behind the main switchboard. But I had forgotten about all those amps coming from our huge storage batteries through the copper bus bars of the switchboard. ZOT! I found out that I was a very good conductor of electricity, all wet like that! It knocked me right on my butt and really gave me a bad headache. Like Coca Cola says, "Zing, what a feeling!" It sure makes you stop and think for a minute.

February 24, 1969

Dear Gramma,

I was certainly glad to get the pictures of snow that you sent – I had actually forgotten what December in South Dakota looked like! It's been three winters already since I've enjoyed snow.

I really liked the candy that Aunt Lujeanne sent. I didn't have to worry about it melting on the boat, because as soon as I opened the box there appeared a dozen hungry mouths around me with outstretched hands. Feeding frenzy!

Our Stewburner has been at home out in town for the past two days. He married a cute little Filipino girl a year ago and now they've got a new baby boy! He's really tickled about that. It's a chubby seven-pound baby; two pounds of baby and five pounds of ears. Criminy. I visit them real often and they seem like a happy couple. Cookie is going to be a preacher back in North Carolina when he gets out of the Navy.

Some fellow from Disbursing called me yesterday and told me I haven't been getting Foreign Duty Pay since I've been down here, and I should have been. So next payday my check should be almost double! Over $100! This is great news. It comes at a good time, too, because I've got some pesky civilian bills back home to pay this month.

In our spare time, like right now, we do a lot of fishing over the side of the tug. Indeed, our Filipino houseboy is simply nuts about fishing with a hook and line. All we use is a spool of line, a hook, and some shrimp for bait. The water is so clear that you can actually dangle the bait right in front of the fish's nose. Some of the fish we catch are really pretty. Such colors! The houseboy knows which ones to toss back, as some are dangerous to eat. This morning I caught a baby sea barracuda. The houseboy takes all the fish home to cook for his family.

Spare time on the tugboat.

They tell me that now is the time to be putting in my request chit for my next duty station already. They call it a dream sheet, and we are supposed to list our top ten choices. But I still can't make up my mind what I want to do. I'd be glad to get on a DESRON destroyer home-ported in Japan; I wouldn't mind an LST ferrying troops and supplies across the South China Sea; and I'd be tickled to death if I got on a river patrol boat in Vietnam! I've got so many things to choose from. Maybe I'll just put in for all of them and see where the chips fall. We'll see…

March 2, 1969

Dear Tootie,

Right now we don't sail our tug because we have two weeks to fix it up. We will paint it and clean it up good. The enginemen will work on our engines and I will work on all of our motors. Just routine stuff. True, we will have to work longer hours every day, but at least we don't have to work at night! I can't wait until we get to sail out into the harbor again, because it's so much fun!

Did you know we have a boy on the tug called Charlie Brown? And we have a guy called Pineapple, because he is from Hawaii. We have a real tall guy called Lurch, but he is in the brig right now because he tried to run away from the Navy. We have this real fat guy who is called Tubby because he eats so much candy all the time. And do you know what they call me sometimes? "Little Stevie Wonderful"! Ha ha. Most of the time, an electrician like me is simply called "Sparky," though.

Well, I suppose you've still got snow piled up to your ears, huh? It's getting so hot down here that in the afternoon we can't even go down to our bedroom below decks because it's like an oven down there! But the weather sure is good for swimming. I saw a shark today that was five feet long. That's taller than you!

March 7, 1969

Dear Gramma,

Thanks for the postage stamps! I was sitting here with a whole stack of letters that I had written, waiting to be mailed, but I had no stamps to mail them with. Now they're on their way to the States. Thank you! Every day we get off work too late to go to the post office, and their windows are closed on the weekends. So that presents sort of a postage problem for us, doesn't it?

I just heard that we won't be out chugging in the harbor for quite a while – about three months! Tugboats go into the yards periodically for a complete overhaul…and now it's our turn. We've been off the line for two weeks now and I'm already going out of my mind from boredom. Sure, our whole day is passed in a multitude of activities, but I sorely miss working out in the bay and cruising around on the green water. The other guys are tickled to death, because now we get liberty every single night. But to me this only means I'll be spending more money on dumb things – just to break the monotony!

Everything on the boat has already been cleaned, painted, rewired, greased, etc., so I have my hands full working on all my motors and generators and lighting systems. But now that we're in the yards, the Filipino civilians will be doing the majority of the work, and we'll be off duty for whole weeks at a time.

I think maybe I'll ride out on another tug with my buddy and help him handle lines when the opportunity arises. Electricians don't normally get all the physical exercise that deckapes do (ha!), so I'm thankful for any I can get here on the boat.

I sure got a workout yesterday, though; I carried four big six-volt batteries up from our engine room, across three tugs in the nest, up onto the pier, and over to the electric shop. Then I carried four new ones back down. It took me half a day to accomplish this, and afterwards my arms literally trembled for hours from the effort. The batteries weigh about eighty pounds apiece! Consequently, I'm a little stiff and sore today.

Battery acid is funny stuff. It won't actually start to burn your hands for a long time, but if you spill a drop on your shirt, an hour later you will suddenly have a big hole there. After I got done lugging all those heavy batteries, my poor dungarees simply fell apart. It looked like somebody had taken a razor blade to them.

Last week one of the guys off another tug came back from town drunk and decided to go swimming in the bay after midnight. He drowned before anybody even knew what was going on. The next morning they had several Navy divers looking for him, and a couple of hours later they found him underneath the tug, floating about six feet off the bottom. They tied a rope around him and we all helped pull him up. But when he came over the side and flopped on the deck like a wet thing, I got light-headed and left the scene. I didn't even hardly recognize him; he was blue and all bloated up like a balloon. I sure hope I never see anything like that again. Anyway, there followed a big investigation about the whole deal, with no results other than a drunk sailor jumping over the side and drowning. I'll bet his parents were crushed, though. Terrible thing to have happen.

Smitty, my buddy from the old garbage boat, and I have joined the American Legion Post here in Olongapo. We got a year's membership for just sixteen pesos. About the only benefit from doing this is that now we can eat and drink there on our membership card, and not have to pay the tab until payday. So when we're broke – which is more often than not – we can still stop down at the Legion for refreshments. Last night we played Bingo there for hours on end, and I won two lousy pesos. Oh well, two pesos are two pesos; that'll get me into a couple of flicks at the base theater!

There's a little friction on board right now. Mostly, it's between me and a red-haired bully seaman. But there are four or five other guys on the boat who can't get along with him either. It's because he always tries to tell everyone else what to do – and he's literally got the lowest rank on the whole tug! Then he tries to back it up with the promise of physical mayhem, which he is more than capable of doing. We've all complained about him to the craftmaster, but they're both good buddies and he won't even listen to us seriously. I don't see any solution in sight; this boat ain't big enough for the both of us! And the situation makes for miserable work conditions.

This morning I was checking out our flooding-alarm system, so I had to do a lot of crawling around in the bilges under the deckplates of the engine room, trac-

The Filipino peso (worth twenty-five cents in 1969).

ing wiring and inspecting sensors. I looked like a wet, greasy rat when I climbed out. It'll take years to get clean again! I think that's where us snipes get the reputation of being "greasy, slimy snipes." In the old navy they called us "the Black Gang" for good reason. *sigh*

Well, right now we are taking an hour rest period after a very filling meal of fried rice and sweet-and-sour pork. Slowly but surely, delicious Filipino food is pushing out all the American dishes that we once knew and loved. Everybody is having a nooner in their own special way: several are sleeping in the shade on the deck, under the table, on a pile of nylon line, etc. One guy is sitting on the gunwales, fishing with shrimp bait; I suppose he's after those two dolphins that came snooping alongside yesterday. And I am writing letters home, as you can see.

At 1300 comes mail call, and then we have to turn to once again. We got some new furniture back from the base woodshop today. The pieces looked pretty sharp – even if I did design them myself! So this afternoon we'll work until 1600, sanding and refinishing them.

OFFICIAL QUARTERLY MARKS
March 16, 1969
(Assigned to YTM-182)

"FN Stanga is the only Electrician's Mate on the YTM-182. He maintains all electrical equipment on board, as well as lending a hand on deck when needed. He also stands security watches. Stanga is extremely effective and reliable. He relieved an EM2 and is carrying on very well. Stanga offers no problems in any form and gets along exceptionally well with everyone. His military and civilian attire is always clean and neat. His behavior is exceptional and he has never had any disciplinary problems while on board."

March 25, 1969

Dear Family,

I have approximately an hour left before I go wake up my relief, so I'll press my energies to getting off a letter to you folks at home. Having the duty every three days is enough to get a fella down after a while; I'm so dead tired that I doubt I can even stay awake long enough to finish this letter. My head keeps nodding and smacking the table before I even realize it. I'll get four lovely hours of sleep tonight before I have to go on watch again. Urg.

The Filipino workers were installing new insulation in our sleeping compartment and we just couldn't take it any more. It was miserable sleeping in a rack full of fiberglass dust, and on the beach we itched and scratched horribly in our civvies. Finally, they placed us temporarily in some run-down old barracks over on Mainside and made us double up on sharing some lockers.

I don't know which is the bigger hassle. Every morning now we have to get up extra early just so we can catch a truck after breakfast and be back here at the boat on the opposite side of the harbor in time for work to commence. Then at noon we ride the truck clear back over to the main galley for chow. There's one good thing about living in the barracks, though: it's five miles closer to the main gate! Oh yeah.

While going down the ladder into the lazarette the other day I slipped and fell because I had my hands too full. I caught my mouth right on the edge of a steel shelf on the way down, and from all the blood I saw I figured I had knocked every tooth out of my fool head! But they're still all accounted for, thank Allah. As it turned out, I only cut the inside of my lips against my teeth.

For a couple of days I walked around like someone had hit me in the mouth with a 2x4. (Come to think of it, that's about what it felt like, too.) The guys thought I looked extra funny with my lips all swollen up like a duck's. Big joke! The swelling has gone down now, but it still smarts when I eat and drink. I can't whistle at all; I wonder if I'll ever be able to whistle a merry tune again? Oh well, I'm just glad I broke my navy-issue glasses instead of my dang nose.

The division lads packed us off for a day of fire fighting last week. Yes, exactly like we had in boot camp! What next? Actually, if I let myself admit it, I guess I did have a bit of fun there. It was rather exciting to be put into a smoke-filled chamber and then told to find our way out of that cloudy labyrinth. They had placed all sorts of obstacles in our path (including a naked mannequin, which was a pleasant surprise), tricky dead-end passageways, and walls that were too hot to touch. You couldn't see a thing. Luckily, they gave us each a gas mask. But that wasn't half as grand as when they chucked us into the Flaming Pit to put out a hot, block-high raging oil fire! I was nozzle man, and we got so close to the flames I thought I had lost my eyebrows for good. And there went my last clean pair of dungarees, too. *Voila!*

Last payday I lucked out and got a paycheck that was double my usual pittance: $110. So I paid my civilian life insurance, a payment on my writing course, my bar tab at the Legion, and with what I had left over I splurged and bought that new wristwatch that I've always wanted. It's a Seiko diver's watch, and it's got enough bells and whistles on it to plot a course by the stars, I swear.

Well, Smitty got a "Dear John" letter yesterday and he's still walking around in a funk. And what really puzzles him is that she gave him no reason whatsoever; up until her last letter everything was hunky-dory. They had gone steady for seven years and were engaged to be married. I think that story about girls waiting for guys to come home from the service is just a myth along the lines of Santa Claus and the Tooth Fairy. It only goes to show that you can't trust a round-eye.

Some Marine from the assault-craft division was showing me a curious little trinket last night. It's a hand grenade that screws into a light socket, and when the bad guy turns on the light switch – KABLAMMO! I don't know where they'd ever use such a device, but I think it's pretty clever. What fun things will man think up next?

As I was sitting in a Filipino theater house out in town last weekend watching a flick, a cat came walking up the aisle and climbed into my lap for an hour. Miracles never cease. Actually, it's kind of comical to see cats and dogs and sometimes even chickens loafing around inside the cool movie theaters, no doubt escaping the heat outdoors. A very relaxed attitude down here. The Joes really go ape over those wacky movies from India, with their gigantic lurid billboards all over town.

Good old "deadly shipmate" has struck again – and it wasn't even my fault this time. I was hooking up a new flooding-alarm system behind the switchboard, so I had Earl run out on the pier and shut off the main rectifier. As I look back on it now, I should maybe have had him stand by the switch as well, but I figured that normal people operating in and around Navy personnel would know by now that you don't just walk up and energize any switch that you find open.

Well, they waited until I had all my fingers in there and cramped between the bus bars before they turned on the power. Boy, did the lights come on then! I'd sure like to catch the clown who pulled that stunt! It wasn't a terribly awful electrical shock, but it's just that I was in a perfect position to get electrocuted properly.

I can just see the headlines in the *Stars and Stripes* newspaper now:

"EX-CIVVIE AND 150 D.C. TANGLE FOR KEEPS"

or

"SLOW JOE SLIPS SWABBIE THE JUICE"

March 26, 1969

Dear Family,

It's 0400 now and that was certainly the shortest four hours of sleep I ever had! So now I'm up for the day. I sure wish there was something decent in this lousy galley to eat – or even something to make a little weak coffee out of. I'm gonna have to talk to the Stewburner again.

Ah, I can see that the roaches are out in fine form tonight. Unhindered, they run wild in the streets through here. I don't know how many dozen are scurrying across the bulkheads. There's a few walking leisurely across the table not a foot from me. There's so many of them that I've lost heart in squashing them. A couple of the fellas on the boat are missing their white hats; I suppose that this is where they're going to.

Last week I finally got to see Truman Capote's "In Cold Blood." The only thing I didn't like was that I couldn't keep telling myself, "It's only a movie, it's only a movie," seeing as how it was a true story. Otherwise, I thought it was an excellent flick. And filming it in black and white was a stroke of genius and no doubt a major factor in its success. For a while during the movie I thought we were going to be spared the gruesome murder scene itself, but I guess it had to be included after all. I get too involved with movies like that.

I got a letter from Bobby Anderson down in the "sun capitol of the world," Jacksonville, Florida. His "A" school for Aviation Electrician's Mate is 21 weeks in length, and he thinks that's so terribly long! I wonder if he could handle 18 months down here without crying? He claims he stays on the base in the evenings and studies diligently, and only goes to town on the weekends; if so, that would be very out of character for him. I know a lot of guys who'd give anything to be stationed in Jacksonville for the duration of their hitch. I'm not one of them, though.

I finally got Al Larson's address, but he's going to be home on leave soon, so I'll wait to write to him when he's at his next duty station. Wilt and Nicky write real often, too; Nick is enjoying college life in Aberdeen, and Wilt is traveling all over the United States participating in karate tournaments as a black belt.

The sun is just starting to come up now; I guess I'll secure the standing lights and then make myself some graveyard stew. The guys should be here from the barracks in about an hour, and then our work day will commence.

March 28, 1969

A day off! We were certainly feeling energetic today, as we did so many things in our spare time. First we played pool, and I won three consecutive games! Dean and Benton are real good at it, and so I'm usually the first one out of the game. We were playing Cutthroat. Next, we spent a leisurely hour at the miniature golf course on base. We were behind two little girls and they were just cracking us up. And then you should have seen them giggle when all three of us sunk our balls in the water hazard!

It was around the twelfth hole when the courtesy music overhead suddenly went off and they announced that Ike had just died at Walter Reed Army Hospital after a series of seven heart attacks. Didn't seem to make much of an impression on us, though, as I guess we were all sort of expecting it at any time. His condition had been worsening for quite a while. I never knew what kind of a man he was, as I was only five years old when he became President.

March 29, 1969

Dear Family,

How about that? The *USS Enterprise* (CVAN-65) is in port and it's the first time I've ever seen her in the flesh. From here she doesn't look any bigger than any other ol' bird farm, but I know she is, because our tug had to help put her alongside the pier. Now all you can see out in town are those *"bostusin* [rude and crude] Amerikanos" off the *Enterprise* carousing around as if *they* owned the place, instead of us. Lock up your women, the Fleet is in!

I got another bundle of newspapers from Aunt Amy today. All those pictures of local servicemen home on leave, and none of yours truly. I saw a couple clippings of old buddies I went to high school with, though. I see that most of them wimped out and went Air Force.

What I wouldn't have given for a camera on the boat today. We finally got the lazarette chipped out and red-leaded, and were ready to paint. We got a paint sprayer from the shop, but we couldn't get it to work properly. For some strange reason, the paint was going in one end of the hose, but not coming out the other end.

I saw the growing bulge in the hose about half a second before the fertilizer hit the ventilator. White paint exploded everywhere! The guys were laughing so hard at the resulting spectacle that they almost forgot to shut the dumb thing off. I guess I looked like someone had poured a bucket of white paint over my head. Anyway, I sure had a hard time getting the paint off me and out of my hair. My dungarees were a total loss. Why do these things always happen to me?

I had another weird happening the other night for the first time. The three of us , Dean, Benton, and I, went out into the nasty town with a common goal in mind: to drink all the San Miguel beer in Olongapo City. And it didn't take us long to get completely *lasing* [drunk]. I think we warmed up at the American Legion on 7-Sevens and then we moved on to new and better things. We overindulged in fiery tacos at Mom's, found the best strobe light action in Olongapo at the Stardust Club, and danced our feet off at the Pacific Club. But the last thing I remembered was that Reuben and his band were going to play "Hey, Bungalow Bill" for the Three Stooges (meaning us guys). The rest of the night was a total blank for me. This has never happened to me before.

The very first thing that came to mind the next morning (I mean, besides how much my brain hurt) was "How did I get back here?!" The guys swear up and down that we went to a couple more clubs, stopped on the Shit River bridge to throw centavos to the kids in the banca boats, and had a burger at the Spanish Gate café on base before finally heading for bed.

And I didn't seem [to them] to be any different from any other night that I was a *lasingero* [drunkard]. Good grief! And up until now I've always been the one who could remember everything the next morning when the other guys couldn't – the responsible one who got the rest of them back home safely. But they tell me that I even smoked a cigarette – which certainly accounted for the foul taste in my

The old Spanish Gate of Subic Bay, Philippines.

mouth – and I know I never would have done that in my right mind! Oh well, I'm not going to let a little thing like an alcohol-related blackout upset me. You know we're just sailors having fun and letting off a little steam, don't you? Okay then.

I got a notice from the division officer stating that I have to attend an interview on April Fool's Day concerning "seavey osvey," whatever the heck that is. Sounds like Pig Latin to me. Some of the guys seem to think it means I'm getting on a tin can home-ported in Yokosuka, Japan, and will see Vietnam duty after I leave the P.I. Other guys say it means I'm going to be transferred directly to shore duty in the States! I'm not convinced any of them know what the hell they're talking about. Well, we'll see next Tuesday what they want of me.

Nothing much to do around the boat, so I got a few things together and rigged my locker for light. I mounted a battle-lantern bulb inside, installed a toggle switch, and hooked it all up to a six-volt dry-cell battery. Now, when I come stumbling back to the nest in the wee hours, more or less a maladroit, I won't have to grope around noisily in the dark or switch on the compartment lights just to see what I'm doing and wake everybody up. Pretty clever, huh? Ah, the benefits of being an electrician! Now the other guys want me to rig their lockers for light, too. For a nominal fee, of course, I told them, for a nominal fee.

Well, I'm on duty again tonight. What a mental grind it can be sometimes. Good old Benton is sitting across the table from me, laughing his head off at a W.C. Fields article in *Playboy* magazine. He's okay, even if he does have some strange ideas – like defecting to Sweden right after he gets out of the service.

Even though I've got the watch now, I would sneak up to the warehouse and watch the flick on the sly, if it wasn't for that gung-ho warrant officer prowling around the boats tonight and checking to see if the watches are alert and the bilges are dry. Come to think of it, I wouldn't put it past him to write me up for not shaving today. I better get myself

Benton can sleep anywhere.

squared away pronto. We plan to go skin-diving tomorrow; details to follow…

March 30, 1969

Dear Family,

I got ahold of Mike the Tentmaker, our Filipino tailor, and he measured me for a new set of dungarees. Paint, battery acid, grease, dirt, sweat, salt water, and Father Time had reduced me to two shabby pair. They're going to be tailor-made, tapered and form-fitting, with button-down collar, extra pocket on the calf, surname embroidered on both shirt and pants, a zippered fly instead of buttons, and a belt buckle engraved with "South Dakota." This is an acceptable work uniform in Service Craft. All this for a measly five frog-skins. That amounts to a twenty-beer sacrifice, but it had to be done.

Our freshwater expansion tank blew up early this morning. Some unauthorized clown turned on both switches in MY controller box, which doubled the pressure inside the water tank. The bottom blew out and the whole tank shot upward like a rocket until it smacked into the overhead, then ricocheted around the galley. The guy on watch said it was a regular Old Faithful! The galley is a shambles. It's a good thing that nobody was in the galley at the time. Shucks, I'm never around when there's a bit of excitement.

You know, sometimes I think I'll go absolutely bughouse if I don't talk to a round-eye girl within the hour! There's a few running around base, but they're already snagged by other station squids and jarheads. I haven't even gotten within hailing distance of one, let alone talked to one. I never knew I'd get so darn tired of looking at slanted eyes and hearing, "Hey, buy me drink, sailor!" and "I love you no shit!" and "Wanna dance, sailor?" It's enough to drive a fella to drink, I tell you.

After dinner yesterday, we had a few cool ones out at the Legion. Some officer and his wife had their young daughter there and she was dancing up a storm. She couldn't have been more than five or six, but she must have taken a few dancing lessons because she was very good. And when the band played the Chicken Polka she hopped around just like an old hen! Little kids sure are cute sometimes!

In the afternoon we caught the liberty launch and headed for Grande Island. That's when the sun went under the clouds, so we didn't get much of a tan. (On the other hand, we didn't get sunburned either.) Besides that, the water was choppy and more than once our snorkels unexpectedly filled with salt water, which is not a pleasant thing to inhale.

Those *lapu-lapu* [grouper fish] were awfully wary today, and I only speared a single one. I was following a yellow-and-black-striped fish over some rocky ledges when I looked down and saw a shark cruising along the bottom ten feet right below me. He was about five feet long, and I didn't hang around long enough to see if he was interested in me! I was back on dry land shaking the water out of my ears in sixty seconds flat. More or less.

Fifteen minutes later, with spear gun in hand and courage renewed, I went back into the water, looking for game. I stalked fish for another hour before I saw the shark again. This time he was almost on the surface about twenty feet away. There's just something about seeing a shark underwater *with* you that really turns your blood cold and makes you panic! Then when we saw a long water snake swimming nearby, we decided to call it a day and go to the flick. That was enough native fauna for us for one day.

April 1, 1969

Dear Gramma,

Many thanks for the five dollars! I don't know how you do it, but you always seem to rescue me from the brink of bankruptcy at the very last second.

I've got the duty again tonight. It's just a bit sticky out, but the stars are all lit up brightly and the bay is like a mirror. I've got the Armed Forces radio to keep me company, so I'm not as bad off as others in the world.

There's a lot of phosphorescence on the water tonight, much more than usual. It is actually microscopic plankton that glow in the dark. When you throw a rock in the water, all you see is a splash that looks like blue fire. It's really pretty! A better effect is to pour a whole pitcher of water into the bay, a little at a time, and watch the blue ripples spread out. Sure is strange stuff.

Sleeping in the barracks during our overhaul period ain't half bad, but then we have to put up with all the drunks who come in late, turn on the lights, and make a big racket. No consideration!

They had another blackout in town most of the night, and so they weren't letting anyone out the main gate. They're always having blackouts because their electrical wiring is so haphazard. Their telephone poles are a snarl of wires, and their power lines are an electrician's nightmare. Down here they call them "brownouts," though.

The hospital ship, *USS Repose* (AH-16), is here in port after 120 days without touching land. Goodness, that's a long time! I guess the *Repose* sailors had a right to get a little bit spunky out in town then. The *Repose* has beds for approximately 922 patients, and has been stationed off the Vietnam coast.

I had my SEAVEY OSVEY interview this afternoon. What it all boiled down to was just filling out our dream sheets for where we want to go after we leave the P.I. We had ten choices and I put down Vietnam for all of them. So guess where I'm probably going next! The Personnelman said it's in the bag. Most likely I'll get on a supply ship that refuels here at Subic Bay. Or I might get on a river patrol-boat tender. Or it might be just anything. I'm excited.

Right now I've put in nine months in the P.I.; that's half my tour of duty here done already! I'm on the downhill slide. Only 306 days left in the P.I. Gettin' short! (Never thought I'd live to say it.)

April 13, 1969

Dear Family,

(Overheard)

"Hey, did you scrape together a crew for that extra tow job yet?"

"That's a charlie, Chief."

"Got an electrician on board this time?"

"Yeah, a Fireman."

"Oh ferchrissake…who?"

"Stanga."

"Oh, that's okay then. Go ahead and shove off."

"Aye, Roger."

I've come to a brilliant conclusion: four hours of duty is not the same as four hours out on the beach. I've never known four hours to pass so slowly as those between eight and midnight. And to make matters worse, there's nothing on the radio tonight but static and Filipino yodeling. I've been doing crossword puzzles and acrostics most of the afternoon until the novelty has worn off. Like a fool, I didn't bring along anything to read either. So I've broken down and dragged out my writing gear as a last resort.

I enjoyed a new high in motion-picture viewing yesterday out in Olongapo City. I never thought it'd happen down here, but I finally got to see Stanley Kubrick's "2001: A Space Odyssey"! I must say that the photography and special effects were really quite superior, but I'm not even going to pretend that I followed the plot. When the movie was over, I sat there a while in the dark theater trying to make sense out of it all, feeling slightly stunned. But no luck. (Even the book didn't give me any helpful clues.) I guess the only one who knows what's going on in the story is Arthur C. Clarke, and he ain't telling me. But I still enjoyed it, though!

Unfortunately, we're still living in the barracks. One batch of drunks has left for their next duty stations, only to be replaced by a new batch. It's so hot at night in those ramshackle old barracks that sometimes I come clear back to the boat just to sleep on the deck on a mattress in the breeze off the bay. Oh well, at least I know it won't last forever; the end is in sight. The Joes still aren't done with our crew compartment (they've got to paint it yet), but at least they'll be finished ahead of schedule. I just wish they'd hurry up and put this poor old raggedy-ass tug back together in a hurry, so we can get back on the line and chug!

There went a rat! It left the tug and ran right up the mooring line and onto the pier. Going on liberty, I reckon. He was the biggest, boldest, nastiest P.I. rat I've ever seen on this boat. So what's a fellow to do? Putting rat guards on the lines doesn't help, seeing as how they can leap onto the boat as easy as we can. As long as they stay down in the bilges and the chain locker, I guess I don't resent their company on board.

I've been checking into becoming a cop when I get out of the service. Some of the qualifications for a South Dakota cop are easy enough to meet: 12 years of schooling, married or single, 150 pounds minimum, 5'5" minimum, a proper security clearance. The starting pay at present is $350 to $450 a month. I can handle that! Well, we'll see… I just might wind up on a merchant tanker or going to college overseas somewhere. I still don't know what I want to do.

I'm going to get a tattoo. Now wait, hear me out! Sit back down and listen to reason. I figure if I'm going to flounder through four years in this Canoe Club, I might as well have something permanent to show for it, right? After all, what's a little old measly tattoo anyway? I thought I'd put it on my right shoulder; maybe a nice eagle with a US Navy banner or something like that. I could have it done in a clean place down in Manila next time we go there. I know I needn't ask your opinion, because I'll be hearing it shortly anyway! Ha ha.

Dean and I have a bet going to see which one of us can go the longest without a beer. Sounds like a fool's errand to me. It might be a tough bet to collect on, though. After a hard day's work it's sort of needed like a tranquilizer, you know? Besides, good beer is half the fun of being in the Navy!

A fella just dropped by the boat, looking for "Mitchell, South Dakota." He said his sister sent him my clipping from the hometown newspaper and he came around to see if he knew me at all. He was two years ahead of me in high school, but I sure didn't recognize him. He knew all the same kids as I did, but he didn't recognize me either. Still, it's always fun to run into somebody clear down here who's from back home.

Remember that little girl I mentioned in my last letter that was dancing with her father in the American Legion? Well, she's been missing for almost a week now. They lived out in town and just about anything could have happened to her. Sure hope they find her okay, though.

Somebody up there loves me. In less than a month we are getting rid of the only undesirable element on this whole boat. Then we will have one of the tightest crews here in Service Craft. That 22-year-old, redheaded asshole causes so much friction and discontent amongst everybody that each day is pure misery trying to work around him. Four of us, including me, have gotten into fights with him several times, and he simply refuses to believe that he alone is the cause of the whole crew hating him. He's the kind of freak that you can't even reason with successfully, and he gets spitting mad (literally spitting!) at the slightest argument to his out-of-line orders. His eyes get wide, his face turns all white, and he looks like he's really quite crazy.

For the past three days no one would talk to him and refused to work with him. When he sat down at the table we got up and left. Everybody ignores the childish words that follow us. Our blackballing him seems to have finally been effective because he put in for a transfer – and got it! Within a month he goes to Vietnam! I tell you, we were the happiest bunch of swabbies you ever saw when we got wind of that wee bit of scuttlebutt.

The other night at the American Legion, I was having a cool one with Jeff, a tall black-bearded Aussie off the *H.M.S. Brisbane* (D-41) that I had just met there. He had been at the bar all day, so he already had a few sails in the wind. He noticed my new Seiko diver's watch with the glow-in-the-dark dial.

"If'n I were you, mate, I'd get rid of that watch," he said.

"This thing?" I asked, surprised.

"No sir, you wouldn't find ol' Jeff with no bloody clock on 'is wrist!"

"Why zat?" I asked.

"Why, man, it's the radium! It'll get in yer body and give you leukemia or skin cancer!"

"Is that a fact now?"

"I'm not peeing in yer pocket, mate. You slap a Radiac on that and take a roentgen count, and then you'll see ol' Jeff ain't a'lyin'!"

"Oh, we haven't got that kind of gear on board."

"What the – what kind of a bloody ship is it you're on anyway, mate?"

"It's a tug…mate."

"Blimey! Then you come on down to my ship and I'll do it proper. Then you'll see 'ow many roentgens it's a'coppin' out!"

"I might just do that – "

"By the queen, you're not a diver anyways!"

"I'll think about it, Jeff. Can I buy you another one?"

Maybe you've noticed that I've been particularly more detailed in my letters home? That's because I've come to realize that my letters will prove in later years to be my most accurate source of information when I sit down to write of the things that have happened to me. Another good storehouse will be my journals kept while in the Navy. I really make an effort to be thorough in them and leave out nothing – no matter how seemingly inconsequential at the time. My buddies try to keep up their journals as well, but every day sees their entries become shorter and more cryptic, until just terse sentences are left. They swear these will be enough to bring back the particular incidents in full bloom anyway, but they will find out how sadly they are mistaken. It's worth the effort to be painstaking in the first place.

April 16, 1969

Dear Family,

We were occupied all day long with putting our tug into dry dock. The YTM 369 (Smitty's tug) is just going into a four-month yard period, too, so his tug is here in dry dock with us. Now at least Smitty and I will get to stand duty together.

The dry dock is called the *USS Windsor* (ARD-22), and it is self-propelled to boot. It is the only commissioned non-ship in the Navy. Guys even live on it down inside the walls! The walls are eight feet thick and about 400 feet long. I don't think I'd really mind being stationed on this dry dock; it looks like jolly good duty.

Seamen up on top of the walls threw dozens of lines down to us and pulled us by hand inside the sunken dry dock. Then they slowly raised the dry dock by pumping water out of the voids in the walls. All the time, divers were down below making sure our keel would rest exactly on the concrete and wooden blocks and be seated in the cradle. It was all pretty exciting.

So here we are, high and dry, and when you look over the side of the tug, it's about forty feet down to the floor of the dry dock. The tug's bottom is rusted out and covered with stinky barnacles. Our brass prop is dented and bent out of shape from all those times when our fearless craftmaster went aground under the influence of tater juice. So we'll probably be here a good month, I'd guess.

Both Dean and I agreed to mutually forfeit our non-drinking bet last night and went out in town in search of beers. Can't win them all, I guess. In the 7th Fleet Club there were a bunch of sailors off the *USS Saint Paul* (CA-73), a heavy cruiser. One idiot had bought a live rooster from some old lady on the street. He was feeding it dark rum, and the chicken was getting pretty silly...even silly for a chicken, I mean. It was pathetic to watch him abuse the dumb thing. But then he started mistreating it very badly, and I wanted to leave, but my buddies wanted to finish their beers first.

And then, before we even knew what was going on, that damn drunk fleet sailor stretched out the chicken's neck as far as it would go and bit the head off! Blood ran all over his whites and the bar hostesses were screaming and sailors were jumping up in disgust, spilling drinks, knocking chairs over. Total chaos.

I was so mad at him I think I could have broke a beer pitcher over his head right on the spot! But he was with a lot of his buddies, and there were only four of us; you have to take that into consideration. So when he finally got up to leave, which was shortly, I just tripped him down the long flight of stairs into the street, and nobody was the wiser.

They have brownouts in town almost every night for a few hours. It's getting to be a regular thing. The drain is simply too great on the city's generators during the hot season – it's all those stupid air conditioners! Some small nightclubs have as many as ten of them going at full blast; they just about freeze us right out the door. And they say there are close to 300 clubs in Olongapo City.

I got a letter from Karen F. today. I really enjoy her letters; she makes me feel like I'm somebody important who's doing an exciting job. I've got a bunch of *Stars and Stripes* newspapers that I know you'll enjoy reading, so I'll send them along just as soon as I rake up the postage.

April 26, 1969

Dear Vern,

I am enclosing three pictures for you. The first picture is of a YD, which is a floating crane. It is not self-propelled, so it must be moved here and there by us tugs. Above it you can see two Phantom fighter jets taking off from Cubi Point. At the very end of the runway you can see crash boats, which is a detachment of guys on swift rescue boats who have to deploy whenever jets take off or land, just in case of a crash in the water. Thus the name.

In the background is the destroyer tender, the *USS Samuel Gompers* (AD-37). Usually a tender just stays in port and the tin cans tie up to it. The *Gompers* is able to furnish service to six guided-missile destroyers alongside simultaneously. Tenders are supposed to be named after important locales in the United States – like *Dixie, New England,* and *Everglades* – but this particular one of ours was named after a famous AFL-CIO guy, Samuel Gompers…who I've never heard of or know his claim to fame.

The other two pictures are of my tug in dry dock. They had already taken off the propeller to straighten it, so it's not in the picture. As you can see, most of the hull of a ship is underwater when we're afloat. It really looks like a rag right now, but not for long, brother!

The commander of the base said that it's okay to grow beards if we want – but we have to request permission from our immediate superiors first. So now all the guys are keyed up to grow beards for a contest. It'll take time to grow a proper one, but time is one thing we have plenty of.

Smitty and I were going to take a week's leave down in Australia, but then we found out it cost $650 roundtrip for just one person. And that's only the plane fare part of the trip! It might just as well have been $65,000, as it was still way out of our price range. Rats!

When there isn't a blackout in town, or a bar-hog riot, we usually go out and listen to a few good bands. The trouble is that there are over 300 of them and we'll never hope to hear them all. Some of our personal favorites are the Cyclones, the White Rabbits, the Hi-Jackers, the Cavemen, and the Wild Five. They play most of the latest Beatles, Doors, Bee Gees, Stones, and all the other popular ones back in the States. The Electros play vintage Jan and Dean, the Beach Boys, and the Association! Really great stuff! Another band specializes in Jimi Hendrix songs.

It's been raining here the last couple of weeks because *Baguio* [typhoon] Suzie hit the P.I. Right now we're at Typhoon Condition Two. We're still in dry dock and they think they're going to get us out by tomorrow. Heck, they still have to paint the whole tug, put the screw and rudder back on, put in the sea valves so we won't sink immediately, and scour out our rancid bilges before they're done with us. They'll be lucky to get us out of here in another 4 to 5 days! But an LST is waiting to get in here, too.

I've got the duty all day today, so I have to stay on the boat. Duty isn't real hard, just boring, because all we have to do is sit around and watch the Joes work, and make sure they aren't stealing us blind. But that's not the same as being out in town, is it?

Colors just went down, so we had to pop to attention (if we were outdoors) and hold a salute during the long bugle call. They raise the flag every morning at exactly 0800, and then take it down whenever sunset occurs, which varies from day to day. But on tugs we never have to take it down because we work 'round the clock. The flags here are still flying at half-mast for Eisenhower anyway.

SPECIAL REQUEST/AUTHORIZATION CHIT
April 27, 1969

"I hereby request permission to grow a small beard which I will keep clean and short and neatly trimmed. The beard may be only temporary, as I am not sure it will be right for me. But I would like to try it just the same. Thank you.

Respectively yours, Steve Stanga"

Request denied by Division Officer.

April 28, 1969

Dear Gramma,

It's been a long time since I last wrote, maybe a little too long, but I've settled down this morning with a stiff cup of Navy coffee to get off a few letters. I took my buddy's duty this morning so he could go to church, and he will take my duty tonight so I can go to the movie. Fair enough. This is called "cooperation."

We have been in dry dock for almost two weeks now. It's very interesting because it's all new stuff to us, and the change of pace is wonderful. They sand-blasted the hull free of barnacles and rust right down to the bare metal. Thus, our boat is really a mess now; all the decks are buried in sand drifts about a foot high, and the inside compartments have a thick layer of dust over everything. Who's going to clean up this debris to our satisfaction?

There was a little girl who had been kidnapped for the past three weeks, and they had almost given up hope of ever finding her. Everyone around here contributed to a fund to boost the reward, because her father drove one of the tugs where I work. Then suddenly they found her asleep all alone in a movie theater in downtown Manila! The kidnappers must have gotten cold feet; these things don't usually have such a happy ending. Her dad is sure one overjoyed guy now! While they were searching Olongapo City for clues, authorities discovered there were six other Filipino children missing that nobody had bothered to report before. "Body snatching," as they call it here, is a very popular pastime – especially down in Manila. I've even met a few of the ex-snatchers…real hard-looking guys. What a dirty racket.

Naturally, I am learning Tagalog (the national language) all along, and it makes communication a lot easier with these people. And rightly enough, the first words I learned down here nine months ago were *salamat po* [thank you very much]. Tagalog is very similar to Spanish, for good reason, and some of that has come back to me clear from junior high school.

Boy, I sure hate reading about all the riots and protesters in the *Stars and Stripes* newspaper. It really makes me mad to hear that those young bums want to abolish ROTC from college campuses. Those men already in the service who protest and have refused to fight in the war ought to be tried for treason! And if one more incident like the kidnapping of the *USS Pueblo* happens again, we need to show the world that we mean business!

LETTER TO THE EDITOR

"Dear Editor,

I'm just an insignificant sailor doing an anonymous job in a detestable environment 9,000 miles from home, but it does not help my patriotic spirit any great deal to keep reading about the foolishness going on around campuses today. Here I am, sworn to naval duty in these islands for two years, locked away from my loved ones with the bolts and bars of an ocean and a military obligation, and my frustration is compounded daily as I leaf through our base newspaper. But occasionally I am refreshed to see a telephoto showing a fellow student slugging a long-haired protester who is about to cold-cock a drilling ROTC member.

Students (and I use the term very loosely here) who do not sanction the college's curriculum simply because it does not cater to their vain and radical demands have no legitimate gripe against the establishment. If they do not 'approve' of the university's regulations and methods of teaching, they have only to pack up their hair dryers and SDS membership cards and go harass some other school. I'm sure the vacillating college hierarchy wouldn't miss them. It seems to me that it would be a step in the right direction to suspend a serious reprimand above the curly locks of college instigators. Anyone who incites riots and inspires dissension among students should be ejected with no academic credit whatsoever.

Where do some people get the sheer audacity to raise a black militant flag over hallowed halls, to ship blood plasma to the North Vietnamese, and to deceive National Guardsmen into accepting cookies filled with whooping doses of LSD? And on top of that, they want the vote! The years between 18 and 21 are years of great uncertainties, social pressures, and frantic rebellion against things that aren't fully understood – when they should be years of serious reflection and maturing and the determination to strengthen tried-and-true American ideals.

Thank goodness there are still those legions of decent young people who rally round the flag, who still wear the uniform with pride, and who still enter the world of work with a firmness of purpose to become a contributory citizen. There are even scores of unacknowledged events that demonstrate clearly that youth can participate responsibly and intelligently in the intricacies of our wonderful country.

So why all this ballyhoo magnifying a minority of destructive militants, anarchists, and national ingrates? They thrive on publicity! Take away their thunder, put them back in the proper perspective as unwanted rebels, and maybe the remaining 14 million young people of America will regain their sanity and respect.

Steve Stanga, USN
The Philippines"

NEWSPAPER CLIPPING
(San Fernando, Pampanga, Philippines)

"A 29-year-old Filipino, fulfilling a vow of penitence, was nailed to a cross at noon in a Good Friday re-enactment of the crucifixion of Jesus Christ. Juanito Piring, a one-time slum brawler and father of three, stood nailed to the cross under the scorching sun for two agonizing minutes, wearing a tailored purple robe and a crown of thorns. A crowd of about 5,000 shouted and shoved to get a view of the scene just outside this town, fifty miles north of Manila.

Only Piring's palms were impaled on the cross with two and a half-inch stainless steel nails. The man who hammered the nails carefully sought out the soft, boneless parts of the palm. Piring closed his eyes and showed no signs of pain while being nailed to the cross. His armpits, stomach and legs were tightly bound to the heavy, ten-foot wooden cross. Filipinos dressed as Roman soldiers hoisted him onto the cross and brought him down. The man who had driven the nails earlier methodically proceeded to pluck them out, drawing spurts of blood from Piring's palms when the nails were withdrawn.

Piring, bloody and sweat-soaked from the ordeal, stumbled with the help of other men to a shade tree where he rested for a few minutes before he was carried to a friend's house nearly a mile away. It was Piring's second year to be nailed to the cross, replacing a townsman who had submitted to the annual ritual the previous seven years.

It is believed to be the only ritual of its kind in the whole Christian world. It takes place, paradoxically, in the only Roman Catholic country in Asia where the church has forbidden the practice, but has not been entirely successful in outlawing it. Besides the crucifixion, thousands of Filipino flagellants throughout this country roamed towns and villages flogging themselves in a centuries-old practice of penitence for real or imagined sins."

MEET THE CARABAO

The largest domesticated animal in the Philippines is the carabao, a cousin of the water buffalo. Although the carabao looks menacing with its sharply-pointed, crescent-curved horns, it is very tame and used daily in the agricultural tasks of plowing rice fields or pulling carts laden with products. Young farm boys can be found almost anywhere in the Philippines, riding on a carabao, guiding the slow beast through its day of labor. There are over 2.8 million carabao in the Philippines.

This animal is dark in color. It grows to be a huge specimen at times, and half-ton bulls are not uncommon. Both sexes grow the familiar moon horns; occasionally these are shed and new ones are grown. Small white herons ride on the carabao's back and pick off ticks and other parasites.

An interesting fact of the carabao's physique is that it lacks sweat glands. Since it is found in a tropical climate, this special lacking creates problems in its domestication. It forces keeping the animal tied up in some shade and bathed with water in large quantities after working it. Either bathing it or allowing it to wallow in mud or a water hole is essential to keep it alive. This is usually no problem in a land of rivers, streams, and rice paddies. The gray carabao is frequently covered with a layer of cool mud.

Since the carabao is such a highly valued farm tool in a sense, it typically enjoys a long life. It is also protected by laws that prohibit its slaughter with fine or imprisonment or both as punishment. The carabao is a common sight in native art, and folk tales abound with bull tales.

THE ELECTRICIAN'S TEN COMMANDMENTS

1) Beware the lightning that lurketh in an undischarged condenser, lest it cause thee to bounce upon thy buttocks in a most unseamanlike manner.

2) Causeth thou the switch that supplieth large quantities of juice to be opened and thusly tagged that thy days be long upon this earthly vale of tears.

3) Prove to thyself that all circuits that radiateth and upon which thou worketh are grounded and thusly tagged lest they lift thee to radio frequency potential, and causeth thee to make like a radiator, too.

4) Tarry thou not amongst those fools that engage in intentional electrical shocks, for they are surely nonbelievers and are not long for this world.

5) Take care thou useth the proper method when thou taketh the measure of a high voltage circuit so that thou does not incinerate both thee and thy test meter; for verily, though thou hast no Federal stock number and can be easily surveyed, the test meter dost have one and as a consequence bringeth much woe to the Supply Officer.

6) Take care thou tampereth not with interlocks and safety devices for this incurreth the wrath of the Division Officer and bringeth the fury of the Bureau of Ships upon thy head and shoulders.

7) Work thee not on energized equipment, for if thou doest so thy shipmates will surely be buying beers for thy widow and consoling her in certain ways not generally acceptable to thee.

8) Verily, verily, I say unto thee, *never* service equipment alone, for electrical cooking is sometimes a slothful process and thou might sizzle in thy own fat upon a hot circuit for hours on end before thy Maker sees fit to end thy misery and drag thee unto His fold.

9) Trifle thou not with radioactive tubes and substances lest thou commence to glow in the dark like a lightning bug and thy good lady wife be frustrated and have no further use for thee except for thy wages.

10) Commit thou to memory all the works of the prophets which are written down
in the sixtieth chapter of the Bible, which is the Buships Technical Manual,
and which giveth out the straight poop.

– the Electrical Officer

May 1, 1969

And then there was always the running argument about whether or not there
was any difference between Philippine and Manila brewed San Miguel beer. The
question was such a hotbed of debate that it was even addressed in a column in
the *Subic Bay News* by staff-writer Teddy B. del Rosario.

People were calling it the "Dr. Jekll and Mr. Hyde" beer. When it came in a
bottle labeled "Philippine San Miguel beer," by general consensus it tasted just
perfect. But when it was labeled "Manila San Miguel beer," we all agreed it tasted
like rotgut.

The bartenders assured us that the beer all came from the same source. The
bottles, whether they be labeled Philippine or Manila, were lined up, like a chow
line, and got their contents at the brewery from the same spigot.

The explanation of why some people could swear there was a difference in
taste was probably purely psychological. One time, one guy maybe drank one
Manila beer which happened to taste a little green to him, so he jumped to the
conclusion that all "Manila" beers tasted that way. He began telling his drinking
buddies about his discovery and soon the word spread.

Afterwards, even when a Manila beer tasted just fine, the drinker, due to
the psychological effect that the rumors had implanted in his mind, thought the
beer tasted differently. Old wives' tales die hard. This grew to such an extent that
whenever we were served a Manila beer in a nightclub, we would quickly inspect
the label and immediately send it back to be exchanged for a Philippine beer. We
were so adoring of Philippine San Miguel beer that we would not even have admit-
ted it if one of them turned up a bit skunky, too.

May 4, 1969

Dear Family,

Got your letter today – along with a dozen packs of sunflower seeds. Thanks
a lot! I've been studying my butt off for the big test next Tuesday, but I reckon I
can put aside the books long enough this fine Sabbath morning to get a few lines

off to you – just to let you know that I haven't drowned in San Miguel beer or something.

I took the Military Leadership test and passed it. Now all that stands between me and third-class petty officer (E-4) is the Electrician's Mate exam next Tuesday. It's not an easy test, though, so don't be surprised if I fail it. Better men than I have had to take it two or even three times before they finally passed. If it was a simple test, then everybody would be a third class.

I've gotten my glasses replaced, but that wasn't the end of my problems. I had a bad fall in the engine room which made my pilonidal cyst on my tailbone flare up again. It hurts something awful! It's not peaked enough to lance yet, so I have to sit in a sitz bath twice a day. After they lance it again, they say they are going to take me over to the base hospital and have it removed entirely. I also got my shot card updated last week; I got smallpox, yellow fever, cholera, and flu shots all in the same arm! The pain! The pain!

My little buddy, Dean, got his "Dear John" letter just recently from his girl back home. It was a little quicker for Dean than it took for most of us, but it came nonetheless. It only strengthens my opinion of those fickle round-eye girls back home: they just don't care what we're doing over here or in Vietnam. And that's the way too many other people think back home, too. So Dean has the blues.

We just got out of dry dock yesterday and are back here at the Boton Wharf in Service Craft with the rest of the tugs. We won't be able to get underway for a while yet, but we're sure having a lot of work done on the boat during this yard period that has been long overdue.

Three carriers pulled into Subic last week and another one was on its way here. But the base commander made two of them leave again because he didn't want "…another Pearl Harbor incident" with so many valuable ships in one place at the same time. Besides, there are always a lot of fights between the crews when different bird farms are in port together. They simply hate each other – even guys on sister ships! Who can explain it? Then again, who can explain why sailors and Marines hate each other? The Marine Corps is a branch of the Navy, for pete's sake!

NEWSPAPER CLIPPING

"About 1,000 Filipino nightclub hostesses, who want a bigger share of the American serviceman's dollar, plan to demonstrate this week against clubs inside Subic Bay US Naval Base. The PNS said the hostesses, along with waiters and other entertainers, plan to demonstrate at the main gate, then take chartered buses to Manila to continue their demonstrations at the US Embassy and the Presidential Palace. The hostesses and waiters from Olongapo City are from clubs where business is slipping since the naval base set up its own clubs. The PNS said that club operations inside the base have violated Philippine-American bases agreements."

May 16, 1969

Dear Family,

It's an unusually quiet day in the P.I. (I think it's the hush before the storm.) The clouds aren't moving, and the jungle just stands there like it was painted across the sky with a dirty green brush. Thank goodness there's a feeble breeze coming in from the sea, or this peaceful Boton Valley might be as merry as a morgue. Par for the course, Stanga has got the miserable duty again, including the ever-popular midwatch! Oh well, I made my bed the day I signed that paper, so now I'll have to lie in it.

I won't get to find out until next month if I passed my Electrician's Mate test or not. I don't know what takes so ridiculously long. I must say that it was a hard one, though, and I hope my studying paid off. If I passed, then I'll be a third-class petty officer, with a promotion in rank, and a raise in pay – not to mention a new 12:30 AM curfew! That sounds alright by me, but I'm not getting my hopes up yet.

Right now we're getting a stretch of cool weather to make the shade tolerable and tempers bearable. The all-afternoon showers we receive daily help a lot for good sleeping at night, too. The puddles and the mud out in town constantly remind us of the imminent rainy season about to set in with a vengeance. It's still in the high 80's after it rains, but that's relatively cool to us; you can about imagine the humidity that we have to deal with, or maybe you can't. I have a permanent heat rash; I'll not tell you where.

Two weekends ago I was awfully sick; I had severe abdominal cramps and had to run to the head every ten minutes with a dire rear. Then I started passing blood and it hurt something awful. I felt so bad that I couldn't eat for two days. I suspected that maybe I was trying to pass a stone of some sort, but on Monday morning the symptoms had mysteriously disappeared. Whatever it was, I've been all right ever since.

Smitty may have to go to the hospital with something that's got him down, though. The corpsman says his liver is "arching," whatever that means, but Smitty thinks it's his old hepatitis coming back to haunt him again. He's bedridden in the barracks for now. Poor Dean, Earl, Benton, Bobby, Peter, and Scotty have *all* got a dose of the Olongapo Rash – but then that's another story altogether.

A British bird farm pulled in here today; it's the first one of its kind that I've seen. It looks sort of pretty, if an awesome warship can be described as pretty, sitting about a mile across Subic Bay at Alava Wharf. The Limeys have sharp uniforms, too, as do the Aussies and the Kiwis.

Tomorrow, pockets permitting, Dean, Earl and I are going horseback riding down some jungle trails. It's one of the activities provided by Special Services here on base. Good clean fun. Earl is from Minnesota and Dean is from Iowa, and us Midwesterners sort of stick together. I guess it's purely psychological – or else it's just because so many clever fellows come from the Great Plains? Earl's sister's boyfriend got killed in Vietnam, so she up and joined a nunnery in Mankato; they send us cookies and stuff once in a while.

Don't ask me how they do it, but the nightclub hostesses out in town know when a ship is coming into port weeks before we even see a list of the ships we'll be moving to berth! If you want to know when such-and-such a ship is coming in, say you got a buddy on that ship, just ask a bar girl before you bother to ask the Lieutenant – it'll save you a trip and you'll get the straight poop, and maybe she'll let you rub noses later to boot. The clubs will have signs erected reading, "Welcome Enterprise!," even as the ship is still somewhere out at sea. So much for our secret ship movements, eh!

I saw "Romeo and Juliet" out in town last night and I thought it was just an outstanding film! I had never read the story in school, but everyone basically knows what happens. I loved the excellent dueling scenes and appreciated the genuine emotion of the talented young actors. I can't see how any of the Filipinos in the audience understood a word of the heavy Shakespearean dialogue, though, but they sure seemed to be enjoying it nonetheless. I also saw the movie, "The Boston Strangler," starring Tony Curtis, and it left quite an impression on me as well – only of a disturbing nature.

If we don't get chugging out in the harbor pretty darn soon, I may lose what's left of my sanity. It's not exactly cheering to look at the total state of disrepair and piled junk on this boat day after day while we wait for the pride of the Filipino Nationals to finish our overhaul job. If somebody doesn't put us back together soon, I shall totally lose my patience and start to hate the very sight of this boat!

I'm so undecided right now that it's really starting to bug me. Not being able to make this decision of mine is very frustrating. What decision, you ask? On the day I joined up I started thinking about what I wanted to do when I get out of the

Navy, and I'm still thinking. I'll probably still be thinking when they hand me my discharge papers at Treasure Island!

I'd like to go to a technical school for Electronics, and then ship out on a merchant tanker on a European cruise. But then again, I'd like to settle down in a nice apartment with a big old motorcycle, get a good job, and spend my spare time writing short stories and learning Italian. Then again, I'd like to go to a police academy, or maybe re-enlist in the Navy for two years down at Operation Deep-freeze in Antarctica, or even raise sheep in New Zealand. I guess I'll just have to keep thinking about it.

Well, I think it's fixin' to rain pitchforks and hammer handles soon, so I better dog down the hatches and button up the portholes. Try to shake the Spring fever and drop me a few lines now and then, why don't yuh?

May 22, 1969

Dear Gramma,

I've got the duty tonight and I always write my letters then; it helps so much to pass the time. There's not really much to say anymore. I guess I'm either getting immune to everything, or else there really is nothing exciting going on down here! Some guys write home so infrequently that their parents have complained to their commanding officers, and the men have been *ordered* to write home regularly!

I'm desperately waiting for next month when I'll find out if I passed my third class test or not. Just the same, I've seen to it that my recommendation for the next testing period for Electrician's Mate has been sent in, just in case I failed this one. I have absolutely no faith in myself on this last test; it was a tricky one!

Here on the boat, repair work and general overhaul struggles on and on. It seems like it is taking forever, doesn't it?! Right now a couple of us are laying new linoleum tile on the floor of the crew's berthing compartment. After that, we will paint the bulkheads, and then we can move back on the boat! I hate it so much over in the barracks – it's so hot inside and those Marines are so darn noisy! They're taught how to yell and scream in boot camp, and they never seem to be able to moderate their indoor voices after that.

Like a fool, I accidentally walked into the jagged end of an angle iron yester-day and cut my forehead wide open. It went pretty deep and sounded like some-body ripping silk. After I got the bleeding stopped and put a battle dressing on it, the guys tried to send me to sickbay for stitches, mind you! I told them it was all right and that I didn't need any stupid stitches, but they dragged me there anyway and dropped me off at the dispensary. I waited until they were out of sight, and then I walked back to the barracks. I watched Smitty get stitches in his lip after a fist fight once; from then on I can't even stand the thought of having stitches! I'm healing fine already, anyway.

Now that it's the rainy season (officially, as of today), everything is such a dreary, boring gray color. The sky is gray, the clouds are gray, the water is gray, the jungle and hills are gray – and of course all the ships are gray! Sometimes you can't even tell where the sky and the sea meet. But we sure get some beautiful sunsets during the rainy season.

I'm getting short now, only 240 days left here in the P.I. I started counting down the days after I had ten months under my belt. Ten long months, and I haven't even so much as talked to an American girl! Whatever will become of me???

Well, time to make my trusty rounds. I hope you're having nice weather back home; anybody in his right mind couldn't possibly enjoy this climate!

May 26, 1969

The Apollo 10 mission has been completed now. Our little space race is sure advancing by leaps and bounds! It's a big risk, sending men off into space like that, but necessary hazards have to be met teeth to teeth. Apollo 10 was a full dress rehearsal of the moon landing coming up in July. The three astronauts confirmed all aspects of lunar landing procedures except actual descent. They circled the moon 31 times and came within 9.4 miles of the lunar surface. They made splashdown near Pago-Pago in American Samoa. The USS Princeton (LPH-5), a helicopter carrier, retrieved them from the Pacific Ocean. Thirty-six minutes after splashdown the capsule was safely on deck.

I'm sure glad nothing went wrong. I can't help but think that sometimes we're pushing our luck as we try new and bolder things, but there are too many things holding back progress the way it is now. It's a wonderful thing what they're doing for mankind.

June 9, 1969

Dear Dad,

Weather-wise, the paper should read, "Thundershowers with scattered sunshine." Pretty soon it'll rain solid all day and all night as we get well into the depth of the rainy season. I bought an umbrella this year; I remember how soaking wet I got last year without one! But this ridiculous spring-loaded umbrella of mine is one of those perverse things that opens whenever it feels like it…in my locker, in the Blaylock's taxi, in the bar…whenever I least expect it.

This month all enlisted men get a small pay raise across the board. So if I make third class, then my pay will go up $100 with the raise and promotion. I also go officially "over two" this month; figuratively, that's over two years in the Navy. I came in under the 120-Day Delayed-Entry Plan, and that was accredited to my active-duty time, when actually I spent it as a happy-go-lucky civilian. Anyway, that'll be another sixty dollars, which will raise my pay clear up to $268.50 per month – about what I made at the café! And it only took me two years to get there! I won't know what to do with all that extra money.

We have heard rumors about a bad collision between one of our tin cans and an Aussie bird farm, which were on joint ASW maneuvers near here. I think they towed the damaged ship into port somewhere, because I saw the *Manila Times* helicopter fly overhead earlier. I wonder how bad the collision was?

More bad news: another guy drowned here over the weekend. This makes the third guy from Service Craft to drown since I've been down here. It happened the same as the others; he was drunk and fell down between the tugs at the pier. The rest of the crew is sitting around with long faces mumbling that the place is jinxed. So now the division officers are putting cargo nets between all the boats and cracking down on the sentries standing watch.

Might as well get all the bad news off my chest: I got picked up last night by the Shore Patrol out in town and was charged with Public Intoxication. This is really quite unbelievable. I was trying to cross Magsaysay Drive and I got caught in the middle of the street by a sudden rush of traffic from both ways when the traffic lights changed simultaneously. I couldn't go safely forward or back. The Shore Patrol came roaring up beside me; they must have figured that anybody standing in the middle of all that traffic just had to be drunk. So they picked me up and charged me, without even the benefit of a blood test, thank you very much, and I had had only five lousy beers stretched over the whole evening!

When they took me down to the SP headquarters, they acted so surprised when I didn't stagger around or slur my words for them, or act belligerent in any way. I appeared too rational for the average drunken sailor, and it seemed at first like they didn't know what to do with me. I was hopeful of just being sent back to the boat with a warning. But eventually they took away my liberty card for a month – which is alright by me, because I'll be forced to save a little money then. Kind of like being grounded to the base for thirty days.

Things on the boat are going from bad to worse. Now we have to await parts for our engines from the States and they may not come for a couple of months!

What the – are they coming by row boat or what?! I can't take this torn-up roach of a boat for that long, but I suppose I will have to. They tell us that we may not be back on the line until 1970. Great, just about the time when I'll be ready to leave for home. I like to work out in the harbor with the big ships, not sit on my butt and watch somebody else work!

For the amusement of the crew, and as an attempt to boost flagging morale on the boat, I started drawing a cartoon character named "Superskate" ("…while normally disguised as Harold Buships, FA – the champion of snipes everywhere!"). I periodically draw detailed cartoons and they seem to get a big kick out of them.

Don't worry about me taking drugs; I'm very much against it and I don't tolerate anybody who uses the stuff or cut them an inch of slack about it. (That's one reason why I have a couple of enemies on the boat. But they aren't the kind of guys I'd choose for friends anyway.)

The most popular form of drug down here among the sailors is grass, or marijuana. There are also Red Devils, Bennies, speed, and sniffing glue, among others. There is a phone number for Crimestoppers Anonymous where you can be a snitch, but I can't see going that route either. As long as they leave me alone, I figure they'll get caught sooner or later all by themselves. To make matters worse, a few of the station sailors are even rolling fleet sailors to get money for their drugs. You just don't know who you can trust anymore. And with all the venereal disease running wild out there in town, this place falls slightly short of Shangri-La.

My buddy, Dean (from Sioux City, Iowa), wants me to partner-up with him in a hamburger joint when we get out of the Navy. He said we could build it close to a big campus in Sioux City, and I would be the chef. We have in mind a wholesome place where young people and families can eat well at a reasonable price. He has $10,000 in savings and we can both borrow off two different life-insurance policies. It'd be close to home for both of us, and just the thing to get started in if it made any money at all. Oh well, that's a long time from now, but we like to dream.

Say, do you know something that we all need down here, but can't seem to lay our hands on? Safety pins! Can you send some soon? Hope you have a happy Father's Day, Dad! Miss you all…

June 10, 1969

Several days ago they towed in the wreck of the *USS Frank E. Evans* (DD-754), a destroyer which was accidentally rammed by the Australian carrier *HMAS Melbourne* (R-21) on June 3rd at 3:00 in the morning. (The *USS Frank E. Evans* is not to be confused with the *USS Evans* (DE-1023)). The *Frank E. Evans* served in World War II and the Korean War and the Vietnam War, before being cut in half by the *Melbourne.* The forward section of the *Frank Evans* sank instantly after the early-morning collision with the *Melbourne,* containing 74 men still asleep in their racks. It went straight to the bottom within two minutes while the aft section remained afloat. (In 1964, the *Melbourne* had been involved in a collision with Australian destroyer *HMAS Voyager* (D04), sinking the smaller ship and killing 82 of her crew.) At the time of the collision *Evans's* captain was asleep. The OOD, a junior officer who was not qualified to stand watch, having failed at his previous board, neglected to notify him as required when he executed the fatal maneuver. They have the ship in dry dock now here in Subic, and it looks like a terrible mess! Those poor sailors must have gone through pure hell. Workers are stripping down the ship, removing all the salvageable equipment, and then they will strike the ship from Navy records. It really stinks down inside the hulk, and they think there's still several bodies encased in the twisted metal bulkheads that they haven't found yet. The Filipino workers are a pretty superstitious lot, and are more than a little skittish about even working on the ship in the first place.

USS Frank E. Evans (DD-754), at left, after being cut in half.

June 11, 1969

The Apollo 10 space capsule was recently used for training purposes in the Philippines, dropping paramedics and frogmen on it in the sea to assist the "astronauts" and then picking up the capsule with a helicopter. With the training completed, it was decided to give Subic Bay personnel an opportunity to see what an Apollo command module actually looks like.

EM3 Steve Stanga B617389
US Naval Station, Subic Bay
Box 15, YTM-182
FPO, San Francisco
96651
June 12, 1969

Dear Gramma,

It's really raining hard outside at this time. We're well into the rainy season. Maybe now that it's much cooler we'll all be able to get rid of our constant heat rashes.

Please notice the change in my address – I made third class! I got the results back today, and to my amazement I had passed the test! You're the first person I've told… besides the guys, of course, who never doubted that I would pass with flying colors. I am finally a third-class petty officer. (I think that's the same as a corporal in the Army.) This will raise my pay up to $268 a month! I feel like a peso-millionaire! Goodness, I want to celebrate, but I haven't got the funds just yet. Come payday and I'll treat my buddies to a big dinner out in town.

My buddy, Smitty, made third-class petty officer, too. He's a Boatswain's Mate, though. From now on, I will wear a globe of the world (symbol of the EM) and one chevron on my sleeve; Smitty will wear one chevron underneath a pair of crossed fouled anchors (symbol of a BM).

At present, we've got another crippled destroyer here in port that had a bad fire below decks which killed several sailors. These things are happening all the time, but you hardly ever hear about most of them back home, I'll bet.

Say, I've been wondering; do you think a loaf of your world-famous banana bread would survive a week in the mail? I don't know how much bother it is to throw a batch together, but I'd be ever so happy to get a fine treat like that!

June 21, 1969

Dear Family,

It seems like it's getting farther and farther between letters for us, and that ain't right. I'm sure your new canoe doesn't take up that much of the family's time. C'mon now!

I found out on the 12th that I had passed my test, and my advance in rate to EM3 became effective as of the 16th. Now I can start giving orders for once! Ha ha. Naw, I don't think I'm the kind of guy to abuse my authority. With my increased pay, I started a savings account at the American Express down here for the things I want: a stereo, a camera, a motorcycle, a tattoo… And I'm having an allotment taken out of my paychecks to send home *two* savings bonds a month now instead of one! Be sure you make the proper change in my address now; I worked hard to get EM3, and I'd like to see it on all my letters.

Well, I got my liberty card back from the chief yesterday, so I'm not restricted to the base anymore. I intend to hang onto it this time. My new liberty hours will run until 12:30 AM now. But I doubt if I'll stay out that late anyway. It's funny, but as a civilian I thought nothing of staying out until 0400, drinking North Star beer and jumping freight trains, but here in the Navy most of the guys are voluntarily in their racks by 2300. About the only thing you can accomplish by staying out after that time is getting into trouble of some sort.

Things here on the boat are really shaping up fast and it isn't much of a roach anymore. I put the range, the reefer, the lights, and the vents back together again. I helped install a new commode, a hot-water heater, and a galley sink (hey, plumbing is kind of fun!), and we all have new bunks in our compartment. Next week we get us a new cook and then we can move back on board for good. (Stew-burners aren't very hard to get ahold of in the Navy, either.) We paid off the Joes in cigarettes to paint out the compartments for us. They'll do anything for tasty American cigarettes; they can't stand the dog turds that they make down here in the islands.

I just happened to look over my shoulder and I see the jungle is getting pretty black as a wily thundercloud tries to sneak down the valley and catch me out in the open. Even now it's starting to sprinkle, so I'll retire inside the galley to finish this letter. So much for tanning today.

Benton's old tin can pulled in here a couple of days ago, and he gave me the grand tour around it. I had never been on a destroyer before. It's quite a place, I must say! Everything is so neat and tidy and compact and, well – shipshape! Their galley, believe it or not, is not much bigger than our tiny kitchen back home, but they serve almost 200 men out of it. Really something! And all the officers were so friendly (that's a switch). I hope to get on a tin can someday, too.

Poor Dean-o, he'll never learn his lesson. This payday he got paid over $200 in back pay and he's already got it spent. Him and money just aren't close buddies for very long. "A fool and his money are soon parted" refers directly to him. He must have a girlfriend in every bar out in town. And he gives his money away to every girl that says she loves him no shit.

He came back drunk the other night with only forty dollars left of his paycheck and told me to hang onto it for him. "No matter how I beg or how much I plead, do NOT give me that money!" he instructed me. The next day he had already asked for the money five times by noon, and then got really mad at me because I wouldn't give him back his dang money.

Well, I held out for two days under this kind of pressure and abuse, and then finally gave it back to him just to shut him up. I told him that he was going to spend it foolishly no matter when I gave it back to him, so he might as well have it now and be happy. So he came back this morning, flat broke, and mad as hell at me for giving his money to him. *sigh* I can't win for losing. Now he's got until next payday to think about it. Nobody can talk any sense into him.

I quit going to that silly sitz bath, as I didn't think it was doing me a bit of good. The pain in my tailbone has gone away since I started working out at the gym anyway. The pilonidal cyst has subsided on its own.

I sure would like some recent color photographs of the family and the old homestead. Right about now I'm really missing the little kids! I'm always taking out their pictures and making myself terribly homesick.

June 26, 1969

Dear Vern,

Hey, man, since the family has gotten that dang canoe, you're the only one who writes anymore. I'm grateful for that.

As you know by now, I made third-class petty officer. Of course, after sewing my new stripe on, everybody got to "tack it on" good and proper with their big hairy fists (par tradition). Ouch! Then they threw me over the side into the bay with all my clothes on. For a moment beforehand they held me suspended over their heads above the water, as if possibly changing their minds. Then those piss-ants on the other tugs, eager to take part in the fun, started yelling, "No balls! No hair! No stones!" So over I went. I swore my everlasting revenge upon them all. For the finish of my initiation I had to pass out Swisher Sweets cigars to everybody and his dog. I'm sure glad I don't make third class every week!

We've finished the work on our crew's compartment, so today we moved back on the boat for good. It sure does get hot down in that hole sometimes, though. The sun beats on the main deck without mercy for hours, and you can feel the hot metal radiating down on you in your rack. We also got a new cook, a southerner, and all he's served us so far are ribs, ribs, and more ribs. He'd better shape up fast! Us working boys gotta eat better than that!

One of my shipmates, Earl, who lives out in town with a girl, had an exciting experience the other night. He was sleeping in his apartment and suddenly he heard loud voices and shooting. He looked out the window to see five guys shooting it out with his landlord next door. Two guys started running up the steps to Earl's room and the landlord shot them both in the back. Those Joes go crazy when they get a gun in their hands! Earl was scared, so he locked the door and stayed inside until morning. Boy, everything happens out in that town, huh?

We have been trying different clubs lately to see if we can find some good new bands. Many of the bars have two go-go dancers and they are usually the best-looking girls in the whole club! You just have to sit there and watch them, though; you can't even cuddle with them. Rats!

But there's usually enough other snakes around to talk to. They always want you to buy them a drink for four pesos. The "drink" is usually iced tea, for which the bar gets half the money and the girl gets half. That's all you hear, like a damn tape recording, "Sailor, be nice – buy me drink, buy me drink." Christ! It really gets on your nerves after a while. Do you know that even a Coke for a bar hostess costs a dollar? What a racket. We just can't afford too much of that. Once in a while we'll break down and buy them a drink, though, and then they just love you all to pieces!

After 5:00 in the afternoon, it costs you five dollars to "check out" a girl and leave the club with her. (Again, the bar gets half and the girl gets half.) After that, she's all yours to do with what you want. If she doesn't want to go with you, then she stands to possibly lose her job in that club. It sure is a different world down here, bro.

I can stay out until 12:30 AM, and then the main gate doesn't open up again until 0530 in the morning…but that's only for going from base into town. Yes, you are allowed to stay out in town overnight, but you have to be off the streets prior to curfew – many is the time my buddies are caught minutes before curfew, running hand in hand with some bar girl through the back streets of Olongapo, looking for a place to "sleep" for the night – and if you try to come back on base before 0800 you can get thrown in the brig. They're really strict about that. Crazy rules!

I made a vow today: I'm going to kill every fly in the Philippines, or at least Subic Bay. They've walked on my food and bugged me while I'm sleeping long enough! I will be merciless. I'll get such a horrible reputation as a fly killer that when I come after them they'll just lay down and die. The daddy fly will say to his offspring, "You see who's coming now? It ain't no use to struggle, kiddies. Just lay down and die." And parent flies will threaten their offspring with ME if they don't behave. Maybe the word will even spread back to the States, and when I come home the filthy suckers will migrate to wherever I'm not. Flies of the world, beware – this is war!

EVANS DECOMMISSIONED; TO BE USED FOR TARGET
July 1, 1969

"The *USS Frank E. Evans* (DD-754) was decommissioned in a ceremony aboard the floating dry dock *USS Windsor* (ARD-22). The aft section of the destroyer cut in half by the Australian aircraft carrier *Melbourne* on June 3rd had been at the dry dock since being towed to Subic Bay after the collision. The forward section of the *Frank Evans* sank after the collision with the *Melbourne*. Seventy-four American sailors were lost. No crew members of the Australian ship were hurt. The *Frank Evans* was commissioned on February 3, 1945. Her namesake was Brigadier General Frank E. Evans, USMC, a much decorated fighting man who served during the Spanish-American and First World Wars. The vessel was officially stricken from the Navy list on July 1, 1969. The skipper of the destroyer said it is a fitting tribute that the *Frank Evans* can provide service even after decommissioning. The ship's hull will be towed out to sea for use as a target in gunnery practice."

July 2, 1969

Dear Gramma,

Your box of goodies came this morning! I was certainly surprised that the package came so soon, and in such good condition, too. The banana bread was like you had just taken it out of the oven, only it wasn't piping hot. It was moist and fresh and simply delicious! We all shared the first loaf for dinner. "Tell your gramma that she makes some gooooooood banana bread!" said one southern boy with a drawl. And it really was. I like the chocolate-chip cookies, too; I got four of them before the other guys got ahold of them. But I don't mind sharing. Thanks again for all your consideration and the trouble you went to for me. A fella couldn't ask for a better Gramma!

Smitty and I had a serious fight two weeks ago and haven't seen each other since then. This has been building up for a long time. As soon as he made third class he started throwing his weight around with other guys. Just by being in his company, he has gotten me embroiled in fist fights with fleet sailors out in town, because he can't seem to keep his big mouth shut when he's been drinking.

But that's not the worst of it. He's always been completely obnoxious and ill-mannered to the Filipino people, and it just got to the point where I didn't want to be around him anymore. I thought we were buddies good enough that I could talk to him about it, but when I mentioned it he flew off the handle. I guess some people just don't like to have their faults pointed out to them. At least my other buddies treat the Filipinos like human beings, and don't always assume a superior attitude with them. After all, we are guests in their country.

Well, today I had my first minor crisis as a petty officer. The chief engineer left me in charge of Benton and Earl (who are still Firemen), and wanted us to get the new flushing pump installed. But getting work out of those two goldbricks is like trying to squeeze Lord Calvert from a rock. Impossible.

I explained to them what the job was, and how to get set up for it. An hour later they were still sitting around and hadn't started. I kept telling them to get on the ball and get busy, but they would only ask, "Is that an order, *Sir?*" I finally just gave up and did the job myself; rounded up the necessary tools, installed the heavy pump, hooked up the plumbing and the wiring, then cleaned up afterwards.

Being a petty officer is supposed to be rewarding in that you delegate people to work for you, or at least with you, but these two lazy bums are too much bother to get a fire started under them. Benton is the kind of guy who gets migraine headaches every time he does something constructive for the Navy. And Earl looks at his time in the service as four completely wasted years, and he isn't about to be helpful on any voluntary basis.

That's the trouble with many of the guys on this boat; they literally have to be forced to do something unless they stand to benefit from it directly. And you should just hear the names I'm called because I'd rather pass the time by working instead of sitting around. Thank goodness there's still a few of us on the boat who care enough about what kind of tug we have to live on.

The guys had a good laugh today, as I was the goat once again. I was climbing down into the engine room and I accidentally upset a Filipino worker's toolbox which was left sitting in my way. All of his tools went tumbling down into the bilges under the main engine. The bilges are full of oil, dirt, grease, foul water – and I think some of the guys pee down there out of sheer laziness.

Boy, did I feel like a fool. The Filipino workers had gone home for the day. So I got out an extension magnet, fished all the tools out, and cleaned them up. And all the time the fellas were hanging around and laughing their heads off, heckling me rather than helping out.

One of our seamen was handling line the other day, manually moving a paint raft around to the other side of the tug, and he wasn't paying attention where he was backing up. He backed right into an open hold and disappeared through the deck – just like in the old slapstick movies! Apparently nobody else saw the hole either. Luckily he landed feet-first, but he caught his arm on the way down and sprained it pretty bad. Danger lurks everywhere if you are not alert.

I was never prejudiced against Negroes until I came into the service. (Maybe that was because we didn't have any colored families in Mitchell when I was growing up?) Strange to say, but my best buddy in boot camp was a black kid named Albert from Georgia.

But all of the Negroes down here are really something else to behold. They all have this sickening holier-than-thou attitude, and their vanity is unbearable. They wear outlandish clothes, and their speech sounds totally foreign from the English language. They go out of their way not to fit in, and then complain when they don't. Besides, most of them sympathize with the Black Panthers and other Negro militant groups.

I know it ain't my place to find fault, but the Navy breeds such a hate for the Blacks in a person that it almost seems intentional. And in turn, the Negro cultivates it and keeps it growing, widening the gap between us. About one-third of the town is relegated to the Negro and all the businesses there cater to "soul brothers;" the rest of us are told to keep out of that part of town, called "The Jungle" or "Jungletown." I'm concerned that my current dislike for colored people might carry over into civilian life, too. It might be sort of hard to break a strong four-year habit.

I guess I'll have to call off my skin diving for a couple of months, or at least until the rainy season is over with. All this rain and its subsequent runoff have made the water pretty dirty – even as far out as Grande Island. The last thing I need is to go swimming in murky water so a shark can sneak up on tasty little ol' me!

July 19, 1969

Dear Gramma,

How are things back in the World, anyway? I hear President Nixon has made tomorrow a national holiday in anticipation of the moon landing. I hope his optimism isn't going to be upset; space exploration is still risky business. But I think it's all pretty exciting and it'll make a wonderful piece of history to tell my kids. The guys on the boat think I'm half crazy because I get so worked up about it, but their trouble is that they're too apathetic about the important things going on in the world today. They don't realize that big steps affecting our future are being made every day, and they could simply care less. They're a new breed of fools.

My buddy, Dean, just made Storekeeper third-class this week. So now they'll yank him off our boat and re-assign him to some air-conditioned warehouse somewhere over on Mainside, because there isn't a billet for an SK3 on a tugboat. I wish they'd leave us buddies alone, but it isn't to be. Anyway, with his raise in pay he can support a lot more girls out in town than before. He'll enjoy that.

On watch tonight Benton and I had a contest swatting flies in the galley, as part of our joint goal to drive them into extinction. He got 31 and I got 88. A week ago we caught a five-inch-long cockroach under the stove. It was making a loud snapping sound, and it gave me the willies just to look at it. I threw it over the side and it swam away in a huff.

Curtis, one of my buddies from the old garbage boat, writes that he recently got wounded over in Nam. His river patrol boat got hit with a mortar shell which killed one guy and made a mess of the boat. Curtis was spared being hit by shrapnel, but sustained a lacerated finger when they went to General Quarters. As he was running to his battle station, some yahoo slammed a watertight door on his hand. The corpsman stitched him up and told him to get back to work and quit whining. But the finger was also broken and the splint made holding a beer can nearly impossible. Now he'll have a fancy scar, and there's crazy talk about possibly getting the Purple Heart medal, and then he'll have a *real* war story to tell his buddies back home.

I am enclosing one of the new one-peso bills that the Philippine National Treasury just started circulating. They look almost phony, don't they? The faint picture within the blank circle is supposed to make them extra hard to copy. I don't know who would bother to counterfeit a peso bill worth twenty-five cents anyway.

The *USS Sanctuary* (AH-17), a hospital ship, is in port now. It is air-conditioned throughout, has a helo platform and 760 beds. I'm sure you've seen pictures of hospital ships, haven't you? They're all white with big red crosses painted on either side of the hull. Really beautiful ships! They pull in here every once in a while after several months on the gun line in Vietnam. Some have almost a thousand bunks on them for sailors, soldiers, airedales, and Marines. Hospital ships are named after words that suggest rest and comfort, like the *USS Repose, Benevolence, Tranquility,* and *Haven.* The *USS Consolation* was renamed *"Hope"* by the People to People Health Foundation, a private civilian group that uses the ship as a floating laboratory and medical school in Southeast Asia.

Meanwhile, it rains and it rains, but I manage to keep my spirits from getting too dampened. We're living and eating back aboard the boat now, so it's not so bad. At least we're out of those miserable barracks.

July 21, 1969

Dear Family,

It took us all afternoon to get the mailbox key out of our locked craftmaster's stateroom, but we wanted our mail awfully bad and he wasn't coming back to the boat until tomorrow. Mail deprivation does strange things to a person. I finally snagged the key out of his desk by reaching through the porthole with a bent coat hanger. I had three letters waiting for me when we opened the division mailbox, so I was glad I made the effort to get the key.

Yes! I finally got your long-awaited letter! I figured that you were all wrapped up in that new red canoe of yours and probably didn't even stop for meals anymore. Out of sight and out of mind, eh?

Find enclosed a picture of Dean, my best buddy in the whole P.I. He's 22 years old, and has only been in the Navy a year. He's about the most considerate guy I know and he's a steady, hard worker on the boat. He caught the clap a couple of weeks ago (for the second or third time), but he's getting medical treatment once again, and I don't hold that against a guy.

He's such a complete and total fool with money, though. When he gets money in his hands on payday, dollar signs literally appear in his eyes. And when he regains consciousness three days later in a hotel room he's flat broke and he hasn't a clue why.

For example, Dean recently rented an apartment out in town, furnished it, and was all ready to move in with a girl when she threw him over for a Marine. That's the lowest blow! But he just let her keep the apartment anyway. What a *malaki lapu-lapu* [big fish]!

He is currently rotting away (his own words) here on the boat for a month because they pulled his liberty card after he got picked up for Public Intoxication. And the funny thing is that he was the one who laughed the loudest when I got picked up by the Shore Patrol for the very same thing a while back. Anyway, it's probably the best thing in the world that could have happened to him.

Good buddy Curtis recently wrote from Nam; his letters are always full of misadventures and hi-jinx:

> *"One dark night on the Mekong River near Can Tho, I was bow sentry*
> *armed with a sawed-off twelve gauge. The guy on Starlight watch*
> *called me and said he saw a whole bunch of movement in the jungle*
> *on our near shore. Since it was a free-fire zone and there was not*
> *supposed to be anyone out there but Charley, we went to General*
> *Quarters and opened up on the patch of jungle with the fore and aft*
> *quad 40mm's. It was quite the light show! At daybreak they sent in*
> *a bunch of 9th Infantry Division Army troops to check it out. They*
> *came back laughing their heads off and said, 'You dumbasses, you*
> *blew the hell out of a herd of water buffalo!'"*

Mail call is never dull if there's a letter from Curtis in the bag.

I read in the *Stars and Stripes* about that hippie who was high on LSD and jumped off the Golden Gate Bridge. They pulled him out of the water singing "America, the Beautiful" with just bruises on his ankles. I guess he's supposed to be one of the few to ever survive the jump, eh?

You might know I had the duty on the Fourth of July, just like every other holiday that comes along. I sat here on the fantail and watched the fireworks over the bay. But they were so darn far away, and some of them must have been damp, because they were not too impressive. They had a big USO show and all kinds of games and celebrations and good chow. But the guys had to pay to get in, and they weren't allowed to bring their Filipina girlfriends along, so many of them simply skipped it. What a rip.

Well, the Apollo 11 crew is on the moon right now, aren't they? That is, if we can trust stories passed from mouth to mouth. (Our radio is FUBAR again.) Do you know what the first thing was that the astronauts heard when they stepped onto the moon? "Hey buddy, change your dollar to pesos at the Golden Gate Money Exchange, authorized by the Central Bank of the Philippines!" It's an inside joke. (The first thing you encounter when crossing through the main gate and over Shit River bridge is about twenty money exchangers all yelling to you at the same time.)

There's a rumor that President Nixon will visit Subic Bay after he leaves Manila. He really shouldn't waste his time. You know, I was thinking; if Nixon plans to pull all the troops out of Nam by the end of 1970 like we're hearing, I wonder if I'll even get to do my tour of duty over there? We seriously doubt that he'll actually carry it off, though. Next thing you know they'll try to abolish the draft, which will play right into the hands of the SDS. I think that if everyone just treated SDS as the joke that they are, they wouldn't last for long. If nobody took them serious, they'd just fizzle out and fold up.

It was a long weekend with no Stewburner, so I was the designated cook for the last couple of days. Friday night we had shrimp cocktail, Salisbury steak, and Greek salad. The food disappeared fast. Saturday night I made tuna-salad sandwiches and split-pea soup; that didn't seem to last very long either. Tonight I think I'll whip up ribeye steaks and scalloped potatoes. Got to keep in practice, you know. Meanwhile, the crew is just eating it up!

We had another contest swatting flies in the galley and I won with a grand total of 170 casualties. I could have gotten even more, but I was going a little kill-crazy and thought I had better get a grip on myself.

Other than going prematurely bald, I'm in fairly good health. But I currently have a bad case of athlete's foot. That's your reward for using a communal shower all the time in the Navy. I have these huge cracks in the skin between my toes. It never stops itching and I'm about ready to go out of my skull just restraining myself from scratching.

They're rapidly putting the boat back together again, but it'll still be a couple of weeks before we'll be chugging. The electrical work is done, and all that remains is putting the two main engines back together. Getting them together again is the easy part; getting them to *run* is another story. We've lost the most hated guy on the boat; he was finally transferred! And now we're one big happy crew just like old times. Life is good.

We had a minor problem last week which had us all thoroughly confused at the time. We got a new pump and motor that wouldn't work right. When the pressure in a certain holding tank (used for flushing our commodes) dropped to forty pounds it turned the motor on, which built the pressure back up to fifty pounds and then turned itself off. This is fine and dandy; this is how it is supposed to work. But every time someone shut off shore power to connect up their tug, the whole flushing system would turn off and would not turn back on again automatically when shore power was restored! This about drove us crazy trying to figure it out. In the end, I jury-rigged up a couple of special switches of my own design that turned the unit "on" whenever shore power was on. The chief engineer was so happy that he gave me the next day off.

So now I lay here in my rack, propped up on one elbow (which is rapidly going into a coma) with the radio pounding the Big Beat into my ear. Fly-Trap is asleep in his rack, where he spends 95% of his time, flat on his back with his mouth wide open as usual. I can see the doomed flies buzzing in lazy circles, hypnotized by his quivering uvula, and being drawn ever inward.

Some tardy liberty hound is in the shower singing "Why Don't We Do It In The Road?" And through the bulkheads I can hear the perseverant Filipino workers tinkering away down in the engine room. The rest of the crew is already out in town, consuming vast amounts of San Miguel beer, listening to the best in Filipino-accented rock 'n' roll, and doing heaven knows what with those bar girls. I'd be out there, too, but I'm saving every penny I can for a nice stereo.

August 6, 1969

Dear Family,

Just thought I'd set a world record and write twice in a row for once! There isn't anything monumental going on right now, but writing letters is certainly more mind-stimulating than swatting flies on watch.

It's been raining without once letting up for a week now; I don't even remember the last time I saw the sun. Ever since Typhoon Viola whipped through here a week or so ago, the wet part of the rainy season has really set in with a vengeance. I don't mind, though; every night that I stay on the boat I am saving money. The last five days I made forty dollars extra by taking other guys' duty for them.

The pressure is on. The division officers are doing everything they can to have the Filipino workers put us back together and chugging by the end of the month. That means the rest of us are really crackin', too. A day doesn't go by that we don't crash in our racks for a quick noon-hour nap, or collapse bone-weary, greasy and grimy at the end of the day. For the past two weeks just about nobody has gone on liberty after work – they're simply too tired to get showered and dressed and make the five-mile trip to the main gate. We feel like zombies, and morale is at an all-time low.

I saw "My Side of the Mountain" the other night at the base theater. I talked Benton and Dean into going with me, and now they're mad at me for making them lose two irreplaceable hours of drinking time. Half of the theater walked out ten minutes into the flick. However, I stayed to the end and enjoyed it tremendously. When I tried to talk about the film later they just shrugged their shoulders and muttered, "Well you gotta remember you were brought up in South Dakota…"

I wasn't surprised to learn that Subic Bay produces more mental cases than all the other Naval Stations in the United States combined. That I can believe! Subic Bay is enough to drive anybody berserk. But I've only got five months left down here, and I'm just going to do my job, keep my mouth shut, put up with our pea-brain fearless leaders, and try to get out of here in one piece.

It's frightening how common drug abuse is down here. It's probably just the environment. Right now there are four potheads sitting on our fantail smoking marijuana. This goes on almost nightly. The smell of marijuana is so distinctive that you'd think they wouldn't dare smoke it so close to the warehouse. Idiots!

If they haven't got the money for grass, then they pass around a rag soaked with model airplane glue. I read a pamphlet on that once, and I don't believe those fools really know what they're doing to themselves. A lot of the bar girls use Speed and Bennies (whatever they are), and even some of the bands get doped up on Red Devils before they play. At least my buddies and I have got the common sense to leave all that crap alone.

I've finally found the kind of nightclub out in town that I really like, that plays the kind of music I really go for. I wish I had found it months ago! It's a small, quiet spot and a welcome change of pace from all the hard rock bands screaming out Jimi Hendrix lyrics in the other bars and ruining your hearing. This bar exists under the deluding name of the "Can Can Club;" but the cozy, Italian-accented interior seems completely out of place in that decadent town. It has red-checkered table-cloths, individual candle-in-the-bottle table illumination, complimentary Spanish peanuts all night long, courteous waiters (!), mood lighting, clean restrooms, and soft-spoken well-mannered intelligent girls for companionship. You can actually carry on a conversation in the place!

The club features a seasoned four-man combo (i.e., piano, drums, guitar, and saxophone), made up of middle-aged merchant marine guys who have settled in Olongapo with Filipina girls. They play a combination of jazz and mood music – "I Left My Heart in San Francisco," "St. Louis Blues," the Mills Brothers, that sort of thing. Naturally, I'm the only one of the crew who really likes the place, so I'll prob-ably end up going there all by myself more times than not. That is alright once in a while, because if you spend 24 hours a day with the same people you will eventu-ally get on each other's nerves big time.

I finally got my athlete's foot situation under control, but the balding process continues without check. What a joke! Is it merely a coincidence that I began to lose my hair precisely at the same moment when I started wearing a hat 16 hours a day in a tropical climate? I think not. Do I have a viable lawsuit here or what? I think so.

I need to get away from it all pretty soon. I haven't seen open countryside or been out of sight of battleship-gray buildings in so long that I'm about ready to go bughouse for a little solitude! I hope I can get some camping done with you guys after I get out of here.

I know this is about four months too early to mention it, but I'd sure appreciate it if you and the other relatives didn't send me anything this Christmas. I'd just have to turn around and mail it all back home when I got ready to leave the Philippines anyway – and heaven knows I've already got much more than I can carry now. You do see my point, yes-no?

August 10, 1969

Dear Gramma,

You asked about the peso. A Philippine peso is equal to 100 centavos and is currently worth about twenty-five cents American. I don't know how much a Mexican peso is worth, but I think it's only half as much. Down here, one peso will buy a haircut on base, or a hamburger; a movie ticket out in town, a taxi clear across Olongapo, four bottles of pop, and lots of other things. Prices for clothes are basically the same as back home; but out in town it's slightly cheaper, and may even be tailor-made as well.

You could write a book about the sidewalks of Olongapo City. Masses of humanity thrive on the crowded sidewalks. They make baskets there; eat rice there; sleep there; fight roosters there; stack cases of San Miguel beer there; pick sailor's

Olongapo City today, Luzon, Philippine Islands.

pockets there; park jeepneys there; beat rugs there; children play games there; servicemen get sick there; Filipino soldiers patrol there.

On the sidewalks they also sell cheap watches, Red Devils, marijuana, Joe cigarettes, Tootsie Roll Pops, cold weenies, popcorn, monkey meat on a stick, switchblades, Campbell's soup, Sampaguita flowers, sweepstake's tickets, sunglasses, rosaries, Last Supper pictures, black-velvet paintings, and genuine plastic carabao horns – just to name a few. It's impossible to move leisurely down the sidewalk without being pestered continually.

The sidewalks are not for walking on, they're for walking around; the streets are for walking on, and then you risk getting run down by a jeepney.

I never went to see Nixon when he was in Manila, as it was too far away. I was relieved when the moon men got back to earth safely, though, but I am so disappointed that we never got to see any of the live transmissions from the moon, or any recorded pictures afterwards for that matter. All we got to see down here were a couple of blurred gray photos in the base newspaper.

Now I'm excited over Mariner 7 which is orbiting Mars as we speak. I may never live long enough to ever leave this old earth, but I believe in my heart that I'll live to see the day when we make contact with alien life from another planet. And that's something I am really looking forward to!

We might have this old tug chugging by the end of the month. It's just my luck to get stuck on the oldest tug down here. It was built in 1941 by the Pacific Coast Engineering Company in Oakland, California, and I think that it's just about had it.

Some guys really have it made: they got assigned to the new tugs which just arrived in Subic. They are only a year old and are air-conditioned, modern, with fluorescent lighting, tiled compartments, new equipment and furnishings, etc. They even have radar for chugging at night. Boy, it must be rough…

Do you remember my next-door neighbor, Bob Anderson? I talked him into joining the Navy. He is just finishing Aviation Electrician's school in Jacksonville, Florida, right now and then he'll be stationed in Maryland with a plane squadron. He'll go on flight tours to Europe and see all kinds of foreign countries. My other buddy, Al Larson, is going to be stationed in Pensacola, Florida. I have yet another buddy in San Diego, Doug Seiner, who is going to Corpsman school and studying to be a Medic. I figured they'd all want to gang up on me for talking them into enlisting, but so far they seem to really like the Navy.

BOTON VALLEY

August 15, 1969

I opened my eyes, as usual, about 15 minutes before reveille went down. A sort of biological clock wakes me up about the same time every morning. I lay lethargic in my rack, marveling at how quickly eight blessed hours of sleep could pass by. I stared at the girlie pin-ups on the overhead above my rack; they were the first things I saw every day: Raquel Welch, Nancy Sinatra, Julie Christie, Chris Noel, Ann Margaret, and Barbarella. Morning, ladies!

But I made an effort to roll out of my rack at that exact moment, or never rise at all. I stood clutching the chain-supports, prying open each groggy peeper in turn, and tried to force down that detestable thought of having to shave my stubble.

Instead, I quickly donned a fresh pair of dungarees and left the crew's compartment before the day's first installment of grumbling started. Maybe it's the frightful hour of the morning, and maybe it's the equally frightening environment, but my shipmates, god love 'em, seem obligated to begin each new day with a great deal of complaining about this or that.

Finally finishing the monotonous chore of shaving for the millionth time, I drew a cup of strong coffee in the galley, mellowed it down somewhat with sugar, and retired to the fantail where I could sit alone in the cool dawn breeze and view the beautiful sunrise. A new day's beginning, a world awakening, men and machinery coming to life – it is a remarkable and profound thing to witness sometimes.

Slowly but surely, the remainder of the crew started appearing above decks, hair awry, eyes bloodshot, alternately munching toast, yawning, scratching, stretching, farting, and stumbling over things, some of them with whopping great hangovers from the night before. They're not always as quick and eager to greet the rest of the world. It is comical to observe.

And so another working day in this man's Navy had begun. It's a real challenge every day here on the tug; I start out wondering what little odd jobs I might have to do, and end up without enough time to finish them all. But once I've started, time flies quickly enough, and before I know it it's time to knock off ship's work. I'd much rather spend my time working than pretending to work and being apparently busy, like some of the other guys.

To begin with, I went throughout the boat and replaced all the blown-out light bulbs, which is a daily ritual of mine. This craft consumes light bulbs just about as fast as the bilges devour tools. This brought an end to my reserve supply of bulbs, so this in turn involved tedious paperwork, looking up Federal stock numbers, and a trip over to the warehouse to renew my stock. This could very well be the only bit of actual electrical work that I accomplished all that day. The rest of the time was divided between working on projects with the other snipes, eating and skylarking.

The snipe's realm is the Hole, of course, and the mess down there can really get on a person's nerves after a while. The grease you get on your hands will probably never come off for the remainder of your life; I certainly haven't been able to get it out of my hands yet, I know. And there are engine room gremlins lurking among the pumps and motors which tear your clothes unmercifully and mysteriously open valves and run off with fuses. Today they decided to torment us while we installed a new fire-pump shaft.

Everything went forward as planned while we lifted a section of the 01 deck up and lowered the 800-pound shaft down into the engine room. But as soon as we tried to hoist it into position, the gremlins successfully jammed our block 'n' tackle and sabotaged our fresh air supply; the ventilation fan crapped out, the temperature soon soared, and tempers flared.

After a grueling hour of pushing and pulling and scraping knuckles (and considerable guy talk), we finally got the shaft seated in place. Despite the sweat and the heat, I don't really mind strenuous physical labor once in a while.

About this time the Stewburner hollers down from the galley, "Slop's on!" We're the kind of garbage-guts that only need to be told once that chow is ready. I don't even think that we bothered to wash up first; it seems that food always tastes a little better mingled with honestly-earned sweat and conscientious dirt. Like always, I ate too much.

As is normal custom on our boat, we hold a two-hour siesta over the noon hour, and silence reigns about the boat. It's sort of an added attraction to the day to be able to count on getting a nooner from 1100 to 1300. Laying in your rack under the breeze of an electric fan, listening to the radio turned down low, and soon you drift off to sleep.

During our nooner today I had a pleasant dream about Suzie. It was good seeing her again, but it left me in a pensive mood the rest of the day; I wanted to be with her. Sometimes the Navy seems like nothing more than a big interruption of my life, much like a series of irritating commercials in the middle of my favorite TV program. But before you know it, some chowderhead is shaking you and saying, "Time to get up, Sparky, time to turn to."

All afternoon the snipes tried to ready our port engine in preparation for lighting it off. One complication arose after another. The gremlins were having a regular field day: water materialized in the fuel; oil tanks overflowed; valves defied to be opened or closed; leaks appeared in abundance; a couple thousand gallons of fuel could not be located at all.

At one point we started the fuel pumps so we could light off the auxiliary. Very quickly I began to smell a great overpowering whiff of fuel oil. A plumbing union connecting two fuel pipes had come off and we were rapidly filling the bilges with straight fuel oil! Christ.

In the end, they lit off the engine and it ran spasmodically for a half hour before dying. I had completed my electrical task involved in the operation, and went topside to assist the deckapes in their work.

People on this boat would give you many and diverse arguments as to what exactly is the highlight of each day. Some of our sailors see no highlight whatsoever as they wallow along in their sub-zombie funk just counting the days until they can get out of the military. Others will say that chowtime is tops; others will say that the best time is when you can hit the beach on liberty; and still others will say that it's the grandest feeling to step out of grimy dungarees and slip into a hot shower. I maintain that mail call is the zenith of my day, even though more times than not there is nothing for me.

Liberty call finally rolled around. The liberty hounds all took quick mini-showers, jumped into their civvies and bolted for town, leaving behind me and two duty men. I was much too fatigued to think about anything else but catching the flick and then testing out my new bunk springs. The movie, shown on a bed-sheet screen under the stars behind the warehouse, was one of those ridiculous spaghetti-westerns, where the invincible supershooter merrily guns down hundreds of bad guys in two hours, apparently without even reloading once.

Today I celebrate 13 months of duty here in the Philippines. I don't know if I should say "celebrate" or not, although the months went by fast enough and not altogether disagreeable.

And now I think I shall call it a day and get ready to turn in. A shower, a bowl of graveyard stew, and the prospect of sleeping in tomorrow appeal greatly to me at this late hour. To sleep, perchance to dream – aye, there's the rub! Don't let it be said that Stanga never got up with the sun, or sweat, or has known weariness.

August 16, 1969

I am an extremely light sleeper. And even though I slept like the dead last night, something stirred my brain when I heard steps on the ladder and I awoke immediately. It was almost noon – I had slept for 12 straight hours and had traveled many boulevards of dreams. Since my top bunk hangs directly under the main deck, it was growing rather warm. I could just see the sun bearing down all its tropical fierceness upon the steaming gray steel, making the compartment below an oven.

There certainly isn't a great deal of activity about a tug on a lazy Saturday morning…unless it happens to be the duty boat. Besides the watch standers, the rest of the motley crew must have stayed overnight in town with their girls. A very pleasurable pastime, to be sure, but eventually quite expensive. I showered and dressed, had a simple meal of soup and sandwich, and struck out for Olongapo City myself. I had no trouble at the main gate, and quickly crossed over Shit River, an artificial canal of the Kalaklan River built to separate the naval base from the town.

"Royal Swedish Warm Bath," the sign read. "The first ever in Olongapo City – Swedish-style massage, modern steam baths, cocktail lounge, barbershop…175 Rizal Avenue." I promised myself that I would have to investigate that fine establishment before I left the P.I.

I met Dean in the American Legion and together we went to a nearby barbershop for a shave and a haircut. Filipinos have evolved a strange auditory system; they only hear what they want to hear, and they conveniently filter out everything else. I'm well aware of their frustrating handicap, however, so I took special pains to specify *only* a haircut and a shave. Nothing exotic.

To my amazement, a girl barber started to work on me – I had never been shaven by a female before! I closed my eyes and relaxed to enjoy the experience thoroughly. I soon grabbed the arms of the chair in a death-grip as she started scraping off epidermis layers like she was strip-mining in Wyoming or something!

Midway into this vivisection, I opened my eyes only to find that a different girl was operating on me. Later, Sweeney Todd himself took over the desecration and slapped mud all over my entire face. Under the fan this soon dried rock-hard and I felt my face shrivel and pucker underneath the mud. Suddenly I was smothering under a steaming hot towel. My torturers were not yet done with their Gestapo treatment. The fiends coated my raw and tender skin with some sort of liquid-fire aftershave called *Diyablo Losyon* [Devil's lotion]. Sparks flew from my teeth as I ground them to ivory dust.

At last my ordeal was over with. I pulled out my two pesos and handed it to the demon barber.

"No, no!" he cried, "Seven pesos!"

"But your sign right there says two pesos for a haircut and shave," I said, pointing at the sign just three feet away from him.

"Oh no, seven pesos for *facial!*" he announced proudly.

You just can't win for losing with these people. I paid him the blood money, and we moved off down the street.

I had a couple of bourbons in the Legion while Dean went to his apartment to fetch his latest female attachment. She's a shy, well-built, hostess from the Cairo Club, and Dino was giving her his usual "Diamond Jim" Brady routine. They finally came strolling in after a considerable amount of time had gone by, looking extremely guilty. Dean is such an animal sometimes.

We ducked into Kong's Kafe for a bite to eat. My taste for Filipino food inspired me to order a plate of shrimp-fried rice and a side of *lumpiya* [egg roll}. *Masarap* [delicious]! A taste delight, to be sure!

Dean's girlfriend had the worst manners at supper. She ate as if someone were lurking behind the pillar, ready to snatch her plate away. She was having a disgusting bowl of unholy baluts. It's positively sickening to see the nightclub hostesses gobble them down all the time, crunching and sucking until the egg is empty. Lips that touch balut do not touch my lips.

We mutually decided to indulge in a movie, and after flipping a coin we ended up going to see "Highway Pick-up." The title was very misleading and the film was a major disappointment; the only "highway pick-up" was when a farmer gave a lift to a fugitive criminal who was hitchhiking! Hardly what we had expected; our minds had been running in a different direction altogether. And to make matters worse, the film was in black and white. We suffered through two hours of stuffy heat, cramped wooden chairs, and dreadful overacting before we left.

Before we decided to go our separate ways, we stopped at the Oceans 11 Club for a couple of straight Cokes. The band was reputed to be the most talented group in town, but I was more interested in watching the people dance under the fascinating strobe lights. Their rapid blinking creates a hypnotic and dreamlike quality. The reusable, xenon-filled tube was originally developed for action photography, but I preferred its application in nightclubs, where it gives the illusion of slow motion to everything; this enjoyable sensation is further heightened by a few cocktails.

So we said our goodbyes, Dean took Lupi home with a twinkle in his eye, and I caught a Blaylock's taxicab back to the base. It was a fine evening for driving, so I had the driver just cruise around for a bit and leave the meter running. We got out on the old hospital road and I had him really open it up. I miss the good old days when I took my motorcycle on perilous midnight runs. I ran up a small fortune in cab fare before I finally had him drop me off at the boat.

For as tired as I was, I still sat on the fantail and watched the light show over the bay. A storm was brewing in the west. The sky was laced with blue-white lightning, and distant thunder followed seconds later. I seemed restless and pensive. I just couldn't get Suzie off my mind. And whenever I start thinking about the first love of my life, I start remembering all the good times that we had had together, and eventually my heart hurt at the remembering.

August 17, 1969

I had the first watch at 0800 this morning and it was a relief to finally drag myself from that bed of nails. I had dreamed about Suzie nearly all night. And even though it was very good seeing her again, it was still frustrating nonetheless to wake up and find that it was only a dream after all.

It was a warm, bright, fine Sabbath morning and somehow it felt appropriate to hear hymns on the radio; it sort of puts the week into perspective. It's been well over a year since I last saw the inside of a church, and years longer since I actually prayed. Maybe it's only a period of agnosticism that most people experience sometime in life, but right now I feel strongly that there is no place in my life for religion.

The galley was a total mess: greasy dishes piled high in the sink, a dirty grill, food spilled all over the tabletops, and still more food trampled into the floor. No wonder the roaches thrive. The guys must have really swilled down when they got back from town last night. I decided to kill some time by cleaning it up. I cannot abide filth and disorder; it's too depressing to live in a pigsty 24 hours a day. But, sadly enough, most guys on this boat wouldn't care if they had to wallow in trash all day long. I know, I've seen their lockers.

Afterwards I worked for an hour on my blueprint-reading correspondence course, as I still tentatively plan to study architecture in college when I get out of this Canoe Club. I received my highest marks in high school in Mechanical Drawing class, and it was always my favorite subject throughout my learning years. Even though I was rejected as a draftsman when I entered the Navy (the field was already full), I still think I have what it takes to make it my vocation in life.

I spent the remainder of the day in various ways: I lay on the fantail and absorbed a few million gamma rays; I read a bit from Tolkien's "Lord of the Rings;" napped for a short time, and wrote some letters home.

Dean and Bobby came back from the beach totally intoxicated and barely intelligible, and made unbelievably bizarre Dagwood sandwiches, as only drunks can do. And then, after undoing all my earnest work in the galley, they changed shirts (after first rolling on some fresh Old Spice deodorant) and tore off to town once again. Such meager lives they live. Later in the evening, it rained horrendously and completely drowned out the warehouse movie.

Nowhere in the world have I seen more beautiful and awe-inspiring sunsets than those I have seen over the Pacific Ocean! While stationed in San Diego, Ron and I used to walk five miles almost daily down to Ocean Beach simply to see the sun go down in a blaze of color. But never have I viewed such postcard-perfect magnificent sunsets than those I have seen here in the Philippines over Subic Bay! Clouds streaked every color of the spectrum, golden reflections on the sparkling waves, and the grand finale of a day well-lived is worth the time taken to behold it.

August 18, 1969

yawn I wonder whatever possesses me sometimes? After I completed my watch last night I stayed up the rest of the night reading, writing, and playing solitaire. Somewhere in between all of this I consumed a whole pot of coffee – and I don't even like coffee! It gives me the shakes.

I guess I've always been a bit of a night owl, though; night is my element. Besides that, it's about the only special time that I can have all to myself. I recall that when I had my apartment back home I would often pass the entire night away by writing, going for walks, or holding long telephone conversations with Susan. Those days seem so far away and irrevocable; surely pleasant times such as these are not gone forever?

For some unexplained reason anyway, I was in excellent spirits all day long, albeit on the tired side. Along about 0500 this morning I determined to be cheerful and easygoing all day unto everyone, no matter what they tried to do to me.

Talk about a bunch of sullen sailors on this boat, though! Every day I try to boost the crew's morale in some small way. Since they are so darn disgruntled about their present condition (i.e., non-civilian) and positively abhor the Navy, I feel it's completely up to me as an individual and self-proclaimed morale officer of the boat, to help all I can in making life aboard this tug easier and lighter. Is it not more pleasant to move in good humor through life?

There was not much by way of electrical work to be done today, but it still managed to keep me occupied until liberty call went down. In the forenoon I made minor repairs on our electric grinder in the engine room. Some low-life (presumably a Filipino yard worker with an axe to grind) cut the power cable and ran off with an expensive electrical plug.

I performed a measure of PM on my huge lead-acid batteries, watering and charging them. I also held a field day in my motor room which had become littered with every conceivable type of trash: empty boxes, burned-out light bulbs, lengths of frayed cable, peeling friction tape, twisted strands of wire from who knows where, dead flashlight batteries, and oily rags slowly reaching their flash point. The snipes must think my motor room is a catch-all for the junk they're too lazy to carry up to the dipsy-dumpster on the pier.

This afternoon, a jumper cable burned through from carrying too many amps, and I had to splice it back together again so our illustrious snipes could continue working on their engines. I guess I didn't actually raise a great deal of sweat, but I feel I accomplished a few things today for the American taxpayer and earned my keep. I used my muscles and my mind, I moved things around, and work of a sort was done.

Consequently, I was simply too exhausted this evening to accompany the fellows into town. Instead I rode the bus up the hill to the Sky Club, where I had supper while I watched "The Green Berets," starring John Wayne. I got too wrapped up in the movie as usual. When a soldier fell into a pit of punji stakes I flung an empty beer can at the movie screen, upon which I was escorted to the nearest exit by the MP on duty. Down the hill and back on the boat, I labored over my scrapbook for a bit. Everyone should take time out to keep a scrapbook. It's absorbing, amusing, and should be rewarding later in life.

Ah well, another day draws to a sober end. It is not intentional that my journal entries are becoming shorter and shorter, but that is only coincidental with these warm, lazy days here in Boton Valley. It's late and I'm unshowered and tired. It's a feeling something akin to intoxication, and the only remedy is a hot shower and a cool fluffy pillow. *Gut nacht* [good night].

August 18, 1969

Dear Family,

It's been a hectic week, and writing a letter home is just the ticket to give me a breather. I am happy to hear that you are saving the newspaper clippings concerning the moon walk for me. I was fortunate enough to lay my hands on about ten colored pictures of the moon walk in the *Detroit Free Press.* Just the other day I was quizzing the guys on the boat as to who was the first man to walk on the moon last month, and nobody could even tell me, nor did they especially care. Apathy runs rampant around here.

So what do you think of the religious riots over in Ireland lately? They interviewed some of the kids on the radio and they were really hysterical about what they say they believe in. I wish I had a cause that I'd be willing to defend to the death, but I'm not sure if I do. I feel very strongly about patriotism, but then again, I'm not on the battlefield, am I?

Lurch, one of our enginemen, got himself in an odd bind the other day. He always sleeps flat on his back with his mouth wide open (hence his other nickname of "Fly-Trap"). He is totally oblivious to his horrendous snoring; I pity the poor woman who ends up as his spouse. Well, the other day he was lying on the fantail, soaking up some gamma rays, and he fell asleep. Now he is sunburned on the roof of his mouth! That doesn't happen every day!

I'm just relieved to see that he was here at all this morning. He was going to revenge Easy, who got cut up by some Filipinos out in town. I remember when Easy came down in the compartment two nights ago and stood there before us, blood on his shirt and swaying with liquor. He had a large "X" slashed deeply across his chest and a similar gash on each cheek. He'll be scarred for life, no doubt. And so last night Lurch borrowed my souvenir switchblade to do a little "carving" of his own out in town. But I guess his intended victims were keeping under cover, because he couldn't find any of them. Just as well, I say.

In less than a month this old tug will be out there in the harbor chugging again after almost half a year of stagnation in the yards. Praise Allah for that! I tell you that I don't think I could have taken another month of our tug gathering dust and rust. Once we get chugging, we'll be on the line until the time I leave the P.I.

When I do go out in town anymore, I usually go to the Can Can Club to hear that good combo play easy-listening music. They already know me by name and always play my requests when I come in: "I'll Be Down to Get You In a Taxi, Honey," "My Baby Just Cares For Me," "Up A Lazy River," etc. They're a welcome relief from all that psychedelic hippie noise out there. In the Can Can Club I can stay anchored to reality.

Well, I may as well tell you what happened to me last week. It's a long story, so bear with me. For a while there, two other guys and I faced a General Court Martial, Executive Mast, Court of Appeals, a stiff fine, a reduction in rank, and possibly even a stretch in the brig! Thank goodness that's all in the past now. But I was sick to my stomach for four days with anger and frustration and worry.

But I'm getting ahead of myself. It happened this way: last Friday Benton had the duty. Sometime during the day he forgot to turn on the bilge pump, and water started slowly leaking into the engine room below the deckplates. We soon developed a slight port list, so he went down and turned on the bilge pump. For some reason the drainage pipes had become clogged and it wouldn't pump the water overboard. But he wasn't aware of this.

The next day Dean had the duty. He noticed the list was worse and tried to pump the bilges, too. He also found that the lines were plugged, and so he informed the division office. They took no action. But at least the water was not rising anymore.

On Sunday I had the duty, and after I ran the bilge pump all morning long I deduced that it was doing no good whatsoever. By then the water was within four inches of my generators, but it hadn't risen in two days. I informed the office, too, but again no action was taken by them. A chief advised me to leave it until Monday morning when the full crew would return to the boat and definitely get the situation under control.

Come Monday morning, then, we were down in the Hole working to free up the clogged pipes when suddenly chiefs and officers swooped down upon us and started to hyperventilate. And the next thing we knew, us three petty officers were on report for "improper watch-standing" and "dereliction of duty"! I am not kidding about this.

Well, we finally cleared the obstruction from the pipes and quickly pumped the bilges dry so that we were once again on an even keel. But we were still not off the hook. There was no damage done, and there had been no imminent danger, but our commanding officer was determined to hang us, come hell or high water. We were going to fight him all the way to the brig if we had to! The whole boat was on the verge of – dare I say it? – mutiny, and sparks were a'flyin'.

Our commanding officer is a real candy-ass and a total sadist, and there isn't a man jack in the whole division who doesn't despise him. How do jerks like this rise to a position of responsibility in the US Navy anyway? Is it a prerequisite? He had already been beaten up several times out in town, and we hear there is presently a standing bounty of one thousand pesos hanging over his head for any Filipino who wants to make a little easy money.

Finally, another officer managed to see through all the bullshit and get our story straight, then he convinced our CO to drop all charges. He looked as if he was going to bawl with frustration because he couldn't bust somebody. I'm just glad that it's all over with at last, and we have been cleared. We dodged a bullet that time.

August 19, 1969

It hasn't rained in two days and that is quite unusual for the middle of the monsoon season. Right about now we should be having typhoons and thunderstorms and week-long deluges left and right. It was well into the 90's today, and I'm sure I gave up a full quart of vital body fluids in sweat, maybe more. Back home we never batted an eye when the South Dakota heat reached 105 degrees; but this South Pacific heat is so much worse due to the extreme humidity. I am certain that this is the main reason behind my premature balding, too.

Again, there was not much in the way of electrical work today, and I managed to squeeze in an hour of skylarking in the shade with Dean. He's really a confused fellow at heart. All he has on his mind is rutting (that's the only word I can think of to describe him) with the females of Olongapo City. But he is doing this so much that he contracts some sort of venereal disease about every other week. He confided in me that once he had intercourse 17 times in one night with the same girl! I don't think that this is normal, but who can really say exactly what is normal for human beings in Subic Bay? He has the ability to help himself out of his predicaments, but he doesn't seem to want to. He is generous to a fault with his girlfriends – or is the right word "naïve"? But then he doesn't have enough money left from his paycheck to buy necessities such as soap and shaving cream and underwear. Oy.

Later this evening a floating derrick came alongside us. It picked up a Bell helicopter off a barge, swung it carefully over the top of our tug, and set it down smartly on the pier. It was fascinating to watch.

There was no mail for me again today, but I didn't especially mind, as I am presently caught up with all 32 of my correspondents and would appreciate a breather from writing without feeling guilty about it.

August 20, 1969

I was like a man dead to the world this morning. Even though the lights and the radio were turned on in the berthing compartment, and the rest of the crew was already up and about, I still had to be woken up. This is very unusual for me; I must really have been sleeping deep.

I'll put it to you straight on the line: I didn't accomplish a single thing by way of electrical work all day. On the other hand, neither did anyone else. There just wasn't anything to work on. "Ex nihilo nihil fit" (out of nothing comes nothing). So I worked on my blueprint-reading correspondence course instead.

There was a council for the Service Craft potheads on the fantail later this evening. It continues to puzzle me just exactly why those dope fiends choose this particular tug to smoke their grass on – unless it's because nobody on the boat gives a good goddam if they do it or not. The moment I started noticing drug abusers was the same moment that I joined the service – a cause-and-effect relationship if ever I saw one.

It's so pitifully easy to obtain drugs out in town that any weak-willed serviceman can hardly be blamed for trying them. Besides smoking marijuana, other dopers also experiment in rotting their brains with stimulant pills that keep you awake long after your body urgently demands sleep. "Speed" users are easily identified as those wild-eyed, shaking, scrambled eggheads who are banging away furiously on the table as the band plays – while the strongest thing they've had to drink all night is a Pepsi.

A self-propelled crane was moving along our pier at a pretty fair clip this morning, and as it passed narrowly between two power poles its bouncing hook caught a rectifier on one of the poles and ripped it clean off! Power cables snapped, tubing bent with a shriek, and cement cracked. Power went off immediately everywhere in the area. When I think how close the men in that crane came to 400 amperes of current it makes me shiver! A measly two amps are enough to kill you under the right conditions.

There was another fire out in town early this morning. Two years ago almost half the city was scorched; nine months ago the whole marketplace burned down; and today the holocaust was on the busiest street in the densest section of nightclubs and hotels. We lost a couple of our favorite clubs in the blaze.

Seen from five miles away, the flames reached high into the air. The Navy base fire department was called out, and around noon the fire was extinguished. This time they found a few bodies in the ashes, though. For some reason, I get nervous every time I see smoke billowing up in the distance. I can't imagine my fear on the day that I see a nuclear mushroom cloud on the horizon!

August 21, 1969

This is a late entry. I was in no condition last night (i.e., the 21st) to sit down with pen in hand and relate the day's happenings. Benton and I decided to have ourselves a proper night on the town. You can't deny it, sailors will be sailors.

When we heard that the office was thinking about finding some work for us to do, Benton and I really got our motors running in high gear and set a new land speed record for getting cleaned up and hitting the bricks in 15 minutes flat. Now you see 'em, now you don't! It's the earliest we've been out in town in ages.

Benton is one of our brightest enginemen, and rightly enough he is from the auto capital of the world, Detroit. He is a handsome devil; he has a smooth baby face and curly blank hair, and is a hit with all the bar maids. He's a regular guy, with more than a little suave and class, but he's got some mighty peculiar ideas when it comes down to manners, religion, and patriotism; and he smokes way too much. I guess it takes all kinds to make a world, eh?

Anyway, before the sun even had a chance to set, we had guzzled down six beers. That's fairly inhaling them in 90 minutes! This we did at the American Legion. There were a few old alcoholic vets there, staggering from table to table and telling their admirable war stories to anybody who'd listen, in hopes of a free drink. Sometimes we obliged them, as we liked to hear the old stories.

Then we moved on to new and better things, to nightclubs that had more cold beer, warm girls, and live bands. It's wonderful to be 21 and a little drunk, cutting loose overseas in an ally's country, cock of the walk, knowing that any girl in the room would take you home with her if you wanted.

We glided aimlessly from club to club, floating about six inches off the sidewalk. If I can remember correctly, the clubs that we terrorized last night were the Empire, the Stardust, Acapulco, Can Can, Ding's, Mom's, and the Sherry Club. Some of the clubs offered raunchy floor shows; others were nothing more than dark caverns in the wall with scary girls waiting to pounce on you. Boy, we flat did some steaming, drinking heavily at each port of call.

In the Empire Club we had two old harridans that wouldn't stop clinging all over us, so we moved along. In the Stardust we enjoyed the strobe lights. In the Acapulco we did a little romancing and dancing. In the Can Can we consumed about five pounds of salted Spanish peanuts and Benton got sick. (He swore it was on account of the offensive music there.)

Out front of the Panama Club, between the club and the sidewalk is a crocodile pond with a couple of old crocs lounging around in the murky water. Two Joes sell baby ducks to anybody who has a few pesos to spare, then you can toss them into the crocodile pen and see what happens next. Nobody seems to think anything odd about this thriving enterprise at all. While I have no conscious memories of ever buying any baby ducks *myself* to feed to the creepy reptiles, I do recall pausing on the sidewalk whenever we were cruising around out in town and happened to catch a fleet sailor shelling out a couple of pesos for a baby duck; just to watch for developments. Usually the crocs were so lethargic and already stuffed with baby ducks that the little fuzz balls were perfectly safe. After awhile the Joes would retrieve the ducklings and sell them again to the next passing fool. What a gig.

Inside every bar out in town is an offensive and minimally-maintained toilet, usually no more than a trough hanging from the wall or a hole in the cement floor. It was normally manned by some Filipino male of varying age.

After the customer was done peeing on his own shoes, or worse, the headboy's job was to offer the guy a washcloth or towel or even some cologne in the nicer clubs. And for this service, plus the nauseating stench of warm urine in an unventilated room, we were expected to give a gratuity.

I bought a tout sign off one headboy in the Penguin Club which read in beautiful printing but awkward English, "As in the presence of me, in this very disgusted place, I stay here not because of intention to slaughter you but I am being forced by a change of time to do this in order to live. We have to use our own possible last means that will give us little chance to live even how much degrading or miserable. From this short expression of what I am here. I hope it will make it clearly for you to understand me better, so that you may act in sympathy of me, instead of against me. As you see, I work here by providing those head facilities and by maintaining this place for your own personal comfort without receiving any salary. I am only depending on the tip you give. This, a plead to you. Please, be considerate and generous. Thanks"

This was one of the more involved signs that I have seen in an Olongapo toilet, and we usually were not even finished reading it before we were done with our business. I don't mind extending a little charity to a headboy now and then for providing those head facilities, but most of them provided nothing but attitude and a cloth rag topped off with bacteria, and still had the nerve to hold out their palm afterwards. We were American servicemen, for pete's sake; we were not made of money!

In Ding's Club we were really insulted by an outrageous excuse for a band, and departed sooner than later. In Mom's we indulged in a dozen fiery tacos out in their beer gardens. And in the Sherry Club we finally found a band to our liking and some girls that we could both appreciate. All in all, it was a legendary and thoroughly enjoyable night. A night to remember.

However, I still don't remember just how we got back to the boat and into our own racks – and neither does Benton. (Sometimes, if we are aware that we have over-indulged, we will walk the five miles back to the boat instead of taking the taxi, with an irresponsible amount of beer stowed away inside us, and wear off most of the liquor before we even go to bed. By doing this we feel much better the following morning.)

But I faintly recall a wild taxi ride last night, and boiling some hot dogs in the galley a little after midnight, while the security watch talked Benton out of going swimming in the bay with all his clothes on. I don't know where my brain was during this whole time, but it sure was beautiful there, man. What surprised me even more was the fact that it appeared I had more money left in my wallet than when I went to town!

I had inclinations of sitting down and scrawling Suzie a letter last night when I returned from town and had Benton all tucked in, but the need for sleep won out in the end, so I hit the rack instead. Seems like I'm always thinking and talking about her whenever I start drinking, and maybe that's only natural because she is always at the back of my mind, even if I won't admit it all the time. I miss her something crazy! Like the lovesick fool that I am, I secretly hope that she still thinks about me and misses me from time to time. But mooning about it will get me nowhere fast, so I decided to write her a long letter this weekend and lay all my cards on the table.

August 22, 1969

One of the prices you have to pay for reveling to excess is the delightful after-effects the next morning. For as much San Miguel beer as I sopped up last night, I should be tipsy until three days from now. Instead, I am stone sober. But it feels like somebody is crushing my head in a vice and has rubbed sand in both my eyes. The whole Filipino army must have marched through my mouth sometime during the night – horses and all!

Nevertheless, I spent the morning in shaky good spirits, thanks to Mister Bufferin. I grabbed a paint brush and put the finishing touches on my motor room. I don't mind painting a whole lot (off with the old and on with the new, and all that tommyrot), as it leaves my mind totally free for out-of-body wandering.

Besides, touching up the details and fancy work with bright, cheerful colors is not exactly what I'd call work. Well, the other members of this crew would, but then again they think it's work having to wipe themselves. I take real personal pride in my work, and a job done by me is a job done right the first time. I am determined not to let my relief electrician inherit the sort of second-rate crap that I got stuck with.

Seeing as how our fearless leaders got an early start on their own weekend, we voted a little early liberty for ourselves as well. Benton and I immediately donned our civvies and headed for town – will we never learn?! We indulged in a double feature at the Grand Theatre. They always play the Filipino National Anthem before the movie commences; I stand right along with the Joes and sing the words which are shown on the screen. This mortifies Benton.

The first flick was a zany Jerry Lewis comedy, which I always enjoy. The second show was "Funny Girl" with Barbra Streisand. The movie was absolutely precious, but it had a really lousy ending. I only wish I had walked out of the theater ten minutes before the credits and spared myself the conclusion.

Later, while having an actual soft drink with Benton in the D'Lover's Club, this same old bar hostess came over and sat on my lap that has been pestering me every time I go in the place. They must have drawn straws for me or something. It's hard to tell her age, as they keep it curiously dark inside the club, but she certainly does have an enticing scent that she wears. She held my hand lightly, and started stroking the back of my hand with her thumb – just the way Suzie used to do. Good grief! I just couldn't take it, and when I withdrew my hand from hers she arose and left in a huff. It was too much for me. It brought back too many memories.

Afterwards, while coming back through the main gate, there was a small skirmish between a drunken liberty sailor and a loudmouthed Marine sentry who was baiting him and giving him the business. The sailor finally passed out and slumped to the ground, where the Marine just left him lying. For ten minutes people stepped over him before some kind soul finally moved him off to one side.

August 23, 1969

It's the cool of the evening, and they're playing Golden Oldies on the Armed Forces radio. I feel like just forgetting about this insane duty and flaking out on the fantail under the stars. But that would really be "dereliction of duty" then. I mean, who in their right mind is awake at 0230 in the morning when they're dead tired? Somebody in the military, no doubt.

Man, it certainly was a scorcher today! Old Sol really poured on the coals. The compartment was unbearable, and topside there was scarcely a breath of air moving on the bay. It was humid, sticky and parching, and there wasn't a decent comfortable spot to rest on the entire craft.

Tonight's sunset was one of the most beautiful that I've seen in weeks, however. From between majestic towering chasms of cotton-candy clouds came brilliant pink shafts of light against a bright blue background. And like an ass, I just left my camera in my locker while I sat and admired the view!

Much to my pleasant surprise, I received a letter from Suzie today! I didn't open it right away, as I looked at her familiar handwriting on the envelope and simply savored the moment, halfway dreading what I might find inside, but always hoping for the best. I didn't know what to expect from her, and a hundred different scenarios raced through my mind. My heart actually beat faster in anticipation when I finally opened the envelope and read:

> *"I laid awake last night and no matter how hard I tried I could only think of you. I've been dreaming about you a lot, but I couldn't get to sleep last night. I laid there thinking…I was nearly in tears…then I got your ring from the jewelry case and put it on. It felt so good, like it really belonged there. I think it does. And then I cried myself to sleep. I miss you so much…"*

An indescribable warmness crept over me as I finished reading the rest of the letter. All in all, it was a truly sweet letter from the heart, and she made me feel rather exhilarated. My spirit soared. That she would finally write back to me, just when I was about to write to her, fits into the pattern of how we both react after months of separation. I answered her letter immediately.

The reason she dumped me like a leper many months back was on account of my Filipina "shack-ups," as she called them in her letter. You see, I also wrote regularly to Suzie's older sister, Laury, and made the asinine mistake once of confiding to her about one of my Olongapo girlfriends. Now, Laury is completely trustworthy and capable of handling intimate confidences, and we have operated on this basis for a long time. But Suzie happened to accidentally run across one of my letters to her sister. She promptly condemned me without mercy, and I can't really say that I blame her one bit. On the contrary, I blame myself entirely.

And now she was giving me a chance to explain my side of the story, and she is willing to listen and is going to try to understand. I really don't expect her to, though, as there's such an unmistakable age difference between us. And where five years doesn't matter much in love, it definitely creates problems in the way we both look at life.

One strong reason why Suzie finally decided to hear me out at last is because she is disillusioned with a girl who is very close to her; it seems that sex had suddenly entered her best friend's life and Suzie was so confused by it all. I tried my level best to be rational with her, while not cutting my own throat again. I don't know if I succeeded in explaining anything, though. I might have just made matters worse. Only time will tell.

I've got duty tonight with Benton. He is certainly unlike anyone I've ever met before. All too often he allows himself to get what he calls a boredom headache and drifts off into his own little fantasy world. A common trait among this crew.

There – it happened again! Just now, as I was sitting here at 0500 in the morning, listening to mellow songs with dawn approaching, a sensation of unexplainable happiness and well-being swept over me. Total euphoria! This usually occurs to me around this time of the morning, especially when I've been awake all night long. Certainly is peculiar, though.

August 24, 1969

"To you Benton,

Please excuse me if I disturb you just a minute only. I want to tell you something don't get mad to me. I want to invite you on Sunday at White Rock Beach if you don't mind you tell your friend, Steve and Dean, to go with us. So that we are happy. I want you to answer me soon.

Until then, Stacy"

As you know by now, I was awake all night again. Sometimes you have to sacrifice a couple of hours of sleep that you might have gotten, because such a short nap after a long day would probably do more harm than good, and leave you more tired than before.

I got Benton out of his rack at 0800 and we proceeded to get ready for a party at the beach. It was a fine, sunny day and there wasn't a rain cloud in sight. We had some premeditated drinking lined up, and were anxious to get to it.

We met Bobby, our chief engineer, at the Legion, and had a few cold ones while waiting for Dean and his girl to arrive. By 1015 we knew the Sad Sack wasn't going to show up, so we shoved off to Bobby's apartment to pick up Stacy and the rest of the girls. I really hadn't expected Dean to come, anyway. He'd rather spend seven days a week in bed with Lupi than get out of the house and spend one day recreating with his buddies. What a meager existence. What a sap.

The girls who lived above Bobby's apartment came downstairs with all their useless paraphernalia that girls always carry everywhere. Bobby and his woman came, and also brought their house mouse, Geema. She is sweet 17, painfully *mahiyain* [bashful], and just as cute as a bug's ear! But Bobby's woman, Alice, works her like a slave around the house and pays her next to nothing. Still, Geema is unusually happy most of the time, and that's one of the things I like about her.

The ride to the beach was scenic overkill! It was my first time in that part of the Subic hills, and the bay looked quite panoramic from our jeepney. A ride in a Filipino jeepney is an experience unto itself. Nowhere else in the world have I seen so much reckless lane-wandering, passing on curves, speeding through populated areas, or such narrow roads. It's kind of like a fairground ride.

The resort is called White Rock Beach. The beach itself was quite a letdown; it looked like some British estuary after the tide had gone out, and smelled about the same. Black mud stretched perhaps fifty feet before reaching the water. But we were going to swim in a freshwater pool anyway. We all changed into our bathing suits in the bathrooms and found a nice table at poolside in the shade.

The resort looks like one of those Miami Hilton pools that you see in the movies or something. You just don't expect such splendor in the middle of the jungle! One side is hard pressed by sheer cliffs, and on the opposite side is a beautiful Chinese-pagoda-style hotel. Real coconut trees surround the pool and there is an excellent view of Subic Bay. There are two big boulders, painted white, placed in the middle of the huge pool, with cement mermaids perched atop them. Some Navy wit had climbed up and put a bra on one of the painted mermaids. From the deep end of the pool rose an alarmingly high diving board.

We dove and swam and frolicked with the girls, and had quite a few chilled beers in the shade. Alice and Stacy kept jumping off the high dive like they could never get their fill of it, and Geema was like a regular fish in the water, and rarely came up for air.

As the day wore on, and the daredevils got more beer in their system, they did some pretty hairy stunts off the diving board! We worked up a healthy appetite and bought some chow from an old lady barbecuing chicken over a small smoking hibachi grill at one end of the pool.

About dusk we stowed our gear and shoved off. We took a taxi over to Bobby's apartment to have a proper supper. Alice and I walked to the *sari-sari* [convenience] store where I purchased about twenty-five pesos worth of groceries and a bottle of strong Tandawy rum for later. We drank and made sailor small talk while the women whipped up some goodies in the kitchen for us to eat. After our delicious feed, I helped Geema do up the dishes.

Then we proceeded to finish off the bottle of rum. Much later I noticed poor Geema – who doesn't smoke or

Banca boats in Subic Bay.

drink, and who had had a lot of sun; she was having a hard time keeping her eyes open or her chin off her chest, so we said our goodnights. Benton and I somehow stumbled back to the boat. All in all, it had been a swell party. Another day in paradise.

August 25, 1969

May the sun's eternal fires be snuffed out forever! I am so godforsaken sunburned that I probably won't even be able to lay in my bunk tonight! I'm as red as a spring radish – especially my nose – and I've already got blisters on both shoulders! My legs and back are also burned, as is the top of my head. Oh woe is the fool! I gently rubbed on some baby oil, but it didn't alleviate the pain any noticeable amount. The heat irritates it the worst down in the motor room, which is coincidentally where I had to work all morning.

Over the noon hour, while everyone else enjoyed a two-hour nooner in their bunk, I sat in the shade and played solitaire, seeing as how I was much too sore to lie down anyway. Baby-faced Benton is likewise burned to a crisp.

When the heat in the crew compartment had subsided later, I dragged myself below decks (a bad sunburn really exhausts you) and climbed very gingerly into my bunk. As yet, I cannot take a shower – either hot or cold – because the slightest water pressure on my skin feels like it is flaying me. I hope it still doesn't hurt this bad tomorrow!

August 26, 1069

I was really sawing logs this morning when reveille went down, and it took every bit of effort I could muster to crawl out of the rack without breaking in half. My blisters had burst during the night and had started to water all over my bedding. My sunburn was still quite painful, but much less in severity than yesterday.

Something is wrong with this crew lately; we just don't seem to have a friendly word for each other anymore, and it's not very frequent that we all go out on liberty together like we used to. I think this yard overhaul period is getting on everybody's last nerves. Maybe things will cheer up around here after we go back on the line.

I spent all morning down in the Hole, painting the overhead and bulkheads an uninteresting eggshell white. I believe I got more paint on myself than I did on the bulkheads. And it was very frustrating when the paint drops fell with deadly accuracy right in my eye. Painting isn't really work, as such, but it is a fine way to hurry the day along without doing anything too strenuous. The engine room is really a mess, but it's slowly shaping up. The whole space will take a few more days – there's so many pipes and cables and valves that I have to paint around.

Nobody bothered to lend me a hand at painting, either, even though it wasn't even technically my responsibility! It's supposed to be an "all hands" evolution, but the rest of the snipes are a bunch of lazy slobs. I could throw down my paintbrush right now and nobody could do a stinking thing about it.

In the afternoon I decided to just sit around on my ass and see how everyone else liked it for a change. I guess nobody paid any attention to me, and I quickly felt like a fool, so I soon got up again and continued painting. I'm determined that even unappreciated efforts won't dishearten me.

August 26, 1969

Dear Karen,

Such an electrical storm we had last night! And it looked like it was directly above us. Quite a light show! The air felt so charged up that at any moment you expected the sky to split wide open for the Second Coming. A lightning bolt hit my rectifier on the pier and we went "dead in the water" for over an hour before we got power restored. Then it rained to beat the band and chased away the heat, and everything calmed down for the night.

I heard something interesting on the radio yesterday:

> A Chinese sailor fell off a ship at sea and was left behind as lost. He swam around for a while until he saw a giant sea turtle. He climbed onto its back and floated along in this manner for 15 hours before another ship picked him up. And all this time the turtle did not dive once. Really strange...

We've got a big personnel inspection coming up next Friday. So we have to drag out our whites for laundering, shine our dress shoes, polish our brass belt buckles with Brasso, scrub our white hats, bleach our T-shirts brilliantly white, buy new belts and socks and ribbons as necessary, and roll our black neckerchiefs as skinny as a rat's tail. The admiral himself is inspecting, I'm afraid. I think they do this to us periodically just to remind us that we're still in the military – and not the US Canoe Club. As if we could forget.

August 27, 1969

I've decided that it's more dignified to just go ahead and keep painting in the Hole and not get mad that the other fellows aren't working. If I just do my best and carry my share of the load, there's no reason why I shouldn't sleep good at night. My conscience is clear. It's no skin off my snout if they'd rather pass the day slowly by just sitting in the shade; what goes around comes around. It'll eventually catch up with them. Karma usually does. Painting the engine room is my baby now, and I'll have something to be proud of when I'm finished.

Since today was payday, everyone else pulled a little early liberty and went to town. I stayed behind, as I had the duty. First of all, I washed the dinner dishes and cleaned up the galley. I swear we've got some real animals on this ark! Maybe they enjoy living in a sty, but I don't.

I was looking up at the full moon tonight and it looked simply hypnotizing. And then I lowered my eyes and looked about me. I decided, with an awful shudder, that I positively hate the sight of this base anymore! I've been in Subic Bay way too long. Everything is so sickeningly familiar that I can't stand the very thought of it. And yet, I know that I will miss it terribly after I leave. How ironic. I guess I'm just homesick.

August 28, 1969

I happened to be awake at 0530, so I got up anyway. The sun was just peeking over the jungled hills, wondering what had transpired in its absence, almost afraid to know. The Stewburner had prepared the proverbial S.O.S. for our breakfast, which I love, so I was in and out of the galley before the rest of the crew even got up.

My sunburn has stopped hurting, but now it is beginning to peel and it itches me to distraction. I don't know which is worse, the awful sunburn or the relentless itching!

As I did yesterday, I spent the entire morning painting down in the engine room. Benton came down after a time, which surprised me, and I watched him out of the corner of my eye as I worked. He spent the better part of an hour just locating and cleaning out a stupid paintbrush! And in the end he didn't even use it anyway. Eventually, he just drifted out of the engine room without accomplishing a single thing. I pity someone who has such an obvious lack of initiative as he does.

All over the base last-minute preparations are being made for the big personnel inspection to be held tomorrow, and I went into town for a decent haircut. Now I am prepared for the inspection; I didn't leave it all 'til the last minute like some *other* people did.

August 29, 1969

We were roused bright and early this morning so that we could prepare for the big inspection. To add to the commotion, we were constantly running into each other in the crowded compartment. But we finally managed to get all squared away to our satisfaction, and left for the inspection site on the far side of the base, looking oddly like proper sailors, innocent enough to make our mothers proud.

The officers were gracious and let us face away from the rising sun as we stood in formation, but it soon grew very hot on the backs of our sunburned necks. As we went through the customary procedure we alternately stood at attention, at ease, and parade rest. A poorly-rehearsed band of Filipinos played some soul-stirring marches as the inspecting officer walked slowly up and down the ranks of the different divisions with his motley ensemble of bootlickers right on his heels.

Finally we snapped to attention as he came down our row. It's a real heart-stopper to come vis-à-vis, eyeball to eyeball, with the Admiral of the whole Pacific Fleet! But, as usual, I passed again. Three guys off our boat got pinched for haircuts, though. He handed out several Medals of Honor to Vietnam heroes and then we were dismissed.

Normally, after an Admiral's Personnel Inspection, all the men are given early liberty – but not our chicken-shit division, oh no. They wanted us to do a normal day's work. All the same, we changed into our working clothes and escaped to Dungaree Beach. There we had a few cold brews and sat in the sand for a while. Then we came back to the boat, ate dinner, and racked out. There was literally no work to do, so we slept until we were darn good and ready to get up. Totally rebellious.

The CIA suddenly swooped down on the YTM-521 and apprehended two felons. These two guys were running a slush fund from their tug; that's where they lend out money at a terribly high interest rate. (In the first place, lending or borrowing money is illegal in the Navy! But everybody still does it.) They had beaten up one fellow because he couldn't pay them on time, so he went to Base Security for help. Now these two guys (one white and one black) are charged with Assault and Battery, Usury, and Extortion. After a spell in the brig, they will be kicked out of the Navy on a DD. Was it worth it, I wonder?

Latest scuttlebutt says that they're finally going to decommission the battle-ship, *USS New Jersey,* because it supposedly never accomplished the job that it was recommissioned for: namely, to shell North Vietnamese positions, I guess. They say it cost over $20 million a year for upkeep alone, and every time a 16-inch gun went off a Cadillac went out the barrel. It's hard to justify that kind of expense. I figured it was nothing more than just a big prestige ship anyway, meant to awe the world.

August 29, 1969

Dear Family,

Thanks a lot for all those sunflower seeds; that ought to last me until I leave the P.I.! No kidding. I gave a couple of packs to the sunflower seed-eating fools on the boat, and kept the rest under lock and key in my locker. The safety pins are much appreciated, and everyone enjoys reading "The Plain Truth" for a change of pace; it gives us something new to argue about.

Well, it shouldn't be long before we are chugging again. (Déjà vu…how many times have I said that now?) All we are waiting on are ten huge storage batteries to start the main engines with. We've heard all kinds of scuttlebutt concerning them: some say that they just left the States by ship; some say they're floating around someplace right here on base; and some say they're obsolete and can't even be ordered anymore. Who really knows? I just want to get back out there in the harbor!

While throwing away my money on frivolous luxuries at the base exchange recently, I bought a new product from Gillette. It is called "The Hot One," and it is a self-heating shaving cream aerosol bomb. Have you seen it yet? This is not to be confused with the shaving cream can that you have to hold under the hot-water faucet to get warm. This is all self-contained and it actually comes out of the can piping hot! Pretty nifty, huh?

They've been having quite a rash of USO shows here lately, which is a happy circumstance for us servicemen. Last night was a real talented and comical older group from Canada which cracked corny jokes and harmonized in barbershop quartet mode. My favorite number was "Grandma's Boy Is Back in Town."

The smallest inconveniences around here bring on the loudest grumbling from the guys on this boat. These poor excuses for sailors seem to think that the Navy purposely contrives new ways to harass them – as if the war was being run for their own personal convenience!

My drifty friend, Easy, who I went to "A" school with back in Dago, you remember, was caught with marijuana in his locker the other day. So now he's getting kicked out of the Navy on an Administrative Discharge. He sure fixed his wagon good this time, as that sort of thing never leaves your permanent record. But he says he's happy, because he wants to get in the Army now and go to Vietnam (where the marijuana is cheaper, presumably). I wonder if he'll even be able to join the Army now.

Furthermore, you recall that Easy came back to the boat one night two weeks ago with blood all over him, claiming some knife-wielding Joes had carved an "X" on both of his cheeks and his chest? Well, it turns out that Easy did that to himself while high on drugs! The guy needs more than just a discharge, I'd say.

Now that the monsoon season is rapidly petering out, I can get back in training and get out on the athletic track again. That's two rainy seasons that I've seen come and go – only four and a half months left here in the Black Hole of Calcutta! And then I'm homeward bound for a leave – I hope!

August 30, 1969

I'm a little groggy from having duty again last night, but I've still got another day to go before I can hit the beach. I remember once when I had the duty for five days in a row; I was in a sleepy stupor for a week afterwards!

I had planned on catching some rays today (as if I really needed any more), but the sun never once made an appearance. To put the icing on the cake, it also rained off and on. This wasn't so bad in itself because it cooled things off extremely – even so that I had to dig out my work jacket during my early-morning watches.

In the afternoon I went over to the main exchange and did a little shopping. I bought Geema a nice girl's wallet for her 18th birthday, which is tomorrow, and had it wrapped up pretty.

I hear on the news that a lot of people have already died on US Highways, and it's yet so early into the Labor Day weekend.

August 31, 1969

I woke myself up at 0900 and got cleaned up after three days of just letting it all hang out. I took my swim gear and Geema's gift and headed for town. I had a straight 7-UP at the Legion and then walked over to Bobby's house to meet the rest of the fun-seekers.

The POD was to go swimming at White Rock Beach again. Geema was her usual self; you so much as looked at her and she'd blush beet red. I like that quality in a female; I think it's an attractive feature if not carried to extreme. Geema said she really liked her new wallet; I hope she wasn't just being polite.

"Alice" (nee Trinidad Val Millaflores) was her usual self: vague. And Bobby was his usual self, too – drunk 24 hours a day. Also present was a homely girl named Norma who lived upstairs and worked in a very dark club, the D'Cave.

A young boy was there, about 19, by the name of Jule, who was Alice's cousin. He was well-groomed, had excellent manners, spoke good English, and seemed quite intelligent. In short, nothing at all like the normal Filipinos I was accustomed to meeting in my circles.

We also had a small cohort there from across the street, a midget hunchback by the name of Caesar. He was a swell little guy with a great sense of humor. Caesar is the man to see if any Filipino hoods are giving you grief, and he'll make it right! After each having a beer, we headed for the beach.

At first we feared that the day was going to be ruined because it started to sprinkle, but then it stopped and the sun peeked out now and then. So it turned out to be a fair day after all, and we had a great time at the pool.

There was a live band there for some private party, but we all benefited from the music just the same. Alice finally talked me into jumping off the high diving board, thus driving my pills up into my body cavity. We stayed only long enough for me to get slightly sunburned before we went back to Bobby's house.

Since I didn't have to work on Labor Day, I figured that I'd just drink to my heart's content, and then sleep where I fell down. So we all proceeded to get royally plastered – with the exception of Geema and Jule, of course, who remained the sole voices of reason. We did all the silly things and exchanged all the heavily meaningful talk that drunks do, and then went to bed sometime after midnight.

I lay on the vinyl couch for an hour, reading a book by myself in the quiet house. But when I was finally ready for sleep, I couldn't drop off because I could hear rats running up and down inside the walls. Finally, I saw the shadow of something move in the darkened kitchen. When I looked harder in the dim light, making a genuine effort to focus my rum-besotted eyes, I saw three of those despicable vermin. While my head smoked, I sat on the edge of the couch with my umbrella in hand, and waited calmly. I had to laugh to myself, because rats normally make my skin crawl.

I waited until six of those hairy bastards had invaded the pantry before I sprang upon them in all my drunken rage. They went scuttling in every direction at once, while I tried to beat them into the table and the sink and floor, sending crockery flying and tipping over chairs. But in the end they all escaped and my umbrella was in shambles. Geema peeked out of her room with huge eyes and then went back to bed. Bobby and Alice had never stirred during the whole melee. Satisfied that I had saved the household from a fate worse than death, I sprawled across the couch and slept.

September 1, 1969

Something woke me up at 0530 this morning. I think it was because my face was stuck like glue to the vinyl of the couch. For a moment I couldn't remember where I was, and then the whole night suddenly came back to me in a black wave. The sun was coming in the window and falling on my face, so I sat up. Mistake number one.

My head, apparently weighted down with cinder blocks, tried desperately to break off the top of my spinal column and fall to the floor. I gripped the couch firmly in an effort to keep it from foolishly spinning around the room on its own.

Why do I do this to myself, I asked for the millionth time?! I went into the kitchen (which looked unusually chaotic for some reason) and got a glass and a jug of cold water, and sat down at the table to try to revive myself a bit. I stared at my mangled umbrella in amazement. Geema peeked out of her bedroom for a second, and I knew she was in there holding her sides laughing. Very slowly I began to feel like a human being once again (a stupid human being, to be sure), instead of the walking dead.

Jule woke up and the three of us went to the *sari-sari* [convenience] store to get some provisions for breakfast. It was a beautiful, cool morning! A great day to be alive! Or just recently off life-support, at any rate. We saw Caesar in his little half-pint shoe stand and we hailed him; he seemed no worse for wear from last night.

Geema prepared some omelets and fried Spam, and the three of us sat down to our sumptuous repast. Bobby arose then and made a beeline for the reefer to get a bottle of cold beer; he was shaking that badly. Breakfast did not interest him. How can his body take it, I wondered.

We all went downtown and saw two movies in the afternoon. After that, I went back to the base, where I watched two more movies at the base theater, followed by another USO show. I didn't have the energy to do anything else. I topped off the evening with a cheeseburger and chocolate malt at the Spanish Gate cafeteria, and was in my own bunk by ten bells.

September 2, 1969

I halfway expected to be dragged kicking and screaming from my rack this morning, but to my surprise I woke up early, quite alert and fully functional and eager to start a new day. I had not woke up once during the whole night, not even when the other drunks came back to the boat. Feeling slightly rebellious, I skipped my morning shave. I wasn't going to shave today unless I got a direct order from the War Department!

While making my first-of-the-week rounds of the boat, I discovered countless light bulbs burned out everywhere, including five in the engine room and all eight in my motor room! So that was my first project this morning.

I passed another hour just puttering around in the Hole, picking up gear adrift and holding a general field day on my own. If I didn't recognize the items that I found, or thought they had no practical value to anyone, I threw them over the side. Quite a few things got the float test in that way and ended up down in Davy Jones' Locker.

SRF workers secured shore power to replace a smashed rectifier on a power pole. This curtailed any work for us the rest of the morning. But who's complaining?

In the afternoon, Benton was supposed to be painting the engine room with Earl, but Earl was sleeping it off on the floor of the pilot house, and Benton was much too busy making trips to the gedunk bar for snacks. What a couple of wastoids!

I helped Dean and Scotty lay non-skid on the 01 level forward of the pilot house. This is a mixture of cement, gray paint, and sand that you apply to the deck with a heavy white-washing brush. When it dries and hardens, it forms an absolutely gripping surface that you're not supposed to be able to slip on.

September 3, 1969

I had the reveille watch this morning and therefore had to wake everybody else up. This is not a pleasant job at any time, because then everybody is pissed at the reveille watch for the rest of the day for interrupting their sleep. Once this was done, I made myself scarce and worked down in the motor room. Finally, it seems, the chief engineer has ordered somebody else to paint in the engine room besides me! Or at least I saw Benton with a paintbrush in his hand once or twice, but I cannot confirm that he actually used it.

I cleaned out a huge spare-parts box that had been gathering for years and stowed it elsewhere, throwing away a lot of stuff that might conceivably have had some future use to someone somewhere on earth, but for right now it was just junk taking up valuable space and adding to the general weight of the boat. *Adios!*

I took a long nap before I attended the warehouse movie: "Citizen Kane." I had seen it two months previously over at the base theater, and I didn't like it then either. But having nothing else better to do, I sat through it again with Scotty and Benton. (They thought it was a great movie, however, which made me question their grip on reality.)

Back on the boat, I fried myself a tender sirloin steak with sliced onions. That sort of appetizing aroma will bring them running from all over the neighborhood, and it certainly did.

September 4, 1969

This was supposed to be the Big Day, but it was a complete flop in more ways than one. Our tug was scheduled to have dock trials all day long today. This involves running our engines and turning the screw at various revolutions, forward and reverse, while we are firmly secured to the pier. But we didn't quite get that far. First of all, my storage batteries were too low in their charge to light off both engines, so we had to wait around while I gave them a quick trickle charge.

Meanwhile, the starboard generator was running but we weren't getting any electrical output from it. Finally we got the port engine started, but then we weren't getting any electrical output from that generator either. SRF electricians were called in and they tooled around for five hours before they got the wiring hooked up correctly – exactly the opposite of which the previous Filipino yard workers had hooked it up!

In the meantime, the port engine stalled, and we couldn't get a fuel suction to start it up again. While we were working on this, the starboard engine began to "hunt;" it would speed up too rapidly and then slow way down almost to the point of stalling. The governors were going crazy, and the enginemen were almost in tears.

There wasn't much an electrician could do down there at the time, so I just stood by helplessly and observed the organized chaos. Every minute that passed found a new malfunction in the engineering plant. Finally everybody just gave up and shut down for the day. By then it was well past liberty call and we were all quite bushed. It was mighty good to get into a hot shower after that ordeal. Tomorrow's another day.

I hear on the news that the leader of North Vietnam, Ho Chi Minh, has died. Reports say that the new leader maintains he will not be influenced by the old leader's doctrines, though. I wonder how that will affect the war? We shall see what we shall see.

September 5, 1969

TGIF! They tried to hold dock trials again. I say "tried" because nothing much happened today either. We never even turned over the motors, much less the reduction gear or the screw. Difficulty after difficulty sprang up at every turn, and frustration was festering within all of us. The same troubles we had yesterday returned sevenfold.

Was it too much to ask that something went right occasionally, just by accident? All thoughts of dock trials soon disappeared when the starboard engine stalled, because we had no hope left of starting it back up at the time. They had run my batteries into the ground. We then happily secured for the day.

A while back I paid $3,000 (not out of my pocket, of course, but out of yours) for a new set of ten storage batteries to start our main engines. Each one was about the size of a spinet piano. They flew them here from Sacramento, California. That's the most money I think I've ever spent! Our tug's total overhaul costs come to over $200,000 so far, though.

Earl, Lurch, and a bunch of the usual suspects had a pot party in the pilot house this evening. They like to smoke their grass up there because the nightlights are deep red and cast the whole pilot house in a ruddy, crimson, surreal glow. Besides that, their perch in the pilot house commands a wide view of the surrounding area, enabling them to keep an eye peeled for any officers roaming around.

Lurch gets sleepy and drifty on marijuana, while Earl gets quite jolly and good-natured and high-spirited on it. So it can't be all that bad, I guess. Actually, I've been considering trying it once myself one of these nights, just to see what it's like – for the sake of forming an educated opinion, you understand. Sorta like a scientific experiment.

September 6, 1969

This is another late entry. I was in no sober condition to sit down and compose a journal entry for this date, so I am actually writing this on September 7, *comprende* [understand]?

Anyway, it was a bonny Saturday and Benton and I hung out together. We had a big fracas right away first thing in the morning, as the three tugboats in our nest were shuffled around in different order, so that the duty boat was placed outboard. To accomplish this, you have to disconnect shore power cables, freshwater hoses, and throw off all lines and wires. The tugs switched positions, and then we had to hook everything back up again.

We still made it to the base theater in time for the matinee. It was "Ivanhoe," starring Robert Taylor and Elizabeth Taylor, and there must have been a thousand kids in the theater. I got a kick out of the kids' reactions whenever Ivanhoe skewered an evil knight or when a knave would fall from the castle walls with an arrow in his chest. Vicious little beggars!

But when a mushy love scene appeared on screen they would grow noisy and restless and start moving around like so many rats. And rats, as you know, make my skin crawl.

After the movie, we went to the gym and worked out for a couple of hours. Then we sat in the steam room for as long as we could stand it, followed by alternate hot and cold showers until we felt like we were spotlessly clean. A session in the steam room leaves you feeling like you can breath through your skin; your pores are completely cleared!

In the bowling alley later, we had a burger and a Busch beer to undo what we had just done in the gym. Both Benton and I weigh in at 148 pounds at present, but this fluctuates daily with our San Miguel intake.

In the afternoon we went to another movie at the base theater. It was a comedy entitled "If It's Tuesday, This Must Be Belgium," which was hilarious! We came back to the boat, still laughing, got cleaned up and changed out of our sweaty clothes. Scotty had fried some Southern-style chicken for dinner and it was absolutely delicious! Maybe we ought to make him our new Stewburner?

In the evening, Benton and I planted ourselves firmly in the China Seas Club on base to do "…a little serious drinking," as we called it. The band played at intervals, and later there was a terrific floor show. There was this one talented Filipino boy of eight who sang just like Andy Williams – he came back time after time for many encores.

The very last song of the night that the band always plays before retiring is "The Green, Green Grass of Home," as it is a real tear-jerker, and the men are in various stages of self-medication by then, so they get all moist-eyed and thinking of home, and head off to their bunks.

We really put away some liquor last night! They say you shouldn't mix your alcohol, but we had bourbon, vodka, brandy and whiskey. On top of that, I bought my very first bottle of champagne, which we quickly made short work of. Alcohol really loosened our tongues and we rapped quite a bit. And then, after breaking the stems of our wine glasses so that our toasts could never be undone, we escaped into the night. Somehow, we got back to the boat safely and climbed into our trees.

September 7, 1969

This is a late entry. Yes, I was out partying again! You act as if it's a Federal crime or some kind of moral outrage. I really don't know why we did it again – feeling as messed up as we did this morning after last night. I stayed in my rack as long as I could to try and sleep it off, but it still felt like my head was full of water where my brain should be. (That would explain a lot of things, though.) What else could I do but pull myself together and go to Bobby's house for a birthday party?

Geema was especially *maganda* [beautiful] today! She had on a new yellow dress that squeezed in and puffed out in all the right places. And she had her hair braided into pigtails like a red Indian. It was a pleasure just to look at her, and several times she caught me looking at her like a lost pup, I'm sure. Geema had two beers before her mother stepped in and put a stop to that. (Her mother, I found out, works in Gerry's Club.) We sat around and listened to music and talked. About 5:00 PM half the girls pulled out to go to work in the clubs.

Later, we all piled into a jeepney and went to one of the clubs ourselves, where good old Steve pumped pesos into the jukebox so everybody could dance. At first I couldn't get Geema to dance with me, so I danced with her mother and Alice and even little Caesar! He's a wild card. They call me "the dancing fool of the Orient," since I can never seem to get enough of dancing.

But finally Geema got up and danced with me, and smiled up at me the whole time like a love-struck child. Those goofy girls working in the club kept shaking my hand and saying that they'll see me at the wedding. I didn't know what they were talking about.

Later, Jule said to me in a low whisper, "Have you told your feelings to her? She's ready now. Geema feels same-same for you." (That's the way they talk.)

Well, believe it or not, that really came as a big surprise to me. It made me feel...nervous.

Back at the house, Bobby and Alice got into their fourth or fifth argument of the evening, which is so tedious, and he stomped off to the bedroom to pout for a while. Caesar went home because it was getting very late; while Earl, Alice and I sat in the kitchen and conversed. Geema and Jule had both gone sensibly to bed.

Then, as is Earl's habit, he pulled out several joints of grass. And before we knew it, both Alice and I were helping him smoke them. I smoked five marijuana cigarettes in a half hour, but it didn't seem to do anything. Possibly I wasn't doing it right. I really didn't care for it, nor the tacky taste it left in my mouth afterwards. So much for my abbreviated drug career!

When I think back on it now, I'm ashamed of myself for doing such things in front of Geema every weekend. She must think I'm a hopeless *lasingero* [drunkard]! And so would my sisters. Well, next week is going to be a dry and sober one, I vow!

They wanted me to stay overnight and I was so tired that I almost did, but I knew it would be better for me if I went back to the boat. For some reason, Geema was out of bed again, trying to convince me to stay also. She didn't want me to leave, and every time I got as far as the street she'd call my name. But when I came back to the door each time, she would hide her face and say nothing. I think she wanted to say something, but didn't know how. Anyway, I finally hailed a jeepney, and she stood in the doorway waving as I drove off. I just didn't know what to make of it all. But it was after 0100 and I was almost asleep on my feet.

September 8, 1969

"What shall we do with a drunken sailor?" That is the question. I've had hangovers before, but this one must take the purple ribbon! Usually, I just shut up and tolerate the hangover until it passes. But that drinking bout last night has made me swear off the rotgut for quite a while!

I was so tired all day, but I couldn't sleep because my head started spinning every time I closed my eyes. And to make matters worse, I have the duty tonight. Don't I plan things well? I didn't have the energy to do a single worthwhile chore today, and late in the afternoon I got stomach cramps. I was terribly hungry, as I couldn't remember the last time I had eaten, but I couldn't bear to put food in my mouth. I spent most of the day at the scuttlebutt, slopping up cold water. What a wastoid!

September 11, 1969

Dear Family,

Hi. We seem to be having a post-rainy season fling this year; that old wet weather just doesn't want to give up. There have been two more typhoons since I last wrote, but nothing serious. We've been having mechanical troubles here on the tug, and now I'm kind of glad we aren't out there working in the *ulan* [rain]. A big share of our major malfunction is electrical, so I have my work cut out for me each day from 0700 to 1600. Nothing I can't handle in due time, though.

My buddy, Dino, is leaving the boat in ten days. Since he has made third-class Storekeeper, he will be transferred to the division warehouse where he can work in his rate. But he'll only be a half block away from us, though, and we'll get to see him every day just like usual. Right now he is playing house with a different Filipino girl! He has an apartment out in town with a bed, a table, and a chair. One chair between the two of them. Boy, what a meager existence! He loves it, though.

I got letters from both Bob Anderson and Doug Seiner this week. Doug is a Corpsman at the Naval Air Station Hospital in Lemoore, California, wherever that is, somewhere between Los Angelos and San Jose. I almost dropped my skivvie-shorts when I got Bob's letter from Iceland! His patrol squadron had deployed there and that's where he linked up with them. He writes:

> *"This place is like South Dakota in the wintertime. It's colder than Hell here, but I like it because it reminds me of home... It's flat except for the volcanoes. The wind blows 24 hours a day; it's cold, windy, and rainy. I haven't seen the sun since I got here and I doubt if I will. They say there's a girl behind every tree here – but so far I haven't seen a goddam tree!"*

He's not alone, though; the first week he was there he met six other guys from South Dakota!

I was thinking seriously about extending my hitch by six months in the Philippines, thus giving me a full two-year tour of duty down here. That way I could come home in the middle of summer vacation and the family and I could do all sorts of fun things together.

But they turned down my chit because they usually only approve a request like that if you're married. It's probably just as well; I don't really know if I am mentally equipped for an extra six months in this *place* (for lack of a better word). So it looks like I will come home in the dead of winter. That is all right, because I haven't seen snow for over two years now, and I kind of miss it. Yes, I said it.

Every weekend I make a huge pot of my special Fahrenheit Chili and it lasts for two days and delights the crew. I've finally got the recipe perfected and everybody just loves it! Sometimes even the guys from the office who have duty come down to the boat and feed their faces. Scotty, our lead seaman, ate so many bowlfuls that he couldn't sleep Saturday night – ha! I figure I just might give my prospective wife a run for her money in the kitchen.

Benton was messing around with my generators the other day and he didn't tell me about it beforehand. So when he got shocked he comes all crying to me, whining about how bad he got zapped. He caught ten amps and got a nasty burn on his left arm. Pure carelessness. The guys on this boat are so darn scared of electricity that it's pitiful. It's like they think electricity is supernatural or something.

Clark, one of my old shipfitter buddies, was put in the naval hospital today. He was trying to light a gas oven in his apartment out in town and it blew up. He got burns over forty percent of his body – not his face, thank goodness! He's only allowed one visitor a day for five minutes. What next?

I may have just recently jumped from the frying pan into the fire. A couple days ago I was escorting our new engine room houseboy around the base as he was checking in. We had to go through a lot of paperwork at several different locations on base.

At one stop they had me sign a paper for my craftmaster (his signature); at another place they had me sign a paper for our chief engineer. And so, of course, when they wanted our division officer's signature I signed that myself, too.

Well, when they went to verify it with a phone call, he misunderstood the situation and said it was a forgery! I really should have known better. So far he doesn't know that I was the one who signed his name, and for safety precautions I had the paper destroyed by a very understanding secretary.

But I overheard the division officer say to the chief, "I'm gonna git the sunuvabitch who forged my name!" Oh lordy. That rotten SOB would do it, too. But that was two days ago and nothing has happened yet. Maybe I will skate by once again? This time I learned a valuable lesson. Too bad we lost our shot at an engine room houseboy, though. He would have come in very handy.

The other day I pulled up to a stop sign in a taxi, and at the opposite corner sat another taxi. I thought it was someone that I knew sitting in the back seat. And sure enough, as we passed each other I recognized a boot-camp buddy of mine, and he saw me. We just had time for a smile and a wave before he was gone, and we went tearing off in opposite directions. He was dressed in whites, so he is in the fleet, on one of any number of ships presently in port. I never did locate him. What a maddening thing to happen!

Another old buddy, who used to be on my tug but who is now in the fleet as well, pulled into Subic yesterday on an ammo ship. I just happened to be at our favorite nightclub last night and we bumped into each other there. We had a good reunion; he'll be in port for a month! Happiness is seeing old service buddies.

September 17, 1969

Dear Gramma,

I've been spending nearly all of my spare time working on correspondence courses. It's such a welcome change of pace from going out into town constantly. I've just finished "Blueprint and Map Reading," on which I got an "A," and now I am starting "Illustrator Draftsman."

Hopefully, it will help prepare me for my college years, but it's awfully technical. It asks questions like, "How many equilibrants are on the thimble scale of a micrometer caliper?" Whew! The second half of the course is more along the line of my graphic abilities, which I know I will enjoy. I recently ordered three more courses: "Basic Music," "Builder," and "Mathematics." These are all entered in my service record and someday I might be called upon to use what I am learning.

yawn I am so tired! Two nights ago I had the duty and so I was up all night. Last night I took Dean's duty for him because he got stomach cramps. And tonight I have the duty again and will be up all night for the third night in a row. I hope I can make it. It's not so bad in the daytime while we are busy, but at night I have to drink lots of coffee and walk around just to stay awake. Luckily, I've always been a night owl, but even they get tired, too! Tomorrow I'll get 15 blessed hours of sleep.

I guess I will start mailing most of my junk home to you pretty soon; my locker is already bursting at the seams. I'm just like a pack rat. I accumulate things so fast, and I like books so much that I can't bear to give them away. Will you have Swede put them with the rest of my stuff already up in your attic? I think everything will be pretty safe there. Thanks!

My, it certainly is a fine night! There's a real cool breeze coming across the bay, everything is quiet as a tomb, and I've got the radio working in tiptop condition. They're playing good old easy-listening mood music without commercial interruption. There's a whole reefer full of dinner leftovers: roast turkey, dressing, and luscious turkey gravy. (Not as good as yours, though!) Now I ask you, what more could a guy want? Outside of a little sleep, that is.

Sometimes I don't think that these Filipinos down here are playing the game with a full deck of cards. I mean, I don't think they've got all their marbles. For instance, the other night I was going to the movie out in town and the admission price was forty cents. I gave her two quarters and I was the only one in the ticket line, and she asks, "How many, please?" I looked around behind me; I just didn't know what to say. (I *wanted* to say, "A hundred and twelve – the rest of the people are still getting off the bus." But I refrained myself.)

Two guys just left our boat to go to Vietnam, and next month another fellow leaves. Then we will get replacements for them. We've been pretty lucky about having a tight, cheerful crew so far, and I only hope our new replacements won't be complete jerks and will fit in nicely.

This old tug isn't running yet! After I got all the electrical discrepancies squared away, the snipes started having a lot more trouble with the engines again. Now they have entirely dismantled one engine and I figure it will be another two weeks before we have sea trials. Good lord, it's already been eight months and I'm impatient to get back out there in the harbor!

They had a wonderful USO show here on base the other night, and the enlisted men's club was really packed. It was the first show I had seen with American girls in a band. They sure looked mighty fine! There was a redhead, a blonde, a brunette, and a raven-haired beauty. All the sailors and Marines did a lot of sighing, you bet! They had a great show and we kept bringing them back for encores. They had just completed 300 shows over in Vietnam.

September 26, 1969

Dear Family,

It's really nice to wake up and find a letter on your pillow! Today I got a letter from Wilt, who is back at college in Brookings. We've been hatching a plot for some months now. I know it might seem a long ways off, but I'm referring to the first summer that I get out of the Navy – the summer of '71. We're going to have one last fling at having an adventure and bringing back some of the good old times like we used to have.

We'll get a couple of good backpacks, maybe some pistols, sleeping bags and the lot, and spend part of the summer just hiking around out west. We could cover the Black Hills, Yellowstone, and maybe the Bighorn Mountains in Wyoming. I'm not sure if we could legally hike through the South Dakota Badlands or not, although I would love to. Anyway, I think we could have a lot of fun, and I'm pretty sure I could hack the hiking part of it physically. I'm really looking forward to whatever we decide upon – one last hurrah before we settle down to earn a living!

Can you believe it, we had another damn Admiral's Personnel Inspection this morning, and my face is raw hamburger from shaving so close. We had to stand at attention out in that blazing sun for over an hour, and about two dozen guys passed out.

After the inspection was finally over, four of us went golfing at the miniature golf range on base. It's got 18 wacky holes covering almost an acre. Every other hole is especially tricky and they had signs saying "Tough par – no profanity, please!" But sailors will be sailors. That new AstroTurf stuff is really something! What will they think of next? Once I got a hole in one, which was unbelievable. I looked and looked all over the place for my missing ball – I never dreamed of looking in the cup! Well, I beat the pants off the other guys and now they're calling me Arnold Palmer.

I am *so* excited! After eight months of rotting here besides this pier, next week – if nothing else goes wrong – we will finally be chugging out in the harbor once again! Only then can we fully live up to our reputations as lovers, fighters, and tugboat riders. Our dock trials have all been successful so far. The sound of those roaring engines was music to my ears. All of our electrical and mechanical troubles are squared away, and this old tug is seaworthy again! Let's hear it for the YTM-182!

We got rid of our old craftmaster and got a first-class Negro in his place, who's a first-class shipmate as well. Actually, he used to be my craftmaster on the garbage boat, so we're old friends. I had a for-real date with a nice girl planned this coming weekend, but now I've got to turn her down because we have to work instead. I can't complain, though, because it's only the first weekend we've had to work in about eight months.

They pulled two sailors out of the Kalaklan River last week. Both of them were riddled with stab wounds. How do you tell their parents or wives about something like that? What next?

I've been working out at the track a lot, and taking appetite-suppressant pills – they really work! I want to get down to 140 pounds and stay there, but I can't seem to get below 148. It's like I've hit a brick wall.

The other night I met a couple new guys in the Legion and we went barhopping together. One was a guy in the Australian Navy and the other was a sailor from Iran. Boy, you talk about your strange bedfellows! But the language barrier was no problem – everybody likes cold beer, warm girls, and good music.

I see a bunch of choppers coming in over the hills; they're probably having their silly war games across the bay again. The Marines really eat up that kind of stuff; it gives them something else to yell about. Of course, Marines don't really need anything to bellow about, it just comes natural to them. All they do is walk around hollering at each other and grunting like animals. Sure, I poke a lot of fun at the Marines, but if you need somebody to take and hold a piece of ground until hell freezes over, then you'll want a Marine. Nobody else will measure up.

The base theater guild, made up of servicemen and dependents, put on a live three-act play the other night. I haven't seen one of those since high school. It was pretty funny and they were terrific at improvisation. I still get all embarrassed whenever somebody forgets their lines, though, and you can hear a pin drop in the audience until they get it sorted out. On their limited budget they had an imaginary wall as part of the set, and everybody kept accidentally walking through it. Cracked us up!

October 11, 1969

Dear Family,

Well, my glorious 21st birthday on October 5th didn't amount to much on the surface. I sweat all day long down in the Hole and then stood duty all night, which is not out of the ordinary. But I've got to keep in mind that I'm no longer a civilian, and the Navy isn't being run for my personal convenience – or so they remind us all the time.

Our boatswain's mate, Scotty, fried a delicious chicken dinner especially in my honor and I got the biggest breast piece; and one of the snipes gave me ten pesos to spend out in town. One of our brand-new seamen, a Porter T. Pepperworth (did you ever hear of such a name?! I am afraid to even ask what the "T" stands for.), he took my early-morning watch for me so I could at least get four hours of sleep that night. What a guy.

Instead of 21 swats on the butt, I got 21 slugs in the arm. Ouch! Thank goodness the rest of the crew didn't know about my birthday or they probably would have gotten feisty and thrown me over the side again, or something else equally as fun.

The next night, the band at the American Legion played "Happy Birthday" for me. All I lacked was a birthday cake with candles, huh? I appreciate the cash gift you sent, and you've got my word that I won't spend it on you-know-what.

I'm sitting here this evening up in the pilot house where I can catch a breeze from across the bay. Porter has got the duty with me tonight, and he's on the fantail writing letters to his girlfriend back home in Louisiana. (I sure hope he doesn't get a Dear John letter, too.) He's a two-year Navy Reserve; he entered the Navy only a month ago and he'll still get out before me! Drives me crazy!

That reminds me: on the 9th of this month I marked two years in this goofy outfit. I'm officially over two now. The rest is downhill all the way, as they say. I had won a 15-dollar-jackpot on the slot machines the other night at the Sky Club, so I used that to go out and celebrate being a "short-timer in the P.I." with a fine oriental meal of curried chicken and rice.

Every now and then we do get a bit of genuine drama around here. We had a minor earthquake last Friday night about 2100. It didn't do any damage here, but the tremor sure lasted long. I was in the bowling alley at the time, and all the girls there commenced to hollering like girls will do sometimes. It's the fourth earthquake I've experienced, but it never fails to put my heart in my mouth.

Yesterday they towed the sorry remains of the *USS Frank E. Evans* (that destroyer that was cut in half by an Aussie bird farm during a collision near here in early June) out to sea, and United States Naval ships used it for target practice until it sunk. Now she's nothing more than a memory and some exciting footlocker talk among her survivors.

Another news item well worth mentioning would be the fact that last week we attempted sea trials. It was the first time since February that this old tug left the pier under her own power! Not only that, but our sea trials were successful! The craftmaster blew one prolonged blast, followed by two short blasts on the horn – a happy signal which means "cast off"!

I had to stay down in the Hole to control the main switchboard while we were underway, but I managed to sneak up topside once and feel the breeze. It was sure good to see green water rush along our gunwales once again. Every face was nothing but smiles. We had a spot of trouble with the engine governors speeding up once, but nothing serious. It should be only a matter of days now before we'll be working the big ships in the harbor. It's about time, too!

Last Monday night was the most beautiful night I've ever seen in the P.I.! It started out with a magnificent sunset in a blaze of color. The heat quickly lifted as soon as the sun was down, and the night became so cool and comfortable that I just couldn't bring myself to hit the rack all night.

About midnight I went for a long walk down an out-of-bounds creek, threw a bunch of rocks and kicked some beer cans. Just sort of got away from it all, you know? I found a 15-foot-tall shoot of bamboo grass and brought it back to the boat with me.

I found the security watch asleep on the fantail, and from the 01 deck above him I reached the long grass shoot down towards him and touched the back of his neck lightly. When he turned around to see what was tickling him, I shook the tassel vigorously in his face and scared the holy bug-snot out of him, and he jumped backwards over his bench. He said his whole life passed before him; he thought the Hottentots had got him. Serves him right for sleeping on watch – that's a court-martial offense, fool!

Our Filipino houseboy is Ernesto Danato, but we call him "Ernie." At 32 years of age, Ernie is hardly a boy anymore. He's been a fixture on this boat for eight years around Americans, so that we no longer even consider him a *brownfoot*. He is employed by the crew to do our laundry and dishes and general cleaning and such, duties which he quietly carries out while we ride the boat on jobs around the harbor, then he goes home each night to his little shanty house out in the *barrio* [district or neighborhood], complete with all the modern inconveniences. He'll go drinking with you, he'll fight his own countrymen alongside of us (if you are in the right), and he'll lend you money whenever you need it. He has a few champion roosters in the cockfight circuit with which he hopes to become a peso-millionaire. He's going to have three of us guys to a picnic out in the country soon. Sounds like fun!

Lately, I've seen the movies "True Grit," "The American Dream," and "Popi" – all three of which I enjoyed tremendously! The Kingston Trio is going to be here on the 16th at the Sampaguita Club. (How much do you want to bet that I'll have the duty that night? That seems to be how my luck runs.) Besides my correspondence courses, I've also been reading a textbook on psychology, which is a real eye-opener, especially the chapters on abnormal psych.

Since 1937 the Sampaguita flower has been the national flower of the Philippines, symbolizing peace and purity. It smells much like jasmine, and it's everywhere down here.

My athlete's foot is back worse than before, and I'm trying to get rid of it with every product on the market. Besides that, right now I've got a bad heat rash all over my back. Now that the rainy season is over, I suppose we will start sweating like threshers again. If tomorrow is as nice and sunny as today, we're going out to Grande Island to do some skin diving. This will be the first time since the last hot season.

I got a letter from La Salle College in Philadelphia, saying that they would accept me to their fine school when I was ready, but I kind of wanted to spend my first couple of college years a little closer to home. To get a job worth anything at all, I've probably got to graduate from a brand-name school, though.

While I was sitting in the theater last night waiting for the USO show to start, I couldn't help but notice this cute little girl in front of me. She was peeking at me over the back of her chair, not saying anything. I smiled at her, thinking of my own tiny sisters at home. Finally, she stood up in the chair on her ten-inch legs and said, "Hi, my name is Kathy."

"Hi."

"I'm four years old."

"Really?"

"Yeah, and I suck my thumb." (To prove this she jammed her stubby little wrinkled thumb into her mouth. After a few seconds she pulled it out again and looked at it.) "And when I go to bed I suck it all the time."

"Oh? Do you have any big sisters?"

"No. I only have one big brother...he's a Mareeen!"

"I'm a sailor."

(She screwed up her nose like she had just swallowed a bug.) "I like you anyway," she said after a pause.

"How come you like me?"

"Cuz you got four eyes."

What could I say? I get no respect.

October 15, 1969

Dear Gramma,

Now that the hot season is sneaking up on us again, I've been kept busy rigging ventilation fans in all the portholes to suck in fresh air to cool the boat. Yesterday our houseboy was fishing off the tug and he caught a young shark! He cut him up and fried little shark filets for our supper. It was a real treat.

Hey, how about those Russians up there in space? I sure hope they get their space station put together and get back to Earth all right. Man is going places fast! There are still those people who will forever say, "If God had wanted man to fly, He would have given him wings." On the other hand, if God had wanted steel to float and move through the water, He'd have put fins and scales on it. Right?

Our tug had to meet a ship a little farther out of the bay than usual recently, and we hauled her carefully over to the dry dock. It seems she had run over a palm tree log floating in the ocean and smashed a big hole in the ship. She was a minesweeper, so she had a wooden hull.

We've got two new seamen on board who get seasick while we're gently bobbing up and down tied to the pier! Ha ha. And the ebb and flow of the Subic tides are not even as dramatic as other ports. The tide here rises and falls only about six feet, twice a day. But they'll get their sea legs soon enough.

OFFICIAL QUARTERLY MARKS
October 16, 1969
(Assigned to the YTM-182)

"Stanga is the only electrician on the YTM-182. He maintains all electrical equipment on board and assists on deck in general tug make-ups. He stands engine room watches underway and nest-security watches while in port. Stanga shows a great deal of proficiency and reliability in his work. He works well on his own and shows much ingenuity when encountering something new. It is not unusual to find him working on his liberty time. Stanga responds well to orders without hesitation and sets a good example for his subordinates. He has never been a disciplinary problem on the YTM-182. Although not often presented with the chance, Stanga is very effective when handling men, and gets good results from the people working under him. Stanga presents a neat appearance at all times. He has a good sense of humor and gets along very well with everyone he meets. He contributes to the crew's morale by both his personality and his artistic abilities. He is a good shipmate."

October 25, 1969

It's nice and quiet tonight – I'm thinking about starting a cemetery here. An occasional F-4 Phantom II Navy jet will take off from Cubi Point and kick in the afterburners right over us, filling the air with a roar that sounds positively lethal; but other than that the only sound to be heard is the whimpering of a lonely one-peso bill in my wallet.

The whole crew – all ten of us – went out on the town last night. I spent a 100 pesos all by myself, but I don't remember when I've had so much fun! That's the way this crew should always be – work together and party together. I gave my last thirty pesos to some girl named Wendy about 0600 this morning before I came back from town.

Bad news! The San Miguel brewery in Manila is on strike and the situation is grave indeed. Beer is getting scarce and the price has skyrocketed up to 200 centavos per bottle! Here's the only good thing that ever came out of the P.I. and now they're trying to screw that up, too.

I bought a straight razor out in town, along with a shaving mug and brush and shaving soap. I had to sneak the razor back through the gate in my sock, though, because the things are illegal to possess. I sure do like the shaves I'm getting with

Aerial view of Cubi Point, Subic Bay, Philippines.

it, though; I won't butcher myself with those worthless adjustable safety razors anymore. I also stopped using my electric razor months ago because it really irritated my face all day. This darn hot weather is murder on razor burns. But any way you look at it, I still positively hate to shave! T'ain't natural!

Dean says he's going to marry his current girlfriend down here. He's only lived with her a couple of months and he claims he's fallen head over heels for her. But she's a bar hog after all, and pretty weird to boot, and she's forever stealing all his money. As a friend, I told him straight out that he was an asinine fool. Why, Dean was the one who laughed loudest when our chief engineer decided to marry his live-in bar hog! The last thing that Dean's mother told him when he left Sioux City was not to bring a Filipino girl back to the States. And besides that, she's already got one kid that he knows of. Does he have a death wish or what?

I'll admit that I've met some very beautiful girls down here who really know how to treat a guy right and make him feel like a king, waiting on him hand and foot, and more than once I've entertained the idea of bringing one home. But I've also seen what some Filipino girls look like at age forty and beyond, and I'll settle for a round-eye anytime.

October 26, 1969

Dear Family,

I guess I kind of got sidetracked again. We went to the cockfights on Sunday afternoon. I had never seen a cockfight before, and Ernie didn't want me to leave the islands without having attended one, so off we went. I'll have to admit that it was a very unusual – and unsettling – experience.

We entered a large *bitawan* [a seating gallery], much like the auction pit at the Palace City Stockyards back home in the States. There were men and boys there of all ages and wardrobes, from black-haired lads with cheeks of tan in shorts and rubber shower sandals, to men in those tacky iridescent-green mobster-style suits. Arriving early, we had a ringside seat, so to speak, and got in on all the sport's action. Ernie wasn't fighting any of his own cocks that day, or we would have been right down on the arena floor.

Basically, a cockfight is simply fighting between gamecocks armed with steel knives on their feet. After all the cockers showed off their birds to the fans, at a secret signal everyone in the crowd suddenly started yelling across the arena, giving odds and taking bets. You've got to be able to remember everyone you made bets with, usually by facial features alone, or someone was sure to cheat you. Then they start the actual cock fighting.

They brought out the first two cocks, and poked them towards each other, letting the cocks peck each other in turn to get their blood hot. When the neck feathers were flared like cobra hoods, then they took the sheaths off the knives and let them go at it. The pointed knife is attached to one of the cock's own leg spurs; it was about two inches long and sharp as a razor. Some roosters, small or one-eyed or partially crippled from previous fights, were given handicaps and got to use two knives in the battle.

Sometimes an individual match lasted 5 to 10 minutes, but this was unusual; others were as short as five seconds. When released from opposite sides of the ring, the roosters plunged at each other without hesitation, and then jumped about five feet into the air to attack. The shouting from the crowd at this point was absolutely awful, as shrill Filipino tongues broke out all at once at the top of their lungs. I was not expecting that.

There was a flurry of fighting roosters in midair. By the time they were back down on the floor, a rooster could have as many as ten wounds already! The knives flew so fast that the human eye could not follow them. One stab through the heart or deep under the wing could *bitay* [kill] a cock instantly. Otherwise, they'd both continue to cut each other up before one received a mortal blow and dropped to the sawdust for keeps. They would just not give up! Sometimes both cocks died in the fight and then all bets were off.

If a cock sensed a more dominant rooster, and turned chicken to run away, the other was automatically the winner by default; this happened a few times. If both of them were barely on their feet, the winner was the one that could peck his opponent twice before they quit. The cocker whose rooster won got about 1,000 pesos – and the other guy's rooster for supper! Then he usually had to stitch up the horrendous wounds on his own bird. A rooster that can win 18 or 19 fights is rewarded by being used for stud from then on.

There was a *llamada* [the favorite bird] in each match that had the most money riding on it and an underdog. Ernie and I did most of our betting on the underdogs with great success. If both birds were heavily wounded and tipping over, but still with no clear winner, the cockers would sprinkle them with cold water and they would often revive enough to finish the match.

I never saw people enjoy anything more than that Sunday afternoon crowd enjoyed that particular sport. It was the same with the old *Papa-Sans* and with the boys of twelve. There certainly was an atmosphere of high brutal excitement at all times, and a couple of fist-fights broke out amongst the spectators who were swilling San Miguel beer.

Meanwhile, I grew increasingly uncomfortable. We saw about 25 bloodied cocks bite the dust in five hours. Cockfighting is really an inhuman sort of entertainment, I decided; there was no question about it. Still, it seemed a far less cruel sport than fox-hunting or bull-fighting. I don't think I could handle a bull fight.

I did not stay to see the end of the competition that day. I endured it as long as I could, but it was just too gory an exhibition, and I was starting to feel light-headed in the thick cigarette-smoke atmosphere. I made a confession to Ernie along those lines, and so we departed and took our winnings downtown. We had won 150 pesos (about twenty dollars apiece) and were quite pleased with ourselves. We took dinner at the best restaurant in Olongapo and then treated some lady-friends of ours to drinks. It was a great day!

October 27, 1969

Dear Family,

This funky tugboat broke down already – the recurring trouble with the engine governors once again – so we only got to chug a few days. Oh cripes, they can't expect to keep this old crate chugging forever – it was built ten days after Pearl Harbor! It's costing them a small fortune to keep it going. But I hope we chug a little while yet before I leave the P.I. Meanwhile, I've got to take the test for second-class petty officer soon, so I need to study for that.

We got to go shopping for the tug last week. Every quarter we get to draw supplies from Serve-Mart on Mainside that we can't get at our own warehouse here in Boton Valley. Serve-Mart is like a huge K-Mart with everything under the sun in it. We usually get to spend around $600 on the boat for tools and equipment, etc. Anything that we have left over on our tab can be spent on personal stuff for ourselves! When we finally got our bill tallied up at the counter we found that we had $200 left! Boy, did we go hog-wild then! It was just like Christmas come early.

We were fortunate enough to get to see the Kingston Trio after all! At the last minute I wormed out of my duty so I could go, too. We had to get to the club five hours early to get front-row seats. So we passed the time by doing arm exercises with dark brown vessels of bubbly liquid and arguing about politics and the Moratorium. By the time the show got underway we were floating about three inches off our chairs, and only the weight of a San Miguel beer bottle was holding us down and keeping us from becoming totally free spirits. They put on a terrific show, even though the speakers and mikes were obviously "made in Hong Kong" pieces of crap.

Barely a month past the rainy season, and already the grass is turning brown. Next will come the intolerable dust blowing around. We're going skin diving real regular now. The water is nice and warm, but is just beginning to clear up after the rainy season runoff. I shot a few *lapu-lapu* [grouper fish], but bounced the spear off rocks more times than not.

One day the *USS Camden* (AOE-2) left the harbor, steaming out past Chiquita Island where we were diving. We didn't even realize the large ship was passing nearby until the wake hit us; the waves threw me helplessly all over the rocks and the coral cut my hands and feet. I'm still picking out sharp pieces of coral that work their way up to the surface of my skin.

Tomorrow night is the big poker night here on the boat; there should be about eight of us. Last time I lost five pesos. That's not too bad, eh? Anyway, that's the most I've ever lost in one game. If I don't learn anything else in the Navy, I'll learn to play two dozen different kinds of poker!

Do you really think Paul McCartney has been dead for two years? That's the current rumor. I read a long article in *The Detroit News* and all clues point to his being dead. Wouldn't that be some kind of crazy, bizarre hoax? All these years they have supposedly used a look-alike substitute so the Beatles wouldn't fold up. Anything is possible nowadays, I guess.

And how did you guys spend "Moratorium to End the War in Vietnam Day"? Did you run down Main Street with your little black armbands and your signs reading "Yankee, Come Home!"? Or did you do just what everybody down here did – went about their normal daily routine? I don't think all the hoopla and rallies and demonstrations, peaceful as they were, did a darn bit of good.

In my opinion I think this troop withdrawal thing is wrong, wrong, wrong! Sure, everybody would like their sons home where they belong, but that's no reason for us to pull out and *give* Nam to the Cong. I don't think we should just stop the war, I think we should win it! And it's got to be now or never. Drop the Bomb on Hanoi and ask them where they want the next one! Everybody thinks we aren't fighting for our own country in Nam, but in reality we are. Then again, this is only my opinion. As usual, I tend to get carried away with myself.

November 9, 1969

Dear Family,

This is such a beautiful day, you just wouldn't believe it! Lucky for you that I've got the duty today or you might not be getting this letter for a few more days. I sure as heck wouldn't be hanging around the boat on a day this nice if I didn't have to!

Actually, we had planned on spending the weekend down in Manila, but at the last minute I wound up with the darn duty. (Still no tattoo – rats!) So anyway, I'm catching up on letters this afternoon while soaking up that good old South Pacific sunshine. What, snowing already back home, you say? Wow…what is snow?

Monday begins the Filipino National elections, and for a few days the gates will be closed to us. It's for our own protection, though, because there is always so much rioting and destruction during these so-called "elections." The incumbent President, Ferdinand Marcos, is not very popular around here and he has been accused of everything from ballot stuffing to assassinating opponents. How he manages to stay in office with all the opposition stacked against him is beyond me.

The other Presidential candidate is very popular with the people; he likes the United States presence in the Philippines, and plans to make English the national language here. He is by far the people's favorite and is expected to win this election. I sure hope so.

I heard that the first lady, Amelda Marcos, was attacked on stage while she was giving a lecture by a knife-wielding Filipino maniac who only managed to stab her in the hands as she held them up in front of her to protect herself. This is like the Wild West down here.

Pardon the onion smell on my stationery, but I just finished making the guys a batch of my world-famous Fahrenheit chili. Every weekend I get to voluntarily do the cooking for the crew, as the Stewburner spends Saturdays and Sundays in town with his native family, and this affords me one of my little pleasures. I just like to see them stuffing themselves, know what I mean? I make easy things: goulash, tuna and noodle casserole, split-pea soup, pineapple upside-down cake, fried chicken, cheese royales, and raisin white cake. Little treats like these are much appreciated by the guys, who would otherwise have to eat bologna sandwiches and drink bug juice all weekend if left to fend for themselves.

Well, I hear the Apollo 12 countdown has already begun. This time the three astronauts are going on a ten-day moon mission. I sure hope everything goes all right! With every new space shot that we make, the odds increase for a massive failure.

We've got two new men on board (we're constantly rotating men within the division, plus we were short-handed by recent departures). One is a fireman from Virginia. The other is a deckape, Denny Overby, from Michigan, to whom I took an instant liking. We call him "Overhaul" because that seems like the natural thing to do.

On Thursday and Friday we didn't have too much work to do, so we spent both days just sitting in the shade and arguing about this and that. And, as it always seems to happen, the talk eventually turned to the subject of religion. I maintained that when a person finally follows a specific religion in life, nine times out of ten it will be the same one that his parents have. A person may not want to admit it, but I say that's the main reason why an individual chooses one particular faith over another.

The guys didn't want to admit it either – even though they were *all* of the same faith as their parents, and also the same political persuasion as their parents! Ha! I rest my case. There is nothing at all wrong with this practice, but I was merely trying to point out that most people don't really take the time to rationalize and choose the religion and way of worship that suits them personally. They accept what's handed to them without a great deal of thought. I like to discuss things with people and get their opinions on different topics. That's the only way you can grow intellectually.

People are communicating more and more nowadays, and I think this is really good. After all, this is the Age of Aquarius. Astrologically speaking, the Age of Aquarius is a cycle of the earth which began about 1920 and will last for 2000 years for all people, not just those whose Zodiac sign is the water bearer. Aquarians are described as unconventional, argumentative, clairvoyant, rebellious and unpredictable. Astrologers say their positive attitude toward human welfare during the Age of Aquarius will mean a time of higher involvement with others.

Overhaul and I went to my favorite club, the Can Can, last night and relaxed over a few cold ones. He actually likes the place, too! Some hostess stepped on an extension cord with her spike heels and shorted it out, and for ten minutes they were all running around like chickens with their heads cut off, wondering why the band's amplifying equipment suddenly didn't work. I finally got up and spliced the wire for them so we could get the show on the road. Good old American know-how! Anyway, I got a free beer out of the deal, and they dedicated a song to me: "Waltz Me Around Again, Willie."

I got in a big argument with Scotty the other night out in Pauline's Club. It wasn't much of a fight to speak of, as the other guys soon separated us. He was calling one of the new men an idiot and a *lapu-lapu* [grouper fish] for buying a hostess a drink. And so I told him to "…mind your own business, you stingy slob." Bingo, the magic fighting words.

Actually, I had already explained to the new guy that the hostesses will ask him to buy them a drink from time to time, but he isn't obligated to do so if he's low on pesos. I further explained that the bar pays no salary to the girls and that the only money they get is a small commission from the drinks that sailors (or Marines) buy them (half to the bar and half to the girl). I told him that a drink costs one dollar for her and that she only gets a watered-down Tom Collins or something similar. So Porter knew what he was doing when he bought the girl a drink.

Scotty berated him sharply, saying that they're only hogs after his pesos. (They might not be the most virtuous girls in the world, but it would get mighty lonesome without them around; they serve their purpose.) Scotty said he wouldn't be caught dead buying some hostess a drink, but he certainly expects them to sit and keep him company all night for nothing! He only enhances the reputation that station sailors are cheapskates. The rest of us are victims of circumstance, guilty by association.

I asked him just exactly how the hell are the girls supposed to make money for food, clothes, rent – and half of them have kids to support as well – if sailors weren't generous sometimes? I don't wait for a girl to ask me to buy her a drink, I offer. And then I'll slip her a few pesos under the table all for herself. Her company – someone to talk to and dance with for a couple of hours – is alone worth the few measly pesos that I can afford. Besides that, I've made a new friend in the P.I. then, and showed one more foreign person that not all Americans are callous, loud, and cheap-charlies. Anyway, Scotty and I made up right away the next day. We like each other too much to stay mad for long.

They had another USO show last week that I was fortunate enough to see. It was a group called "The Community Eight;" I've never seen a funnier comedy team in all my born days. Their music and their two long-legged blonde singers were really well-adapted to the GI audience, too. One of the blondes played the accordion like it was the Mormon Tabernacle pipe organ. We encored them four times.

Along the line of work, we don't have too awful much to do around here lately. We're having trouble with the engines yet, and we're still sitting here beside the pier. Next week we go alongside the tender, *USS Delta* (AR-9), to get a bunch of minor jobs taken care of. Leisure time and the pursuit of happiness are alright up to a point, but rigor mortis has set in a long time ago! I have only one hope: that I get to go out chugging again before I leave here.

Smitty left for Nam this week, and realistically I will probably never see him again. I still haven't received my own orders yet, but I'm expecting them any day now. We haven't been doing much in our spare time but going to movies and basketball games. The old town has gotten sort of dull after 16 months down here. I never thought I'd say it, but I think I'm really going to miss this place after I leave. I guess you can't help but get a little attached to a place after a year and a half.

November 19, 1069

Dear Family,

I've got the duty tonight. Overhaul is sitting at the other end of the table, writing a letter and singing, "How's About a Little Kiss, Cecelia?" over and over and over. I'm still trying to figure out what makes him tick.

Lately, every time it came around to my turn for duty I've gotten a standby. Mainly because I don't like to stand watch when I could be sleeping. Getting a standby is as simple as waving five bucks in front of one of the other guys and then jumping into my civvies. This is fine as long as my money holds out, but I figured one night of duty now and then wasn't going to kill me, even though tomorrow is payday. Anyway, the town is an absolute madhouse on paydays, and it's hard to get a decent date when every swabbie has money to burn.

Speaking of dates, find enclosed a picture of me and Elby in Gerry's Club. I sure wish I would have met her when I first came down here – we could have set up house or something. She is always so bubbly and cheerful and full of fun; that's why I like her, I guess. She likes me because she says I'm "good to her." Well, I don't much care if she likes me or my pesos better; we have a good time when we're together. She's 19, or so she says; it's hard to tell with these girls.

Well, on the last news dispatch I heard that the astronauts are safely (?) on the moon and will make their first walk in about an hour! I've been following this moon shot pretty closely. That sure was a tense moment right after liftoff when the rocket was hit by lightning! They sounded like a bunch of happy kids when they finally landed on the surface. Whereas Apollo 11 only brought back a few rocks, these guys are going to return with over 100 pounds of lunar soil. Just think of it.

The Filipino national elections are finished, and President Marcos has been surprisingly re-elected once again. I was hoping the people would elect the underdog this time around. The first thing Marcos wants to do is pull all the Filipino troops out of Vietnam (yeah, all three of them), and open diplomatic relations with Red China. So I guess that's what the people wanted, as they went ahead and re-elected the guy.

Meanwhile, the three-day voting period created havoc and mayhem here on base. Since the gates were closed to us, we were forced to entertain ourselves on base. Can you imagine thousands of thirsty fleet and station sailors and Marines trying to get a drink at the few base clubs that we have? Every night that the gates were closed, the situation got worse and worse.

Finally, on the third night, a couple hundred Marines took over one club all for themselves. Then a bird farm pulled in and a few hundred sailors descended upon the same club, fighting and smashing. Two Marines were killed and one Filipino girl got her stomach cut open with a broken beer bottle. What next?

On a cheerier note, this old tugboat is chugging once again! We've been on the line for almost a week now, and have worked quite a few ships already. It sure is nice! The new deckapes are really getting the hang of things pretty quick, too.

"Boats" Washington, who was my craftmaster back on the YG-52, as you will remember, has proven to be quite capable as a tugboat skipper, too. It's a relief to know that while we're making up to a big ship he won't kill one of us in the process. Our last craftmaster was forever ramming ships and piers and barges, and making us quite uneasy.

While we're underway on a job, I run the forward capstan and its stout wire, which takes a special knack, and occasionally I pop down into the Hole and check the switchboard gauges. The main line that is used to tie up to a ship is at the bow of the tugboat, and is actually a thick braided wire. It is extremely heavy and inflexible. I will be the first one to admit that I am not man enough to raise the wire up and take a turn around the bull bitt by sheer muscle power. But some of the deckapes can do it. When not using our nylon lines to move a ship, we fake them down in neat spirals on the deck to dry out.

One of our new firemen is leaving us already. He has to return to the States to marry a girl. Boy, is he ever nervous! For a year before he came into the Navy he lived with some girl, and they had a kid together. For some reason they told everybody that they were married. Well, it finally caught up with him. Now he either marries the girl or pays her twenty-five dollars each payday for child support. And he only makes thirty-five dollars a payday to begin with! So it seems he will be a husband soon. He's already a daddy.

I've got the distinction of being on the boat the longest. It's hard to believe that I'm considered an "old-timer" to some people here —

Hey! I finally got my orders yesterday!!! And guess what? I'm going to Vietnam just like I had requested! I'm going to be on an ammo ship – the *USS Iredell County* (LST-839). The old salts tell me that LST stands for "Large Slow Target."

She's home-ported in Norfolk, Virginia, but I doubt if we'll ever get there. We'll be going pretty far up the Mekong River most of the time, and expect to see some action. And maybe once every two months we'll pull into Subic Bay for a little R&R! Coincidentally, the *Iredell County* just happens to be here in Subic Bay right now, so I went over and took a gander at her – mighty fine! I'm real satisfied with my orders.

Right now I don't know if I'll be getting leave or not between duty stations, but I'm sure going to try. I'll probably have to pay my own plane fare from here to Omaha and back, and that won't be cheap. I'd be broke for the rest of my natural life! But maybe I can get a military "hop." That's free, but it's awfully risky, too, and sometimes it falls through at the last minute. Anyway, I'll do my best to get home…but no promises.

(Later) Well, I'm back now. I suspended my letter-writing for awhile as I listened to the moon transmissions over the radio. I just can't believe that it's really happening even as I sit here and stare up at the full moon. The first moon walk of the Apollo 12 mission is over with now, and so is my watch. Tomorrow is another working day, so I'd better get my four hours of shut-eye.

November 27, 1969

Dear Gramma,

Ah, this is the way to enjoy Thanksgiving Day – stuffed to the tonsils with good food and have the whole afternoon to loaf around! Although our division didn't get a four-day holiday weekend like the rest of the base did (due to the nature of our work), we did get all of Turkey Day off.

Our Stewburner didn't even have to get out of his rack all day if he didn't want to, as he also had the day off; but happily he slaved away in the galley all morning and really outdid himself on a fabulous dinner: roast turkey with all the trimmings; I peeled the potatoes for him. Your delicious banana bread was counted among the treats; the boys really went for that! Many thanks from me and the crew for helping to make this a special Thanksgiving! You should have seen their eyes when I opened the package you sent. Now all of us can have our fill of cookies, candy and nuts for the holiday.

I really liked the pamphlet on "Moral Disease" that you included with your last letter, really. Personally, I think that a sin is what I know to be wrong and do anyway. But I cannot imagine that a god, as fair-minded and understanding as the god which we are taught to believe in, would punish a person for doing something he does not consider a sin. Man was born with a mind for reasoning and a will to choose, and I cannot believe that He would condemn a person for doing what he thinks is right. Just the other night Overhaul said to me, "Stanga, you're a man that I'll remember the rest of my life. You're the only one I've ever met who can talk about something controversial and not be so darn biased!"

Our craftmaster forgot to send in my recommendation this month for second class, so I have to wait until next month to take my Military Leadership test. Also, the Navy has cancelled all exams for second class in February – they have too many at present – so now I'll have to wait until next August to take it. I'll sure be losing a lot of money on that deal, but on the other hand it'll give me a much longer time to study.

Now the only problem that arises is the little matter of getting home for leave. I have thirty days of leave coming to me. I've been checking around with lots of different guys who have gone home on Emergency Leave, and there appears to be hope for me yet. Fortunately, I have a good friend who has a good friend who works at the Naval Air Station. When the time comes for my leave, he said he could put me right at the top of the list of 130 people waiting for a free military flight to California. I know this isn't fair to the rest of them, but at present I am only thinking of myself.

If this doesn't work out, I have a good friend who has a good friend who runs the computers at the air terminal flight-processing complex. He could program me onto a flight, possibly escorting an engine part or something to the States! I guess it pays to have friends, huh? I'll be darned if I'm going to pay $650 or more for a round-trip commercial flight. But I'm bound and determined to get home, even if I have to swim!

December 3, 1969

Dear Family,

Hey, that's a switch – my pocket full of pesos on a payday, and I'm not out in town contributing to the Philippine economy! I'll betcha he's probably got the duty, you say? Nope. I'll bet he's lost his liberty card again, you say? Nope. I just want to sit here in the breeze and relax a bit in the peace and quiet, unwind and get a good night's sleep for a change.

I listened to a rerun of the Lottery System drawing for the draft on the Armed Forces Radio Network a little while ago. It seems to me that this slightly more complicated system will be quite fair and easy to accept for all concerned. I found out that my birth date was number 24 on the list, so I would have stood a good chance of getting drafted into the Army as it was.

Our forward capstan crapped out. I had never had any trouble with it previously, and then all of a sudden it started blowing expensive buss fuses every time I turned it on. Well, I worked on it for a whole day and didn't accomplish a thing. So I finally called in three first-class electricians from the shop for assistance. They messed around for *two days,* trying all sorts of stupid things, almost electrocuting each other in the process at one point, before they finally gave up. So I took another crack at it and had it fixed inside of two hours. Boy, what a bunch of chowderheads. They've been in the Navy three times as long as I have, and they probably couldn't even change a fuse without consulting the manual.

The cook got early liberty this afternoon, and rather than face utter starvation, I threw together a gallon of Hungarian goulash for the crew. As a matter of fact, the guys are feeding their faces on it right now…and it's almost gone, too! I get a lot of compliments on my cooking. I live for compliments. But there's always some joker who reaches for the salt or the catsup before he even tastes it! Oh the urge to kill…

This time we're on the line for good. (Where have I heard that before?) We've been chugging for a couple of weeks now, with no major malfunctions in machinery to speak of. Oh yes, we have our little trying moments – like when the engines suddenly run away while we're making up to a ship at ten knots – but it's all in a day's work.

Yesterday a strong wind caught us and put us under a helicopter carrier's fantail at about a 25-degree list, and we were almost in their screws! When the wind takes you, all you can do is hang on and go with it! When we tipped that far over, our table on the fantail slid clear across the deck, smacking against the gunwales and dumping everything on it into the bay: my Scrabble game, dictionary, some coffee cups, a loaf of bread, and the best damn crescent wrench I ever owned! Oh brother! I had my eyes peeled on the nearest life-ring, that's for sure. Afterwards we went down into the crew's compartment and picked up our lockers off the deck.

When you stop and think about it, I guess there's really never a dull moment around here, is there? Maybe we've just become used to a lot of weird things happening, huh? Only the day before last, a merchant tanker called the *Loma Victory* ran aground off Leyte Pier. Boy, when a captain pulls a boner like that in broad daylight, in shallow water where he isn't even supposed to be in the first place, he must feel like a real jackass. Three tugs pushed and pulled on that old rust bucket for an hour before we finally broke the suction in the mud and dragged her clear. That's an hour of our liberty time that he screwed up! Little things like that seem to pop up every other day or so.

Hey, I just noticed about a dozen candy canes hanging from the electrical cables on the overhead! I wonder who Santa's helper is?

THE CLINOMETER

My ever-faithful friend, Daniel Webster, defines "clinometer" as a device used to determine degrees of angular inclination. Just so.

The different types of practical clinometers, from simple to elaborately intricate and expensive, are extremely profuse. A typical clinometer may appear as a half-moon (belly at the bottom) steel plate marked at regular intervals along the curvature with degrees. A weighted needle free-hangs from the compass point of this semicircle. It always responds to gravity, and as the clinometer scale moves fixedly with the vessel, the exact degree of list could be easily ascertained.

Another common clinometer is represented as a partial arc (belly at the top this time) with respective graduated markings. The arc is in the form of a curved, sealed glass tube incompletely filled with liquid and containing a single bubble of air. The liquid is usually yellow-colored ethanol, which is used because of its low freezing point, -114 degrees Celcius. The bubble of air, following the laws of nature, will strive to remain at the zenith (or meniscus) of this tube at all times, much like a carpenter's level. Thus, as the ship heels over left or right, the floating bubble will accurately denote the degrees of list, also.

Our small harbor tugboat did not own a regulation Navy clinometer – it having been carried away a year before in the Great Water Fight of 1969 between the snipes and the deckapes. But I digress.

As we grew more unsettled while walking about the tug and not having the vaguest idea of whether the imagined list was the boat's, or our own from the previous night of carousing out in town, typical sailor improvisation took its natural course.

Our scuttlebutt was located almost directly on the center line of the boat, amidships. When resting on an even keel, the jet of water rose from the bubbler guard of the drinking fountain in a graceful fluid arc and fell about five inches down onto the anti-splash rib of the basin.

If we were ever in doubt of whose list we were laboring under, we simply depressed the push button of the water fountain and noted where the stream landed. Landing to the left or right of the anti-splash rib meant either a port or starboard list, respectively. As to the actual degree of the list, any decent swab with a half-trained eye could stand on the fantail, looking forward towards the horizon, and just approximate close enough.

December 10, 1969

Dear Gramma,

We worked until dark last night and believe me it's pretty nice to sit in the bay breeze and watch the lights of Subic as we cruise around the harbor. For some reason it makes me feel good inside. And when you have a tight crew with a bunch of great, fun-loving guys it's going to be mighty hard to leave them all behind. I think I'm fortunate to be able to have a good time no matter what kind of work I'm doing.

This year we're going to try something new. Last year on Christmas we were duty-boat and had to work almost all night long. Everybody was tired and grumpy and irritable after that. Well, there's no guarantee that we won't have duty-boat again this year, but we're going to try and make the best of it if we do. I got the guys to go along with drawing names out of a hat and buying small gifts for each other; maybe a gag gift or something to cheer us up with some laughs. They're all excited about it now. I got one of the snipe's names who never takes a shower; maybe he could use an industrial-strength can of Right Guard?

Today I put up a string of colored Christmas lights around the pilot house and smokestack. They're the kind that blink in sequence. It sure looks sharp when we chug around the harbor. So far Port Control hasn't said anything about our non-regulation lighting, so I guess it's alright with management, as they haven't kicked us out of the harbor yet. Overhaul and I bought a real live pine tree from the Navy exchange! It's a four-foot Scotch pine which only cost us $1.50. We transplanted it into the crew's compartment.

I got up the other night for a drink of water and found the security watch asleep on a pile of line. So I walked around the nest in my skivvies, checking out the situation, and I found about an inch of water in the YTM-421's crew compartment! I could just see somebody getting up in the morning and stepping out of bed into knee-deep water. The watch had been taking on fresh water and had forgotten to close the valve when the tank was full. So I woke him up, chewed him out, and started him bailing water before I went back to bed. As a petty officer, I could have put him on report for several offenses, had I chosen that route.

I finished reading "The Generation Gap" pamphlet that you sent me. I thought it was very intelligently written, for a religious article. At least they tried to present the pros and cons of the topic. I enjoyed it, and when I finished I gave it to "Preacher" Williams. He's one of the enginemen off the YTM-188 who's always preaching at us and carrying around a New Testament in the back pocket of his dungarees. Most of us have very little tolerance for dedicated bible-beaters. He ought to enjoy the article, though. Thanks.

Well, it's starting to get light out now and it's almost time to make my hourly rounds. Then I'll wake up Benton so he and I can light off the engines in preparation for the day's work. I love the smell of diesel in the morning. The Stewburner just came on board with a watermelon! How much do you want to bet he's going to call that breakfast, too? I can see it's going to be one of those days…

December 16, 1969

Dear Family,

A weekend is a terrible thing to waste. Tonight is the division's Christmas party, but several of us are not going. Party – pshaw! It's more like a division brawl. It's a hassle from the word "go." I can't stand to even be in the same room as some of those officers. Plus, we would have to be all squared away in our whites the whole time. No. Thank. You.

At present we are moored across Alava Wharf from the tender *Delta*. The *Delta* is the first ship to tie up at the new $1 million Alava Wharf extension. The 600-foot dock extension, completed in late October, will provide docking space for 5 to 10 extra ships.

Every day for a week sailors from the *Delta* came on board our tug and did jobs that we couldn't get done at our own division shops, due to lack of equipment and money. They're going to put screens on all the portholes (our latest attempt to stymie those wretched Filipino flies), and weld braces and install additional ventilation down in the Hole. That sort of thing. Right now we're only about five blocks from town, instead of five miles, which comes in handy. Too handy! Tomorrow is payday and we've got early liberty! What could be sweeter?

One of our deckapes got a huge fruit cake in the mail from his grandmother. She had preserved it with a whole bottle of brandy and a whole bottle of bourbon! Gads! All the walnuts had soaked up the brandy and the pineapple chunks had soaked up the bourbon. I couldn't eat very much of it, even with a Coke chaser. We sure did have the holiday spirit afterwards, though. I like fruit cake, but I wasn't hardly old enough to eat this one!

Some guys have their buddies back in the States send them whiskey in Listerine mouthwash bottles, so they can have a little "cheer" while they work, and nobody is the wiser as it looks just like Listerine. I'll bet a Corpsman would be surprised at our avid quest for oral hygiene, though! ("Hey, c'mon Larry, lemmee have some more of yer mouthwash!") Never a dull moment.

We saw a movie the other night called "Eva," which was originally meant to be a dirty movie, I think. Of course, beforehand they just advertised the raw scenes, to draw more people into the theater. But I went to see it because it started off with a baby being born. I had never seen such a thing before, and I was mighty curious about it. I must say that it left me with quite a lasting impression – actually speechless.

I'm having some clothes made by Mike-the-Tailor. They're specially tailored to fit my unusual form, and the design is my own. It's so darn cheap, and the old Filipino exhibits very good workmanship, too. I'm having him make dungarees, civilian trousers, shirts, and some tight thirteen-button dress-blue bell bottoms.

They've had some pretty disgusting accounts of the My Lai massacre in *The Detroit News*. You stop and try to think how such things can actually happen, but then you realize you won't really know unless you were there. Of course, a lot of the newspaper accounts differ, and you can't really be sure who is telling the real story. People ask: how could young American men, fresh out of high school or college, pump slugs into old men, women and children? They apparently didn't know either..."It had to be done...I was ordered to...it was either shoot or be shot... they was nothing but gooks anyway..."

At first the South Vietnamese government issued a statement saying that no massacre even took place! I knew a Seabee a couple months back who had just returned from Vietnam. He was a gunner on a patrol boat, and he said that a lot of that kind of stuff goes on. They would stop fishing boats and sampans and tell some woman that her papers were no good. Rather than run her into the authorities, they offered her a "reasonable alternative." And while her husband watched, she had to give herself to the sailor. Don't know how much of that is true, though.

I've read that this sort of thing went on all the time during World War II as well. But I don't think it's the war that is the cause of it all. A person has got to be slightly twisted to begin with – the war just brings it to the surface and shows his true base nature. And if the person has any kind of morality or decent upbringing or humanity left within him, he may come out of it a better man, sadder but wiser. Even I can see the stupidity and horror and absolute sin of war and its senseless slaughter of innocents.

Our chief engineer is a big crybaby – a 24-year-old crybaby! He has neither willpower, common sense, nor the capacity of happiness in simple things. He is drunk all damn day every day (I am not exaggerating about this), and he has proven time and time again what manner of fool he is. His trouble is that he doesn't even care!

The drunker he gets, the more he fishes around for pity: "I don't know why I get drunk, Steve! I just can't help it! I ain't no good and I know the guys all laugh at me. You run this boat, Steve, you know that. You're doing your job, plus mine! The guys like you, and you get the work done with them. If it wasn't for you, they would've had my stripes a long time ago – I'm so incompetent!" Cry, cry, cry, and so on. Right now he's passed out in his stateroom cradling a bottle of vodka. Somebody should take a picture. Oh well, he's making his own bed; he can't get away with this forever. You really have to pity weak people like that.

Our black craftmaster is probably a confirmed alcoholic as well – but a damn good skipper when he's dry. A couple days ago we had to ride the boat after he had been drinking. I'll bet we hit every obstacle in the harbor! He rammed a gasoline barge and the Joes on it ran for their lives. Then he backed into some pusher-boats and cracked our rudder, which promptly filled up with sea water. Next he yells at me because the boat is steering kind of funny. I yelled right back. He bumped into a minesweeper – minesweepers are wooden and tugs are steel – so now they've got a nice hole in their hull. And at one time or another during the course of the day he had us all on report for insubordination, mutiny, disrespect, disobeying a direct order, being a junkie and a communist and a KKK, and anything else he could dream up in his alcoholic logic. A regular Captain Queeg. But he's making his own bed, too, and his day in the spotlight will come.

We all packed up and went to the Olongapo Festival the other night. It was the first carnival I've been to since I left the World behind. It was, uh, very different, but we all had a good time. They had so many strange midway rides (just simple contraptions of steel and wood that the local natives got such fun out of anyway), as well as games and sideshows. And everything was so darn cheap! That was the best part.

We played a roulette-style game and, for the second time in my life, I actually won something at the fair! I gave the Teddy bear to some tiny Filipino girl, who was ecstatic. I won a couple hundred sticks of chewing gum at the BB-gun range, which was promptly devoured by a herd of urchins that had taken to following us around. There were dozens of those little rug-rats, with their pockets and mouths bulging with gum, but still hollering, "Hey sailor, gimmee gum!"

Benton and I rode most of the midway rides, which did nothing but make us hungry and thirsty. And the vendors don't peddle simple stuff like peanuts or popcorn or hot dogs. Oh no; they sell mangoes, hard-boiled eggs, baluts, monkey meat on a stick, bananas on a stick, and fried squid on a stick – which really isn't all that bad! Every booth sold San Miguel beer, too. But they didn't have a bathroom in the whole place that we could find, and we almost lost our...minds.

We tossed the rings for a while and managed to loop a few drinking glasses, which we could put to good use back on the boat. (The "girls" who worked in that particular booth turned out not to be girls after all, when we looked a little closer; they were Benny Boys! Cripes.) We took in one girlie show and then finished off the evening with a variety show.

The first attraction was some little kids doing acrobatics. It was very late at night and they looked like all they wanted to do was crawl off somewhere and sleep. They went through their routine in listless motions, bordering on exhaustion. Besides, somebody had painted them up like pathetic little mannequins. I just don't go for that sort of thing.

They were followed by a sleight-of-hand artist and a prestidigitator. They put on a cool magic show that I still don't believe I witnessed! A man cut off a lady's head and made another girl float in midair. I know it was all a trick, but I was sitting in the very front row watching for wires and gimmicks, and it sure looked real to me!

Well, I've got some stale bread and a big stick, and I'm going to see if I can't bag me a couple of wharf rats tonight. They're worse over here at Alava than they are back in Boton Valley. God, how I hate rats!

December 26, 1969

Dear Family,

Due to an utter dearth of writing paper, I believe I shall use this page out of the ship's logbook, which is probably a court-martial offense, no doubt. Everything else seems to be. I received your package of goodies right on Christmas Eve – what perfect timing! – and everyone stuffed his face. The ginger snaps sure hit the spot with a cup of strong Navy coffee. The treats were all gone by nightfall, though. Many, many thanks!

Well, guess which tugboat had to work all night on Christmas Eve again? You guessed it: the 182. We had smuggled a bottle of "cheer" on board in case of this eventuality (it was the chief engineer's gift to the Stewburner, actually), so we didn't mind it all that much. We were so tired by Christmas Day that we slept most of the afternoon away. By the time we were all up and about, we decided to open our presents. The 182 is the only boat in Service Craft with a Christmas tree; what a bunch of Scrooges around here.

Anyway, we got a sampling of gag gifts for each other. I received a crazy pink sport shirt with purple stripes (that I soon grew quite fond of). I bought a monkey bank – not a piggy bank – for one of the snipes. (We call the girls down here "monkeys," so it's sort of an inside joke.) Porter, our resident cowboy from Louisiana, got a big straw sombrero and a tin sheriff's badge. Overhaul got an outrageous tie, which we could hardly get off of him later; he wore it everywhere! Bobby got a wooden hand carved out of monkey pod showing the Universal Sign of Ultimate Scorn. He loved it, of course.

Benton got a pair of trousers back that he had sold to Porter earlier on. Larry got fifty boxes of matches, as he's always bumming a light off somebody. The cook got a bottle of vodka, which he shared with the rest of us; Scotty got a case of Budweiser; Washington got a bottle of pills (for his social disease); and the houseboy Ernie got a cigarette lighter with something nasty in Tagalog engraved on it. We all had a lot of laughs. Benton even put up one of his smelly old socks with a note pinned to it reading,

> *"Dear Santa,*
> *I've been a pretty good boy.*
> *~Benton (bottom rack, port side, aft)"*

And Porter stuffed it full of toilet paper and peanut shells while he was on watch! Ha!

I got a brainstorm and we all went out to eat at the swankiest place in Olongapo, Nina Papagayos. We ate in the Roman Room under a painting of the Forum, where we dined upon: zuppe, ravioli, bread sticks, an anchovy-tuna-olive salad, hot cross buns, all the fresh Parmesan cheese in the world, and a twenty-five-peso bottle of imported Chianti wine (ca. 1955).

I picked up the tab for the wine as my treat. And I almost fainted when they brought the wine and asked me if I would care to taste it first before they poured around! It was really a feast! Every time somebody reached for a cigarette, a waiter materialized with a light – *Voila!* Goodness, such class. And in a town like this! All in all, the sumptuous repast set us back over 100 pesos, and we went away fat and sleepy and well contented with the world.

I got some new spectacles this week. Finally fed up with those miserable black plastic Navy glasses which hurt my nose and ears, and made me look like a trunk murderer anyway, I got a new pair made out in town at Acebido Optical. They came to only about seventy-five pesos – you can't beat that! They're perfectly round, with gold wire-rims, like Beatles glasses. I'm just now getting used to them. The boys think they look pretty cool on me, but the division officer, Mister Tactful, said they make me look "...crazy as a loon."

Well, our regular craftmaster went home on Christmas leave, so we got a new guy who is awfully green on tugboats. They had us moving big barges and cranes yesterday, and wouldn't you know the wind was blowing like a son of a gun! That's the last thing we needed with a greenhorn at the wheel. First of all, we ran aground right on top of a huge electrical cable that was submerged and clearly marked with a large sign warning us to keep away; I thought for sure that we had had it then!

Later, while approaching the famous bird farm, *USS Constellation* (CV-64), the wind caught us again and we went head-on into a cement pier. It smashed a few things on the crane we were hauling and snapped a bunch of cables. The crane's hook broke loose and was swinging around wildly like a demolitionist's wrecking ball. Luckily it didn't hit anything.

Then the wind swung us sideways and caught a pusher-boat between the crane and the pier. It shoved that old pusher-boat up high and dry on the sea wall and bent up its screws, while its poor crew hung on for dear life with a look of sheer terror on their faces. And all this time the sailors on the "Connie" were watching us from the railing and laughing their asses off. Boy, did we feel like complete fools then! I don't know how much total damage was done yesterday, but today we got a new craftmaster. Never a dull moment.

Wilt, who is at college at this writing, sent me a keen T-shirt that had "South Dakota State University" emblazoned on it. The first night I wore it out in town I was stopped by three different sailors from Aberdeen, Belle Fourche, and Armour! Talk about your small world. That was a thoughtful gift, huh?

They've got a big carnival here on base next Sunday (guess who has to work), and the American Legion is planning a New Year's Eve bash (guess who has to work). One of our guys is getting married to a Filipino girl on January 15th, and wanted me as best man; he was disappointed to hear that I was leaving for the States on the 14th. Such is life.

There's still no definite word about my leave yet. It looks like I'll have to make my own way home from pillar to post, from milkstop to milestone. You may not hear from me again until I walk in the door! I had to laugh out loud when you said you didn't see how they could send me to Nam without a leave first. Ha! The Navy can do anything it wants to, and doesn't have to justify it to anyone.

Thanks for sending more pictures of the family. Everybody looks at the pictures of the little girls and then at me and asks, "So what happened to you?" I get no respect. Write soon. Belay that last – your letter probably wouldn't reach me before I left for home anyway.

December 30, 1969

Dear Gramma,

It's perfectly shameful how long I can put off writing letters the way I do sometimes. But this last month has been unbelievably busy for me. Preparations for leaving a year and a half of tugboat life behind are not easy. As the day of departure draws nearer, I grow more reluctant to leave all of this. Sure, over the past months I griped half-heartedly at this mean environment in some of my letters, but I wasn't fooling anybody but myself. The only consolation I have is that I am supposed to be back here several times in the near future to see all of my old friends. Now I can leave much easier with a lighter heart. At least I know I'm still half human inside when it hurts so much to part company with comrades.

Only today have I finally received all the information concerning my upcoming leave. I have wrangled a flight to the States (via Anchorage, Alaska), and from California I will have to take a commercial flight to Omaha. I will stay overnight with Amy and John there, before taking the bus north to Mitchell. I completely check out of here on January 12th, and as of 1200 on January 13th I am a free man for a month!

That afternoon, my buddies and I will take a Special Service's rental car to Clark AFB where they will say their "so longs" – not goodbyes. At 0800 on the morning of the 14th I will have a big, beautiful silver bird carrying me homeward bound. At first I thought money would be a big problem – or the lack of it, to be more precise. But now they're going to advance me $600 out of my paychecks for the flight home. I am excited already!

We've really got a tight crew now, all ten of us – Negro, Filipino, American Indian, and Caucasian. Benton made third-class Engineman today, so we will be throwing him over the side shortly. This morning I was supposed to take my Military Leadership test along with two of the deckapes, but someone (who drinks a lot on the job) messed up and lost *all three* of our recommendations again (this has happened twice now), and so we couldn't even take the test. Grrrr! This is beginning to look like a plot. The man is a total incompetent!

And how are you weathering the fierce South Dakota winters there in your stout farmhouse in Lake County? It seems to me that grand old house of yours is quite snug and dry and cozy no matter what's going on outside. Someday I would like to live in a house just like yours, with a small acreage and maybe a few out-buildings, and a garden where I could grow as contented as my beans. A house with fine old hardwood in it and a hundred memories in every room – a serene, pastoral view of country and more country beyond that, and a few independent cats loafing around. I've always loved the rural life, and I didn't realize until lately just how little I like living in an urban area.

I hope there's all the snow in the world waiting for me when I get home on leave! I realize it's no picnic for the daddies who have to clear the walks and drive-ways and get stuck in the snow, though. That reminds me: I've always wondered how the men who drive the snowplows get to work? Hmmmm. I hope to see you all in a couple of weeks.

December 31, 1969

I kept a running total of all the San Miguel beer that I drank during the year of 1969. This came to a grand total of 1,075 beers (a high of 146 during the month of March in the middle of the hot season, with a low of 38 beers during July in the rainy season). This averaged out to be about three beers a day. At an average of twenty-five cents per beer, this came to a total cost of around $269 for the calendar year. My liquor bill was about half again as much.

IV.
MARE ISLAND CALIFORNIA

12 FEBRUARY 1970 – 10 MARCH 1970

EM3 Steve Stanga B617389
Code 810
San Francisco Bay Naval Shipyard
Vallejo, California
94592

February 18, 1970

Dear Family,

Pray for your son. If I do not go completely berserk in the last two weeks that I have left here, it will indeed be a miracle. This Mare Island place is so barren and bleak that you absolutely wouldn't believe it. A large mothball fleet is moored here, and it's really a SNAFU. There is nothing of interest to do here and at first I thought I would surely perish from boredom. But I resolved to make the best of it.

I just want to say that I really enjoyed my leave at home, even though it went by awfully fast. The weather was perfect – I even enjoyed the snowstorms! The little kids haven't changed at all, only gotten more adorable. Timmy sure has gotten a somewhat spunky spirit, huh? Probably from dealing with three sisters.

I was surprised that I didn't catch a cold or something, with the drastic change in climate from the steamy Philippines to the tundra of South Dakota. I had come home to relax and slow the pace down for a while, and that is exactly what I did. I hope the next 17 months go by fast, so I can be home with you all once again. But I guess there are better things to do with time other than try to speed its passage.

Coming back from leave, I got a noon flight out of Omaha, so that I could sleep in late at Amy and John's. I had a real good flight with some marvelous chow. I had a window seat and I got to see just about everything, as we had fair weather and clear visibility. You'd think I'd be tired of seeing that same old stuff as many times as I've been over it, but no.

At Travis AFB I was told that I could have stayed at home for two more days. Rats! I really hated to leave as it was. To get down to my temporary duty station at Mare Island in Vallejo I had to secure a private chauffeur, because I couldn't locate any other mode of transportation. That cost me a healthy twenty-five dollars, the racketeer!

My room is the worst part of this miserable "hotel" existence; I am sick and tired of living out of my sea bag. There is nothing to look at on the walls, and the ceilings are a good twenty feet high. We have no pillowcases on our pillows, and only one lone, unfinished table. More like a cell, I'd say. There is no radio, and the icebox in the room needs defrosting and smells bad. There cannot be anything more melancholy than an empty reefer. All you can hear are the radiators knocking, and sometimes you positively have to get out of the room or go bughouse.

So I am here at this poor excuse for a base library, where I accidentally ran across a stray typewriter. It sure is making a nasty, clacking noise in this vast, drafty hall, though. Most of this week has been rainy, gloomy and totally depressing, but today the sun is out hot and strong.

People are constantly checking in and out of here like Grand Central Station. Soon there were six of us in our cell, who all seem to be regular sports. Together, we try and safeguard each other's sanity while we await transport to our ultimate destinations. One of the men pantomimes that he has a traveling flea circus with him, which is quite comical to observe. I guess you have to be there.

One of the guys has a little German car, so we buzzed down to Frisco last weekend to knock around a bit. We saw the long-awaited hippie freaks at Berkley, and viewed "Paint Your Wagon" at a Cinerama in Oakwood. Terrific show – don't miss it!

Frisco is really a remarkable city; everything is on such a huge and grand scale. The skyscrapers still fascinate me, but I think it's gotten much too big for real people to live in, though. We stopped at the USO Club there. I taught the guys how to play Probe, and they thought that it was possibly the most enjoyable table game they've ever seen.

All we are doing around here are rotten, Mickey Mouse work details. It wouldn't be so bad if we were actually doing something constructive with our time. But we tear masking tape off the windows and scrape paint spots off the floor, and clean the heads and stand around with our fingers in our…ears. After boot camp, I vowed I was never going to clean another dang toilet, and here I am doing it all over again.

Today they had us doing some actual work, though; we were painting the overhead and bulkheads of some barracks. We discovered the TV lounge right down the corridor from our cell, and the base theater is right across the street. So things are looking up a little.

There is no curfew here, and you don't even have to show your ID to get out the gate. We have three-day weekends and every noon-hour and evening off. We have no duty or watches to stand while we're here, and we are paid an extra dollar a day just for being stuck here for a month. So what am I complaining about, eh?!

Since I've been down here I've been keeping myself very occupied and not allowing myself to get too bored. I've given a lot of thought to applying for "Operation Deepfreeze" down in Antarctica. And if I am going to spend two years minimum down there, then I'd better be able to cope with lots of leisure time.

I've been reading paperbacks left and right, and just today I got ahold of another book by Rachel Carson. I have even managed to write a few stories in the solitude of my cell while the rest of the guys were gone, all about some of my more memorable Navy experiences.

The Navy is a small world. I've already run into a guy that used to be in Service Craft down in the P.I., and a guy that I went to "A" school with in Dago. And this one clown in our cell, Fireman Frank, knows a lot of guys that I do from my old tug! Every single one of the guys here has been in Subic Bay at one time or another, so we have a lot to bat the breeze about. The Navy really is a small world. (Repeated for effect.)

I'm being conservative since I've been here; I maybe spend a quarter a day. (I almost said peso.) Imagine that. It's probably because there's nothing to do here. But I just found out that we can have beer up in our cell and keep it cold in the reefer. There goes my last hope for clean living.

Well, that's about all the news from my end of the tunnel. Maybe you can still get a letter off to me before I leave here on the 10th of March? The rest of my mail will eventually catch up with me at my next duty station anyway. Movie call is fixing to go down, and I don't want to miss "Goodbye Columbus," so I will sign off here.

As always, more or less, Steve

P.S. I wish you could have seen the sunset tonight. I didn't think it was possible that a sunset could look beautiful over mud flats, tin sheds and telephone poles, but it sure was!

February 21, 1970

Dear Family,

Greetings! It's turning out to be an extra long and leisurely holiday weekend for a change. We worked overtime painting on Thursday, so they gave us most of Friday off. Monday, being President's Day or something, I believe, is also a holiday and so we don't have to work then either.

This payday turned out to be nothing less than a joyous occasion. For some unknown reason I received a grand total of $300...$200 of which I want you to put in the bank for me. I withheld enough money for a cassette tape of the "Paint Your Wagon" soundtrack, and a sketch pad and pencil.

I've taken your advice, Dad, about sketching things around me wherever I go, and it's a good way as any to pass the time. As you can see, this letter is profusely illustrated. The picture on this page is what I can see out the back window of the library. Pretty dreary, huh?

I am presently fighting off a tremendous head cold and runny faucet-nose. You might know – I spend almost a month at home in the dead of winter, and then I come out here to golden California and catch a friggin' cold! And a handsome cold sore on my lip, to boot.

I sometimes find it hard to sleep, so I sit up in the TV lounge with the other insomniacs and watch the late, late shows. We really got a kick out of Pat Paulsen the other night; I know he's got my vote for President!

I wrote a letter to the Christian Children's Fund, Inc. in Richmond, Virginia, and requested information. I saw their ad on TV and decided to look into it. It's an organization that sponsors some needy child somewhere in the third world through me and my small monthly donations. It will provide the child with clothes, extra food, medicine and school supplies, and stuff like that. I told them I would be interested in sponsoring an 18-year-old Filipino girl – just kidding, folks! Ha ha

True story: Four guys were going to Vietnam together. Each one of them bequeathed a third of his $10,000 serviceman's group life insurance to each of his three companions. In case one of them should die, then the rest of his buddies would come back from the war with a little spending money. Should two of them be killed, then both of their policies would be split evenly between the two survivors. Sort of like a tontine, where the remaining subscribers would collect more and more as each subscriber died off. Should three of the buddies be killed, god forbid, then the lone survivor would inherit the whole of $30,000 to start out his civilian life. What next?

Tomorrow we will be going for an excursion down to Frisco and/or Oakland. The weather has been absolutely ideal and we all have got money burning a hole in our pockets, I guess. Anyway, we were thinking about seeing that Ripley's Be-lieve-It-Or-Not Museum down at Fisherman's Wharf for starters.

One of the fellas in our cell has a girlfriend down in Oakland. She is an Eskimo and lives with another girl who is a full-blooded Canadian Indian of some sort. The Eskimo girl is as fat as fat can be, with little black hazel nuts for eyes – but a nicer personality you couldn't hope for! (Besides, she's probably skinny way down deep inside, next to her bones.) She swears she was clubbing seals and harpooning whales by the age of 11, but she had never seen a polar bear where she was from, which was around Kodiak, Alaska.

Well, as usual I time my letters to finish just about the time the flick is going to start. Tonight's feature presentation is "A Man For All Seasons," an Academy-award winner that I have already seen four times, and would hope to see four more times. What an excellent film!

I sure am getting tired of wearing my dress blue uniform every day after work-ing hours, but it's the only way you can go anyplace around here. I haven't seen a newspaper or heard the news since I got out here, so I don't have the foggiest idea of the *status quo* of world affairs. Sometimes I kind of like it that way, though. How's the weather back home? Are you stravaging along in another winter bliz-zard, or has spring come early to Dakota this year? Not likely, eh?

February 25, 1970

Dear Family,

Earlier I fell asleep in the TV room watching Tarzan and I just about didn't make it over to the library tonight to type this letter. Well, it's been two weeks since I left home and it already seems like two months. I was kind of looking for some mail today, but then again, I don't have any idea how long mail takes to get forwarded here through the Navy postal system.

Do you know the way to San Jose? We do! Us four adventurers all piled into Jim's little Opel automobile and struck out in an easterly direction. (This is the same new car in which I threw up a sweet dessert wine, Chateau Lasalle, all over the back seat one night. I scrubbed it up the best I could, but you can about imag-ine the aroma inside the car on a warm day.) We had full intentions of going to Yosemite National Park to see the big redwoods and the dramatic mountains, but we never quite made it. All the way we were having steering control issues; the car would shimmy something awful at a certain speed.

And so, about fifty miles short of Yosemite (we had traveled all damn day, too!), we decided to turn back while we still could. But I don't think that any of us were too terribly disappointed, because we got to see a lot of beautiful country along the way just the same. It was a nice road trip. We took turns driving, and I was almost a nervous wreck by the time I got off the freeway.

That same weekend we went down to Oakland and saw "Butch Cassidy and the Sundance Kid" starring Robert Redford and Paul Newman, which we had all wanted to see for quite some time now. And believe you me, it was well worth the drive!

Later that same day we picked up the Eskimo and her Indian friend and took them to see "The Magic Christian" starring Peter Sellers and Ringo Starr. It was a very funny show and I'm glad I went. Movies are your best entertainment.

Yesterday we drove down to Berkeley for some more good movies to see while we still had the cash. As you know, Berkeley is a campus town and is just crawling with hippie types. In the space of one city block we counted no less than 27 hitchhikers, and they were mostly girls. Walking along the sidewalk, we were constantly assaulted with: "Can you spare any loose change for something to eat, buddy?"… "Pot? Hashish? Bennies?"…"You looking for a girl, sailor?" Boy, what a disgusting town! It was worse than Olongapo City.

We finally found a movie that we all wanted to see, but the theater was a major disappointment. It was a hole-in-the-wall pigsty with hard, wooden folding chairs for seats, and a by-god actual king-sized bed sheet for a screen! But the price was right. We saw the old classic, "War of the Worlds," for just fifty cents a head.

I guess you get what you pay for, though. One person sitting about a dozen rows ahead of me had such a monstrous Afro hairdo that I could hardly see past him/her. And being that the unisex toilet was immediately beside the screen, it was sort of distracting whenever anybody flipped on the light to go in and out – or flushed the john – which they seemed to be doing a lot of, for a theater that didn't sell any refreshments.

Afterwards we looked for a place to eat, and Jimbo suggested a Straw Hat restaurant. Now, I had never eaten at a Straw Hat before, so I didn't know what to expect. But it was a fun place with huge, thick, wooden tables, candles and beer kegs. We ate pizza and drank dark lager beer imported from Finland while we watched a silent Harry Langdon movie (on a proper screen, no less).

I think we had our best time that night right there in that marvelous place. After the comedy had concluded, they turned on the player piano and passed out the salted peanuts. The atmosphere was indescribably fun! We're going to try to go back there sometime soon.

Oh, I don't think that I mentioned that there are a couple of AWOL guys staying with Jim's friends down in Oakland. One ran away from the Army, and the other is a medic who ran away from the Navy. They're a couple of real creeps, and a bigger pair of whiners I've never seen. Jim is thinking about turning them in to authorities. There's a fifty-dollar-reward on the GI, but the bounty on a medic is worth quite a bit more. I say more power to Jim; anyway, he needs the money.

For some mysterious reason they've put me in charge of an eight-man working party here. Now I'm so busy just seeing that everyone else has something to do that I don't do much of anything but run around and baby-sit. It's kind of nice flexing my third-class stripes for a change, though. Rank has its privileges. And when our bosses aren't watching, we even manage to sneak in a few games of Hearts or Spades.

Just today we went over to the commissary and restocked our reefer with three cases of pop, four loaves of bread, bologna, cheese, lettuce, mustard, salad dressing, olives, chips 'n' dip, etc. We hardly even go down to the galley to eat anymore, mainly because it's a lot more enjoyable to eat while we're watching TV in the barracks.

My cold has gone away, but the attractive cold sore still lingers on. And to tell the truth, that new shampoo doesn't seem to be doing much of anything for my dandruff but irritating the hell out of my scalp. Maybe I'll go over to the dispensary for something that really works. My fingers are peeling, though, because we get to swab the floors almost constantly.

I can't think of anything else to add right now. I probably will as soon as I seal the envelope, though. I think the guys have got a heated Hearts game going in our cell, and I want to get in on the next hand. I'm pretty good at cards, I'm pleased to say. That's just one more skill that I learned in the Navy!

March 8, 1970

Dear Family,

Well, I finally got my Port Call and will be leaving Travis AFB on the morning of the 11th. It's a beautiful day out here today; the sun is coming down through the library windows and it really feels good across the back of my shoulders. Both of my hands are raw and chapped on account of all the painting we do and the paint thinner we use to clean our hands. I think they're going to be permanently green. When I get out of this Canoe Club I am just going to quit shaving altogether, too. I hate it that much! Who started this barbaric ritual anyway?

Holy cow, one of the guys in our cell is going to be on the same ship as I am! His name is DeGroot and he is a Boatswain's Mate. As for myself, I was pretty tickled to meet somebody that was going to be a future shipmate, but he took the news with as much enthusiasm as a wet chicken.

He tells me that he heard scuttlebutt that our ship is going to be decommissioned! What a bummer if this is true! I don't want to be on a ship that is off the line – I've had enough of that crap in Subic – I want to be on a ship that sees some action! But I seriously doubt if this rumor is true; why would they assign new men to a ship being taken off the line anyway? Seriously now. If it is true, then I'm going to do my level best to get an immediate transfer. Just that short period of overhaul on my tug was enough to drive me near crazy.

The chief called us down to the MAA shack last night and we all thought he was going to chew our asses for something or other, although we couldn't imagine what it might be. But all he wanted to do was explain why us guys were sent here to Mare Island for a month in the first place. Most of us assumed that we were simply here awaiting convenient flights to our next distant duty stations.

But he explained that we were assigned temporary duty here, working and such, to pay for a plane ride that we had already received. Ahhh. The Navy didn't fly us all home for leave out of the goodness of its heart, he said, but because us overseas guys deserved a break. (We were coming from an overseas duty station and going to another overseas duty station, and by all rights we should have paid for our own flight back to the States for leave.)

So here we are at MI to pay back the free ride home that we all got. Turns out they had us pay it back in the form of labor instead of out of our future paychecks. That's reasonable, I guess. I wasn't looking forward to paying back that expensive plane ride anyway. I was impressed that the chief even bothered to explain the situation to us; most wouldn't have taken the time.

We were getting ready to go out on the town the other night and I was lending the guys some of my bay rum cologne. This one clown dabs a little daintily behind each ear – and then takes a healthy swig of the cologne! I guess he was trying to be funny, like one of the Three Stooges. But he instantly went screaming down to the scuttlebutt to soak up a bunch of water. He eventually threw up. Ha! What a maroon.

Last weekend we decided to go north to Sacramento instead of south to Oakland to seek fun and/or adventure. We all piled into Jim's little Opel and struck out. In Sacramento, we went through the state capitol building and looked at the exhibits and stuff there. It was all very impressive. We then went on an old riverboat that was moored on the Sacramento River. It was the kind with a big paddlewheel. A couple of the guys got quickly bored with these activities, but that's to be expected.

We drove around the campus of the state college and looked at all the fine buildings and delightful girls, mostly the girls. I finally talked them into going up to Folsum to see the old historical town there and the territorial prison that Johnny Cash always sings about. I think we liked that the best.

At Placerville, we saw some old mines with mills and flumes. It was exactly like the Black Hills there. We drove past vineyards and between miles and miles of orchards and fruit groves. All the blossoms were out in full bloom and the smell alone was enough to make you drunk.

The next day we did go down to Oakland to a party that the Eskimo had planned. As it turned out, I wish we hadn't. There was good news in that one of the deserters had been turned in and taken away by the FBI; somebody else got the reward, though, not us.

The party was very sociable and congenial and all was going well until Mike, the medic who was AWOL from the Navy (and a real live crybaby if ever you saw one), tried to pick a fight with some nice college graduate from the University of Hawaii, a little wiry guy by the name of Chico.

Denny and I took that opportunity to walk down to the corner bodega for some more Chateau Lasalle wine, and when we came back to the house there had already been a big damn fight. The guy from Hawaii was wiping a drop of blood away from his nose and breathing slightly heavy, while Mike was in the head—screaming for some girl to turn him loose or else!

Finally Mike busted loose from her and dashed noisily out of the house – he looked like he had been run over by a Mack truck. Mike was twice as big as the guy he had picked on; I like to see the little scrappy guy come out on top once in a while. We all calmed down and pretty soon the party mood picked up again.

Mike came back later, much to our dismay, and fell on his knees in front of Chico, begging forgiveness, slobbering and making a complete ass out of himself. The guy had no pride whatsoever. And then, before we knew what was actually happening, Mike had pulled a steak knife out of his shirt and stuck it at Chico's throat, who was soon backed up against the wall!

Chico just looked at him coolly and said, "Man, don't do anything that you're gonna regret." Mike was screaming his head off like a madman, with spit flying. At that time Denny and I jumped him from behind, each pinning an arm, and he threw the knife into a corner, and then started bawling some more in earnest. That was when Chico called the cops, and we decided to call it a night and get the hell outa Dodge! I only hope that the authorities finally got a firm grip on that nut case. Okay, it begins to dawn on me that just possibly I am running with the wrong crowd.

We got a new guy in our cell who hails from North Dakota. Him and I are doing a lot of things together now, since the other guys have recently left for their various ships and shore stations – Jim went to the Philippines!

Yesterday we walked out into Vallejo to look for a good place to eat; somebody in town recommended The Golden Bubble. It turned out to be a topless joint, but unfortunately for us it was only noon, and the good-looking waitresses hadn't come on duty yet. Anyway, the North Dakota Kid had a Club steak and I had a New York cut. They sure were tender – the steaks, I mean. Just what we were craving.

After that, we walked quite a few miles around Vallejo to get rid of our stuffed feeling. Compared to San Diego, Vallejo isn't nearly as pretty – or friendly towards sailors. Little kids playing on the sidewalks laughed at us and called us names. One even tried to pound our toes with a hammer as we passed by! We get no respect.

I tried reading "Wuthering Heights" last night, but I guess I just wasn't in the mood to read about people throwing knives at each other, pushing folks off cliffs, and hanging puppies from the backs of kitchen chairs. Maybe I'll tackle it again when I'm older and wiser. I was tired of watching old movies on TV, weary of playing my harmonica, and burned out from losing dumb games of solitaire. So I went to bed early, feeling a little homesick already. I need to get out of here.

March 9, 1970

Dear Gramma,

The chief gave me the day off for working so hard this week, so I thought I'd write one last letter to you before I leave the States. I'll only be here two more days and then I catch a flight to Vietnam to meet my ship. The North Dakota Kid will be stationed in the Philippines, so I can see him whenever my ship pulls in there.

Lately, we've just been painting and cleaning the building in which we stay. We've completely painted out 25 rooms, which is one room per day since we've been here. And the chief says that just our cleaning alone saves the Navy over $1,000 a month from having to hire civilians to do it.

I check out tomorrow, so my working days here are basically over. Somehow I've got to get to Travis AFB by Wednesday morning; they don't provide transportation for us from here to there, which really doesn't seem fair. I mean, after all, the Navy sent me *here* in the first place! The Air Force base is about forty miles away. There is rumor of a shuttle bus available to me, however.

Well, the next time you hear from me will hopefully be from sunny Vietnam, settled in on my new ship. I'm getting kind of anxious to be back in the South Pacific once again.

V. VIETNAM

13 MARCH 1970 — 15 JULY 1970

COMING INTO THE COUNTRY

13 March 1970

I was flying from Clark Air Force Base in the Philippines to Saigon to begin my tour of duty there. I had volunteered for duty in Nam out of a sense of patriotism only secondarily, but primarily for the terrific Battle Pay (also called Combat Pay or Hazardous Duty Pay), which amounted to an extra sixty dollars per month. That was a lot of spending money in those days of low enlisted men's salaries. And besides, my original request for a gunboat off the Gaza Strip in Israel had been denied.

The jet airliner flew high over the clouds where all was deceivingly quiet and clean and peaceful. My first glimpse of South Vietnam was a great, winding ribbon of muddy water through a break in the clouds. It was the mighty Mekong River. The Mekong Delta is so infiltrated with channels of this river that you are tempted to wonder if Vietnam is just a bunch of islands strung together.

Suddenly, everything outside my window disappeared, including the wings of the plane, as we began our steep descent through the thick cloud cover. The US Marine in undress khaki sitting beside me said that we would be making a rather hasty landing at the airport.

"Charlie likes to take potshots at the planes landing here," he enlightened me with a grin.

Yea, even in downtown Saigon! It was a little disconcerting to see the Marine then cross himself and start to pray silently.

Soon the plane nose-dived and we dropped like a stone. About fifty feet above the landing strip we broke out of the clouds into the open air once again and quickly touched down. We went tearing along the dotted line towards the terminal at what seemed like a reckless speed, considering the short distance we had to go.

The terrain that I could see on my side of the plane, coming into the country, was flat and desolate, with just a hint of remote jungle. Here and there old Mercedes trucks sat beside crumbling tin sheds and fuel tanks, and in the misty distance one could see the ghostly shapes of the really big Air Force long-range bombers waiting at the far end of the field, shimmering in the heat, ready for business. I wondered if those meteor-like holes in the ground were really bomb craters? Charred, wrecked planes and twisted jeeps had been just shoved off the runways and left to rust in the medians.

There were sandbags and barbed wire everywhere. A small ramp tractor drove silently by the windows of our plane in the opposite direction, dragging the mangled fuselage of an Army helicopter behind it, and I suddenly remembered where I was. This was a goddam war zone! People got killed dead in places like this!

I told myself, "Well, here's another fine mess you got yourself into, Spud." I was uneasy in a brand-new way for once.

We disembarked into the humid fog clinging to Tan Son Nhut (pronounced "tonn son NEWT") International Airport and were immediately hustled inside the terminal. Strange, but the air didn't smell any different there than, say, the Philippines, and I couldn't hear the ominous thunder of bombing just over the horizon like I had expected.

The interior of the airport was an absolute ruin: peeling plaster left huge open wounds on the walls, and the concrete floor was scored with wide cracks. Everywhere were tiny penny-skinned men and women in flat reed hats – looking not unlike your average Filipino. It was terribly muggy. I noticed we were rarely without the sound of choppers passing overhead.

Inside the terminal, the Vietnamese police took all of our American money away and exchanged it for roll upon roll of miniature paper currency looking exactly like Monopoly money called MPC. There were even paper bills for nickel and dime denominations!)

We were to use MPC whenever we were on military installations, we were told. If we wanted to buy something off the Vietnamese economy, we had to exchange our MPC for piasters. We had to pay piasters to the Vietnamese civilians,

Five-cent MPC.

but MPC to the Vietnamese serving in the military. Vietnamese civilians working on military installations, however, were to be paid in MPC, they explained.

It was all very confusing, especially to a newcomer. And even though the American dollar was the admiration of the world and universally accepted, in Vietnam it was a black-market offense to even carry them around.

They herded us onto a battered bus with bars over the windows and took us across town to the processing center. And thus I got my first look at the ancient city of Saigon. Basically, the living structures and the people didn't look too alien, but there was one major difference. In place of the sidewalks on either side of the downtown streets, there were walls of sandbags, 55-gallon steel drums full of sand, bunkers, guard towers, and a seemingly endless snarl of barbed wire. Soldiers of both colors walked everywhere in the heart of the city, armed with the ever-popular M16 rifle. It was then I realized that here was a country deeply entrenched in real war…and to affirm my cheery thoughts the bus next passed by acres and acres of close-set gravestones.

And what an incredible hullabaloo there was! They say that Saigon is supposed to be the noisiest city in the world. In addition to that dubious honor, it certainly appeared to be also the most crowded. I had never seen so many cars, trucks, buses, taxis, motorcycles, scooters, and bicycles ricocheting down one street before! And all this was accomplished without apparent loss of life. The black-haired, almond-eyed females looked so slim and pretty in their *Ao Dais* [national dresses].

No doubt an air-conditioned bus was a great luxury, but it put us in a sort of refrigerated shell and shut us off completely from the full effect of the city's unique environment. Possibly an open-air bus would have been more appropriate, but then I instantly thought of what security problems that would present. Maybe the sounds and smells of the great Fish Market would have been offensive, but at least it would have given us a tangible atmosphere to grasp and make a more realistic experience that we could relate to years later.

Saigon's population had swelled to approximately three million – mostly North Vietnamese refugees that had fled to the south. Driving along, we saw the huge Saigon Black Market; the Vietnamese Navy yards (containing some of the 1,400 ships that the United States had simply given to them); the many sprawling cemeteries; the Presidential Palace (much more beautiful than our own White House and much more heavily guarded, too); the refugee camps for all the homeless Vietnamese; the Viet Cong interrogation camp; and dozens of elaborate Buddhist temples.

The influence of the retreating French was still visible everywhere: in the shops, the road signs, the architecture, and the low-slung European automobiles reminiscent of World War II.

Our processing camp was in the center of town, right on the border of the twin cities of Saigon-Cholon. From the outside, the headquarters appeared to have once been a grand oriental home, but the years of strife had decidedly taken their toll; I learned that last July the Charlie terrorists had bombed it quite adequately.

The camp, nicknamed the "Annapolis Hotel" by some wit, was surrounded by an eight-foot-tall wall of sandbags. And on each corner of the building sat a heavily fortified bunker with automatic weapons poking out of it. Jeeps, mounted with fifty-calibre machine guns, patrolled constantly.

Inside the camp, our orders were checked and rechecked and we were given detailed orientation about Nam from American clerks in olive drab. We endured long, tedious lectures that tried to impress upon us endless patience for the Vietnamese people who had their own way and speed of doing things. We didn't have to like them, they instructed, just respect them and treat them as our equals. Fat chance of that.

We were briefed on how to operate the M16 assault rifle and riot guns. Billet assignments and meal cards were handed out. A Marine Sergeant informed us that we would be at the Annapolis Hotel for only a few days while we awaited transportation to our ultimate destinations. I was to be a brown-water sailor the whole time that I would be in Nam. That is, I would spend the duration of my stay in-country aboard a supply boat on the Mekong River.

In the meantime, no matter what branch of the service we were attached to, we were all expected to stand security watches at the Annapolis Hotel armed with loaded weapons – mostly .38 and .45 revolvers – in the berthing quarters, in the bunkers, and on the roof. We drew jungle-green fatigues from Small Stores to complete the GI Joe charade.

Every four hours we had to muster together to see if everyone was still with us and had not gone AWOL. Otherwise, our leisure time was our own time. There was absolutely nothing whatsoever to do. Boredom reigned supreme. People were constantly coming and going. Most just read paperbacks and wrote letters and slept. The "hotel" was awfully crowded and enough bunks could not be found for everybody at the moment. So that first night in town I spread my work jacket and slept on the linoleum. There never was a place less like home than Vietnam.

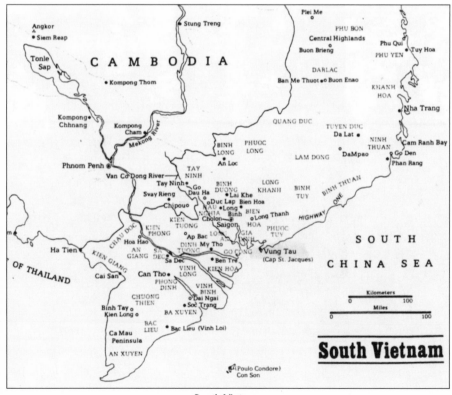

South Vietnam

SAIGON

March 13, 1970

Dear Family,

At present, they aren't exactly sure where my ship is, but when they locate her they will fly me there directly by chopper. I ran into an old electrician buddy whose billet I filled on the garbage boat in the P.I. He was as brown as a Hottentot and extremely happy. His ammo boat had gotten hit by Charlie's mortars last week, but no one was hurt. Tomorrow his four years in the service are up, and he's homeward bound, the lucky duck.

No postage is required for letters here in Vietnam. Servicemen can simply write "free" on the envelope in place of a stamp. Even an envelope isn't a necessity for the letter to be delivered; I could write you a letter on the back of a brown grocery sack and send it to you as is. Just another benefit from drawing Vietnam duty.

March 17, 1970

Dear Family,

It's been five long days now and still no word about where my ship is working. Oh c'mon, *somebody* has to know her whereabouts! If she is truly being decommissioned, then they will be taking her back to the States to do so. But if it is simply being recommissioned, or in the process of being turned over to the Vietnamese, either way it looks like I'll be in for a transfer in the near future. Here are two hands that want to do something for the war effort and nobody wants them. *sigh*

I had the brig watch one night from midnight until 0400. I was supposed to guard this one swabbie so he wouldn't try to commit suicide again. I don't know what he had done to himself initially. About 0300 he wanted out of his cell to make a head call, and I was a little apprehensive about this, but nothing unusual happened. Hell, I didn't plan on using the .45 automatic pistol anyway.

I don't think I've spoken more than ten words since I got here. I don't know anybody, and so far I haven't seen anybody that I might even want to know. I've had only two working parties, since I'm a third class; there are so many seamen and firemen around here that they use them for the work details instead.

This hot climate does not induce much of an appetite. For the past five days all I've had to eat is a cup of coffee in the morning and a hamburger at noon. Sometimes I'll go wild and have a cheeseburger instead. Maybe a couple of beers in the evening. I get 12 hours of sleep every night, and I really feel fit.

I wrote Wilt a letter and asked him to send me any vocational literature he could acquire on such topics as forestry, weather stations, spelunking, animal research, mapping, exploring – and just plain outdoor work. I don't know of any forest ranger schools, as such, but there must surely be some around. Your camping adventures and Wilt's ranger job in Cody, Wyoming, have inspired me into regarding this as a possible career choice when I get out of the service.

March 18, 1970

Everybody here reads all the time – that's a good thing! I am presently reading "The Sand Pebbles" by Richard McKenna. I saw the movie, starring Steve Mc-Queen and Richard Crenna, and it was a real showstopper. This could possibly be the best book I've ever read in my life!

I even met a guy once who served aboard the present-day *USS San Pablo* (AGS-30), a former seaplane tender, now a deep-sea hydrographic-surveying ship. His ship was named after the US Navy gunboat of the same name, an ancient relic left over from the Spanish-American War – and the same *San Pablo* from the book "The Sand Pebbles"!

> *"The words kindled Holman. Sometimes when he was drunk he would feel that he was right on the edge of unrolling the master blueprint of creation. It was just a way of looking at things, a sideways slant of the mind's eye, that he could only get into when he was drunk, and he would always pass out before he got drunk enough really to see anything. But it was more exciting than a woman. Whatever he said and what other people said seemed loaded with strange and wonderful meaning. He listened to himself as to a stranger."*
>
> *– The Sand Pebbles*

CAT LO
March 19, 1970

They hauled me out to Tan Son Nhut airfield and ushered me aboard a C-123 "Provider" cargo plane bound inland for the village of Cat Lo. From there I was to take a swift patrol boat out to my ship, which was already working upriver on the Mekong. I sat on the folding bench seat with my sea bag between my feet along with a couple of other men, and stared out the large open hatch in the rear of the

USS Iredell County (LST-839).

plane. A Sea Bee stood silhouetted in the hatch, looking much like a recruiting poster, watching the brilliant green jungle pass by beneath us, resting the stock of his M16 rifle on his hip. Conversation was impossible in the noise from the engines.

I eventually crossed the quarterdeck of the *USS Iredell County* (LST-839) just as a carmine dusk was settling over the jungle. The LST is the most numerous of the larger types of amphibious vessels. Its great advantage is the ability to run up on the beach and unload combat cargo through the massive bow doors.

In the designating of Navy ships, LSTs are always named after famous counties in the United States (or parishes in the case of Louisiana), and the word "County" is added as part of the name. My ship was named after Iredell County in North Carolina. She had seen battle on the beaches of Europe during World War II, but had been in Nam since 1967, occasionally receiving enemy fire and incurring personnel casualties during her resupplying duties with the riverine forces in-country.

Until further notice I would serve as electrician's mate aboard the old *Iredell County,* hauling oil, fresh water, C-rations, ammo, beer, mail – and sometimes body bags – to our base camps up and down the Mekong River.

EM3 Steve Stanga B617389
USS Iredell County (LST-839)
C/o FPO San Francisco, Calif.
96601

VUNG TAU

March 22, 1970

Dear Family,

I am on my ship at last! And if it doesn't sound too corny, I'd like to say that it really feels good to get a deck under my feet again. I had to wait at Cat Lo for two days while my ship was upriver, but at long last I am a member of her crew. If you have a map of Vietnam you may be able to find out where I am. Vung Tau is the coastal base for all the Second Squadron LSTs here in-country.

The *USS Iredell County* (LST-839) was made during World War II. Her sister ships are the *USS Iron County* (LST-840) and the *USS Hunterdon County* (LST-838)— which is over here somewhere. She is 328 feet long overall, and displaces 1,653 tons. The main engines are GM diesels of 1,700 b.hp, able to propel the ship through the water at 11.6 knots on just two shafts. We can accommodate up to 266 men in a pinch, but a normal crew complement is usually never more than 119. She is armed with eight 40mm AA "pom pom" guns.

There are presently 112 men on board this "T," including yours truly. There are only four electricians, so we've really got our work cut out for us. Everybody is going out of their way to help me get settled in. All day today I just wandered around trying to get my bearings below decks. I finally got it all mapped out in my mind's eye. We are allowed to wear T-shirts and cutoff dungarees all the time on board. But for liberty we have to wear a clean, unmended dungaree uniform. This is really nice. But the greatest thing I found out is that we can grow beards! The electric shop, the messdecks, and the berthing compartments are all intensely air-conditioned, which is absolutely wonderful in this heat! But the engine room is like the seventh level of Hell. A lot of the guys on the boat are from Kansas; I don't know why that is. Several of them have pet monkeys. The chow is great so far; we have steak once a day, and plenty of beer-calls.

A few short days from now I will be upriver on my first "brown-water run" to supply bases and small support craft with ammo and other supplies. We'll be going upriver almost to the Cambodian border. Liberty in Vung Tau is real good, but the beer there costs around ninety cents a can for some fool reason! (At least on the ship it's free.) So we usually buy a bottle of Old Grand Dad bourbon from the Navy exchange and take it out in town with us for the evening. If we're feeling particularly fearless we'll buy a bottle of Old Card Table – two drinks and your legs fold up.

I would have thought by now that I was pretty savvy to the tricks of conmen and pickpockets, but they got me again. On my very first day of liberty out in Vung Tau a skinny, cross-eyed Vietnamese boy ran off with my wallet! He used a razor blade to slash open the bottom of my dungaree jeans pocket, and the wallet dropped out right into his hands as I walked along with my buddy. I didn't even feel a thing, or know that anything was going on until another Vietnamese man yelled suddenly from the sidewalk, and the boy high-tailed it down an alley with my stuff. By then it was too late. I only lost about eight dollars and a bunch of precious family photos, but I'll have to get all my military IDs replaced.

Alas, it is indeed true that this ship is going to be decommissioned sometime in the near future. She will make the long 45-day trip back to the States, so I guess I'll finally get my taste of crossing the ocean sooner than I planned. After that, I'm going to try to get back over here to earn some decent Battle Pay.

I'm sorry this letter is so short, but I wanted to rush it off on the next mail launch. I'm glad I'm finally settled down in one spot and am not carrying that miserable sea bag all over creation anymore.

BINH THUY

March 29, 1970

Dear Family,

I'm in hiding. It's about thirty minutes until holiday routine goes down and I'm hiding here in the log room so they don't find something for me to do in the next half hour. They're notorious for doing that. They get so mad when we all go into hiding. But what can they do, send me to Vietnam? Take away my birthday?

I guess this is Easter weekend, I'm not sure, but that might explain the holiday routine. I was surprised to discover a typewriter down here, so at least my letters should be legible for the next few months!

We are on our way back to Vung Tau now after completing a five-day run upriver. Yesterday we were about twenty miles from the Cambodian border and there was quite a bit of shooting and shelling on the mainland.

I got to see both Moose Turner and Curtis, my old garbage-boat buddies from Subic Bay. They are getting out of the Navy in a couple of days, so I just about missed them! Moose is on a PBR tender, the *USS Sphinx* (ARL-27) which services river patrol boats. He got the Silver Star medal for saving two Vietnamese kids in the river under fire. Sounds like something Moose would do.

Curtis is on the *USS Satyr* (ARL-23), another PBR tender. He is about 25 clicks from the Cambodian border and is presently engaged in Operation Giant Slingshot. Curtis and Moose have never bumped into each other after leaving the Philippines; their ships always seem to be in different parts of the Mekong.

Stationed midway between Moose and Curtis is the *USS Benewah* (APB-35), a self-propelled barracks ship and PBR repair shop, which is the flagship of the whole MRF. But the only time Curtis has set foot on that ship was when he went aboard for a USO show at Christmas time.

Certain areas are known as "free fire zones," and they are heavily infested with Charlie. All the villagers have been evacuated out of there, and nobody is supposed to be in these areas at all. We may fire with impunity instantly on anybody we see in these zones, as they are most likely up to no good there.

Just to show you how treacherous the Mekong River is, one fine day the Engineering officer had the bridge when we dropped anchor for the night. I don't know what he did wrong in the anchoring process, maybe nothing, but come morning they couldn't raise the anchor again to get underway. I mean to say, we maneuvered with both screws and jockeyed this way and that for awhile, but nothing we could do would budge the death grip our anchor had on the bottom of that old river. So there we sat, a Large Stationary Target for the Cong while the shipfitters rigged their cutting torches and cut the anchor chain. Rumor had it that the cost of the anchor would come out of the officer's paycheck, but I seriously doubt it.

We had liberty in Binh Thuy (pronounced "bin-TOO-ee") and I met an Army ground pounder who was from South Dakota. Matter of fact, he lived in Mitchell and graduated from high school the same year as I did. And I had never seen him before in my whole life! But he knew all the same people that I did, so we had a nice soggy visit. Consequently, I forget his name at the moment.

Quite often when we dock at a small river town, the Stewburners set up the chow line on the bank and we can dine al fresco. Afterwards, we form a line to scrape our leftovers into the garbage can. On the other side of the can is another line, of Vietnamese peasants waiting their turn to pick something out of the garbage! We had heard that the natives were very poor upriver. But talking about it and seeing it firsthand are two different things. We felt like insensitive clods if we cleaned up our trays!

Lately, we've been anchoring upriver at night because it's simply too treacherous to try and navigate in the dark, even with radar. So sentries are posted all over the ship with guns, and they are supposed to shoot "zippos." (Zippos are pieces of junk and branches that float down the river past the ship.) Charlie often floats along underneath them with a snorkel tube and sets mines by the ships. Just the other day we had a mine go off right behind us in the river. We had passed it by and then it went off! At night one of our launches cruises round and round our ship constantly while it rides at anchor, periodically throwing concussion grenades over the side at random to keep off enemy swimmers. These are really loud, and it's hard to get any sleep then.

I'm going to rig some AC outlets in our berthing compartment so we won't have to use up a million batteries in our tape recorders all the time. By the way this ship rock and rolls when we are just off the coast, it should be a real joy ride back to the States across open ocean, I can see that now.

We've got a puppy here on board, and a no-account monkey name of Fred who'll never amount to anything. They're loads of fun to watch, though; they like to wrestle each other and frisk about and be jolly all day. We took some heavy seas over the main deck a while back and the puppy almost got washed overboard.

The monkey runs around loose. Sometimes you'll see a brown furry ball come streaking through the compartment and you'll know that Fred just went by. He climbs all over, though, as monkeys will do, and I'm afraid he might climb up into the radar some day and get instantly crispo. He likes to sit on your shoulder and look for fleas in your hair. With monkeys this is a sign of affection, I'm told. He's also got a cute trick of untying your shoe laces and tripping you up.

You know, sometimes I have to wonder just how in the heck some of these guys would ever get back to the ship when they get so drunk out in town, if they didn't have buddies like me to take care of them. Some of these clowns just go on the beach and drink until they pass out. They don't give any thought whatsoever to getting back safe and sound; they just take it for granted that somebody will carry them back and tuck them in their rack. They figure that somebody else will always stay sober enough so they can do their own thing and crash. I bet they'd really be surprised if they came around the next morning right in the same bar where they passed out, with their pockets emptied and the ship nowhere in sight!

They had us working until 0200 one morning on a miserable generator, because it was vital for running the radios. What a bummer. We couldn't get the damn thing to work right at all. It kept over-speeding and running away. We were hot and tired and hungry and frustrated and out of ideas. Finally we noticed some stupid little thing that we had all overlooked before, and then we had it running in a jiffy. But at least we got "late sleepers" the next morning for working so long into the night.

The other day our AC generator crapped out; the air conditioning and all the ice machines went off immediately, along with the fluorescent lighting. That was just awful! All day we sweated profusely everywhere we went on the ship. We had horrible visions of lying in a puddle of sweat trying to sleep that night.

On the messdecks sat about sixty rowdy guys with cups in their hands, waiting to pounce on the first ice cube that would come tumbling out of the ice machine as soon as power was restored. They all sat there beet-red with strangled faces, and it would have been comical if it wasn't so dang pathetic to see a bunch of swabs reduced to uselessness just because they were deprived of alternating current for a few hours in a tropical climate.

Later, as I was sitting in the berthing compartment under a fan set on "high," one of the deckapes came running through, holding up a half-melted square of ice and screaming, "There's ice on the messdecks! There's ice, I tell yuh!" Like they had just found gold at Sutter's Mill or something. Fourteen sailors were maimed in the mad rush that followed.

This morning I was talking to an engineman from Laramie, talking about what we wanted to do once we got out of this canoe club, and he said that the University of Wyoming had a very good Wildlife Management program if I was serious about going into that field – one of the best in the country. From the way he describes it, the country around Laramie really sounds beautiful, too; the famous cowboy town is located on the high plains. It's a five-year course and the GI Bill will pay for everything. I think it sounds perfect for me and now I'm really enthused. Maybe I won't sign up for Operation Deepfreeze after all.

This morning we had a General Quarters drill and went to our battle stations. That was kind of exciting. At noon we are having roast ham plus strawberry crème pie! And all the cold, cold milk that we can drink! Wow! This afternoon I'll have to go down in the Hole for a four-hour watch over the main switchboard. It's so loud down there that I often get headaches, even wearing earplugs. Later I hear they're going to spring an Abandon Ship drill on us. Oh goody.

"The ship's usefulness lies in her ability to put part of herself up on land and take herself off again. But to give her this very strange talent she has been strangely contrived. She is 328 feet long but has a draft of only 13 feet and has no keel, meaning that in any kind of sea she rolls like no other ship ever devised by man, and she has a blunt bow which likes to club the sea instead of riding through it.

These various specifications make her about as ungainly a vessel as you would ever see in a harbor or at sea, and also one of the slowest and least maneuverable. With the hull newly scraped of barnacles, the shrapnel holes smoothly patched, the hull painted, a favoring wind, and her engines straining, she can do 11½ knots. Usually she cruises at 8. Naturally this also makes her an excellent target.

One of her other chief characteristics is her generous amount of free-board. More of her is out of the water than in, so that she is blown by the wind almost as much as she is moved by the current of the water and in this respect is more like a sailing vessel than any ship in the Navy Register.

The ship is called an LST, for Landing Ship Tank, complement of nine officers and ninety men. The essence of diesel fuel was eternally the prevailing scent aboard the LST. The captain doesn't care what kind of clothes the men wear, and there are some pretty weird combinations aboard. Sandals are the most popular footwear aboard.

The landing craft are the forgotten ships of war and in a way the outcast Navy, the glamour having been staked out by vessels such as destroyers, carriers, and subs. But of all ships, LSTs are the most indispensable part of the Navy in War."

– "The Ninety and Nine" *by William Brinkley*

VUNG TAU

April 1, 1970

Dear Gramma,

It's four o'clock in the morning and it's useless to try and get any sleep before reveille at 0630. I just spent the last hour polishing my dress shoes for the big inspection tomorrow morning. I wouldn't have to do this stuff in the middle of the night if we had time to do our personal chores during the day. But all day yesterday we cruised around off the coast of Vung Tau and had one drill after another. We went to our battle stations and they simulated casualties and fires and such… all…day…long.

After that I had to go right down in the Hole for a four-hour watch on the main switchboard. Those three generators are so loud down there that I can't hear properly for two hours afterwards. But I think I'm gradually getting used to it.

We're here in Vung Tau to pick up supplies and ammo, and soon we'll be off on another fun-packed five-day run up the Mekong River to give supplies to the small support craft. After this next run we will be making a long trip down around the southern coast to an island called An Thoi. They say that we may have to go in shooting! Good grief! On our first run up the river we caught a little small-arm's fire, but nothing serious, and our boys soon silenced the troublemakers with our 40mm's.

Most of us don't have the slightest idea of what is going on in Vietnam, and can't make sense of what we're doing over here, outside of some vague patriotic notion that we're somehow protecting our country. I guess it really doesn't matter; it's something to do.

I see I'll have to cut this letter short. The lights are dimming and then getting real bright, which means the generators are hunting, so I had better get down there and check things out, seeing as how that's my job. There's supposed to be a watch down there in the Hole, keeping an eye on things, but he's probably reading a comic book.

CAN THO

April 2, 1970

Dear Family,

We had ORI two days ago; that's an Operation Readiness Inspection. And a Commodore did the honors! We steamed around in circles while they simulated all manner of drills. They had General Quarters, Man Overboard, Abandon Ship, fires, engine casualties, etc. They had us running around like a bunch of clucks, but it was kind of exciting. They threw over some fifty-five-gallon drums and the gunner's mates on the 40mm guns blew them about thirty feet out of the water.

In After Steering they simulated steering loss, and this other swab and I had to rig it up for manual rudder control before we ran aground. The ship's record to do this is 12 seconds, and him and I beat that by a full second! Proudness! A lot of the guys think that all these drills are Mickey Mouse and useless, but I suppose they serve their purpose. All the same, they get just as tiresome as anything else that is endlessly repetitive.

Yesterday we had a Change Of Command on the main deck. They hold this ceremony when the Old Man is leaving and we're getting a new captain. You might know, for the past week it has been lightly overcast, cool and pleasant. But the only time we have to stand at attention outside in our uniforms, the sun comes out like gangbusters and there isn't a breeze stirring! Boy, did we sweat then!

The COC program just consisted of a prayer by the chaplain, speeches of admiration for the crew, handshakes all around the top brass, and short talks by officers saying inane things that they really didn't mean anyway or could possibly know, like how tight the crew and them were, and how squared-away the ship was, and blah blah blah.

After that ordeal, getting back to work was a welcome relief. The new Old Man is going to be a bit of a stinker, I suspect; we're going to be steaming all night tonight – and we don't usually chug at night. So that means that good old Stanga has got the midwatch…again…great!

At one point upriver we were informed that military clergy from all denominations would be visiting our ship the next day. If we wished to have a religious conference or service with a particular man, then we had to indicate thusly on a sign-up sheet. Naturally, I did not participate, preferring instead to get my churching from Old Grand Dad.

Somebody earlier in the war had scratched an ornate Star of David on the side of my bunk; anyway, it was there when I came on board and was assigned a rack. I paid it no mind. When the gig arrived with our visiting clergy, one of them was a rabbi. And before I knew it, I was being summoned to officer's country to meet privately with the rabbi! What the – ?!

It turns out some buffoon had noticed the Star of David on my bunk and had alerted the Old Man. The rabbi was insistent that I receive instruction or whatever, and despite all my protests he was convinced that Stanga was a Jewish name – instead of the good German name that it actually is. But I was let off the hook only after I exposed some other Jewish guys in the crew, ha ha.

We did quite a bit of exhaustive work today, working on the feeder pump motor for the boilers. Without it we would have no hot water for showers and shaving and such. That's a bummer, too. The deckapes are always giving us snipes a ration of shit about how much we skate, but they didn't bug us once while we were restoring hot water to them, you bet!

Stewburner takes a break.

Fixing the motor was no sweat, fairly elementary work; but it was sure a damn hassle getting it in and out from underneath that hot boiler! I'll bet I spent half the day roasting away in the bilges today, usually hanging upside-down with sweat running *up* my nose. Oh well, one way of losing weight is as good as another, I guess.

I've got a new girlfriend out in town. Her name is My. She is six years old and even tinier than sister Julie! But she is really cute and well-mannered. She begs from bar to bar, and inevitably hits the bar where my buddies and I hang out. She knows I'm a soft touch. I give her a 100-piaster note whenever she comes in. I also buy her a Coke and some rice to eat, too. She says that both of her parents were killed already in the war and that she is an orphan. That may or may not be factual, as most of the beggars make the same claim.

A steady stream of little kids flows in and out of the bars all night, begging from the servicemen there with the help of a laminated card of barely-disguised propaganda. One night I bought one of the actual cards itself from one kid. It read:

> *"Friendly American, because of your country's policy of foreign inter-vention in a civil war, I have lost my parents and need to beg to live. Please help me live!"*

A lot of those bar-maids out in town seem to think that they own you as soon as you walk in the joint, and they get all uppity when you try to move on and hit a few more clubs during the evening – no doubt to visit another bar-maid, they suspect. "You big butterfly! You number ten sailor!"

sigh You can't win.

I hope my tape recorder comes in the mail pretty soon. Just about everybody on the ship has one, and listens to their own brand of music on headphones. They are really nice when we are in the electric shop working on motors, etc. It reminds us that there is still a World back home somewhere.

The entire crew is split in half into a port duty section and a starboard duty section. The port duty section got liberty in Vung Tau last night – our one-day stop – and then we pulled out of port this morning. Consequently, the starboard duty section never even got to leave the boat and is kind of ticked off today. (Kind of?!) You can't imagine what it means to hit the beach after we've been on a long river run, if nothing else just for the sake of getting off the ship onto solid ground and unwinding a little bit. Well, I must say that we unwound extra loose in Vung Tau last night. I bought a South Vietnamese flag out in town for a souvenir of the war.

We are loaded for bear this time! We are heading for the island of An Thoi with a tank deck crammed with *beaucoup* [a lot] ammunition; this is supposed to be the roughest seafloat run that we'll ever make. We'll be at our battle stations for nine hours while we are there, and we are not looking forward to *that* at all.

My battle station is in After Steering, and my function is to provide manual rudder control should our automatic steering get knocked out. After Steering is incidentally the worst place on the ship when the shells start flying, as the enemy purposely tries to cripple the steering; the safest place being down in the Hole between the massive bulks of the main engines.

We are carrying twenty tons of C-4, which is a kind of plastic dynamite. They say it only takes about two pounds to sink an aircraft carrier. We are also loaded with lots of rough napalm; enough combined heat to generate thirty-million degrees. I can't fathom such a temperature. And then there's the small-arm's ammo – they stopped counting it after 125 million rounds!

Of course, it would seem negligible to mention the 100 crates of explosive hose, mines, grenades, rockets, pyrotechnics, and large-caliber projectiles. All it would take is just one mortar shell from Charlie in the tank deck, and we can kiss it off. To say that we're nervous wouldn't tell you much.

Landing Ship Squadron Two

SECOND TO NONE

Our last cruise around Point de Ca Mau, the southernmost tip of South Vietnam, didn't start off any different than any other cruise. Even though the men of the *USS Iredell County* called the ship a "Large Slow Target," none of us ever really doubted that we'd reach our destination safely.

Besides the usual crates of C-rations, barrels of oil and cases of beer, we were also carrying enough black powder to level a small Midwestern town. The rounds of automatic weapon ammunition ran into the millions. There were concussion and fragment grenades by the thousands. There were antipersonnel land mines by the hundreds. And we had enough plastic explosive on board to generate the necessary heat to melt down the *USS Enterprise* into a ball of silly putty.

Now couple all this fire power potential with the thousands of gallons of fuel oil we had on board, and you got yourself a nice little weenie roast. Small wonder some of the men didn't sleep well last night.

Morris pretty well summed up everybody's sentiments as he stood on the tank deck, hands on his hips, surveying the veritable Everest of ammo stacked before him, and said to me, "Well, Sparky, it's been good to know yuh."

It almost spoiled my ability to function as a member of the world's greatest military machine.

Everyone refamiliarized himself with his abandon-ship station. They wanted to know exactly where to run in case a Chinese-made VC rocket ever came slamming in through the bulkhead. It didn't dawn on the big sillies that nobody could possibly survive such an attack, except by *accident,* what with all the ordnance exploding at once. But just the same, they wanted to try for the lifeboats anyway. They say a ship and its cargo belong to the captain, but the lifeboats belong to the crew.

We were sitting ducks in the Mekong River, so we were ordered to get underway at once. The ship left Vung Tau at first light and headed south through the South China Sea, around the Ca Mau Peninsula, towards Islande d'An Thoi in the Gulf of Siam, where we would off-load our sinister cargo. The water in the delta was brown and choked with sediment where the Mekong emptied into the sea. At that point of the delta, the river was eight miles wide or so.

The Mekong is the largest river on the whole Indochinese peninsula. It originates from glacial sources in the lofty Tibetan Highlands in China, and empties 2,600 miles later into the South China Sea. It drains more than 307,000 square miles of Thailand, Burma, Laos, Cambodia, and South Vietnam. Ships with a 15-foot draft can only sail about 350 miles up from the mouth of the Mekong. Farther inland, river travel is interrupted continuously by rapids and sand bars.

As we pulled ever so slowly away from the coast to get into deeper steerage, no one noticed the wind coming up; it was usually windy at sea. No one noticed the waves getting rougher; it was always rough sailing in our flat-bottomed "T." Soon it would get windier and rougher. In just a couple of hours an oriental typhoon would descend upon us and toy with a hundred souls for fourteen hours.

It was about four o'clock in the afternoon when the sun disappeared for good and it started to rain in earnest. By six o'clock the wind was driving the rain positively horizontal. The ocean swells were gigantic! Our rust bucket of a ship would slide down a steep trough and bury its bow in the wave. A mighty shudder would race through the whole skeleton of the ship, and you'd swear the bow was never going to come back up out of the white water!

During particularly rough weather, it was popular to gather in the athwartship passageway to watch the swinging needle of the clinometer tell us how extreme

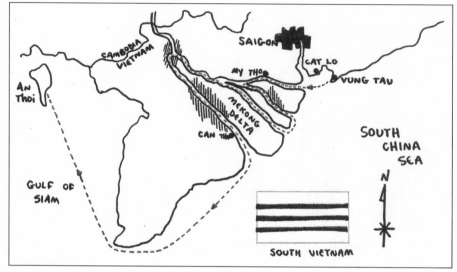

South Vietnam

the ship rolled from side to side, hoping that we weren't going to set any new records.

Before the storm was full upon us, we were ordered into the hold to secure the cargo for very rough weather ahead. Full oil drums were already rolling from side to side, awash in seawater that had breached the big bow doors. Cases of C-rats were tipping over and crashing into the water on the deck. Stacks of ammunition were falling into each other, but with small danger of actually detonating.

First things first, though: we turned our attention to the many unstable pallets of Black Label beer that were stacked from the deck to the overhead, and in imminent danger of tipping over. As far as we were concerned, the Canadian beer was our most precious cargo.

So we worked feverishly while other cargo crashed down all around us. Only when we had all the beer firmly secured, did we turn our efforts to the remainder of the cargo to restack it and lash it down. All the while, the storm was becoming more and more wild, and swabs who normally never got seasick were now violently ill.

By 6:30 PM it was as black as a moonless midnight outside. Sailors were forbidden to cross the weather deck for fear of being swept overboard. Only the inside passageways could be used to reach the forward compartments.

Every loose article on the ship became a deadly missile hazard, capable of being hurled at a crewmember. Normally quiescent materiel became audibly restless. Chains clinked, the contents of lockers rattled, books flew off shelves, and small long-lost items sidled out of their dark hiding places and slid across the deck.

We had to stay out of An Thoi harbor until the typhoon moved on across the Pacific to torment somebody else. Damage to ships during a typhoon is usually maximum with ships moored in port.

Ten hours later we limped into the scenic port of Duong Dong on the island of An Thoi. The entire crew was exhausted, and had that gaunt, tired, and P.O.'d look. One window on the bridge was broken out. No. 4 life raft was missing (mine, naturally), having been torn loose in the storm and swept away. The tank deck was littered with flotsam. But our cargo was intact, and so were we. Once again the crew had lived up to our ship's motto: "Second to None."

Vietnamese and American soldiers off-loaded all the cargo, and after a single night of rest in harbor the *Iredell County* fired up its engines and headed back home to Vung Tau. The return trip was not nearly as eventful as the previous one had been, thank Allah. The sun shone warmly down upon the laughing aquamarine waters, and the ship cruised along on an even keel.

C-RATS

Even though C-rations had been officially phased out and discontinued many years ago, the military was still awash in vast stockpiles of them. So when we delivered other commodities to fire bases up and down the river, we always asked them if they could use a pallet of C-rations as well. As for ourselves, whenever we got a little peckish between meals on the ship, we could always rip into a package of C-rations to staunch our hunger until chow time.

The green bags of C-rats came packed in nondescript cardboard boxes with only the barest minimum of information printed on the outside. Besides the main entrée, you were sometimes delighted to find such additional treats as a can of fruit cocktail, hardtack bread, peanut butter, crackers and jam, bouillon cubes, envelopes of instant soup, instant oatmeal, instant fruit drink, cheese sticks, raisins, dark and bitter enriched chocolate squares, and the elusive petrified fruitcake.

Each package of C-rats also included a smaller accessory packet usually wrapped in brown butcher paper and which contained a varied assortment of oft-needed items not necessarily related to a combat meal: chewing gum, toilet paper, envelopes of instant coffee or cocoa, salt and pepper packets, sugar packets, powdered creamer, a small packet of cigarettes and moisture-resistant matches, salt tablets, water-purification tablets, hard sucking candy, a P-38 can opener which many guys took to wearing around their necks with their dog tags, and a flat wooden spoon for eating the meal itself.

The contents of the bags were always varied and always a mystery. But you could expect many different combinations of meat parts plus vegetable bits. What sort of meal you received was pretty much Russian roulette until you actually opened up the can. "Oh crap, I got turkey and carrots again. Anybody wanna trade?"

Most of the canned food items were bland, unappealing, monotonous, packed with preservatives and salt, overly soft in texture and unpalatable. The food could sustain you, but it often tasted like hell. Imagine if you will a can full of mushy day-old Gravy Train.

The olive drab tin can might read, "Combat field ration, Type II, one each, contents meat and vegetable pieces in gravy, made in New Jersey…" Typical selections presented to us for our dining pleasure were chicken and noodles, chopped ham and potatoes, frank and beans, spaghetti and meat sauce; their "beef stew" was probably my favorite. Once in a great while a rare can of mutton would appear, which was very unpopular. The ham and lima beans unit was usually thrown directly over the side, which proved conclusively that we were men of taste after all.

LONG BINH

April 9, 1970

Dear Mary,

The cooks fix something to eat for the guys who have the watch at midnight; they call it "mid-rats," meaning midnight rations.

Sometimes little girls like you come out to our ship in canoes and sell us watermelons. But some naughty boys from the ship poured water on them once. They got yelled at for doing that.

Today we are still painting in our electrical shop. One guy stood up too fast and left his hat sticking to the wet ceiling.

Our monkey likes to take our pencils out of our pockets and chew on them. And if they don't taste good he throws them into the water. What he really likes to eat are sunflower seeds!

VINH LONG

April 10, 1970

Dear Timmy,

We drank 24 cans of Pepsi while painting our electric shop. We painted it black and white and gray, and it looks pretty sharp. Then we shined the floor and polished the work bench. There are four guys who work for me; they call me "Boss Sparky."

There are a lot of helicopters here. They fly right above the jungle treetops and shoot rockets at bad people running around on the ground. Some of the helicopters are from Australia; they have a big kangaroo painted on them.

Did you know that we sleep in Northampton bunk beds with four people on top of each other? I sleep on the very top bunk and the ceiling is almost touching my nose! It's very hard to get in and out of bed. I can't fall out because there are steel bars along the side, which we have to hang onto at night if the boat is rocking a lot.

This morning I woke up just freezing to death; I checked the air conditioner and, sure enough, somebody had set it on "Freeze Out." It is so cold in our berthing compartment that I sleep with three wool blankets and my socks and T-shirt on! But it's better than roasting all the time, that's for sure. The engine room is directly below us, and that makes the floor deliciously warm for our cold feet first thing in the morning.

HA TIEN

April 11, 1970

Dear Julie,

Hi Teeny! We are out on the ocean right now and are taking the ship back to port. The ocean is real, real blue; the river is real brown, though. Did you know that ships have sisters, too? We saw our sister ship yesterday, which had a big helicopter sitting on it.

What did you do for Easter? Our cooks hid some Easter eggs all over the ship and we looked for them, as we just love hard-boiled eggs. We still haven't found them all yet…but we can smell them.

Our monkey ran away when we were tied up to the pier yesterday. I guess he retired from the Navy. We get ice cream sometimes on Sunday. When we do, we each get to eat a whole box of ice cream! We can have all the free pop we want, too.

THE BITING GAME

We used to play this stupid game while I was aboard the *Iredell County*. I don't recall if it had any official name or anything, but it did involve a lot of biting. Yes, that's what I said: biting. Human biting human.

The game was more or less invented by a comical little Italian engineman with a long surname who we all called "Pizza" for short. Boredom on board ship often manifested itself in bizarre ways. Enlisted service, particularly naval duty at sea, places strange and unnatural stresses and peculiar conditions upon men. The result in this case was the infamous "Biting Game." The game was played vigorously by grown men for weeks on end. We made up the rules as we went along.

The game simply involved biting somebody, as often as possible, and in as many different creative places as you could imagine. The intensity of the bite itself should always be well within reason, and blood was never drawn. Of course, there were scores attached to the various types of bites, but I have long since forgotten them. And everybody was fair game, except the unpalatable officers.

1) THE MOVIE BITE – People were often bitten in the dark, while the movie was in progress. Consequently, the guys became very jumpy whenever anybody moved suddenly during the film.

2) THE SLEEPING BITE – Simply put, biting someone while he was sleeping. Not necessarily even hard enough to wake him up, but you needed a reliable witness otherwise to prove that you had done it and to receive the points.

3) THE TRIPPING BITE – Pretending to trip over a door sill or a pair of boots or some other impediment, then falling against the witless victim and completing the bite. (My speciality.)

4) THE LONG-DISTANCE BITE – Merely making a biting motion at somebody across the room. Must be visually observed by the bitee, however. This scored the lowest.

5) THE TOE BITE – Biting somebody on the toe.

6) THE TOE/SOCK BITE – Biting somebody on the toe, *through* his dirty sock. This scored more points than just the common Toe Bite. It was done very quickly, however.

7) THE MUTUAL BITE – Biting somebody back while he was still biting you. Sometimes we had to throw cold water on a couple of biters to get them separated.

8) THE ICBB (Inter-Continental Ballistic Bite) – Here, a person would enter a compartment and first yell his intentions to his victim, then rush screaming through the room, to fall upon his victim and complete the

bite. Seldom was the victim able to avoid the forthcoming bite, short of locking himself in the head.

9) THE RICOCHET BITE – The biter would bump into a locker, etc., seemingly by accident, then ricochet off a few more objects in the room, skipping over several potential bitees in the process, only to finally land on someone totally unsuspecting, preferably biting him on the calf of his leg. This was considered among the more difficult bites to accomplish, and brought the biter premium points.

10) THE BUTT BITE – This was only accomplished by a single person – the deranged engineman himself, Pizza. Nobody else had the guts, nor the desire.

11) THE PERSONAL-BELONGINGS BITE – Points were given for this only if bite marks were actually left on some article of the victim's.

12) THE BACK BITER – This coveted bite also drew a lot of points. It got so bad that people became paranoid and were always looking over their shoulders. They would avoid standing in lines (mealtime was a favorite opportunity for back-biting), and like Wild Bill Hickok they never sat with their backs to the door.

13) THE GANG BITE – This infamous tactic is accomplished if no less than four people attack and bite the same person simultaneously. Every biter gains fifty points, while the victim loses fifty points from his weekly total.

14) THE CHAIN-REACTION BITE – One person would get bit, and then quickly pass it on to the person closest to him. In thirty seconds, as many as 15 people could potentially be bitten! Sometimes it got out of control and almost turned into a real feeding frenzy!

Sounds too bizarre to be true, eh? Truth is stranger than fiction. Once the ship headed up the Mekong River and entered the free fire zones, however, the biting game gave way to a more serious game: human killing human.

VUNG TAU

April 14, 1970

Dear Family,

I received the tape recorder and cassette tapes all in fine shape, and immediately filled the compartment with very welcome music. But before I go any further, please tell me that the rumor we have been hearing down here is not true. We heard that Paul McCartney has announced the breakup of the Beatles! Is it true?! It's all that anybody can talk about, and would be a bitter pill to swallow.

The sunflower seeds in your package were really an additional surprise, even though I was instantly mobbed at the exposing of them!

I think the last time I wrote was when we were upriver in a lot of shooting. That seems like so long ago. Right now we are going into Vung Tau after carrying fresh water, C-rats, and ammo to the boys in Ha Tien. At one point we were actually closer to Bangkok than we were to Vung Tau! We were at our battle stations for about six hours, and I almost lost my mind staring at the bulkheads and Becker's pointed head in After Steering that long. The twin screws were directly beneath us, too, and the constant vibration was terrific!

We received some small-arm's fire from the jungle at one point, but our 40mm mounts shut 'em up pronto! The inside of our electric shop looks like the bulkhead has goose bumps or something, from bullets hitting the hull of the ship. Rumor has it that it costs the United States taxpayer $1,000 per head to get a Viet Cong to defect, while it costs about $1 million per head to actually kill a V.C.! Just one more run up the delta and then we head for Da Nang to pick up supplies for the long trip back to the States.

We saw one of our sister ships, the USS Hunterdon County (LST-838) upriver. Sister ships are those ships that are built side by side in the shipyards, as you can probably guess. (The USS Iron County, LST-840, is also our sister ship, you may remember, but she is already decommissioned.)

The Hunterdon County has a raised helo deck built amidships, so her whole main deck forward of the bridge is a flight deck. On it sat a couple of Jolly Green Giant helicopters, which are anything but jolly. They're nasty, nasty helos, which you wouldn't want to make mad. The ship had just received a Presidential Unit Citation for extraordinary heroism in action against the enemy.

We've got a new Old Man, and he's got everybody hot on painting out all the spaces before we get back to the States. He tries to hand us this cock-and-bull story: "...and remember, men, the more we get done now the more liberty you'll have in Seattle!" Oh bull. Nobody is buying that tired old line of BS. We all know full well we're just going to end up painting everything all over again.

So, for the past three days Becker and I have been slaving away up in the forward machinery space, directly underneath the main deck – what an oven! It's all the way forward in the bow, and the cramped compartment contains the massive machinery which opens and closes the big bow doors and operates the ramp. That's where most of the ship's motion is when we're underway, too, so we were bounced all over the place while we were trying to paint. Oh brother! But it looks neat as a pin now.

I showed the movie, "Midnight Cowboy," to the crew last night, but it got mixed reviews. The only reason I picked it up in the first place was because it had Dustin Hoffman and Jon Voight in it. I felt Hoffman really lowered himself and drastically altered forever his screen image by playing such a scumbag as Ratso Rizzo. Possibly he was only trying to flex his acting ability, I don't know.

Other people will hold that this only shows Hoffman's versatility as an actor. Columnist Al Blanchard writes,

Constant maintenance is necessary.

"The weak-stomached will heave and will ask if we are to go this far in depicting the sickening aspects of life...I would not take my wife to see it because I would be ashamed...That Hoffman can make a crud like Ratso a sympathetic character should win him an Academy Award, though."

Last night I had the midwatch, and afterwards we were rolling so heavily that I only got two hours of sleep. Tonight I have the midwatch again, and then two hours in the rack before reveille. Tomorrow I'm going to feel like a piece of hammered cow-pie. I'm beginning to think that I live down in the Hole! It's my home away from home. I know my ears will never be the same again.

Today, us snipes were right in the middle of a rare two-hour nooner, when some fool yeoman comes into the compartment and turns on the lights. We were all ready to flay him alive and make him a eunuch, but then he yelled, "Mail call!" So we let him live a while longer.

We have on board this ship what must surely pass for the dumbest asshole in this man's Navy. I have seen none to compare with him anywhere in my travels. But to listen to him, you'd think he was the saltiest sailor that ever sailed the Seven Seas. He is an expert on everything under the sun, and has seen everything and been everywhere. He is faultlessly obstinate and totally pig-headed in his opinions, and is always 100% right. Also, he never showers.

First of all, he's from Riverside, California, and so you see he's already lost half the battle right there; sailors will not cut any slack for macho-acting guys from *California.*

He came back from liberty one night, dead drunk (he probably had two beers, tops), and fell down an escape trunk and cut his leg real bad on the ladder. Why he was going down into the engine room at that hour is beyond us. About two weeks later we found a letter lying around from his girlfriend back home that read in part, "Oh Martin, I'm so sorry to hear that you got shot in the leg!" Geez louise. Fortunately, he is getting transferred back to the States in a week. And we are having a going-away party …immediately afterwards!

My opinion of American girls is going down, down, down. My good friend, Mark Morris, is going home on leave in three days; he was going to surprise his sweetheart. But instead she surprised him this morning with a traditional "Dear John" letter. Ooh, that had to hurt. I was the only one he told about it and he was pretty upset. So am I.

He's told me a lot of things about him and her since he made his confession to me a week or so ago. We were all juiced up one night and were coming back to the ship late, staggering down the lanes of a Vietnamese village. Well, you know how drunks get; alcohol loosens the tongue, frees inhibitions, and opens up new channels of thought.

"Stanga," he said, "You're alright! I wanna tell yuh something. When you first came on the ship I figured you for some kinda hippie jerk. I saw the round glasses and I said to myself, 'Round glasses, huh? Must be a hippie jerk.' But then I got to know yuh, and when the other guys ask me what kinda guy you were, I told them you were a regular guy! You're third class, Sparky, and I'm just a fireman. But I'll do anything you say cuz I respect you. You're the best damn third class we got on board!" His opinion of me was very much like my own, but it was comforting to hear it so heartily confirmed by another.

Tomorrow is payday and our duty section has got liberty in Vung Tau. It'll probably be Mark's last night in town – ever – so all the snipes are giving him a farewell party. Oh, I can already feel my head come Thursday morning.

I had my first engine room emergency last week. No. 1 and 2 generators were on the line and I was sitting under the blower watching the main switchboard. The roar of the generator engines was positively deafening, but I thought I heard a tiny noise, a different noise that didn't quite fit in with the regular engine room growl. Maybe an engine shifted an rpm or two, I don't know.

I got off my stool and put my ear beside each engine in turn. Then I heard a definite unusual tapping noise inside No. 2's heads. It got louder and louder even as I listened. Remembering what I had been trained to do – not to panic! – I dashed over and stripped the board down to the bare essentials: radio, steering, lights, etc., shutting off everything else on the ship.

By then, the thundering knock in the engine was the only thing I could hear in the Hole. I tripped the generator off the line, upon which the engine started to run away, with no load on it. I ran back to the engine and wrestled with the throttle...it was jammed. The banging noise was right beside me in the first cylinder, and any minute I expected a con rod to come flying right out the side of the engine, creating death and dismemberment. I had heard all the engine room horror stories.

So I hauled off and kicked the throttle loose and the engine died quietly. Lights dimmed dramatically as No. 1 generator struggled to hold the extra load. Dials were going berserk and the amps were soaring! I grabbed a rheostat in each hand and set my universe safely back to 250 volts.

By this time all the officers in the world had come tumbling down into the Hole. They smiled and gave me the thumbs-up sign, and we lit off No. 3 engine. No. 2 was a smoking beast. We took the heads off and surveyed the damage. Somehow a spring had come off a rocker arm and gotten into the cylinder. What a mess! I took the time to breathe again. At least I hadn't dropped the load and put us on the beach.

My switchboard in the LST engine room.

April 21, 1970

I have sponsored an 11-year-old Brazilian boy through the Christian Children's Fund, Inc. out of Richmond, Virginia. It will cost me twelve dollars per month. My small payment will provide him with nutritional food, extra clothing, school supplies, and medicine. We can exchange letters and pictures. Although he writes only in Portuguese, the organization will provide me with a translation, and vice versa. I am really looking forward to corresponding with him! His background is as follows:

> Name: Silas T. dS—
> Born: December 8, 1958
> Sex: boy
> Grade: 1st year Primary (education delayed)
> National language: Portuguese
> Favorite play: Soccer
> Lives in: Belo Horizonte, Minas Gerais, Brazil

"Silas' family background is one of extreme poverty and privation. His father earned a mere pittance when he was able to work; then he became seriously ill and this disqualified him for the only work his limited ability could handle. The mother was unable to cope with the many problems confronting her, and the boy was left to his own devices most of the time. It soon became obvious that something should be done for this youngster. We were happy to welcome him into our Family Helper Project. Your sponsorship will mean much to him."

NEWSPAPER CLIPPING
April 22, 1970

"APOLLO 13 CREW TELLS OF BRUSH WITH DEATH IN SPACE. An oxygen tank in their service module exploded on April 13th, 202,000 miles from earth. The explosion crippled the Apollo 13 spacecraft, forced cancellation of its moon landing and imperiled the lives of the three astronauts for four days while they fought to bring their craft safely back to earth. They faced the real prospect of slowly suffocating to death in space. The only way to survive the situation was to transfer to the lunar module for the trip home, where there were limited reserves of oxygen remaining. Apollo 13 passed within 137 miles of the moon. As the astronauts approached earth, they jettisoned the service module, where the explosion had occurred."

SNIPES

Ask any sailor and he'll tell you of the legendary and long-lived feud between the snipes and the deckapes. Snipes inhabit the realm of all engineering spaces on a ship, and in particular the Hole. And naturally, the deckapes do their sweating while chipping and painting on the main deck. And never the twain shall meet, right? Wrongo!

To a snipe, it's a rare and welcome treat to come topside for some pure, fresh sea air – and the deckapes will nail him every time: "You goddam greasy snipes get the hell offa our clean deck! We just swabbed that!"

But we'd bide our time and return tit for tat. A deckape would come down into the blast-furnace heat of the Hole to borrow some tools (probably to replace a light bulb, or something else just as lame). He'd stand there like a schoolboy and stare in awed silence at all of our intricate equipment: the engine and generators, boilers, coolers, dials, gauges, pumps and valves, steam, fuel, and water lines, and everything else that he knew absolutely nothing about. He'd absently pick up a screwdriver or crescent wrench when he thought nobody was watching, and then we'd immediately jump him: "Put that *down,* you damn dirty deckape! You don't know nothin' 'bout machinery!"

And in the snipe's territory, the deckape is wisely silent and well-rebuked.

When some of the air-conditioning units crap out in several locations of the ship at once – as it most frequently does – you can safely bet your last Washington that it's still running smoothly in the snipe's berthing compartment! An occasional deckape, on some flimsy pretext, will pass through our cool compartment and linger to ask, "Hey you snipes, why zit always cool over here and we have to sweat all the time on our side?"

We would razzle-dazzle them with some engineering bullshit, and the deckape would retreat humbly, lost in the wonderfulness of Snipes.

And where's the best place to read letters from home? You guessed it. And it's us snipes who keep 'em flushing.

In the Old Navy (pre-World War II) we were called the "Black Gang," for obvious reasons. We were constantly covered with a mixture of grease, dirt, sweat, paint, fuel oil, and carbon dust. Somehow our food always seemed to taste better with honest dirt on our hands mingled with salty sweat. The deckapes wouldn't sit close to us on the messdecks during chow, as they claimed that they got sick easily.

Some character, unrecognizable from human form, would climb out of the Hole; unshaven, hair askew, shirtless, ruddy-faced, greasy, sweaty, dirty, paint-spattered and fuel-scented, with cracked and blackened fingernails, soggy dungarees, with a rag and a wrench crammed into one hip pocket, a paperback book in the other – and you'd know that a snipe was stumbling topside to take the air.

We are the underpaid and the unafraid and the unattractive and the unbeaten and the unbuttoned and the uncaught and the uncombed and the uncomforted and the unequipped and the unkempt and the unlaundered and the unsunk who do the unnecessary for the ungrateful. It ain't the most glamorous occupation in the world, but I'm kind of proud to be a snipe.

DA NANG

April 26, 1970

Dear Gramma,

Right now we are about one day out of Da Nang and should pull in there tomorrow. We left Vung Tau three days ago and have been sailing north along the coast ever since. Hard to believe there's a major war going on just over *there*. The water gets kind of rough out here at night and then it's hard to sleep, but I imagine it ain't half as rough as it will be on the way across the Pacific Ocean.

There should be a lot of mail waiting for us by the time we reach Da Nang, and that's what everybody is looking forward to and talking about. Mail means a lot to us! It is a real life saver. It helps relieve the tension of a work day and the long days stretching out ahead of us. We live for mail call.

Today is Sunday and there's been holiday routine all weekend. Yesterday I didn't have any switchboard watches in the Hole, so I didn't even bother to get out of bed all day. Thus, I caught up on a lot of sleep that I've been missing lately. I read two whole books today, which is an accomplishment even for me. Tonight I feel wide awake and ready to answer a few letters. I'm typing this from the electric shop, where my tape player is keeping me good company.

For the past two weeks we've really been busting our humps painting out all the spaces on the ship for the big Captain's inspection that we were to have last weekend. They even lengthened our workday by an hour and took away our nooners to get ready for this inspection. Ha! Some inspection! The Old Man walked through each space, as if he were heading somewhere *else* in a hurry, and didn't even give them a sideways glance! What a waste of time.

Everyone's beards had to go last week before we left Vung Tau. You can imagine the amount of griping that this order produced, of which I may have been among the loudest. More Mickey Mouse regulations. Oh well, I can always grow it back if I still want to when I start college. Some of the guys have had theirs for over a year and we hardly recognized each other that first morning when we all shaved. It was awful comical to see white patches on everybody's tanned faces; half of the guys looked years younger afterwards. Lots of laughs!

We were talking about Grammas the other night on the fantail, because Grammas are something that most of us have in common. We decided that Grammas make the best Christmas and Thanksgiving dinners, but Gramma's house smells like good cooking all year round. Nobody makes pumpkin pie or banana bread or chicken gravy as good as Gramma can. And we all agreed that only Grammas can make a quilt that was truly wonderful. When I get married I'm going to have my wife learn how to make those nice warm quilts from you. Promise?

You probably won't hear from me again for quite some time now. There aren't any mailboxes out at sea.

This was during the period of heaviest Vietnamization of the war, when we were turning everything over to the South Vietnamese and pulling Americans out *en masse.* The song "We Got to Get Out of This Place" by the Animals was our national anthem, and we stood and sang it at the top of our lungs whenever it was played on the jukebox. I was just getting settled into a mindless routine of cruising the Mekong and barhopping in the river towns when our ship came up for decommissioning. Surprisingly, most of us were highly disappointed when our tour of duty in-country was ended prematurely. I was no exception.

SOMEWHERE IN THE SOUTH CHINA SEA

May 2, 1970

Dear Family,

I suddenly realized that it has been an awfully long time since I sat down and wrestled this old clunker typewriter over a letter to you. But when you come right down to it, we've really been turning and burning with work ("all assholes and elbows" as they are wont to say), and sleeping like the dead when we weren't on duty. No more do we get settled down with dreams of Raquel Welch when it's time for another watch down in the Hole. That sort of puts the short sheet on let-ter-writing, but it sure as heck makes the time go fast! Still, it seems like a terrible inescapable cycle of work, eat, stand watch, and sleep, etc. I won't be able to mail this until we get to Guam, so it'll be another ten days before you can read this.

When we had our departure ceremonies in Vung Tau, a lot of fine things were said about LSTs in general, and our squadron in particular. Winston Churchill once said that we couldn't possibly have won World War II without the "Large Slow Targets." After our worthless Captain's inspection was concluded, they broke out the homeward-bound pennant from the flag locker and ran it up to the top of the mast. It fluttered out in the strong off-shore breeze over forty feet long!

So we got underway on our first leg home. Our ship is the Flagship for the entire squadron of four LST's returning to the States; that means we'll be carrying all the big wigs and we'll have to be halfway squared away at all times, and be on the alert for saluting any brass we might encounter in the passageways.

We steamed for five long days until we pulled into the harbor at Da Nang. We had a ton of mail waiting for us there, just as we had hoped! Da Nang is a very pretty city, and it reminds me much of Frisco. It's built up and down the hills, and in the evening the fog comes rolling slow and thick down the mountains and then spreads out over the water. I could just stand on the fantail and look at the city all day, but the fool officers always have other plans for me. Da Nang is too close to the DMZ to suit me, though.

We loaded up with all kinds of junk in Da Nang, like old trucks, half-tracks, jeeps and trailers, which was to end up in Del Mar, California. This stuff was genu-ine grade-A crap; it was equipment that was all shot up and decrepit with bro-ken windows and flat tires, etc. But we were not about to leave it behind for the Commies to use. Then we took on a company of Marines who were to escort the equipment back to the States. It's gonna be fun to watch the big bad jarheads get seasick!

We stayed in Da Nang until just a few minutes after midnight on the morning of May first. That way we can collect our extra sixty-five dollars combat pay for the entire month of May, also! Sometimes our officers are halfway smart!

Now we are steaming at flank speed, only logging seven or eight knots if we're lucky. We're heading towards Guam with the other three LSTs in the Second Squadron. There's no land in sight, and as yet it's not too rough sailing. They say the water is about five miles deep here; I just can't fathom that! ha ha!

I got awarded two more medals over here; they are both Vietnam campaign service medals – strictly for decoration. When we get to Bremerton we are sup-posed to get the Presidential Unit Citation medal, too. That will make four medals that I am authorized to wear, but nobody pays much attention to them anyway. They do dress up a uniform, though.

We're at the point now where some of the guys jokingly suggested sabotaging the main engines so we would have to turn south and pull into Subic Bay. Did you know that this LST has never once made it past the P.I. without having to go there for repairs of some kind or another? There isn't a guy on the ship who doesn't love the P.I. It's a sailor's paradise!

By the way, we'll get a couple of days of liberty in Hawaii and San Diego before we hit Washington. Good ol' Dago! That's where they've got those nice little tattoo parlors. (At last!)

Yesterday we went to our battle stations and had some maneuvering drills and target practice. The ship ahead of us threw some 55-gallon drums over the side and as we came abreast of them we were to train all four mounts on that respective side of the ship on the bobbing barrels. We were supposed to sink them with our single and twin-mount 40mm cannons.

Well, the seas were awfully rough at the time. One minute we'd be shooting right down into the water off our bow, and the next minute we'd climb up a swell and be shooting over the top of the barrels, kicking up whitecaps half a mile away. We never did sink them and the Old Man was ticked off at our poor showing. We thought it was sort of funny, ourselves. Good old Navy combat readiness.

I suppose you've already heard about all those Vietnamese bodies that came floating down the Mekong River out of Cambodia? I've heard rumors that there were close to 500 of them! They all had their hands tied behind them, shot in the head, and then thrown into the water. Sometimes as many as fifty were wired together in a bunch. I seriously wonder what's going to happen next in this insane world.

I've got the reveille watch this morning in the Hole where I can get my brains scrambled and my eardrums ruptured. So I guess I'd better climb into my tree and crash for a few hours. We had all the lobster tail we could eat for chow tonight! I haven't had that since I got into this chicken outfit. It was certainly delicious and everybody made a fine pig out of himself. Gotta run now, there's two other swabs who want to use this typewriter, too.

"And oh, the marvel of it! The marvel of it! That tiny men should live and breathe and work, and drive so frail a contrivance of wood and cloth through so tremendous an elemental strife!"

"The boat's stem touched the hard shingle. I sprang out... At the same moment I swayed, as about to fall to the sand. This was the

*startling effect of the cessation of motion. We had been so long upon
the moving, rocking sea that the stable land was a shock to us. We
expected the beach to lift up this way and that, and the rocky walls
to swing back and forth like the sides of a ship; and when we braced
ourselves, automatically, for these various expected movements,
their nonoccurrence quite overcame our equilibrium. "*

– 'The Sea Wolf" by Jack London

PACIFIC OCEAN, 2,090 FATHOMS

May 20, 1970

Dear Gramma,

When we pulled into Guam, we were manning the rail in our freshly-starched whites. We had spotted Guam earlier that morning, and drew slowly closer and closer to it throughout the afternoon. It rose low and flat and mean out of the middle of the ocean like a magic trick. It looked hazy green from afar, but as we got nearer we could make out the brown of the treeless mountains, and the white and gray of the naval shipyard.

A tug came out to meet us and put the local harbor pilot on board. For the rest of the afternoon we steamed at about one knot up into the harbor, twisting and turning in the narrow channel between the sand bars, coral reefs, and World War II wrecks.

But first things first; before anybody could flee the ship we had to hook up our life-support system: shore-power cables, freshwater hoses, and steam lines. One by one we shut down the huge engines and noisy generators and rattling pumps, and for the first time in almost a year the Hole was totally silent. Very eerie!

It was comical to observe each other trying to walk on terra firma once again after being so long at sea. By then it was late in the evening, and the mail truck had just pulled up. This was what we were all waiting for, and it turned out to be well worth the wait.

We spent our three days of liberty in Guam, usually at the exchange in the morning, at the beach during the afternoon, and in the club at night. They had a huge Navy exchange in Guam! I made one major purchase: I fell in love with a beautiful Winchester .243 game rifle and shelled out only ninety-six dollars for it. I figure I will get to use the rifle sometime in Wyoming between university classes. (I have to keep the rifle in the gunners mate's magazine under lock and key during the remainder of the trip.)

The enlisted men's club featured a band that was imported from the Philippines and so everybody really enjoyed them. You can't imagine how much everyone discovers that he likes the P.I. – once he leaves it! There was only one girl working in the club the first night (they weren't expecting us so soon, apparently), so she had to dance with five fellas at a time! Had this been the Philippines, there would have been large signs welcoming us as we pulled into port, and a club fully staffed and ready to rock and roll.

That left the rest of us poor neglected swabbies out in the cold, so we went next door to the restaurant and had a big steak dinner instead. This was the first really tasty civilian food that some of us guys had had in over a year, and we almost wept because it was so delicious! It made us realize what we had been missing in Nam. A lot of the guys telephoned their parents, wives, and girlfriends from Guam during our stop, too.

The engines seemed to have gotten a good rest since we were in Guam, because they haven't given us a bit of trouble since we left. It makes a watch so much more enjoyable – if a watch for four hours in the Hole can ever be described as enjoyable – when the engines aren't always acting up.

The officers laid down the law and said that if anyone was caught reading on watch he would receive the midwatch for the next three nights running. Everyone still reads, though, but we're a lot more sneaky about it now; we've even set up complicated warning signals to tell us whenever any gung-ho officer is on the prowl.

If you don't read on watch, you're very likely to fall asleep, which is a much more serious offense with even more gruesome consequences. There's absolutely nothing else to do but sit there and stare at the gauges and dials for four hours, and occasionally take engine readings. It can get awfully boring otherwise, with nothing to occupy your mind. Oh sure, you could always do something demented like getting a rag and wiping the oil off the main engines, or getting a bucket of soapy water and scrubbing the grease off the slippery deckplates. But nobody is that crazy!

We had an anchor pool, betting on the exact minute that we would moor in Guam, and some Scope Dope won the $300 pot. We'll be doing the same for our arrival in Pearl, Dago, and Bremerton, too. It costs five dollars a chance, and the jackpot gives some lucky guys extra spending money when we hit port.

And lately they've been having Bingo on the messdecks every evening just before I show the movie of the night. It costs two dollars a card and the cards are good for all five games. Each game the winner gets at least ten dollars, or even more if a lot of guys are playing at the time. It's a form of gambling, I guess – only the House doesn't make any money on it. We've all got a whole payday's cash in our pockets and it must be burning a hole there.

We are now en route to Hawaii as we speak. The water has been turning more gray than blue, and the scattered rainshowers are becoming more frequent. There are very large whitecaps on the waves, and the days are generally overcast. It looks like we might be heading for a little rough weather soon. Well, bring it on – the rougher the better!

> *"These waves were of the hue of slate, save for the tops, which were*
> *of foaming white, and all of the men knew the colors of the sea..."*
>
> *– Stephen Crane*

We're getting our sea legs good and proper now, you bet. When we walk down the passageway we're not careening into the bulkheads anymore when the ship pitches. The trick to getting your sea legs is to keep your legs loose at all times. Let them act like living shock absorbers of flesh and bone as the ocean tosses the ship around on the waves. Soon it comes natural and you don't even have to think about it – sea legs!

Sometimes when the bow of the ship rises out of one wave it will come down hard and flat on top of the next wave with a loud SMACK! And you can feel the steel hull vibrating all over the ship. If you're walking at the time, the deck will literally drop right out from under your feet and leave you walking in midair. If you're in your rack, it will feel like someone is trying to shake you out. I'd say that old ocean is a lot tougher than we give it credit for.

Whenever you pass through a hatch from one deck to another, you are supposed to latch the hatch cover securely in an upright position so it doesn't fall down and smack somebody in the head. Someone obviously forgot to do that the last time I passed through a hatch. The hatch was not secured and the eighty-pound cover came down, catching my head between the cover and the knife-edge of the hole. Stars flew and I got a terrible lump on my temple. I'm surprised it didn't crush my skull like an eggshell. I have pretty much recovered from my accident by now, but it still hurts when I chew food. What next?

I got off watch last night and I was bone weary. I had 15 minutes left before they secured the showers and then I was going to collapse in my rack. So in walks the Water King and says, "Stanga! Old buddy, old pal, friend of mine!" Great, I thought, he's got some work for me to do. No good ever came from those words. And sure enough, he did: he said that one of the water pumps down on the boiler flats was running in the opposite direction than what it was supposed to. (Fool things like that are always happening on this ship...must be the gremlins.)

So I strapped on my tool belt and crawled down into that sweat box. It took me about an hour to reverse the direction of the motor, and the sweat kept making my glasses slide down my nose and want to fall in the bilges. I was really getting mad when I dropped a screwdriver and a fuse and a vital bolt into the bilges (I was working almost totally upside down at the time!), and I had all I could do to hold my temper. More than anything else, I wanted to take my tool pouch and dump all the tools into the bilges and then throw the pouch in after them! I laughed about it later, though.

I've got the watch all night tonight and here I sit typing the evening away when I should be in bed getting sleep while I can. Thank goodness I'm young and foolish. I don't have a watch at all tomorrow night, though, so I will have a full night in the rack then – if something else doesn't require emergency repairs, that is. Only 507 days left in the Navy. And believe me, I'm counting.

June 1, 1970

While in Honolulu, we took a taxi down to Hotel Street, which is like Broadway in San Diego or Main Street in Tijuana or Magsaysay Drive in Olongapo City – the trashy part of town. But this reminded us fondly of overseas, so we felt quite at home there. We found a little grog shop with "Sailor Jerry's Tattoo and Skin-Illustration Parlour" in the back.

At first, we just went in there to browse and stare at the freaks, but soon we decided to get ourselves each a tattoo. The place appeared extremely clean and it looked like Sailor Jerry did good work on the customers who came in. We each found a sample picture on the walls which we liked, then told him that we would be back after we poured about a six-pack into each of us…to ease the pain, we planned, yup yup.

We came back a couple of hours later, and six of us took our turn going under the needles. Some of the guys did it just on the spur of the moment, and then regretted it the next day. We found out later that nearly half the crew of the ship got tattooed sometime in Honolulu on the evening of June 1! No lie!

There were some really clever ones, too. One of my buddies got hinges tattooed on the inside of his elbows. One fellow had "HOT" tattooed over one nipple and "COLD" over the other one. And one strange dude had a picture of a tough-looking bluebird wearing a white sailor's hat tattooed on his stomach (yowch!), pulling a worm out of his navel. Wild! Other guys got the traditional girlfriend's name, or Hawaiian hula girl, or coiled snake, or skull with a dagger jammed through it. You know what I mean, the real classy stuff.

I chose an American bald eagle over a US Navy banner, all topped with stars. I had it placed on my upper right arm where I could hide it with a sleeve when I wanted to. The tattoo itself cost twenty dollars and it took 45 minutes of nonstop pain to tack it on me for better or worse. I was sober by the time he was done with me. It was the worst continuous pain that I have ever experienced in my life! It felt like someone was cutting my skin into little strips and peeling it off slowly. Some of the guys actually had tears in their eyes.

Tattoo gotten on June 1, 1970.

My tattoo eventually scabbed over completely as it healed. I washed it gingerly with warm, soapy water, and kept it continually softened with baby oil. I had to be careful at all times not to scratch the itching scab or tear any of it off accidentally, as it would leave a glaring white spot in the tattoo then. It turned out extremely colorful and looks pretty sharp, as tattoos go, I must say.

I had long planned on getting a tattoo as a permanent souvenir of my Navy days. I chose to get one on June 1 – Suzie's birthday – as an easy way of always remembering how long I've had the thing.

PEARL HARBOR

June 5, 1970

Dear Gramma,

So far we have seen downtown Honolulu and Waikiki Beach, the famed Diamondhead volcano crater, and the monument to the *USS Arizona,* one of the battleships which the Japanese sank during the bombing of Pearl Harbor.

The officers aren't constantly hounding us like they usually do. It was getting so bad that you couldn't even do a simple repair job without stepping all over some young officer's toes and enduring his useless advice every step of the way. Good hiding places aboard ship are getting hard to find nowadays.

Our days are all about the same now: eat, work, sleep, stand watch, ad infinitum, ad nauseum. We still get a lot of reading done, though. I subscribe to *Time* magazine, *The National Lampoon,* and the *Alan Watt's Journal.* I am as well as can be expected. Only 491 days left in the Navy.

June 7, 1970

Dear Dad,

This is a Father's Day letter, or the best that I can manage considering where I am at the time – halfway between Hawaii and San Diego. I should have had the foresight to buy a proper card in Hawaii, but when liberty call goes down in a new port everything else leaves the mind.

If I remember right, it was about 18 days between Guam and Hawaii. That was our longest stretch, but it was very pleasant steaming. Something mysterious occurred during our cruise from Guam, and the officers have suddenly relented hunting us down and stopped being such slave-drivers. Consequently, we do less and less work, but still a lot of hiding and seeking for new places to sleep the day away. I wonder what is in the air?

A couple of days before we pulled into Hawaii, the officers sprang a surprise locker inspection on us. They were looking for drugs bought in Nam, and they looked absolutely everywhere: inside cameras, soap dishes, tape recorders, pill bottles, old socks, under mattresses and in dungaree pockets. What they did find was quite a surprise to them (but not us, naturally; we usually know of everything that is going on): pep pills, knives, pistols, ammo, bottles of whiskey, communist propaganda, etc.

They even found their suspected ten pounds of marijuana taped to the over-head of the tank deck, way up in a dark spot between two steel frames. There is a lot of that going on around here, but of what business is that to me? The less I know about it the better. They made a solemn little procession and escorted all the contraband to the rail and sent the junk down to Davy Jones' Locker.

Nothing else was said about it, though, because a couple of the new officers had been caught red-handed, too. But they never found half of the stuff that is actually hidden around this ship...like the electrician's private stock of Old Grand Dad bourbon, which we have stashed down in the gyro room inside the gyro-scope. It sure beats standing at the rail and looking at the flying fish all day with your mouth hanging open. (But not if we're caught, huh?)

As usual, I had the switchboard watch down in the Hole when we pulled into Pearl Harbor. This is my permanent station whenever we set the Special Sea and Anchor Detail, leaving or entering port. The bulk of the crew manned the rails in their whites while the rest of us were on watch. But I finally got relieved and jumped into my whites to go ashore.

The first thing that everybody does in port – after learning how to walk on sol-id ground again – is visit the Navy exchange, since we had a couple of paychecks to blow. I got about $100 worth of camera gear and stereophonic equipment. You can go bankrupt without even knowing it down here. That is why I would never want to live in Hawaii; the prices are double of those back in the States, and triple of those in Vietnam!

Hawaii is very nice this time of the year, the weather being nearly perfectly ideal and constant. The coeds are just starting to come down from the mainland and there are girls everywhere. We got a hotel room on Waikiki Strip, which is the main drag where all the hippies, teeny-boppers and surfer girls hang out. Never a dull moment there! Our room overlooked Waikiki Beach and the Pacific Ocean, and we were treated to a gorgeous sunset from our balcony every evening.

We went to most of the topless and bottomless nightclubs around, but they were a bit of a disappointment compared to the rowdy clubs in the Philippines and Vietnam. I guess I've just grown accustomed to slant-eyes. We did a bit of bar-hopping in downtown Honolulu. One great club had a resident band who could imitate just about any popular band out there today. They had us jumping up and down and singing "I Want to Take You Higher" by Sly and the Family Stone, and "War (What is it Good For?)" by Edwin Starr.

But most of the real swanky clubs didn't even open until after midnight! We got politely escorted out of one of them due to a riotous buddy of ours who never could hold his liquor. He couldn't hold it in his stomach, that is, and decided to put it underneath the table. *sigh*

Now we have left Pearl behind and are steaming steadily towards the California coast, where we will get a few days liberty in San Diego. All of a sudden the weather did an about-face and it's as chilly as it is during autumn back home. I haven't seen the sun since we left Hawaii. The sky and the ocean are both a choppy gray, and the breeze is laced with icy sea spray. It looks like we'll be dragging out the old work jackets again. I wonder if that means we'll be wearing our blues in Dago?

The way things look now, I might be getting my next set of orders sooner than I expected. Now they plan to sell this pig of a ship to the Indonesian Navy (serve 'em right, too) in San Diego and then ship the rest of us back out to the fleet. Our trip up to Bremerton, Washington, has officially been scratched, too. Rats!

But this also might mean that we could stay in San Diego for maybe a month and show the new Indonesian crew the ropes. That wouldn't be so bad. True, I'd just as soon not have to go through all that rigmarole of decommissioning her, but at the same time I don't want just any old hurry-up orders to a new ship either. I would like them to at least consider my dream sheet in which I requested a gunboat or tug or tin can anywhere in the Mediterranean.

Before we arrive stateside we have to get certain shots, which is always neces-sary when traveling from one country to another, especially when returning from a known malarial zone. The guys have to get shots for malaria, Black plague, diph-theria, cholera, small pox, yellow fever, influenza, and the dreadful gamma globu-lin inoculation in the gluteus maximus! I had just gotten my shot card updated when I left California the last time, and so I was the only son of a gun on the whole ship that didn't have to get any shots! That kind of ruffled a few feathers. Ha!

Bob and Al are both coming home on leave in late July, whereas Wilt has just left for Army boot camp to be a Second Looey. As this is the tail end of my luxuri-ous Sunday afternoon, I am going to wind this up – there isn't a whole helluva lot that goes on out at sea anyway. Also, I have the midwatch again, and even though tonight it will be cut short an hour (as we are passing through yet another time zone), it still takes up the bulk of the night. And tomorrow is another working day.

Sometimes it is hard to get any decent sleep in a compartment full of guys with the lights on all during the day, people coming and going constantly, having conversations in the rack beside you, yelling from one end of the room to the oth-er, wrestling, grab-assing, skylarking. Whenever I have to get some sleep before a watch, I just pop in my earplugs and tie a rag around my head for a blindfold. Then I can sleep pretty well, indeed. Four hundred eighty nine days left in the Navy.

SAN DIEGO
June 29, 1970
Dear Gramma,

Our arrival in San Diego was nothing short of routine. We watched jealously as the fighting ships – destroyers, cruisers, battleships – were met by cheering crowds of happy families, balloons, snappy music, and "Welcome Home" signs. Whenever we pull into port, we never merit a band on the dock welcoming us home, and very rarely a loved one. We are part of the inglorious service fleet; we're lucky to find our mail sacks waiting for us in the rain on some lonely pier when we tie up.

Big news: I will be coming home for a thirty-day leave on July 15th! I could hardly believe it when my orders finally came in and I read that! Actually, I don't even have a week of leave accumulated on the books yet, but anyone who has just returned from Vietnam automatically gets a month leave. Isn't that great? I am so excited that I can hardly wait for the days to pass – only two weeks away! I am looking forward to doing a bunch of camping when I get home. I just want to take it easy for a while and catch up on my sleep.

I am very anxious to get to my new ship, though, too. Anyway, I'm relieved that I did not get stuck on a shore station somewhere. Some guys prefer shore stations in the States for some bizarre reason, but I'd much rather be a seagoing swabbie. I love the ocean! (Tell me again why I'm living in South Dakota?) My new ship is the *USS Elkhorn,* and her hull designation is AOG-7. She is a small ship with a crew of about eighty that hauls fuel oil and aviation gasoline.

I saw her several times while I was in the Philippines, and I'm pretty sure that she makes stops in Vietnam, too. I sure hope so – I need the extra money and I want to be over there doing my small part. She is homeported in Pearl Harbor, but that doesn't necessarily mean that we'll ever pull in there. (The *Iredell County* was homeported in Norfolk, Virginia, but she hasn't been there in years.)

I am glad that she is a small ship, because then you get to know everybody real fast and you all know your own job. I long to see the P.I. again, too. I love those jungled islands! I am so tickled to death with my orders right now that there isn't a thing the Navy could possibly do to me to make me mad – except cancel my leave! What a horrible thought.

Since we have been here in San Diego, some kind soul in the crew decided to dig into his own pocket and rent a TV for the messdecks. And so we sit up half the night watching old movies, horror films, soap operas, the news, and all the dumb, dumb commercials. California must have the goofiest TV commercials anywhere! It had been so long since any of us had even seen television that it was a real treat. We especially get a kick out of this one new show for kids called "Sesame Street." It's a hoot.

We watched an old speech by Nixon last night. There was a lot of childish, un-patriotic booing and catcalls from his TV audience, but a lot of what he said about our policy in Southeast Asia seemed to make sense. Sometimes he has a way of sounding quite logical, when I know that can't really be the case.

I was in Mickey Finn's place last week when they played the song "America." They shined a baby spotlight on the US Flag and almost everybody stood up and sang at the top of their voice. But a lot of the civilians just sat there like lumps holding their beers, and that disgusted me. And these were not long-haired kids, either, but supposedly grown-up folks. They're probably the same ones who wonder what's wrong with kids today.

We just spent the last three days manhandling a thousand-pound generator up two decks, across the main deck, down one deck, through five compartments, and then down another deck. And there were only four of us, so we were bone weary in the end. Thank goodness for block and tackle!

Upon moving the big generator away from the bulkhead, we revealed a live Chinese rocket hidden behind it. Asking around, we quickly found out that one guy had bought it for a war souvenir back in Vietnam and was smuggling it home. How did he even get it on board?! We told him to get it off the boat immediately or we were going to tell the Old Man. For pete's sake, what do some people think of?!

So now that we have gotten that generator installed, they tell us that it doesn't work (we told them that in the first place) and that we will have to pull it out again (we also told them this was going to happen). Nobody listens to us enlisted swabs. Typical Navy.

Last week we disconnected all the motors and pumps on the boiler flats and got them ready to take to the shop, as ordered. Today, then, they tell us to hook them back up again – they won't be going to the shop after all. We knew this would happen. Day in and day out we are constantly undoing our own work. But what can we say? It's the officers who are running this little sideshow of the war, even if they don't know what they're doing half the time. Oh well, only 15 more days on this ship and then *home*. Nothing can discourage me at this point…not even cleaning toilets.

There is a very odd-looking ship in the San Diego harbor. When we asked what it was, we were told it was one of the new-style LSTs. These ships are of an entirely new design, larger and faster than previous LSTs. The *USS Newport* (LST-1179) was the first "T" to depart from the big bow-door design developed by the British during World War II. The new hull shape required to achieve twenty-knot speeds would not permit bow doors, thus these ships unload via a 112-foot ramp *over* the bow; this ramp is supported by twin derrick arms. A stern gate to the tank deck allows loading and unloading of gear from the rear. This new design gives them 5,000 more square feet of storage space than the old LSTs. Impressive!

Oh – tomorrow is payday and I will be mailing a big package of books home to you to store for me. I just can't bring myself to leave my books behind. That must be the Swede in me. My books have helped me get through a lot of stress overseas.

Most of the guys here are always reading westerns and murder-mystery novels. I can't see that at all. A good western once in a while is something I enjoy from time to time, but not book after book after book – they should try to vary their reading material a little bit and get a more rounded outlook on life. I mean, you wouldn't think of eating just one kind of food forever, would you? But they're salty old boys and pretty much stuck in their ways.

I am sorry to hear that Aunt Lujeanne is feeling low again and having more trouble with her diabetes. I hope she is all right by the time I get home to visit you all next month. See you soon!

July 1, 1970

Admiral Elmo Zumwalt, Jr. begins his new duties today as the US CNO. He was specifically chosen by the Department of the Navy to ease racial tensions in the Navy, eliminate Mickey Mouse rules and regulations, and make service life generally more appealing. Prior to the appointment of Admiral Zumwalt, the re-enlistment rate had been dropping sharply.

INVITATION
July 15, 1970

"The commanding officers of the *USS Iredell County* (LST-839) and the *USS Clarke County* (LST-601) request the honor of your presence at a de-commissioning ceremony and commissioning ceremony into the Republic of Indonesia Navy on Wednesday, the fifteenth of July, 1970, at ten o'clock onboard the *USS Iredell County* and *USS Clarke County* at the US Naval Station in San Diego, California."

The *USS Iredell County* was then transferred to the Indonesian Navy. It became a "Teluk" class ship called the *Teluk Bone 511,* of 2,100 tons cargo capacity, in the hands of our capable allies south of the equator.

VI.
USS ELKHORN (AOG-7)

14 AUGUST 1970 — 3 AUGUST 1971

EM3 Steve Stanga B617389
USS Elkhorn (AOG-7)
FPO
San Francisco, California
96601

PEARL HARBOR

August 19, 1970

Dear Family,

Thank goodness I don't have to go through all that rigmarole with flights and buses and taxis ever again – I hate moving! The next big silver bird that starts flying under me will be carrying me homeward bound…once and for all!

My leave was the best darn vacation that I've ever had, and I don't regret spending $1,300 for it either. I hated to leave home. It was a long old bus ride down to Omaha; they never once let us off for a drink, a sandwich, a nature break, or to stretch our legs! I had a real good time chewing the fat with Aunt Amy and Uncle John, and they took me out to eat at a great restaurant once again.

I bought a military standby ticket on a flight out to Frisco, like I usually do, but this time I got bumped off. We came back to the airport later and I got bumped off that flight, too. So Johnny bought me a regular coach ticket, but that was full also. I hate it when they always overbook! We were getting down to slim pickings. I didn't want to take the chance of getting bumped off their last flight of the day, so I had him buy me a first-class ticket – as a loan, you understand. Once on the plane, though, they had a coach seat open up, so I took that and got back the money from the first-class ticket. It sure was a lot of heartache and worry and stress at the time, but I finally made it to Frisco.

Things ran a little smoother after that. I found a Greyhound bus going up to Travis AFB and that got me there at 7:40 PM. (I had to report in no later than 7:45 PM! Yipes!) I got a flight out of Travis at 0100 in the morning. It was an old Air Force job; the seats were facing the rear of the plane, there were no windows, and it was darn chilly up there.

They served a sack lunch once during the six-hour flight to Hawaii. I managed to get a little sleep in the air over the Pacific, but it was almost unbearable, with a lot of intermittent turbulence. There was a small dependent girl about Tootie's age sitting next to me who was scared to death the whole trip.

Upon arrival in Pearl Harbor, I hoisted my sea bag up to my shoulder and strode off to locate my ship. I climbed on board at 0630 and they got underway at 0800. I was cutting things pretty close all the way around. Since I had been traveling for what seemed like two days, I was dead to the world. But I still had to check in, move in, and then put in a full day's work before I could turn in. I ended up working six hours, sleeping six hours, etc., for three solid days. Off and on like that until I thought I would perish. But we are back in port now, and I've got two solid nights of uninterrupted sleep ahead of me before I have the darn duty again.

The *USS Elkhorn* (AOG-7) is named after the Elkhorn River in Nebraska. She was built by Cargill Inc. of Savage, Minnesota, and launched down the Minnesota River on May 15, 1943. She weighs 1,850 tons light, and about 4,570 tons with a full load of 17,775 barrels capacity. Being 310 feet long overall, she has a complement of about six officers and 75 enlisted men. She is armed with three-inch guns. The four main engines are diesel-electric; 3100 brake-horsepower equaling 14 knots. Our sister ship is the *USS Genesee* (AOG-8). (The *USS Agawam* was AOG-6, but she was disposed of back in 1961 already.)

Naturally, my duties aboard the *Elkhorn* are no different than on my other ships. I have to take care of electrical equipment and stand engine room watches. I also have to keep all the ship's running lights operational. Even the degaussing gear is the electrician's responsibility here on board; this is electrical gear which sets up neutralizing magnetic fields to help protect the ship against magnetic-action mines. This system is pretty confusing to me, however; thank goodness we rarely have to do anything with this stuff.

Most recently we have been about 120 miles off the coast of Oahu on some classified sonar operation with a new submarine. This old flounder rocks almost as bad as my LST!

We spotted a school of sharks out at sea one day and the guys decided to try to catch one. They tied an open can of mechanical foam onto a rope and drug it behind us in the water as we steamed. This kept the sharks interested, following us until we got a hook and line prepared. The "fly" was a huge, white, furry shop towel wrapped around a two-inch hook. On the hook was a pound of rancid bacon which we got from the Stewburners. They tied this to a heavy line and towed it behind us. When the shark hit, the line broke like single-strand seine thread, and we sailed away into the sunset empty-handed. The shark probably didn't even get a belly-ache out of the deal.

We've got quite a mixture of guys in this here crew: Mexicans, Filipinos, several dozen colored guys, and even a small handful of American Indians (for example, Nelsen Bringsplenty, Alvin Esquivel, and Charley Goodeagle). They're a real fun-loving bunch, for the most part, and I'm surprised how quickly I fit in, like they were missing a puzzle piece or something, until I showed up.

For some reason, out in the fleet the Filipinos always end up working as stewards in the wardroom, being sort of lackeys and butlers for the officers. Doesn't seem quite right somehow. They ought to have an opportunity to seek better rates than that.

I am already qualified to stand switchboard and throttle watches on this ship. How about them apples?! And in only two days at sea! The XO could hardly believe I caught on so fast. Standing throttle watches is rather fascinating right now, but I suppose that will soon wear off. I certainly hope I finish out my last year in the Navy on this ship. I do NOT want to move again.

I hear the *Elkhorn* will be on local operations in and out of Pearl Harbor until January of 1971. Then she will deploy to the South Pacific (i.e., Hong Kong, Philippines, Singapore, Thailand, etc.). They don't think that they'll be going back to Vietnam anymore, though. Rats! The ship is 27 years old, but is really in good shape. They just got out of a long yard period of overhaul here, too. Boy, am I ever glad that I didn't get in on that!

I got a good middle rack and an accessible locker that's at eye-level. What could be sweeter? There's a TV on board, too, but which only works when we are in port of course. Chow so far is mediocre – nothing like the home-cooking I just had! But for every Sunday dinner we have roast turkey with all the trimmings. No complaints from me about that!

I missed the second-class petty officer exam when I was home on leave in February, and now I missed it *again* when I was home on leave this time. So if I want to go up for second class anymore now, it means that I'll have to sign up for another year in the Navy. And you can bet your boondockers that I'm not likely to do that! I reckon I'll just be content to finish out my hitch as a third class.

August 20, 1970

This will be an awfully short journal entry, as I really must get some decent sleep tonight. Mom writes that there were a lot of waterworks at home after I left. I hope the little ones didn't feel too bad about my departure. I'll be back home before they know it.

Sister Jennifer probably took my absence the hardest. She cries and cries whenever I leave home, and mopes around the house for days afterwards. She would even go into my closet and stand amongst my civilian clothes, because they smelled like me.

With part of the $1,300 I had available to spend on my leave, I went down to Knodel Jewelry Store and purchased a set of diamond rings for my future wife at $325. Everybody else thought this was incredibly unromantic, seeing as how I didn't even have a girlfriend at the time, but I was just trying to be realistic and practical. I knew that I would not have that kind of money to burn once I got out of the Navy, but I did have it while I was home on leave this time around. I still picked it out with her in mind, whoever she may be, and that's the thought that should count. I am keeping the diamond rings in Gramma's safe-deposit box at the bank in Salem, where they will remain until such time as I need them.

September 18, 1970

I just graduated from Damage Control School here in Pearl Harbor, Hawaii. We learned how to cope with all kinds of damage situations from fire and first-aid to nuclear attack and structural damage. It was a very interesting school!

But my favorite part was the day we practiced the maintenance of stability and buoyancy exercises. They had specially-built structures that resembled the interior of ship's compartments, with holes and tears in the bulkheads. They would put us inside, then turn on the water…as if the ship were sinking. It was up to us to repair the damage before we lost the ship. So we were usually working in cold water up to our necks, erecting braces from the bulkheads, installing conical wooden plugs, and securing off compartments from the rest of the ship. It was a blast!

September 23, 1970

Four of us fun-seekers decided to spend the weekend at Makaha Beach, where the surfing is internationally popular on the island. It lies clear on the west coast of Oahu, where giant rollers come crashing into shore that have been growing in size clear across the Pacific. In the winter, wave heights often average fifteen feet and can peak as high as thirty feet plus!

We had to rent a car to drive there. During the long hot day we swam and built complex sand castles, and drank a whole ice chest full of Primo beer. The waves were something to behold and fun to play in!

In the evening we drove into Waianae and each bought a bottle of liquor. My brilliant plan was to drink fairly harmless screwdrivers, so I bought a quart of vodka and a quart of orange juice. But I forgot to purchase anything to mix my drinks *in,* so I ended up just drinking straight out of the bottles. I would take a drink of vodka and then chase it down with a swallow of OJ. Needless to say, the orange juice was long gone before the vodka was even half finished. So I drank the rest of the vodka straight! Seemed like a good idea at the time.

Makaha Beach, Oahu, Hawaii.

Come nightfall, we dug a pit in the sand for a roaring fire of driftwood, and when all the liquor was gone we curled up around the edge of the fire and slept in the sand. Some of the guys had their beach towels to cover up with, but I had forgotten mine back on the ship.

The next morning was a true revelation! I can't speak for the rest of the guys, but I was not sure if I was dead or alive. If this was death, then it made me appreciate life all the more. And if this was life, then I wished I could die. My head was splitting in half. My eyeballs felt like they were being forced out of their sockets, and I had trouble focusing. I had the dry heaves most of the morning; my stomach produced nothing but tiny amounts of ochre-colored globules into the sand.

I could tell that I was already coming down with one hell of a chest cold from sleeping exposed on the chilly beach with nothing but swimming trunks and a T-shirt. My hands were blackened and painful; the guys said that whenever the fire died down, I would simply reach in and grab the hot logs and turn them over with my bare hands. Also, I had the foulest taste in my mouth that I could ever imagine; they said that I had smoked a whole pack of cigarettes while sitting around the fire. And me a lifelong nonsmoker!

I remembered none of this, naturally, even after they told me about it. A complete blank, a merciful alcoholic blackout. And to top things off, I was sunburned to a royal Hawaiian crisp. I briefly considered going to sickbay back on the base. It was without a doubt the worst hangover that I have ever had in my entire life!

September 26, 1970

Dear Tim,

On my birthday we will be sailing far out on the ocean for three days. I hope someday you can ride on the ocean and see how much fun it is. Last weekend we stayed at the beach for two days. We built a big bon-fire in the sand and slept on the beach all night. It was really nice, but there were stray dogs and wild pigs in that part of the Hawaiian countryside. We only saw one wild boar, though.

October 17, 1970

I've sent in my admission papers to the University of Wyoming, and am waiting to hear if I've been accepted or not. I plan to major in Wildlife Management.

This second-class electrician buddy of mine, Parker Pratt, has had his personal sports car shipped from California over to Honolulu, so we can tour the island cheaper than renting a car all the time. It is a little red convertible Triumph. Lots of fun!

A shipfitter on board, name of Zielenski, walks in his sleep, and normally that's grounds for a medical discharge. The Navy can't afford to have somebody walk off the fantail when we're out in the middle of the ocean. Last week we were out of port for a three-day cruise, and one night they found Zielenski lying on the deck beside the railing, sound asleep. He was escorted back to his bunk and claimed he didn't remember a thing in the morning.

Some guys have been known to use this ploy to try to get out of the Navy if they hate it bad enough. But they are usually shipped off to a Naval hospital first where they are observed for a while by experts to see if they aren't actually faking it. Those who are found to be shamming end up with some unpleasant disciplinary action taken against them.

But Zielenski insists that he likes the Navy and doesn't want to get out. Who really knows what's in a man's heart? Anybody else would be overjoyed if they could actually sleepwalk and would qualify for early parole.

Anyway, he has an identical twin brother, also named Zielenski, who came on board our ship just a week ago. He works in the Damage Control Locker. So now we've got two of these crazy Polacks running around loose and you can't even tell them apart. Sometimes they switch duty and stand each other's watches. You have to check their IDs even when you have a casual conversation with them, because they're fond of making a fool out of people.

We watch Hawaiian TV early Saturday mornings, which features the old Three Stooges comedies and laughable All-Star Wrestling and the violent roller derbies. (The women skaters fight dirtier than the men wrestlers!) A monstrous, half-witted Indian crew member of ours, named Esquivel, likes to imitate the foolish fake wrestlers, so he runs berserkly about the ship, dragging guys out of their racks, and disabling men left and right, growling, working himself into a lather. He thinks it's funny. We think he's a menace and ought to be put down.

We see about thirty movies a week here on the ship, not including the short subjects and old TV series that are available. I show the movies on the messdecks as soon as the Stewburners have everything cleared away and cleaned up after chow. They enjoy comedies, westerns, murder-mysteries, and Walt Disney, believe it or not. I try to stay away from picking out porno-flicks, as they do nobody any good whatsoever in our situation.

I recently got a letter from Al Larson, urging me to take leave the same time that he does, so we can see each other at home. He is part of the Atlantic Fleet, which is rumored to do next to nothing compared to us, so he thinks I can just pick up and take off any old time I want to. But we're part of the mighty Pacific Service Fleet, which means we must service the larger and more important ships of the fleet, and plan our schedules around *them*. Not the other way around.

Three hundred and fifty eight days left in the Navy. I'll be 22 years old when I get out. (I had just turned 19 years of age when I entered.)

NAVY RELIEF

Payday was coming up soon (not soon enough to suit us) and we were all ready to make large and substantial donations to the Navy Relief program, which aided Navy dependents. It wasn't always this way.

Every payday they would set up a table on the messdecks for the disbursing personnel to hand out cash to eager, poverty-stricken sailors. At the far end of the table sat a representative from Navy Relief, who caught the sailors at the most opportune time – with money in their pockets. It was quite painless then to extract a few bills from us for charity. That particular payday they were trying a new ploy.

For every five dollars that a sailor generously handed over, he would get a whole day of extra liberty, which could be claimed at any time of the workweek! And if there's something a sailor loves besides girls, whiskey, and the sea…it's liberty.

Needless to say, the Navy Relief program started to receive staggering donations. Parker and I had already purchased a whole week of extra liberty apiece, so that we could tour Oahu thoroughly at our leisure before we were deployed to WesPac and other parts unknown.

October 31, 1970

Dear Family,

It's a slack Saturday afternoon here on the ship; a light drizzle outside makes it very nice to stay inside and look out. I'm just getting a few postcards and letters off this afternoon while I'm in the mood and have the time. I've been pretty busy with Ref-Tra exercises to do much of anything else. Explanation to follow.

But Ref-Tra is finally over with, and our Engineering Division ended up with an excellent rating overall. Our final battle problem was last Friday and I shudder when I think back on it. Let me start at the beginning of all the trouble: let's see, I think it was when I enlisted…

Last weekend we got the word about noon on Saturday that all ten of our giant fuel tanks had to be mucked out by Monday morning, when we were going to take a full load of fuel to the other side of Oahu Island.

By mucking, I mean cleaning out all the old oil and sludge and bilge water that had settled on the bottom of the tanks. We always kept our fuel tanks ballasted down with a couple thousand tons of fresh water when we weren't actually carrying fuel, all of which could be shifted around to maintain stability and keep the ship on an even keel.

We couldn't believe our ears at this announcement; usually it took all hands an entire week to muck out the tanks, but they seriously expected just the duty section to get it done in a mere two days!

So down into the foul, nasty tanks we went with the oil fumes and the stifling tropical heat. The bunker sea oil used as fuel on our naval ships is excessively crude and obnoxious, possibly only one refinement grade above liquefied dinosaurs and prehistoric plants, and it made you sick to your stomach just to smell it.

Late on Sunday afternoon it was clear that we weren't going to get done on time, so the officers started throwing everybody down into the tanks who were loitering around the ship during their leisure time. Some drunken sailors made the sad mistake of coming back early from liberty to take a nap, and were ordered directly into the tanks.

The considerate Chief Stewburner, an older black guy name of Loughmiller, kept a steady flow of sandwiches and soup coming down to us from the galley. We were occasionally allowed topside for a bit of fresh air and to clear our heads. For a while there, us poor swabs were down on our hands and knees, sopping up the stinky water with rags and wringing them into buckets. I wanted to find the Executive Officer and make him eat that rag.

Later on I had to take my engine room watch, monitoring dopey gauges and dials. But at least it was better than mucking! I got off watch at midnight and went right back down into the tanks with the rest of the guys.

We finished mucking sometime before Monday's dawn came, and we were mercifully given the next weekend off as reward for our slave labor. But my dungarees and beloved boondockers (the most comfortable pair of shoes I had ever owned) positively reeked of oil and the sickening stench of sour sludge, ruined beyond salvation even by our industrial-strength laundry department – and I dropped the clothing and boots overboard as soon as we next went to sea.

Within hours of crawling out of the tanks we took on a full load (about 600,000 gallons) of JP-5. By unstable, I mean that if it has the slightest inclination to blow the hell up it'll just go ahead and do so, and send us all to that big shipyard in the sky. We didn't much care for the stuff one damn bit.

Anyway, so we had our last days of Ref-Tra – this letter is about Ref-Tra, remember? We didn't especially care for their little scheme to hold gunnery practice with all that crazy fuel on board, but we went out and did it anyway. Ours was not to reason why…

We had an actual casualty this week during one of the gunnery drills. The first loader on the forward three-inch gun mount, an Indian named Brisbois, got behind the gun when it went off. There is a yellow safety line painted right on the deck which marks the maximum distance the gun will recoil, but apparently he was standing slightly inside of this line. Upon firing, the breech-block recoiled and slammed into his chest and shoulder. He got a broken shoulder and some busted ribs out of the deal. And when he hit the deck he also got a concussion. It sure could have been worse, though.

I imagine it felt like getting hit with an anvil or something. We steamed at full speed all the way back into port so we could get him to the hospital. He's going to be alright eventually, but it was a hell of a way for the rest of us to get early liberty that day.

Wednesday and Thursday we steamed around the island to Kaneohe Bay to off-load our fuel. A whole bunch of exciting things happened while we were at Kaneohe. We were moored right in the middle of a porpoise farm; there must have been two dozen of them critters around us at all times. They looked like they were really having a ball, but I suppose appearances can be deceiving.

We were next to an airfield, and in the afternoon we got to see a Blue Angel's air show. They were terrific; and the parachutists put on a good show, too. They would freefall from a bomber with red smoke flares attached to their heels; it gave the impression they were going down in flames.

We also got word while we were at Kaneohe that we would be leaving for Midway Island first thing next Monday morning. That cheated us out of our big engineering beach party that we had been promised for months. It was the only incentive that kept us going long and strong through Ref-Tra! And to make matters even worse, about thirty guys were told that their leaves later this month were cancelled. Boy, you talk about a mutinous crew!

That night the crew was so mad that about half of them went out in town and got stinking drunk. They came back and tore up the ship a little bit, sat on the pier and threw rocks at it, stuff like that. My sea-daddy, McCallen (the first-class electrician that I work for, our boss and nemesis) was throwing tables and chairs the length of the berthing compartment before he finally calmed down and put his wrath to bed. Some of the guys were seriously talking of going AWOL for a couple of weeks, but nothing ever came of that foolishness; commonsense prevailed.

Anyway, it sounds like we'll be taking a full load of fuel up to Midway and will be back in two weeks. Midway lies over a thousand miles northwest of Honolulu.

THEN the Old Man was going to ballast down with water in Kaneohe just to ride back comfortably to Pearl, where we would then have to muck out the tanks all over again and fill them back up with JP-5 to haul to Midway! Thank goodness, he saw the folly of that lame-brain idea and decided against it. Consequently, we wallowed like a fat sow all the way back to home port – but it was better than mucking!

Reveille was at 0400 all week long, and we were really dragging ass by the time Friday rolled around, time for our final battle problem.

I was the sound-powered phone talker down in the engine room during the battle with the Purple Nation, and things were really jumping on the line as they simulated one battle scenario after another. I had an observer on my line listening to every report I made to the bridge and Damage Control Central, evaluating my performance, and he made me nervous.

But our final grade was 95; so I assume that meant we would have survived in a real situation. Us electricians got the highest scores in the whole Engineering Division. The Ref-Tra observer had nothing but good to say about our teamwork. My sea-daddy said that we made him look very good. Anyway, everyone is sure glad it's finally over with! We've had it up to *here* with drills!

I caught a jellyfish the other day. I fished him out of the ocean with a bucket as he floated past. He certainly was a strange-looking thing – I suppose he felt the same about me – and I watched him for an hour swimming around in the bucket. He had a tiny yellow fish that was with him constantly, hovering just inside the tentacles; he opted to stay with the jellyfish even while I was capturing him. I figured out that the fish must be the lure for the jellyfish to get other fish within his reach, whereupon the yellow fish would get the scraps. It was rather interesting. I had a bottle of rubbing alcohol that I was going to put him in, and send him to Wilt in college. But when the thing died on me, it shriveled up to nothing. So I dumped him back in the drink.

We passed a huge, barren rock the other day called Tern Island. It was named thus on account of all the terns that used to cover it like a white, living blanket. But they all died off years ago. The ecologists still don't understand exactly what happened. But all of a sudden the birds stopped mating and just began to die off. They wouldn't pair off at all. And this is kind of tragic because, after all, one good tern deserves another, right?

My partner in crime, Parker, and I have been seeing quite a few very enjoyable movies out in Waikiki lately: "Strawberry Statement," "Downhill Racer," "Getting Straight," "R.P.M.," "Colossus, the Forbin Project," and "Soldier Blue," to name a few good flicks.

We were fortunate enough to see "Tora! Tora! Tora!" in a large, wide-screen theater downtown. How fitting that Honolulu should be one of four different sites for the world premiere of the movie, seeing as how it all actually took place here, and was filmed here. That may have explained the inflated prices, too. I don't know how Parker and I even got ahold of tickets; there were nearly 3,000 people gathered outside the Waikiki No. 1 Theatre on opening night.

Anyway, it was a very intense movie and the full house enjoyed it tremendously, not to mention learning all that little-known history. When the house lights came up after the 145-minute movie ended, we noticed that there were a large number of Japanese in the audience. (Nearly 30 out of every 100 people in Hawaii are of Japanese ancestry.) I was suddenly worried that somebody in the crowd was going to say something incredibly ignorant and ugly to them, being caught up in the spirit of the movie like we were, but fortunately nobody said anything as we filed out quietly. Still, I had to wonder what was going through their inscrutable little minds, though.

The *USS Hancock* (CVA-19) is tied up right on the other side of the pier from us now. She's an aircraft carrier formerly named the *Ticonderoga*. They just pulled in here for emergency repairs and are presently awaiting shipyard availability. One of their pilots flying a Crusader jet crashed right into the end of the flight deck when he was landing out at sea. He was killed when he ejected himself out; he might have been rescued if he had stayed with the plane, but I don't imagine he had much time to analyze the situation. Five of the airedales on the flight deck dived down into the gun-tubs to escape the flying wreckage, and they were injured as a result, too. I was out a little bit ago taking pictures of the ship, but I have to be very careful not to overdo it. Picture-taking is still kind of a touchy subject here in Pearl Harbor.

Still no word from the University of Wyoming about my application. But then, I suppose there is quite a lot of paperwork to kick around. In the meantime, I am keeping myself busy with three algebra textbooks, trying to cram several years of neglected high school math into my defective brain in the next few months. I am well, save for a killer hangover now and then. I send my love.

OFFICIAL QUARTERLY MARKS
November 1, 1970
(Assigned to the *USS Elkhorn*)

"Stanga is assigned to 'E' Division and performs routine maintenance on shipboard electrical systems and equipment. Stanga works well. He willingly accepts assigned tasks, and will usually put forth his best effort in their completion."

ONE DAY IN THE LIFE OF THE *ELKHORN*

Back home, whenever the fuel gauge in your car reads "empty," you casually pull into the closest gas station and say "Fill 'er up!" But on the other side of the world, an aircraft carrier runs dry and there isn't any handy service station out in the middle of the Pacific Ocean.

USS Elkhorn (AOG-7)

That's when a pretty little 310-foot ship pulls up alongside the bird farm and starts rigging fuel lines over to the thirsty ship. She is the *USS Elkhorn* (AOG-7), one of ServPac's floating gas stations. She was commissioned on February 13, 1944, to help in the war effort, and she immediately began delivering her vital cargo to combat vessels of the US Fleet.

And since that time, she has been highly appreciated in many odd corners of the world: New Zealand, Pearl Harbor, McMurdo Sound in Antarctica, Brisbane in Australia, Point Barrow in Alaska, Hong Kong, Sasebo in Japan, Midway, Wake, Marshall Islands, Guam, Shanghai, New Caledonia, Aruba of the Netherlands West Indies, Subic Bay in the Philippines, and many other exotic ports along the way.

During 1965 and 1966, the *Elkhorn* pumped over 14 million gallons of fuel in support of operations in South Vietnam, which won her two consecutive Battle Efficiency "E" awards. This type of record was unheard of for a ship of her type. She is like an oasis in an ocean desert – which comes to you – even though she doesn't give green stamps. When the *Elkhorn* isn't off-loading her precious liquid cargo, she is usually busy with a host of other industrious activities.

In the fall of 1970, the *Elkhorn* was engaged in a fatiguing exercise known as Ref-Tra while taking a short respite from her replenishment duties. At that time, I was stationed aboard the *Elkhorn,* patiently trying to complete my last days of active duty without going totally *non compos mentis* [not of sound mind].

We had drills from sunrise to sunset; every kind of drill a fellow could imagine, and some that were hardly imaginable. Any sort of situation that could possibly arise on board a ship was simulated and presented to us to handle the best we could.

During our four weekly cruises we ventured about 150 miles out to sea off the coast of Oahu in the Hawaiian Island chain. We had been moored so long at the pier that almost everybody had temporarily lost their sea legs. Consequently, on the first day at sea there was a phalanx of men leaning over the lifelines, changing colors like a bunch of nervous chameleons, and giving up involuntary offerings to King Neptune.

The Stewburners kept a large tray of sliced apples and saltines in the galley for the crew to nibble on. The very last thing that anybody wanted to do at the time was eat, but the secret to diminishing the ill effects of seasickness is to keep a little something in the stomach.

Drinking lots of water along with the saltines helped considerably to fill the stomach and ameliorate the queasy feeling. And secondly, if you do have to retch, at least you'd have something tangible to regurgitate; the dry heaves will rip your insides out! Seasickness is a ghastly sensation, and there really isn't much one can do about it when it hits. Doc had some new anti-vertigo pills, but they made a person so groggy that they were next to useless.

One purpose of our cruise was to test the sonar gear on a newly-launched tin can. Our ship towed underwater targets of various shapes and sizes, and the new destroyer tracked them by sonar.

Another day we were pressed to rig a highline transfer between our ship and another ship which was deployed with us. We sent a young dispensable lieutenant across in a bosun chair on the highline while the ships were steaming along at a reckless nine knots. If the ships came too close together, the line would sag, and at the very least the man would get a good dunking in the sea. In the worst-case scenario, the ships could come together completely and the man might get crushed to death. Steering failure at that crucial moment could cause just this sort of accident, but it hardly ever happened.

After the nervous lieutenant made it across safely, we swapped a bundle of movies with the other crew. Halfway across the highline the films were suddenly engulfed in a big swell out of nowhere, but they had been carefully wrapped in plastic beforehand. The Ship of Fools sailed on.

Altogether, we had four grueling weeks of Ref-Tra. The drills seemed to go on forever. Sometimes the Old Man would sound GQ (General Quarters) in the middle of the night, and we had to drag ourselves out of a perfectly sound sleep and rush pell-mell to our battle stations. The crew was constantly bone-weary and on edge, and tempers erupted frequently. To serve as a safety valve for the men, the division officers promised us a party at Keehi Lagoon as soon as Ref-Tra was finished.

A typical day of Ref-Tra started with a 0400 reveille, and from then on we struggled to stay on our feet until 1900, when we would turn in exhausted. Reviewing officers from the base simulated such entertaining scenarios as switchboard blackout, steering failure, engine stall, and crew casualties. A strange reviewing officer approached a sailor and tapped him on the shoulder. "You are being electrocuted," he announced fatally, and with a sigh the weary sailor collapsed on the deckplates and started convulsing until someone noticed him and revived him with the proper first-aid. Or not.

My GQ station was Repair Two, a damage-control locker located in the bow of the ship, directly beneath one of the three-inch guns. One day the gunnery boys had some target practice to sharpen up their marksmanship. They threw a couple of steel drums overboard, half full of gasoline, and commenced whanging away at them with the big gun. Whenever any of the big guns are going to be fired, the entire crew must withdraw to their GQ stations.

Suddenly the first shell was discharged and everything that wasn't lashed down jumped six inches off the deck down in the damage-control locker where I was. Light bulbs shattered and paint chipped from the bulkheads. The thunderous noise was truly teeth-rattling! They shot off 120 rounds before they blew up the gasoline drums bobbing around in the rough seas. In the meantime, cowering beneath the noisy gun, I tried to imagine what it must be like inside a turret on the battleship *New Jersey* with its huge 16-inch cannons!

On the third day out we had a complicated battle problem thrown at us. GQ went down right after breakfast and we all rushed to our battle stations. We set Condition Zebra, which means that all doors, hatches, and portholes about the ship were dogged tightly shut in order to maintain our watertight integrity. During prolonged periods of combat readiness, Condition Zebra may be modified somewhat to permit distribution of food, use of sanitary facilities, ventilation of various compartments, and other necessary functions.

As was customary, we donned our Mark-V gas masks, life jackets, helmets, sound-powered phones, first-aid kits, flashlights, and other paraphernalia that we were told were indispensable for any crisis. Actually, a guy couldn't even squeeze through a normal hatch opening with all that crap hanging off him like a Christmas tree. But who were we to point this out to an omnipotent officer?

The first thing they simulated that day was a rocket hit in the bow, and they added authenticity to the drill by dropping a concussion grenade over the side of the ship. The loud explosion was especially amplified for those of us who were located below the water line at the time. We cautiously left the repair locker and started to hunt for "damage."

Handwritten signs were taped up around the ship, indicating what sort of damage had occurred at that particular location. We found a "large gaping hole" in the hull of the ship, which we hustled to patch using a canvas-covered wooden plug and your basic sledge hammer.

There was also a "raging fire" in the forward bosun locker, where nylon line and deck gear were stowed. Some shyster had thrown a smoke bomb into the compartment to make it more realistic yet, bless his heart. We adjusted our OBAs and went in to extinguish the conflagration. As the sole electrician of the damage-control party, my duties were to secure all electrical power to that room and rig emergency lighting and ventilation. The portable Red Devil blower rapidly cleared out the acrid smoke.

Working by the light of battle lanterns, we employed various meters to test for oxygen deficiency and explosive gases inside the compartment. During this drill, one of the men deftly got his left arm "amputated at the elbow," so we had to lug him off to sickbay.

Thirty seconds after we had brought the "raging fire" under control, we heard ominous words come over the 1-MC intercom system: "Nuclear attack is imminent!" We immediately set Condition Circle William, which was to button up the ship so tight that even radioactive particles of contamination could not possibly enter its interior.

They threw another grenade over the side, and we all braced ourselves for the nuclear shock wave that was sure to follow. This drill was ludicrous in our estimation; if the shock wave didn't wreck our little ship, the base surge alone probably would have swamped us, or we would have been roasted by the nuclear fireball. We broke out the Radiac instruments and climbed into aluminum-foil jumpsuits, which repelled Alpha and Beta rays, just as if any of our meager efforts might have been useful in a real nuclear emergency. I was one of the Internal Monitors, checking the inside spaces of the ship for hot spots of radiation.

The *Elkhorn* had an interesting freshwater washdown system rigged outside the ship. When the firemain motors were activated they pumped water through sprinklers located over the topside areas of the ship. This was supposed to decontaminate the hull from radiation. It was quite obvious that some of the sprinkler heads were plugged up – probably with sea salt – and the firemain pressure was so low that only a dribble of water came out of the sprinklers. Any chances for survival trickled across the deck and out the scuppers. Somebody's head would surely roll for that exhibition, we wagered, and we were thankful the whole thing was only a stupid drill.

Finally, the drills were secured for the day and the *Elkhorn* turned her bow into the wind and headed for the pier. As tired as we were, a few of us were half-way tempted to take a bus downtown to the nightclubs on Waikiki Beach for some liquid refreshment after we moored.

It was then that everything started to go wrong at once. And it was not a drill this time. No. 4 main engine stalled and dropped off the line. Right on its heels came the last asthmatic wheezing of No. 3. That meant we had no propulsion on the port shaft at all, and we were only getting about three knots on the starboard-shaft due to the wind and the rough beam seas.

At that opportune moment in time one of the shafts curiously developed a leak, and the bilges began filling up with sea water. What next, we wondered? Waikiki Beach was sounding better and better, but farther and farther away. I remember thinking at the time that it would be a good idea if someone wrote down all that had happened to us that day, for amusement in our old age, if nothing else. And then I decided against it. After all, I reasoned, who would believe it anyway?

November 10, 1970

Dear Jennifer,

We are out on the ocean now and going back to Hawaii. The island that we went to is called Midway Island. It has real Gooney birds on it! Gooney birds are big and fat and rather on the clumsy side. They don't fly very much, because they always crash when they land. That's why they are called Gooney birds. It is fun to watch them.

November 10, 1970

Dear Tim,

Hi, best brother! The waves are crashing right up onto the ship now, so we have to be real careful when we open the doors! We saw some shipwrecks by

Midway Island. They used to be Japanese ships. Some of them were made out of cement!

November 10, 1970

Dear Julie,

I got "The Love Bug" movie and showed it to the boys on the ship. They really liked it! We are going to sell popcorn during the movie next time. We have to paint the engine room right now, though. It is very hot down there so the paint dries quickly.

November 10, 1970

Dear Mary,

Hi, squirt! Can you find Midway Island on the map? That's where I was yesterday. Midway is about the prettiest island that I've ever seen! Not that I've seen all that many islands. The ocean around Midway is so clean and green that it's an absolute delight just to swim in it. The water is so clear that you can see downward forever, and the ship looks like it's floating in midair.

BOGIE

For a sailor, boredom often sets in on long sea voyages. While crossing the Pacific Ocean aboard the *USS Elkhorn,* we electricians decided to do something about it. So we constructed a huge kite with a ten-foot tail and flew it off the fantail. It reached such an altitude that we could barely see it, and were reluctant to reel it in after all our efforts. With the approach of night, we tied off the kite line on the aft railing and went below decks.

It wasn't until much later that we learned we had created quite a bit of excitement up in the pilot house. The radarmen had picked up a "bogie" on their scopes that they couldn't identify. It had been pacing the ship from the air directly off our stern for quite some time. Finally somebody told them it was our kite, and the watch alerted the Old Man. Greatly relieved, he advised us gruffly, "Well, haul it down and put some navigation lights on it, godammit!"

1,090 FATHOMS

November 11, 1970

Dear Family,

Pardon the pencil and scratch paper, but that's all I have available right now down here in the engine room. I've got a long, five-hour watch stretching ahead of me and it could get awful boring if I just sat and stared at those dizzy dials like they preferred I do.

It is uncommonly hot down here in the Hole since we've got both boilers going full blast, and the readings that you get off the engine pyrometers are up around 700-800 degrees Fahrenheit. That could have a little something to do with the toasty atmosphere down here. The entire engine room is penetrated with the smell of hot oil and steel sliding against steel, and to a lesser degree the bilge-water souring beneath the deckplates – hardly healthy to sailors and other life forms.

It will be another two days before we return to Pearl Harbor. As soon as we get back we are having a zone and personnel inspection by the USS *Tombigbee* (AOG-11). But we're a cinch to pass it, because if we fail it then the *Tombigbee* will have to take our next fueling commitment. And they don't want to leave Honolulu any more than we do. After that, things will pretty much settle down until we deploy on January 6th.

As an auxiliary oil-and-gasoline tanker, we loaf around the Pacific Rim on many dubious refueling missions. Once our load was even refused, so we headed back home without making a sale that time. Weekends in port are usually spent as far away from the ship as possible. Horrendously swindled are the men who have to remain on board with the duty while the others flee ashore at the first cry of "liberty call."

Even though Midway Island is technically part of the Hawaiian Island chain, it is still 1,300 miles away from Pearl, and it took us six days to get there. So, Hawaii lies about 1,200 miles to ESE of Midway, while Wake Island lies about 1,200 miles to WSW of Midway. Midway Island is only about 160 miles east of the International Date Line.

The airfield on Midway was getting low on aviation fuel and so we stood good to our ship's motto: "We deliver!" We carried another 600,000 gallons of JP-5 fuel and our main decks were only sitting two feet above the water line. So it was a real challenge getting across the decks with those waves constantly coming in. They wouldn't let us outside on deck at night whatsoever.

Midway is a wildlife refuge for Gooney birds; have you ever heard of them? They're a type of albatross. They're fat and lumpish and dopey-looking, standing about two feet tall with a wingspan of ten feet. I imagine they're called Gooney birds because every time they land they crash head-over-heels. You can almost hear them muttering as they come in for a landing, "Oh no! Oh no!" After the big crash they right themselves and shake their feathers as if they meant to do that. They're absolutely hilarious to watch.

The whole place is so darn quiet and peaceful that you wouldn't think it was once the site of a fierce World War II naval battle. But then all you have to do is turn around and look at all the hulks of Japanese ships rusting away on the reefs, and you are reminded. We sank four Japanese aircraft carriers and one heavy cruiser in the decisive battle. The United States lost one destroyer and the carrier *Yorktown*.

Midway is made up of two islands in an atoll six miles in diameter: the larger Sand Island and the small Eastern Island (not to be confused with Easter Island, eh). It has an area of two square miles, a coastline of about twenty miles, and a total population of 2,200. But there is a definite shortage of the female of the species. The sailors there must live a very meager existence. We off-loaded the fuel on Saturday; half the crew got one night of liberty at the only nightclub on Midway, and we left by Sunday afternoon already.

For this trip to Midway we found ourselves drastically short of fresh water and had to light off the evaporator to distill our own. We use sea water to cool the fresh water after it has passed through the engines. One of the snipes opened the wrong valve and a lot of our fresh water was pumped straight over the side. (That's the kind of stunt that can get you an instant field demotion.)

So they put us on water hours and secured the scuttlebutt and sinks. Our rare showers had to be strictly "Navy" showers, and not luxurious "Hollywood" showers. (To take a "Navy" shower you have to get wet all over, then shut off the water; lather up and scrub, then turn on the water for a quick rinse. Period. No lingering. No sudsy fun.) We'll be a bunch of scroungy fellows until we get back to port.

We had to get our shots renewed again recently. For four days we got a shot in each arm every day. We got shots for cholera, yellow fever, plague, smallpox, tetanus, tuberculosis, polio, etc. – all in preparation for being deployed overseas. The typhoid shot was worse than all the others put together; it wiped out half the crew.

After the typhoid shot, I was so pumped full of viruses – and portions of viruses – that I felt fairly doped up. It was painful to lift my arm any higher than my waist. Our arms would have gotten pretty darn stiff and sore during the inoculations if they didn't have us painting out the engine room. They think of everything, don't they? They really take good care of us.

Well, we finally got our deployment schedule for January. Besides hitting Guam, Japan, and Bangkok, we'll be spending quality time in Hong Kong and Subic Bay as well! I'm really looking forward to seeing my old stomping grounds again.

As soon as we deploy, all hands are having a beard-growing contest, okayed by the officers. I don't know if there will be any prizes or not, but as much as I hate shaving I'm really going to enjoy those razor-free months! I have been chosen as official photographer on this South Pacific cruise for our ship's yearbook. I still don't know how I got roped into that deal, but it ought to be fun just the same.

In my humble opinion, the crew is dangerously close to what the Navy would term a "mutiny." All the ingredients are there, and all it takes is just the right kind of spark to touch it off. The situation has come on gradually.

A while back one of our seamen volunteered to spray-paint the entire engine room for us so we could get it done by our inspection next week; and all he asked in return was that some of us give him our month's cigarette ration that we weren't using anyway.

But the damned XO (Executive Officer) insisted that us snipes do it all by hand instead, and has been keeping us working overtime in order to get it done. But they could get the whole crew down here right now and it still wouldn't be done on schedule – the engine room is just too mammoth!

When we got to Midway the XO made the crew wear whites into town, when everybody knows that Midway is a dungaree liberty port. After the officer's projector broke down he halted the enlisted men's movies, too.

He secured the after head for two days so it could be painted and tiled. Now the entire crew is reduced to using one shower, one urinal, three sinks, and two shitters. It just can't be done, I'm telling you. Naturally, the officers have their own private head up in Officer Country, so they don't notice the huge inconvenience to us. What do they care?

When my sea-daddy politely asked the XO if he would sit down with us petty officers and rationally talk the situation over, he responded that the whole crew was a bunch of "stupid idiots" (his words) and that my sea-daddy was a "mutineer" even to suggest such a contrary thing.

For this upcoming inspection the XO has ordered us to get such drastic haircuts that we'll look like a bunch of damn squirrels right out of boot camp! The Navy Regulations clearly state that hair may be six inches long, and sideburns even with the bottom of the ear. But the XO in his infinite wisdom has seen fit to rise above Navy Regs and has ordered three-inch haircuts with sideburns off the *top* of the ear!

He's just a punk kid fresh out of the Academy, living in his own little dream world and thinks he's playing god. We wrote a grievance letter to the Chief of Naval Operations, which is our right as crew members, and all the guys signed it. A message painted in red appeared on the bulkhead outside of the ship's store saying, "Death to the XO!" Things aren't very comfortable around here right now.

November 15, 1970

Dear Family,

After we pulled into port we ran shore-power cables, then us three electricians went down into the Hole to complete our painting assignment. We were supposed to have the whole engine room finished by this weekend – or else find another place to sleep besides the *Elkhorn.* Friday we painted until midnight. Saturday we painted all day until 0300 on Sunday morning. And tonight we finally finished at 2100. It was hard work, but we're really proud of it. It's such a beautiful job that our division officer has promised us a whole week of early liberty for our efforts! I'll have to see that to believe it.

This just in: There's been a slight change of plans; starting the 19th of this month we can grow our beards for the duration of our time left in the service! And they'll even discharge us with a beard if we want! All this, compliments of our new CNO, Admiral Elmo Zumwalt, Jr. – or "Uncle Zoomie," as we affectionately call him. Hip, hip, hooray!

PEARL HARBOR
November 29, 1970

Dear Family,

We were given a six-day holiday weekend for Thanksgiving and nobody could scarce believe it! The Old Man must have a brain tumor or something. They kept us barricaded out of the messdecks until 2:00 in the afternoon before they laid out our Turkey Day dinner. We were really famished by then!

And it wasn't a disappointment, either. We had roast turkey and baked ham, dressing, mashed potatoes and sweet potatoes, corn, salad, hot buttered buns, milk, eggnog, punch, strawberry shortcake, assorted fruits, salted nuts, and hard candy. Twelve hours later I was still stuffed to the gills and I swore that I would never eat again.

Some of the guys had brought their wives, families, and girlfriends along, and it was quite an enjoyable affair. The Stewburners had really outdone themselves to prepare a delicious meal and decorate the place so festively. Of course, I would have rather been at home, rubbing elbows with you guys and feeding my face on some home-cooked chow, but that'll have to wait until next year.

Yesterday was the long-anticipated Engineering party at Keehi Lagoon. Oh, the good times rolled then! It rained for a couple of hours in the morning before the party started – just long enough to really scare the crap out of us – but then it cleared off nice and sunny and didn't rain again until the party was long over with.

The cooks off the ship made the baked beans and potato salad and trimmings, also furnishing the hamburger patties, hot dogs, buns, chips and stuff. The seventy dollars that we collected from the crew went into 13 cases of beer.

We ate and drank and played volleyball and drank and played football and drank and played horseshoes and drank and swam and drank and hustled the girls and drank. The beach closed at dusk and we were in no mood to terminate the party fever, so Doc invited all us snipes over to his house to finish off the night.

We ate some more there, listened to Doc's records, played Yahtzee, looked at the inevitable vacation slides, and sang Christmas carols. That was a nice touch. There were a few who were generally disgusted with the old-fashioned cornball sentiment, but otherwise we had a smashing time.

We had our last personnel inspection ten days ago, so we are all free now to start growing our beards. Since Admiral Zumwalt has made them legal, nearly everybody is letting it all hang out. (Navy men never used to be able to grow beards on account that it was impossible to wear a gas mask or OBA properly with a beard on.) So the next time I see you all, I have no doubt that I'll be a lot hairier. Right now the crew is looking pretty shaggy, but Rome wasn't built in a day, you know.

I got tired of my dopey-looking round glasses, so I ordered a pair of new ones at the Navy exchange optical shop. They're hexagonal, with shiny gold wire rims, which shine about thirty-five dollars worth. Before I got them, however, we had our personnel inspection by the Commodore. I passed the inspection okay, but the Commodore stopped right in front of me and told me to get some plastic Navy glasses.

They were free, he reminded me, and besides, "...those round ones make you look crazy." He sure had some nerve making personnel comments like that!

Enough guys overheard his remark and picked up the ball from there, and for days afterwards I was "Crazy Stanga" to the crew. "Hey, how's it going there, Craze?" etc.

This week I went to the dentist and got a little surprise. He said that I basically had a good-looking mouth, but there were a couple of cavities – and all four of my wisdom teeth would have to be extracted eventually, as they were coming in mighty crooked!

On December 9th I will get the Fluoride treatment, on December 14th I will have my cavities filled, but the dental surgery will have to wait until next June! That's how backed-up the Navy dentists are. By that time we'll just be coming back from our deployment overseas. I figured that I would go ahead and get all the dental work done that I needed now while I was still in the Navy and it's all free, right?

We went to a new place in the country called Sea World which was real interesting. They had live shows with porpoises, sharks, whales, penguins, etc. There were also scientific pavilions and the best darn aquarium that I've ever seen. They had a huge, life-size mock-up of a pirate ship that was pretty groovy, too. It cost us servicemen only a dollar to get into Sea World, so we'll have to go back out there with our cameras next time.

Last Saturday Parker and I hopped into his Triumph convertible and whipped out to Konohead Riding Stables where we spent the morning riding a couple of nags along the mountain trails. But let me tell you, those two horses must have done this a thousand times before. They had those darn horses so well-trained that we couldn't get them to do anything they darn well didn't want to.

They just strolled along like they were walking around the barn and stopped to eat grass whenever they felt like it. We couldn't get them to gallop or turn off the trails; it was really sickening. When we slapped them on the butt to make them go faster, they just turned around and looked at us with a long face. But when they saw the stables up ahead of them at the end of the ride they shot off like two bolts of lightning – with us trying to stay in the saddles and hanging on for dear life – they screeched to a halt inside their stalls. We were very disappointed with those horses and told the stable managers on them.

That night we went down to Waikiki and stopped at Lums. Have you ever heard of them? They sell the world-famous Lums hot dog that is steamed in beer, and they also have the biggest selection of imported bottled beers from all over the world that I have ever seen!

We stuffed ourselves on the tasty hot dogs and drank beers from Austria, Bahamas, France, Jamaica, Puerto Rico, Spain, Japan, Hong Kong, the Philippines (naturally), Germany, Denmark, Holland, England, and Mexico. I especially liked the dark lager beers from Ireland, Norway, and Australia. By the time our thirsty group got to the last rounds of Italian beer that night we would have said that dishwater tasted good.

Last Sunday Parker and I drove out to Kaneohe Bay Marine Corps Air Station and attended a Moto-Cross, which is an international cross-country motorcycle race. All the top European riders were there, and it was really an exciting event! The first few heats were by local riders on small bikes, but as the races progressed the bikes got bigger and faster and noisier.

Those guys from Europe would drive like complete fools! Going around corners at seventy miles per hour and flying fifty feet off the jumps! It is really something to hear fifty big cycles leap off the starting line and come snarling past the stands. There were only a few bad spills, and one guy got run over by no less than a dozen dirt bikes before he managed to crawl off the track. Ouch!

Besides riders from all over the States and Hawaii, there were men from Belgium, Czechoslovakia, Germany, England, and Finland participating. There were over 12,000 people in attendance. I was happy to see a guy named Christer Hammargren from Sweden win the big race, riding a Swedish Husqvarna cycle.

The area in which the dirt track was laid out used to be a Marine artillery range, so that'll give you some idea of how rough it was: huge jumps and deep

At the motocross.

mud holes. As a matter of fact, two unexploded hand grenades were found by wandering spectators!

This Friday we were all sleeping in late on account of the holiday routine, but Parker dragged me out of my rack prematurely and saved me from a terrible fate. Our Chief had come back drunk from liberty and was putting all the electricians to work that he could find on the ship, holiday routine or not. So we jumped into our civvies and made our bird in the Little Red Car.

Since neither of us had any spending money at the time, we decided just to do some sightseeing. We drove around the whole island of Oahu, the circuit taking only about four hours. We saw Waimea Beach; the cliff in Pali Pass where King Kamehameha threw off the army he had conquered; a huge mud slide from an active volcano; drove through a spooky and dripping rain forest; and even stopped beside the road and stole some sugar cane from a field to suck on. You can't imagine how beautiful Hawaii is!

We were amazed at the extent of the fabulous Del Monte and Dole fruit plantations around the island. They were quite impressive, even though we had read that Sanford Dole had grabbed the fertile Hawaiian land illegally when he deposed Queen Liliuokalani in the revolution of 1893. He had even defied a pointed request from President Grover Cleveland to restore the queen to her throne, just so he could further his own financial gains. Such is life.

I think I'll sign off now and take a short nap. Maybe that will fix up my hangover. My buddy and I are going to see Paul Newman in "WUSA" at the base theater tonight and then retire early. (Only 314 days left to hold out!)

December 17, 1970

It's beginning to look a lot like Christmas, even around here. There are big decorations up around the harbor on top of the shipyard shops and cranes, and most of the ships are running their holiday lights, which are strung up the mast and suspended between the masts.

Colored lights are all over our messdecks (another electrician duty, I found out), wreaths around the portholes, checkered tablecloths, and of course a Christmas tree over in the corner. It makes everybody homesick as hell. A lot of packages are arriving for the crew right now, full of popcorn balls, cookies, fudge, etc., so we always have plenty of goodies to share.

They changed our working day again. Right now we're on Tropical Hours. Before, we got up at 0630 and worked until 1100, when we'd have two hours off for dinner and a nap in the rack; then we'd work from 1300 to 1530 when liberty call would go down. But on Tropical Hours we get up at 0530 and work solid without a break until 1300, when we'll have liberty call, mail call, chow, etc. It makes for a shorter work day and longer liberty hours, but it's oh so hard to get up that dang early.

Tomorrow is the first day of the ship's Christmas party. They hold it on two consecutive days so the whole crew can attend at least one of the parties. We hold it out at Keehi Lagoon. The ship has spent over $600 on sirloin steaks, kegs of beer, and cases of liquor.

My fellow Sparky, that second-class electrician named Parker, just went home to California for leave. He's going to hide out at a friend's home until Christmas Eve. Nobody else knows he's even coming home. Matter of fact, he specifically told his folks that he couldn't make it home for Christmas this year. Thus, on Christmas Eve his family will be having a big dinner with all the relatives present, and my buddy is going to walk in right in the middle of dinner. What a guy!

About half of the crew has gone home on Christmas leave so far. They have to stagger leaves so that we always have a minimum crew complement on board, enough to get the ship underway if necessary. There are still quite a few of us not interested in spending the money to just go home for a short Christmas break, however.

At present, us electricians are busy installing and wiring up the new washing machine that you taxpayers bought for our ship's laundry. Both AC and DC power cables have to be hooked up to it. Iggie, who does all our laundry, is simply ill with pleasure at getting the new machine. Anyway, this new washer is entirely automatic. It has a control panel on it like a Boeing 707. It does everything but come and get you out of your rack when the laundry is done. It's a huge monster and it cost $6,000 – just for a wash machine!

Certain civilian manufacturers really shaft the Armed Forces when it comes to buying parts and equipment. They know we've got to have the equipment, so they really soak us for it. A small replacement part that you could buy downtown for a buck will cost as much as seven dollars or more when you go through the Supply Center!

We deploy for WesPac on January 6th – heading straight for the P.I, I hope. In the meantime, we're preparing for the long cruise. We've fueled up at Hotel Piers, and gone over to West Loch and loaded aboard all sorts of ammo, including 20,000 rounds of shells for our 20mm AA cannons.

We had to carry each three-inch-wide shell separately, with our hand cradled under the percussion cap. The shells weighed about 25 pounds a piece. If we were ever to stumble and drop a shell, we were told in no uncertain terms that our hand had damn well better hit the deck before the shell did, and cushion its fall! I also got very good at catching stuff with my feet. As if we needed a further reminder, there's a beached and burned-out old hulk of an LST nearby; an accident occurred while ammo was being loaded some years ago, and it was blown up with great loss of life.

The XO is still a real hard-ass and is getting on everybody's case. He made us electricians take down all of our black-light posters in the electric shop...and some of them were real collector's items, too. In retaliation, we threw his fancy toaster thingie over the side after he brought it to us for minor repairs. We told him later it was beyond fixing. He's not supposed to have conveniences like that in his stateroom anyway.

The darn 1-MC speaker is right over my bunk, and it's the first blasted thing I hear every morning and all day long: "Now reveille, reveille. All hands heave out and trice up. The smoking lamp is lit in all authorized spaces. Sweepers, man your brooms, and give the ship a clean sweep-down fore and aft. Breakfast is now being served on the messdecks. Now reveille!"

I've often contemplated jumping up there and ripping out the wires, but then I'd only have to wire it back up again later. My job, you know.

There is a water fountain located next to my rack, also. But there's way too much water pressure, so it overshoots the basin onto my rack all the time. I'm presently sleeping up in the electric shop on top of the work bench until they get the fountain fixed. It's quieter and more private there anyway. There's not always lights burning, cigarette smoke, guys having wrestling matches or towel-snapping fights or loud conversations while you're trying to sleep.

Last week, Parker and I had our Hawaiian Happening No. 1, and went mountain climbing! How about that? We picked out Olomana Peak in the Pali Valley as our first conquest. It is 1,643 feet high over the Great Kawainui Swamp. Its head is stuck up there in the clouds and it looks positively ominous. Of course, both of us were pretty new at this sort of thing, but the mountain didn't know that.

First we amassed all the necessary needs that would be necessary for us to need. We checked out backpacks, binoculars and canteens from Special Services here on base. On the ship itself, we gathered knives, matches, gloves, food from the galley, camera gear, toilet paper, rope and grappling hooks, and even made our own machetes.

Our packs weighed about thirty pounds apiece. It had rained that same morning, so the trail was sort of muddy, and this made it rough going up the steep grades. But the hard climb was well worth it! The view was tremendous; I felt I could see 100 miles out to sea over Kaneohe Bay. We took lots of pictures from the summit. We had a hearty lunch and then took a well-earned nap on the tip-top of the mountain, before starting back down.

December 25, 1970

Mele Kalikimaka [Merry Christmas]! For the Christmas of 1970 we hear that a 78-foot-high Black Hills spruce from South Dakota became the White House lawn Christmas tree this year. But wind gusts that reached up to 54 mph blew down the tree on the Ellipse south of the White House already.

On top of Olomana Peak, Oahu.

January 1, 1971

Hauoli Makahiki Hou [Happy New Year]! This is the morning after the night before. What a miserable way to start out the New Year. I dimly remember ringing in the New Year in some wayside Korean café, eating nasty rubbery things in the dark with a pair of maladroit chopsticks, getting my eardrums ruptured by all those horrid fireworks that funsters put under my chair.

And what a fine morning this turned out to be on the island; a calm, clear day glazed over with the freshness of Spring. Old Glory is hanging from the spar as limp as a dead cat, and it's so quiet that you could hear a rat pee on a sack of cotton.

I've got the duty today. Most of the day was spent in trying to recuperate from my foolish binge last night. I wandered aimlessly around the ship, not caring whether I lived or had, in fact, died. I was slightly consoled in the knowledge that the world is a big place, and there must surely be literally millions of other Sad Sacks walking around today in the same vegetative condition.

I spent the morning getting letters off to relatives. In the afternoon I showed a couple of westerns for the crewmembers who had remained on the ship. In the evening I sat up in the electric shop and sipped some Cold Duck champagne while I wrote yet another letter to Suzie. After all the letters I've sent to her, and rarely gotten any response to, it seemed like quite a futile thing to do. But I was feeling pretty futile myself.

January 2, 1971

Confucius say, "Too much wine put Devil in mouth to steal your brains." Mom never told me there'd be days like this. I woke up this morning at 0600, only to find the compartment rolling and pitching about. Had we gotten underway during the night? No, it was only my brain in trauma. I've had suspicions all along that my head is trying to reject my body, and vice versa.

Before 0900 I had gotten all my correspondence caught up to date. It's a downright miracle what a person can do when he's still under the influence! Right after dinner the Gyro Jerk came back early from liberty, quite inebriated. He must have thought he was in the head, as he took down his fly and urinated all over another guy's rack. Then he calmly crawled into his own rack and passed out. Oh yes, variety is the spice of life. Tell me, what would life be like if there weren't guys like the Gyro Jerk around? (I'm just glad it wasn't *my* rack.)

I sat in the quiet electric shop, listening to serene tapes, drinking Pepsi after Pepsi in an attempt to quench my thirst. Some deckape decided to earn some brownie points and went to work on the deck directly above me. He was using an air-powered chipping hammer and seemed intent on making more noise than anything else. Every concussion on the steel deck racketed through my brain and it soon started to ache considerably. I was at the point of going berserk for the first time in my life, when I made a tremendous personal effort and locked up the electric shop and removed myself clear to the opposite end of the ship.

Admiral Elmo Zumwalt, our new CNO, has been wreaking major miracles for us enlisted men. One of the first things Uncle Zoomie did when he got in office was to get us guys another pay raise. Then he made it legal for us swabbies to grow beards. After that he cut our work day by a half hour (hey, every little bit helps), followed by the termination of Mickey Mouse and chicken-shit regulations.

And now he has made it legal for men on all naval ships to wear civilian clothes on and off the ship. This is huge! It used to be that just the officers could wear civvies on the beach. The rest of us had to smuggle our civvies off the ship in a duffle bag or something, and change clothes stealthily in a bathroom someplace; then we had to go through the whole rigmarole over again when we returned to the ship – and we still ran the chance of bumping into an officer downtown and getting wrote up for being out of uniform. It was a major hassle!

We look forward to each new Z-gram from him. These are far-reaching Navy directives which further improve the lot of the common sailor. Outside of permitting us to grow beards and sport longer hair styles, and dress in civvies while on liberty, Uncle Zoomie also permits women to serve on ships now, allows us to ride motorcycles, and extends authorized overnight liberty to lower-ranked enlisted men.

I guess he is really cracking whips over the right heads, eh. I can't understand why someone like him hasn't come along before this to give the Navy the good shaking up that it so desperately required. It definitely needed to be brought forward into the modern ages.

The roach coach made its approach about 1800 this evening, so we had supper here in the electric shop: pop, potato chips, and hot dogs – yum!

I just finished off a couple of beers to settle my stomach down a bit. They tasted mighty fine, and I fear for the five bottles of Crown Royal Canadian whiskey I have hidden in the electrical locker. I might just have to crack one open before the evening is done. Will I never learn?

Hmmm, the lights are starting to dim and the music on my tape recorder sounds distorted and alien. I guess the generator is getting ready to crap out again. It's getting to be a regular thing with that generator anymore. I suppose that I should drift in the general direction of the engine room and see what it's up to this time.

January 3, 1971

Having spent the last three years in the Navy, I have learned through sheer necessity to sleep in almost any position on any surface. But for the life of me, I cannot get a decent night's sleep in those accursed things that are supposed to pass for bunks. I can just see some deranged designer drawing up the plans for a prototype bunk that will completely deny a person any amount of healthful sleep, will warp and sprain every muscle in his body, and will accomplish nothing but fatiguing a person utterly. Then he will sell it to the US Navy for an outrageous sum and disappear from the country.

I was in a kind of lethargic mood and spent most of the afternoon in my abominable rack, trying to get just a little sleep out of the deal. But the TV was blaring, and through my pillow I could hear the rumble of the ship-service generator below me in the Hole.

The ever-present hum of it is always felt through the deckplates all over the ship. I really hate machines! I hate such obnoxious things as noisy, oily engines, hot and whirring motors, clanging and knocking pumps, corroded valves, rusty pipes, and especially boilers. I'll be glad when I finally get away from them for good.

It was another beautiful day here in the islands, and I felt a little guilty at spending most of the day inside the ship. I mean, once we deploy I'll be spending about a month on the ship without the slightest opportunity of getting off; you'd think that I would get off her every chance I have now. But it was my day to loaf. There's just something about a Sunday that puts a person off his feed a bit.

January 4, 1971

People really shouldn't have to get up at such a despicable hour as 0530 in the morning. It's all right if you're a farmer when it's necessary to put in a full day, but not when we don't even start work for two stinking hours after reveille. It's quite refreshing to get up and start each new day with the sun, but it's quite another thing to get up while it's still pitch-dark outside. Night is the time for sleeping in your bed – not on your feet!

I hate Mondays with a passion; I wish they'd abolish them from the calendar. But then there would always be Terrible Tuesdays, I suppose. I had no trouble keeping myself busy, because today is the last day we have to ready the ship for sea…and of course you know that everything is always left until the last minute in the Navy. I'll bet we'll still have a hundred things to do tomorrow morning before we leave.

With a little luck, tomorrow at this time we'll be floundering around in the swells out at sea – getting seasick all over again – but definitely on our way back to the wonderful Philippines!

I got off watch early and went over to the movie exchange to pick up our 26 sea prints. When we're underway for so long a time at one stretch, it's good for the crew to have a couple of movies a night to keep the morale up. I enjoy showing the movies to the crew, whether I happen to be the duty electrician that night or not.

The Admiral came on board today and inspected the ship just prior to our getting underway tomorrow. Don't ask me which Admiral, because I don't know; there's so many of them adrift nowadays.

I just happened to be in the log room chit-chatting with "Mafia" Del Rosso when the Admiral came on board, so I got shanghaied into presenting the engineering berthing compartment to him for inspection. When he came in I saluted smartly and said, "Good morning, Admiral! May I present the engineering compartment?"

He returned the salute noticeably less smartly, peered at the name stenciled on my dungaree shirt and asked considerably wide of the mark, "Stagna? Stange?"

"Stanga," I corrected.

"And how are you today, Stanga?"

"Fine. Thank you, sir," I assured him.

"Are you eager to get underway tomorrow?" he asked.

"Oh yes, sir!" I answered. "Eager to get back to the Philippines at least. Not too excited about making the long trip, though."

He chuckled and drifted out of the compartment without even so much as looking at it. We had cleaned it for days for nothing. We had scrubbed toilet stools until they sparkled like the First Lady's best china. We had polished brass with quarts of Brasso – and for what good reason? Admirals, big deal!

I'm all ready for the cruise. I've got five fifths of Crown Royal whiskey in my locker that should get me through the trip without an alcoholic fit. A long cruise gets to be such a tedious and irksome thing that you sometimes wish a couple of good shots were handy to bolt down. I'm prepared for that eventuality this time, as are several of the other guys. This will be my last cruise overseas and I'm bound to make it the best one yet! It's very enjoyable getting crocked with a buddy or two that you can really talk to. It's a personal pleasure that I'll not soon give up. As long as I don't get caught. Drinking on board a naval vessel is a court-martial offense, you know.

Next to eating and drinking, I guess that my most pleasurable pastime is sleeping – and thus escaping my reality. I figure that I could crawl in between those cool sheets right now and sleep for the next 24 hours if they would let me, but I have to get up in five hours to stand a four-hour watch. Then I'll be up until taps go down tomorrow night. *insert audible groan here*

EN ROUTE FROM HAWAII TO GUAM, MARIANAS ISLANDS
January 5, 1971, Tuesday

The day started out bitter cold and raining pitchforks and hammer handles. Oh just fine, I said to myself, everything was off to a good start. Mister T, the engineering division officer, wasn't fooling around with the enginemen on this day and he wanted everything lit off and running smoothly by 0800, even though we were not scheduled to get underway from Pearl Harbor until 0930.

There were a million and one "missile hazards" loose in the shops, storerooms and various compartments that had to be lashed down or stowed before we got underway. Meanwhile, it continued to rain profusely.

They set the special Sea and Anchor detail at 0900 – always a half hour early for some ridiculous reason – and down into the Hole we went. With both ship-service generators and all four main engines running, there was quite a thunderous roar in the engine room. It was already quite toasty down there, too.

In the middle of testing the port shaft, No. 4 main propulsion engine died out and we didn't have enough air pressure built up yet to light it off right away. Great, I said to myself again; everything was falling into place like a recurring bad dream.

Snipes were running around like chickens with their heads cut off, although I didn't see any real need for such unfocused and confused haste. All we had to do was to be patient while the compressor built up the necessary air pressure once again, then light off the fool engine.

Finally, they got the nasty machine going again and we gave our readiness reports to the Officer Of the Deck on the bridge. Minutes later, with the first bell from the Captain (one-third ahead), we gave a great cheer – for we were finally on our way to the South Pacific! I gave Parker a knowing smile and two thumbs up, and he grinned broadly back to me in complete understanding.

Sea and Anchor detail lasted another 45 minutes until we got the ship safely out of the harbor. Soon the deck began dropping out from beneath us in the engine room, and then rising again suddenly; we had evidently cleared the channel and gotten into rough water. It was hard for us to tell anything from down in the Hole except motion of a general sort. We had been in port a long time and it was going to take us a few days to get our proper sea legs back.

We shuddered at the weather report over the radio: there were 20 to 30-foot waves to be expected ahead of us. We would pass through the outside fringe of a tropical storm and a cold front, too. There were definitely going to be some sickies on board. And it didn't take long, either, to gather a sizeable amount of poor devils up on the fantail hanging over the life lines.

As for myself, I kept topside as much as possible to keep from getting sick; I was away from the diesel fumes below decks, and the cool sea breeze was bracing and seemed to help settle my stomach. It had finally quit raining, fortunately, but the waves were every bit as bad as the radio had predicted.

I spent the morning wandering around topside, snapping pictures of the huge swells that were assaulting us. We were taking green water across the tank deck. I ate very little dinner and then retired to my rack for the afternoon.

When I got up for supper I was feeling pretty lousy. As I stood there in the chow line gazing at the grease on top of the stewed chicken sloshing back and forth, back and forth, as the ship rolled from side to side, from side to side, I saw what was coming next. I made a mad dash for the closest head and let it all hang out. I had never gotten *that* seasick before, but then again I had never seen the ocean that rough before either.

I felt a hundred percent better immediately and went back to the galley for a hearty supper. I firmly maintain that those sadistic messcooks deliberately choose the greasiest and foulest-looking food for the first day at sea. Nothing bothers their stomachs, anyway – they eat their own cooking, don't you know?

No siree bob! People laugh when they talk about getting seasick, and I laugh right along with them, but it is an extremely miserable sensation. I cannot think of a worse feeling than being badly seasick. Not even a champion hangover compares. Thank goodness it only bothers me the first day out at sea, and then wears off as soon as I get my sea legs.

After supper this evening (for those few who had an appetite), everything started to go wrong at once. The port shaft locked up completely, the bearing sprung a leak, and the shaft alley began filling up with sea water.

Right on its heels came the realization that we didn't have enough fresh water on board to last the voyage to Guam. (Whose job was *that*?!) There was loose talk of enforcing strict water hours immediately. Besides drinking and washing and cooking, fresh water is used for cooling the engines and pumps and motors. (Sea water is used to flush the shitters.)

An hour later there was a fire in the forward anchor winch controller in the IC room. Water had seeped through a stuffing tube (where an electrical cable passes through the overhead to the weather deck above) and got into the resistors and relays. So that put the anchor winch out of commission; I wonder how we are going to moor once we get to Guam? That is, assuming the ship of fools is still afloat by then. Criminy!

January 6, 1971, Wednesday

It's only the first day out that bothers my stomach, hence I felt terrific when I got up this morning, and lorded it over those who were still a whiter shade of pale. It didn't seem as though we were rocking nearly as much as yesterday; we must have passed through the storm. I stowed away a large breakfast, getting as full as I possibly could on fried Spam, homemade sweet rolls and coffee.

I spent most of the morning installing bunk lights in the berthing compartment, making sure my closest buddies were at the top of the list. Most of our new Northampton bunks had small fluorescent reading lamps already attached to them. All that was lacking was to make a few cable runs to get power to them.

From the tank decks to the forecastle, all the compartments inside had shipped water during the storm. Where there weren't actually pools of water awash on the deck, there was a gritty, salty, slippery condensate.

I had the throttle watch all afternoon. I was extremely tired and could hardly keep my eyes open. It's kind of a hypnotic mesmerism down there in the Hole with the heat and the monotonous roar of the engines. Very conducive to drowsiness.

Amongst the officers and chiefs was horrible talk of turning back to Pearl and totally abandoning the trip itself. Our hearts sank just at the mere thought of such a bitter disappointment.

But during the night, they had sent a radio message to CINCPACFLT and he ordered us to turn our bow towards Johnston Atoll. There we would rendezvous with an ocean-going tug out of Pearl which would bring us a spare bearing and a specialist in troubleshooting.

About 1800 we reached our rendezvous with the tug *USS Pawkaw.* At first they were going to highline the guy and the spare parts over to us from the tug, but then they remembered that our winch controller had burned up yesterday. So they sent him over in a raft.

The little motor-driven rubber raft bobbed around like a bright orange cork on those nasty waves. And then there was the problem of how to get the guy actually on board our ship. He took the situation in hand and provided the solution for us.

When our ship plowed down into a wave, and another wave carried the raft high alongside us, he suddenly jumped from the raft onto the tank deck. Such a look of fright he had on his face, though!

They worked about six hours replacing the bearing and then tested the shaft around midnight. It overheated at 180 rpms, so they had to pull it out again to grind it down some. They tested it once more with the same result. At present they are pulling the bearing out for the third time to work on it anew.

Meanwhile, we are crawling for Guam with the *USS Pawkaw* trailing us to fetch back the technician when he is finished here. At least we're pointed in the right direction...towards the Philippines!

January 7, 1971, Thursday

I had the reveille watch this morning, so my day officially began at 0345, whereas the crew's day began somewhat later at 0630. I think that the reveille watch in the Hole is just about the most god-awful thing that could happen to a person in his lifetime. If you can survive this, then you can survive anything life throws at you. What a way to start off the day! Ugh.

Early this morning they finally got the bearing on the port shaft to run "cool" (still too hot to touch, mind you), so we're cheerfully steaming towards Guam and other parts unknown at nine knots. The ocean-going tug has retrieved the technician and has turned back to Pearl.

They tell us that it should only be another ten days before we hit port. We're going to spend only one day in Guam. I would be just as happy if we decided to steam right past the dumb island altogether. Just about everyone has recovered from the initial seasick period, and we're once again the merry band of pirates that we used to be.

I happened to be topside at sunset today, playing my harmonica on the fantail – I'm usually in my rack as soon as "knock off" goes down, but I wanted to get some practicing in – and the view was really terrific! I can see now that I'm going to have to spend more time outside during this cruise, or I'm going to miss something special.

I got to spend the whole day installing more bunk lights in the berthing compartment again. There were several guys in their racks with "late sleepers," and it was kind of difficult working around them quietly. The existing cable that I had to work with was decrepit and brittle; I wouldn't guarantee any of it to last very long.

I finally got them all hooked up electrically and replaced the fuses for that particular circuit (which I had wisely kept in my pocket all along to safeguard somebody else trying to electrocute me).

As soon as I energized the circuit, flame and smoke belched out of one bunk light and left a smelly haze in the compartment. There were riotous catcalls from the guys of "Stanga strikes again!" But upon checking out the situation, I was relieved to discover that it was merely a faulty bunk light and none of my own incompetence at work.

January 8, 1971, Friday

If it isn't one thing, it's another. Us electricians had a passel of constructive work lined up ahead of us for the day, but before we could even so much as get our tools consolidated, No. 1 boiler gave up the ghost.

I swear, if I ever survive this eternal struggle with fouled-up machinery which is called my "enlistment" and still retain my sanity, it will indeed be a miracle on the order of the Second Coming. This Machine Age is going to be the unhinging of me.

I will not bore you with the details of the boiler repair, which took us the remainder of the day. Suffice it to say that after much cursing and sweating, in the end we got it running again.

There was one saving grace about this day, and one alone: the weather was absolutely ideal for a cruise – balmy and calm. It's rare days like this that make you feel lucky to be a sailor with a good deck under your feet.

> *"Oceanographers have the best of two worlds – both the sea and the land. Yet many of them, like many sailors, find it extraordinarily satisfying to be far from the nearest coast on one of the small, oily and uncomfortable ships of their trade, even in the midst of a vicious storm, let alone on one of those wonderful days in the Tropics when the sea and the air are smiling and calm. I think the chief reason is that on shipboard both the past and the future disappear. Little can be done to remedy the mistakes of yesterday; no planning for tomorrow can reckon with the unpredictability of ships and the sea. To live in the present is the essence of being a seaman."*
>
> – *"The Ocean" by Roger Revelle*

January 9, 1971, Saturday

Today marks the passing of another month of naval service for me. I entered the Navy on October 9, 1967, and have thus far survived 39 months of it.

I got a wild hair and decided to hold a field day in the electric shop this morning. Lord knows it needed cleaning fearfully, and since today was only a half working day I didn't want to undertake any major operations. I restowed all the junk that seems to mysteriously creep out of hiding during the night, and dusted and wiped and swept and scrubbed and waxed and polished.

The deck was hopeless, however. McCormick, who has low-grade manure for brains, used trichloroethane to wipe up some spilled paint once, and the tiled floor has had an ugly, bleached-out appearance ever since. I did the best I could, though.

I had a relaxing and much-needed nap all afternoon and then stood five hours of throttle watch in the Hole. Normally, a regulation watch is only four hours in duration, but we changed time zones at 1800 and they set all the chronometers back one hour. Ergo, I was awarded an extra hour of watch. Just my bum luck.

As soon as I got off watch I set up our brand new Bell and Howell movie projector and showed a flick for the crew on the messdecks. It was "Heller in Pink Tights" starring Sophia Loren and Anthony Quinn. Quite enjoyable!

Tomorrow is holiday routine on the ship, being the Sabbath for some, and it will be nice to sleep in for a change. One of the Quartermasters is going to try to teach me how to use a sextant and separate the various stars and planets from the other heavenly bodies. That should be very interesting.

Would you believe that I was actually afraid to sleep in my rack the first night out at sea? When they installed these heavy Northampton bunks three-high, the shipfitters only spot-welded the stanchions and braces into place. And with all this pitching and rolling that we were doing, the welded joints could very easily become fatigued and cracked and bring the racks down.

I sleep on the bottom rack, of all places, and I calculated I have about 700 pounds of racks, clothes, bodies, and personal belongings hovering above me. Can you imagine what that amount of materiel can do to this frail, mortal body?

But now that I've gotten over the fear of being crushed to death in my rack, I sleep fairly well. I just figure that out of eighty-some racks, I won't be the first victim.

2,100 FATHOMS

January 10, 1971, Sunday

They held Catholic and Protestant lay services on the messdecks this morning bright and early, and managed to drag a few conscientious sleepyheads out of their racks. As usual, I did not attend. We do not carry a chaplain aboard, so the officers take turns holding the religious services for the crew. It definitely leaves something to be desired.

I had the throttle watch all afternoon, but passed it quickly and industriously by studying a volume on mathematics, of which I know little about. It has been since my freshman year in high school when I last had math of any kind (i.e., algebra) – a good eight years ago – and I almost flunked out at the time. I will be expected to take college math when I get to the University of Wyoming, so I had better bone up on it now.

For the last couple of days it's been smooth sailing during the day and good sleeping at night, which was quite pleasant; but now we're getting into rough weather again. Overnight the sea has become choppy and we have resumed our innervating rocking.

This is the first ship I've seen that actually wallows. We sit so low in the water normally, and now we're carrying a full liquid load of fuel and water, that we simply flounder around, decks awash in the smallest of waves.

> *"Rarely did he know his position within half a degree, except when in sight of land; for sun and stars remained hidden behind the sky, and it was so gloomy that even at the best the horizons were poor for accurate observations. A gray gloom shrouded the world. The clouds were gray; the great driving seas were leaden gray; the smoking crests were a gray churning; even the occasional albatrosses were gray, while the snow-flurries were not white, but gray, under the somber pall of the heavens."*
>
> *–"Make Westing" by Jack London*

2,485 FATHOMS

January 12, 1971, Tuesday

I imagine that we crossed the International Date Line sometime during the night, as we totally skipped Monday today, and went directly from Sunday to Tuesday. It's a strange feeling to misplace a whole damn day, but it's good to know that I am 24 hours shorter in this chicken outfit. We are now in time zone +12 MIKE, whatever the hell that means. All I know is that every passing minute brings us closer to the Philippines!

The XO did indeed put us on "water hours" today. It seems that according to him each man has been flagrantly exceeding his quota of fresh water and consequently restrictions must be made. What a geek. Now we may only shower between the hours of 2000 and 2200 – and they must be Navy showers – not leisurely Hollywood showers! Cripes, the boilers will never keep up with that demand within two hours.

We are in the habit of tying a rope to a brand-new pair of dungarees and dragging them behind the ship for an hour. This speeds up the soft, faded-out look that we seek and gives them a salty (nautical) appearance. I had just bought a new dungaree shirt, so I decided to give it "the treatment." I ran a rope through the sleeves and threw it off the fantail, tying the line to the railing. When I reeled in the rope an hour later, I was surprised to find only a pair of raggedy sleeves left. No shirt, just two sleeves. But they were faded to perfection!

I seem to be very tired since we left port. What is there about being out at sea that takes so much punch out of a person's body and yet really stimulates the appetite?

I had my routine throttle watch all morning, which went by unusually quick as I employed the hours in reminiscing in my mind about when I was a footloose youth at large in Mitchell, South Dakota, before the military service. Ah, the good old days!

2,455 FATHOMS

January 13, 1971, Wednesday

I know anger very quickly if I am disturbed while I'm sleeping. I had just dozed off at noon today for an hour's nap which I desperately needed, when some clown comes over and wakes me up to tell me some insanely trivial thing that certainly could have waited until I woke up. I told him where to get off and tried to get back to sleep.

Only moments later someone else wanted something from me that just couldn't wait until I was conscious, apparently, so I was again bothered. People certainly don't show much consideration for others around here.

Five minutes later, two guys sat down beside my rack and immediately decided to have a bull-session right then and there. I sent them packing, blistering their hides with words I had learned in the Navy, and then tried to force my anger to subside so I could nap the remainder of the noon hour.

I finally fell asleep, only to be awakened instantly by some guy playing his tape recorder at full volume, assuming (incorrectly) that everybody wanted to listen to *his* music. I gave up and just lay there smoldering.

It's like trying to sleep in a mental institution when you go to bed in the engineering berthing compartment. There appears to be those people who have never learned how to whisper. And there are others who always seem to be holding a conversation with someone at the opposite end of the compartment. The deckape's berthing compartment is even worse; it's like a damn zoo in there!

I made several cable runs this morning and installed some AC outlets by the bunks for the guys who have tape recorders and such. I enjoy doing electrical work of this nature. It is a slow job, but the steps are laid out one by one before you, so it ends up neat and professional-looking…if you have even an ounce of pride in your work. I don't begrudge getting into electricity during my Navy career; I figure it'll save me a few bucks now and then with do-it-yourself repairs at home.

A rather large flying fish, about a foot in length, landed on the tank deck during the night and was found this morning. Some joker affixed him to the top of the barrel of our three-inch gun mount aft, spread its wings in flight fashion where they dried, and stuck a cigarette in the corner of its mouth. We all got a kick out of it when we spotted it over the officer's head during morning muster, and tried to keep our faces straight.

We have quite an international racial mix for a crew on this ship. I can think of half a dozen races that are represented: Caucasian, Indian, Negro, Mexican, Filipino, and one Jewish guy. Some of the guys come from rich and pampered families; others come from backgrounds of county welfare, broken families, and juvenile jail records.

But most of them, like me, are from solid, middle-class working families that make up the bulk of our great country. Before I came into the Navy I never knew an Indian, never met a Negro, never rapped with anyone from south of the border – never even heard of a Filipino – and only knew one Jew to speak of who ran the local fabric store back home. In fact, the only people I ever came in contact with were other "honkies" like myself. But nobody seems to notice anybody else's skin color here on the boat.

They had small-arms' target practice off the fantail this afternoon which attracted a few of the gun-crazies. I made a large dishpan full of yellow popcorn for the crew during the movie this evening.

There was a full moon out tonight, so I sat on the fantail and played my harmonica until my lips were raw. Gazing up at the moon from the middle of the Pacific Ocean, I often wondered what the moon looked like that night to the people back home...particularly Suzie.

3,180 FATHOMS

January 14, 1971, Thursday

What a bleah day! Today we left Pearl Harbor's First Fleet jurisdiction and entered the sphere of influence of the South Pacific's Seventh Fleet. On the large, sprawling progress map in the messdecks there is a little circle with a dot in it that marks our present location roughly halfway between Hawaii and Guam.

Halfway! After all these days of floundering around out here, we are only *halfway* there. The only thought that I keep before me to retain my vitality is that it will only be a matter of weeks before we view the beloved Philippine Islands on the horizon.

Last night we passed from time zone +12 MIKE to -11 LIMA. As far as I'm concerned, this worthless day never existed and could just as well be stricken from my journal.

2,818 FATHOMS

January 15, 1971, Friday

Last night was the first time since the beginning of this cruise that I've gotten a really great night's sleep. We were suddenly becalmed today; the bleakness and the rain squalls disappeared over the horizon much to everyone's relief. The clouds parted and the sun beat down without mercy. We loved it.

Parker and I worked on a large, bulky vent motor all morning that was out of commission. I'll bet it has been twenty summers since that beast was last pulled for maintenance. The deckapes had covered it with multiple layers of haze-gray paint, the bolts had crystallized in position, and the vent casing was almost completely rusted through from salt water. We'll put in a job order to have it fixed properly in Subic's yards, as there wasn't anything that we could do with it. It was beyond our simple repair capabilities.

It may have been that we saw Wake Island about twenty miles off the starboardside today, but nobody would stake their life's blood on it. At twenty miles distance there seemed to be some sort of blurry land mass shrouded in an aquamarine haze. But Wake is such a mean, flat island that it hardly seems likely that we really saw it from that far away.

The ocean plays tricks with vision and obscures distance to the point that you cannot look directly at something to see it – you must look off a degree or two to the side of the object that you wish to view. And still, you are never quite sure that what you are seeing is what is actually there. The sea is notorious for producing unexplainable mirages.

Around mid-afternoon we spotted a definite dark apparition miles ahead of us. As we drew closer we could see that it was low in the water and extremely wide. Somebody suggested that maybe it was a low-lying uncharted island or reef. It wasn't until we were right upon it that we saw clearly that it was a miles-wide oil slick. It was disgusting! We steamed through it for half an hour! The water was very calm where the oil lay on the waves.

There are days that I positively hate the Navy with a passion, but I have never once regretted enlisting. Common sense tells me that I have benefited tremendously from these four years in the service. Anyway, nobody can say it hasn't been interesting.

3,200 FATHOMS

January 16, 1971, Saturday

I say it's a miserable mean thing to have to work on the weekends, even in the Navy. We have the same early reveille as the week days, and we have to find a hiding place until knockoff same as the week days. And when you add a five-hour throttle watch to this drama, it makes it all that much more tedious.

My beard is coming along famously. Let's see, it's been growing now for almost two months. I've really been looking forward to getting out of the service so that I could start my beard, and then when Admiral Zumwalt made it legal for us servicemen I was overjoyed! As a matter of fact, I'm going to keep it on when I get discharged from the Navy, if I can. I don't know who started this ridiculous practice of shaving, anyway – man was meant to be naturally hairy. I like to sit at odd times and comb it; I imagine the sensation is something akin to a cat being petted.

While I was on watch in the Hole all afternoon, one of the seal bearings of No. 4 main engine ruptured and sprayed hot fuel oil into the coils of the DC generator. With 2,000 amps running rampant in there it's a miracle there wasn't one dickens of a fire!

Luckily, one alert snipe discovered the situation before it really became critical. We took the engine out of the propulsion loop and secured it, then explained to the bridge what the major malfunction was.

After letting it cool down a couple of hours (when I say "let it cool down," I mean that we let it get slightly less hot), we strapped on our tool belts and got down to business. We dismantled the generator and cleaned the oil off the brushes and commutator with rags and trichloroethane.

The whole job took about four hours, after which we reassembled it, lit off the engine, and stuck it back in the loop. That makes four times now that we've had to do that disgusting cleaning job on that particular generator since I've been on board. It ought to be taken out and shot.

Sometime during the night we will be transferring from time zone -11 LIMA to -10 KILO. Every moment brings us closer to Subic Bay and Olongapo City. I wonder if any of my old girlfriends will still be working there?

1,835 FATHOMS
January 17, 1971, Sunday

Today was another carefree Sunday. The crew was employed in a variety of pleasurable pastimes, each swab following his individual pursuit of happiness: watching a movie, shooting small arms at tin cans off the fantail, writing those inevitable lonely-sailor letters home, reading the almighty western paperback book, or sleeping soundly in his bunk, totally unconscious of all else but the luxury of having nothing better to do except breathe.

I thought of breaking open another fifth of whiskey this afternoon, but then I decided against it. This was just too nice of a day to dull my senses and crawl into a bottle.

As I sat there on the athwartship's passageway bench, reposing in the shade with a cold Pepsi and looking out over the endless expanse of brilliantly blue sea, I could not help but wonder why everything on earth couldn't be as peaceful as that?

From the middle of the Pacific Ocean it's very hard to believe that somewhere back there are dirty, crowded, crime-riven cities where people must live on top of one another. And somewhere over there are people starving in a world of plenty. And that in just about any direction you might care to point there is a war going on, or preparations being made for the next one. Maybe that's why sailors are loneliest but happiest on the sea.

A pet peeve of mine is whenever I hear somebody say, "oh, just throw it over the side" or "dump it in the ocean." I have made it a personal point never to litter on the land, and the same applies for throwing something in the water. So I put the empty Pepsi can in the trash...and the steward throws it in the ocean later. But my hands are clean.

I get sick and tired of looking at the oily mess of trash floating in the harbors and staining the beaches. There's just no excuse for that sort of thing. The ocean looks so clean and refreshing from out here, but it won't be for long if they keep dumping the world's garbage into it. Agreed, the ocean is pretty darn wide and deep to pollute, but so was the sky – and look at it now.

I hope the Old Man turns on the laundry again soon, which has been secured since water hours were imposed. I have been reduced to wearing a dirty dungaree shirt with a pair of stained khaki shorts. My skivvies have acquired a distinctive personal attitude about them, and I'd wager my socks could go on liberty all by themselves. But I've seen worse times in Vietnam, so I guess I can weather this "trial by dirt" a little while longer.

2,660 FATHOMS

January 18, 1971, Monday

I slept very restlessly last night and finally at 0200 this morning, when I grew bored with just lying there wide awake, I got up and went forward to the electric shop where I listened to music and wrote letters and disturbed no man.

They passed the word over the 1-MC today that one of the Scope Dopes (radarmen) became the proud papa of a nine-pound baby girl. They received the message over the radio from Honolulu, where he had to leave his wife behind to face the experience all by herself. I imagine he's pretty darn happy right now, but it's a shame he couldn't be with his woman when the big event occurred. I don't suppose he's the first one to make that sacrifice, though.

We are fifty miles ahead of track at this time, so they took two engines out of the propulsion loop and slowed this Mustang down to ten knots. Don't ask me why they want to prolong our being at sea. We are due to arrive in Guam on Wednesday morning after over two weeks at sea. It will be good to get fresh milk, clean clothes, and mail. Then on to the Philippines, followed immediately by Hong Kong. So you can see that we have a lot of fine sightseeing ahead of us.

No. 4 generator got sprayed with fuel oil again – this time much worse than before – and we're going to have to remedy the situation in Guam before we head on our last leg of the trip to the Philippines. They won't spend a damn dime to have the yards fix the problem permanently; I guess they'd rather have us electricians ripping it apart every other day to repair it temporarily. That's logical, isn't it? Riiiiight.

January 19, 1971, Tuesday

To those at home…

Although this seems like a long and drawn-out cruise, there just doesn't appear to be any spare time between duty and work. We are due to arrive in Guam tomorrow and I would like to post as many letters as possible there. This seems to be the only answer, crude and impersonal as a form letter may be, and I hope you will all excuse the rudeness just this once. But when I am writing over thirty people, you'll have to put up with a little inconvenience once in a while. It was either a form letter or no letter at all. We've been busy, busy, busy, man!

I sent in my income tax form this week. I also sent along my 1969 W-2 form which most of us neglected to file last year for one reason or another. Between them both I am supposed to get $160 back! That small fortune ought to buy me a nice cassette player. I was planning on buying a .22 magnum pistol while in Guam, but they tell me it takes five days to purchase a pistol (so somebody doesn't do something irrational just on the impulse); I may have to wait until I get to the P.I. for that purchase.

Today is our last day of steaming before we hit Guam in the morning, so they lifted water hours and everyone could take a Hollywood shower with all the hot water he wanted. It was a small, but welcome, luxury. Also, they relented and let the ship's serviceman do some laundry so that we might at least have clean dungarees to wear in Guam.

Spirits are high as we are soon to be once again on dry land – even though it be barren Guam – and parched throats tingle in anticipation of soothing malt beverages.

A week from today we're supposed to pull into Subic Bay – everyone is counting the minutes. Excitement is in the air! I hope I've got a slough of mail waiting for me in Guam. You probably won't hear from me again until I regain consciousness sometime in the Philippines.

ARRIVAL IN GUAM, MARIANAS ISLANDS

January 20, 1971, Wednesday

Us electricians ran shore-power cables to the rectifiers on the pier; the enginemen wrapped up the main engines and secured the generators; the Hole sounds eerie without any machinery running. The boiler techs rigged water, steam, air, and flushing hoses to the pier, while the deckapes doubled up all mooring lines, put on rat guards, and ran out the brow. Walking on dry land again felt queer to our rubberized sea legs. Guam is the same old stick-in-the-mud place it always was.

Waiting for us on the pier were the mobile canteen, the disbursing clerks, and the mail truck – you couldn't even see the driver for the bags of mail piled around him! They serviced us in that order; it's inevitable that a guy will think of his stomach before letters from home.

The pay clerks, armed with loaded .45s, fortified themselves on the messdecks and proceeded to pay everyone in cash. It had been a coon's age since most of us had any back-pocket money.

Mail was an exciting event, as it always is when you've been away to sea for a few weeks. I raked in five letters, two bills, and a newspaper. Some of the guys got close to twenty letters apiece, from faithful girlfriends back home, whose fantastic perfumes had scented all the rest of our mail inside the canvas bags.

As soon as we could wrap up loose ends and break away, we donned our civvies and hit the beach. They have a fairly extensive Naval exchange in Guam, and
we were eager to be relieved of some of our hard-earned cash.

We decided to stop at the base cafeteria and try some landlubber chow for a
change. For the next two hours we sat there drinking beer and ordering cheeseburgers and watching the girls come and go, holding a running commentary on the
attributes of each one. It's surprising what only two weeks at sea can do to a guy's
animal instincts. Pretty soon they stopped serving beer to us, so we drifted lightly
out the door and back to the ship, feeling no pain.

I racked out until movie call. I showed "The Egyptian" for the crew, which
was a five-reeler starring Victor Mature – a favorite actor of mine – and foxy Jean
Simmons. Seemed like Hollywood spared no expense in making the movie either.
It was every bit as good as the book was, too.

EN ROUTE FROM GUAM TO THE PHILIPPINES

January 21, 1971, Thursday

We pulled out of Guam at 0700 this morning after only one day of liberty there.
One day in that place is more than adequate anyway. When they secured Sea and
Anchor detail I rushed topside to get a parting glimpse of the island of Guam.

It was shrouded in a fantastic mist with the rising sun shining through it, and
the first thought that came to my mind was Never-Never Land. There was a huge
headland called "Lover's Leap" (what else?) where they say a couple of young
Guamanians in love supposedly jumped to their deaths years ago to escape the
mates that their parents had chosen for them instead. Thirty-foot waves were
climbing and clawing the cliff and adding their white spray to the thick fog that
already hung there. Beautiful!

They say this ship is not an Auxiliary Oiler-Gasoline at all, but in reality it is an
Automatic Trough Finder. Sure enough, it does seem to have an uncanny knack for
finding the deepest troughs between the seas and falling into them like a sailor just
back from liberty tumbles into his bunk. No doubt some of our wallowing around
is due to the full load of fresh water that we took on in Guam (thank goodness).

We've got a few sickies on board today, having lost their sea legs after only
one lousy day in port. Pathetic. I would venture to guess that most of today's tor-
tured stomachs are due in part to the extensive amount of drinking that went on
at the enlisted men's club last night. They really ought to have known better, but

then again, sailors are not noted for their common sense when it comes to liberty ports.

The Old Man really poured on the coals after we left Guam – so we could get to the P.I. in a hurry, I suppose. All four main propulsion engines were running at full speed and the Hole was simply an inferno! The ambient temperature between any two main engines is upwards of 160 degrees Fahrenheit, which is harmful to sailors and other living things!

Once more a lube-oil leak slimed the No. 4 generator commutator, and we spent all night cleaning it up instead of sleeping. None of the enginemen volunteered to help; if you can't fix it with a hammer, they figured you've got an electrical problem. We had to clean it with gallons of trichloroethane, and when you put that stuff on hot machinery it vaporizes instantly and – wow! It had us flying high as kites in nothing flat.

But the end is in sight. There's no turning back now – the next stop is Subic Bay! Hard to believe it is true. Sailors have a nickname for Subic: "The Asshole of the World." That may very well be, but oh how we love it there! It's a sailor's paradise where morals and law are virtually suspended or ignored; a whole town laden with over 300 nightclubs and nearly 10,000 pleasure girls. Olongapo City – there's something for everybody there.

January 22, 1971, Friday

We have been having some fairly decent meals on board lately. I wonder why the sudden improvement? Could it be that the Old Man finally cracked down on those Stewburners about their swill? I know that it's difficult when cooking for the masses to give food a personal, distinct flavor such as only home-cooking can do, but for a while there the meals were absolutely insipid and wholly unimaginative. I always remind myself, though, that Navy chow still beats eating C-rats in a foxhole.

I couldn't tell you if the sun was out today or not, as I never left the interior of the ship. I spent every minute of free time in my rack. The other guys say that it's starting to get muggy outside…clearly reminiscent of Subic Bay weather. Sometime tonight we are supposed to enter the San Bernadino Straits. We have heard conflicting rumors as to whether the Straits will be calm or rough this time around.

While wasting my life away in my rack, I decided to get another letter off to Suzie. I have no idea if my letters reach Suzie at all, or are intercepted by her mother. It's so difficult to sustain or salvage a relationship with a girl when you're

9,000 miles apart. But I still want to get back together with her. She doesn't realize that I've already waited for her seven long years and am not about to settle for anyone else. Nobody wants second-best.

January 23, 1971, Saturday

We've passed from time zone -9 JULIET to -8 INDIA. You'll have to excuse my typing errors, but it's really not my fault at all. Nor is it the fault of this ancient typewriter either. It is so rough out today that it is fairly difficult to imagine. It is almost frightening how easily the ocean just tosses around this flimsy ship of steel. The typewriter carriage is sliding back and forth of its own accord with every roll of the ship. It's getting rougher and rougher outside even as I type this. I think I'll have to go out and watch the waves for a while.

Earlier today tragedy was narrowly averted in the case of "The Telltale Locker Incident." It was quite rough out by the middle of the afternoon. Parker and I were hanging out in the electrical shop, just trying to find one spot on the whole ship where it would not make us seasick. Our sea-daddy, EM1 McCallen, came bursting

Caution, wet deck!

in and dogged down the door after having been nearly caught by a rogue wave on the tank deck. He grabbed a chair and sat down to catch his breath, leaning up against a locker.

This was a set of lockers for our personal gear; mine was on top and Parker's was on the bottom, and the whole thing opened up like a pair of Dutch doors. While we were shooting the breeze, mostly about the ocean waves outside, my locker door popped open as the ship rolled heavily to one side. Right there, in plain sight of god and everybody, was one of my bottles of Crown Royal whiskey – delicious, yes, but oh so forbidden on board.

As the ship rolled back the other way, the bottle slid back into the locker and the door closed by itself. On the next roll of the ship the door swung back open again, and the bottle slid forward to the edge of the shelf, threatening to leap out at any second, either hitting McCallen on the head or landing right in his lap!

From his vantage point, McCallen could not see the contraband bottle, but Parker and I could. Parker said later that after the second roll he saw my eyes get as big as salad plates as the bottle came to rest on the very lip of the shelf. Parker was gripped with fear, unable to move. But as for myself, I was concerned about losing a fresh bottle of Crown Royal should it land on the deck with a smash. Always calm under fire, I quietly stood up as we chit-chatted, stepped across the room and reached over McCallen's head, securing the bottle in the back of the locker and re-latching the locker door firmly.

Enjoying a fine whiskey as much as our Irish sea-daddy did, I would like to think that McCallen wouldn't have reported me to the Old Man, but to cover his own butt and protect his first-class stripes I'm fairly sure he would have passed the bottle down to Davy Jones' Locker under the cover of nightfall.

It is beyond me why some nights at sea are brightly lit and spangled with stars, while the very next night it is darker than pitch outside. It can get so closely dark at sea that you cannot see the proverbial hand before your face, so that you might think someone had pulled a sack over your head. The ship being in blackout mode doesn't help matters. It makes it all the more eerie when you see the phosphorescent plankton shimmer like blue fire on the waves; it's like a fantastic light show *sans* drugs.

January 24, 1971, Sunday

Sunday is our free time, as much as the Navy allows you free time. They had a poor turnout for lay services this morning; I think organized religion is finally losing its death grip on the human race, thank goodness. The lights were turned out in the berthing compartment all day long, with just the red sleeping lamps glowing, so most guys slept at least part of the 24-hour siesta. I spent most of the day in bed, myself, just drifting and dreaming, occasionally stirring for chow call...

NIGHT CROSSING

Frog-lips climbed wearily up the greasy ladder of the escape trunk, squeezing his head and shoulders through the narrow scuttle. The night breeze was cool and refreshing compared to the blast-furnace heat of the engine room far below him.

He breathed heavily after the long climb, drinking in the dank, saline air. The night tasted raw, green and glistening. So he stood there on the upper ladder rungs enjoying it, halfway through the scuttle, looking like some awesome truncated hand puppet sitting in the middle of the deck.

Somewhere above him came the muffled woofing of the stack, followed occasionally by the whiff of some diesel exhaust wafting past overhead. Slowly his eyes adjusted to the inky darkness of the fantail and he could discern the shadowy shapes of machinery lashed securely to the deck.

The dim light from the passageway below him shined up and cast his sweaty face in a ruddy, devilish glow. It was a youngish face, and yet there was a hardened look in his eyes and a row of furrows knit across his brow that belied his twenty-odd years of life.

An unruly shock of straw-colored hair, cut lopsided by some amateur shipboard barber-wannabe, thrust itself at every opportunity out from underneath his worn and faded ball cap. The cap was long since crushed out of its original shape and spotted with grease and ringed with interesting white sweat patterns, but the bill was lovingly formed into a perfect arch over his eyebrows.

A large, dark mole on his right cheek sprouted the only whiskers that grew on his boyish face. He would never have to shave. One's eyes were inevitably drawn to the pursed, corpulent lips that took up a larger portion of his face than was necessary for any practical purpose. But he wore his nickname comfortably because his shipmates had given it to him with affection.

As his eyes grew accustomed to the gloom, he perceived a familiar figure sitting near the lifelines. Frog-lips wriggled the rest of his lanky body through the scuttle and made his way across the darkened fantail with practiced ease, unconsciously avoiding the guy wires holding the heavy machinery to the deck.

His sea legs maintained balance automatically as the ship rose and fell dramatically with every ocean swell. He plopped down onto the bitts beside the silent figure and mopped his forehead with a grimy rag that he had produced from the back pocket of his dungarees.

"What's happenin', Nelsen?" he asked the quiet figure mechanically.

"Not a helluva lot," answered Nelsen in a husky, lisping voice as if some of his front teeth were missing.

Even in the dark, Frog-lips could see that Nelsen sat there only in his skivvie shorts. He was barefoot, too, and his dog tags tinkled against one another as they swung across his bare chest in the slight breeze.

It was a close, humid night on the Pacific, and sleep was evidently all but unbearable to some of the crew. Through the salty night air a familiar, sweet, pungent smell came to Frog-lips that cloyed in his nostrils.

"Hey, gimmee a hit, huh?" asked Frog-lips eagerly.

Nelsen passed the reefer over to Frog-lips and the ash glowed furiously as he inhaled deeply. He passed it back as Nelsen asked, "What time is it anyway?"

There was a brief pause before Frog-lips answered. He held the smoke inside his lungs until his eyes watered from the exciting burning of it. Fingers of warmth embraced his chest as the drug worked, and his tired muscles relaxed noticeably. When he finally exhaled, the air was heavy with the stink of marijuana, but the breeze quickly swept the odor aft.

"It's oh four hundred," said Frog-lips weakly. "I just got off watch."

"How'd it go on the mid-?" asked Nelsen.

"Okay, I guess. But Jesus Christ, it's hotter than hell down there! The starboard vent crapped out a little after midnight and we couldn't get none of the electricians down there to fix it. They said it'll have to wait till morning."

"Figures. That sounds just like those pricks," said Nelsen with a touch of disgust in his voice.

"McCormick is down there on watch, but he's about as worthless as tits on a boar," said Frog-lips as he spit vehemently over the railing into the swirling sea.

"And those idiots up on the bridge kept giving us bells!" he wailed. "One-third ahead...full ahead...flank speed...all stop. Christ, you'd think we were going to run into something out here in the middle of nowhere! I'll give you three guesses who's up there on OD – and the first two don't count."

"Potter?" guessed Nelsen.

"That's a charley," confirmed Frog-lips. "He's got the mentality of a piss-ant. It never ceases to amaze me how some of those clowns ever get to be officers."

"Well, you can rule out intelligence," suggested Nelsen. "Want the last hit?"

He passed the roach to Frog-lips who inhaled until it burned his fingers. With a deft flip he sent the butt spinning out into the water in a lazy arc. He imagined that he could hear it extinguish with a faint hiss, but he knew that was ridiculous.

The Pacific Ocean slid slowly past as the huge ship plowed clumsily through the water. The cargo tanks were swollen with diesel fuel and aviation gasoline bound for the Philippines, and the four mighty engines strained to make headway against the relentless swells.

Each of the engines was as massive as a Cadillac and unbearably loud as individuals. Noise-Foe ear mufflers were required in the engine room when all four of them were running at the same time, but there was never enough to go around. Already, several of the sailors on board suffered permanent partial loss of hearing – even while wearing the mufflers. From the fantail they could hear the mechanical monsters far below them, thundering and vibrating through the deckplates.

The seas were wide enough and the ship was short enough that it mounted each crest and plunged into each trough with a vengeance, ascending and falling a distance of thirty feet at the very least.

Now and then, huge blankets of plankton floated by. The passively-drifting organisms sparkled and gleamed in eerie phosphorescence like liquid blue fire.

Frequently the stern of the ship would rise clear of the water as the bow dived, and then the twin screws would make a hollow thrashing sound as they partially churned air, and the engines would race briefly. By the faint glow of the aft anchor lamp they could see the foamy wake of the ship trailing away behind them, white in the dark.

"That's good pot," spoke Frog-lips. "Where'd yuh get it?"

"My girl in Subic," answered Nelsen. "She's pretty hooked on the stuff, but that's her problem. Have you got a straight one?"

"Sure," said Frog-lips as he reached into his shirt pocket and brought out a pack of crumpled, damp Winstons, handing them to Nelsen.

There was a sharp scent of sulphur as the match ignited. Nelsen quickly cupped it in his hands away from the breeze and brought it momentarily to his cigarette. From the flickering flame of the match came the solitary vision of his face, floating like a crimson mask in the darkness.

His face was a devastated field of pockmarks, left over from a serious adolescent bout with acne, smoking, and excessive drinking. The sharp, angular features of his facial bones and his hair of jet gave mute testimony to his Crow Indian heritage. And he was indeed missing most of the teeth in the front of his mouth.

Actually, he was only half Crow, not knowing who his father was. Some overly-loud Marine in a bar in Honolulu, obviously delighted by his own wit, had once baited Nelsen, "What's the matter, chief? Couldn't your squaw-mother run fast enough?"

They carried the Marine away with a broken jaw and Nelsen had lost his liberty card for a month. So it goes. His thin ferret eyes glowed like black buttons, and the salt spray of the ocean had whitened his lashes and eyebrows with a briny crust. He looked ten years older than Frog-lips, but he was actually several years his junior.

Abruptly the match went out. Frog-lips thought he had detected a faint expression of melancholy on Nelsen's face in the instant that the match had flared.

"Is something eating you?" he asked cautiously.

The glow of the cigarette bobbed up and down in the dark for a moment before Nelsen answered, "Not really. Wanna read something good?" He passed over a folded and creased piece of paper that he had been holding unnoticed by Frog-lips in his hand all the while.

Frog-lips dug his lighter out of his pocket, snapped it open like a pro, and scratched the flint several times before it caught. By the flickering light of the Zippo he unfolded the paper and read. It was obviously in a feminine hand with broad, scrawling loops, and was unnaturally short and sweet:

"Dear Nelsen,

> *I don't like to tell you in this way, but it is the only way I can reach you right now. I am returning your ring in this envelope for reasons that you probably already know; you can keep my ring. I'm sure that your good friend, Sonny, has told you everything. Did you have him checking up on me or what? Were you halfway expecting this to happen? It's just no good; it'll never work out between us. I can see that now.*

> *I'm going with a great guy now and I'm sure it's the real thing. I'm not going to tell you his name because you'll just do something stupid when you get home. Besides, I'm sure that you have had your share of girlfriends in every port. Don't pretend that you've been true to me all the time, either, because I know better. It's all finished between us. Don't bother to write because I'll just tear it up without reading it.*

> *~ S."*

Frog-lips finished reading the crumpled letter, snapped out the light with a metallic click, and sat there in silence for a few minutes. You never know what to say in times like that. He folded up the letter slowly and carefully and handed it back to Nelsen. Finally he spoke, "Where's the ring?"

"I threw it over the side, I was so pissed off," said Nelsen calmly.

And then, as an afterthought, he flung the letter into the water, too. It disappeared out of sight in an instant, caught in the turbulence of the ship's wake. Frog-lips rather expected Nelsen to throw himself over the rail next, but he knew he was far too level-headed to do something that rash.

"So much for my love life."

Frog-lips was confused. "But what did she mean by 'reasons that you probably already know'?"

"Shit! Who knows?!" exclaimed Nelsen hotly. "And I don't know what the hell she meant by saying that Sonny had probably told me everything. He never told me a goddam thing. I didn't have him spying on her or anything stupid like that, and anyway, he wouldn't have told me if she was stepping out, because he knows I wouldn't have believed him."

The incessant tinkling of Nelsen's dog tags in the breeze finally irritated him enough so that he threw the chain over his shoulder and let the tags lay quiet against his back.

"So it's the old 'Dear John' routine, eh?" asked Frog-lips as he sadly shook his head, genuinely sympathizing with his buddy's plight.

"I was expecting it. Her last letters were pretty weird," said Nelsen, resigned.

"When'd you get this letter?" asked Frog-lips, just to keep him talking about it, not having anything particularly constructive to say.

"The last day we were in port. I didn't even have a chance to go out and get drunk on my ass. I had the damn duty."

"You mean to say that you've had it all this time and didn't even tell me about it?" asked Frog-lips, still confused.

"That's what I mean to say. It wasn't your problem," said Nelsen absent-mindedly. "Besides, I had to think things out for myself."

"Yeah, but it always helps to talk about it, y'know," reminded Frog-lips. "What're you gonna do now?"

"I don't know," Nelsen said as he waved his arm in a useless manner. "What the hell can I do? It's like somebody just kicked the ladder out from under me and left me hanging on the roof. Whaddya think I'm gonna do? I'm gonna get drunk a lot, that's what."

"Well that ain't gonna help," chided Frog-lips, feeling a little like he was preaching.

"Don't give me that crap. I know what'll help and what won't. I've gotta get her outa my system. I suppose I'm feeling like a goddam pansy, but I can't help it. She was special to me, and I really thought we had a good thing going, man. And I don't see why she got all bent outa shape by my so-called 'girlfriends' overseas; they certainly didn't mean nothing to me. I can't even remember their names, fer-chrisake!"

"It's not the end of the world, y'know." But to Nelsen at the time, it was right up there next to the end of the world.

Frog-lips knew the whole story. He had heard it from Nelsen one night when they were both drunk in Pearl. But he didn't think that Nelsen remembered telling him, so he wasn't going to embarrass him by bringing it up again.

Nelsen had had a rough time – rougher than most guys deserve. He had women early in his life on the Rez, and since they spoiled him he became contemptuous of them. He hated the young virgins because they were so damn ignorant and teased all the guys, and he hated the others because they were so vulgarly experienced. He had a penchant for attracting the worse in women.

He was engaged once, to one of the better-looking sweethearts in his home town. And just one month before they were going to be married, Nelsen had found out that she was pregnant…by some other guy. That was when he had enlisted.

But even a low blow like that could have been recovered from in a certain amount of time, like a dirty river purifies itself over a certain amount of miles. Meanwhile, Nelsen's current ex-girlfriend had built back up his faith in the female of the species…only to be eventually dropped flat on his face and kicked squarely in the teeth. It was a well-aimed kick, and Frog-lips knew that it had most certainly done damage that probably couldn't ever be repaired, no matter how much time passed. Nelsen wouldn't be serious about another girl again.

He had seen other guys get hit hard with Dear John letters. Their wounds had never closed and scar tissue had never been allowed to form. Overcome with depression, they had consistently re-enlisted when their hitch was up, and eventually disappeared from the face of the earth.

"There'll be other girls, buddy," said Frog-lips futilely.

"Not like her. She was one in a million. And even after what she did to me, I'd still take her back right now. Sure, there'll be other girls. I've got a long sex life ahead of me. There'll be lots of girls. I'll shack-up with a few, and maybe even get ringed by one. But there'll always be that special one. The one you never forget. Yuh follow me?"

"Yeah," answered Frog-lips. He knew exactly what Nelsen meant. Frog-lips, himself, had not exactly had what you'd call a smooth cruise through the sea of romance. He had received his Dear John letter barely six months after he got in the service.

Personally, he didn't believe that girls waited for guys overseas anymore. He had been seeing too many romantic World War II movies. Out of sight and out of mind; he figured that was the twisted logic of all girls. He thought that he had gotten over his past girl troubles, but he realized suddenly that he was just as bitter as ever.

Frog-lips hadn't been expecting his own letter either, and that made it all the worse. It was the unexpected blows that dropped out of the clear blue sky on your head as heavy as a ton of scrap metal that caused the most pain. Crawling out from under the debris was the hardest part. Who said that guys don't have feelings? And Frog-lips, being just a fresh crewmember on the ship at the time, had not had anyone to talk it out with, and had to work through it by himself.

It seemed funny to him to have gone halfway around the world to the city of Hong Kong, only to come face to face with misery begun at home, through a crushing letter the first mail call in port. And amid all that oriental beauty and exotic scenery, Frog-lips had been twisted in anguish inside. Crowded, jumbled thoughts arose before him, each one clamoring for attention. Outwardly he presented a placid, seasoned surface – even jovial to his buddies – but inside he was a raging maelstrom. His guts writhed with the fierceness of his withdrawal from the girl that had once been immured in his very bones.

Separated from a friend back home with whom he was accustomed to exposing his innermost thoughts, he discovered and was surprised at his own strength. Separated from a large family from whom he had received the necessary moral support, sense of belonging, and admiration that he held as first-born, he substituted an inner discipline for an outer one. And finally, separated from a girl with whom he had shared intimate behavior and grown dependent upon, he realized the awful predicament of being romantically unloved.

He came to know his own mind, what he wanted out of life, and what he could expect of himself. Previously he had regarded himself as a special individual. Now, for the very first time he was content to be just average.

He became more and more realistic, and worried less and less about the things that really didn't count for much in the long run anyhow. He took hold of life by the nape of the neck and slowed down the tempo to a pace that he could comfortably keep up with.

"Hey, did you hear me?" someone was asking.

"Huh?"

"I asked you why you joined the Navy," repeated Nelsen.

"Oh," Frog-lips thought back. "The Army wanted me pretty bad."

"You were drafted, huh? I didn't know that." Nelsen examined that new thought for a moment. "Didja wanna come in the military?"

"Hell no!" said Frog-lips importantly. "I'm anti-war."

Nelsen snorted. "So who isn't? You might as well be anti-sunshine or anti-glacier or something like that. It does about as much good to try to stop a glacier as it does to try to stop wars."

"Don't I know it," mumbled Frog-lips. "It's sickening! I think that's why I'm the happiest when I'm out at sea. It's like being on another planet."

The smokestack behind them made its throaty whooshing sound as the pale gray smoke from the diesel engines continued to belch forth and disseminate. Far off in the east there was a pale blue glimmer on the horizon, as if some huge city's lights were all ablaze just beyond sight. It was a comforting thought to pretend that there was a port so close at hand. New sights, new drinks, new girls...

Far off to the west, where the black canopy of night still hung darkly, there passed the lights of another vessel steaming in the opposite direction. They could have been as close as one mile away, or as much as twenty miles distant; night vision on the ocean was so peculiar at times.

Frog-lips and Nelsen simultaneously wondered to themselves just what the vessel might be: an American freighter? A Japanese fishing boat? A French cable-layer? Or perhaps a Russian destroyer with Russian sailors peering over the railing back at them? They'd never know.

As inevitably happens when people are suddenly drawn close, there is a baring of souls. Without the slightest sign of assent or refusal from anyone, there immediately exists a truce of total sincerity. All the day's light-hearted banter is thrust aside, and the false façade of secure complacency is razed.

When someone has seen a bit of the world, has tasted the bitter gall of memory, and has been bent nearly double under the weight of heartache upon heartache, one is eventually drawn to ask the question, "Do you believe in God?"

It was Nelsen who had asked. Frog-lips wasn't surprised at the question. It went with the mood of the moment just as chilled white wine goes with fish, and Mutt goes with Jeff. In fact, he felt that he would have asked the question if Nelsen had not. It was not especially addressed to Frog-lips in particular, but rather seemed as if Nelsen were thinking out loud.

"I don't know," said Frog-lips slowly and truthfully, picking his words carefully, as if it were the first time that he had pondered the idea. "It's not like I haven't given it any thought. It's just that one minute I feel there is a God, and the next minute I'm sure there isn't."

"Well, it doesn't do any good to lose sleep over it," said Nelsen with finality.

"That's what I figure," agreed Frog-lips. "Since we probably ain't gonna find out for sure anyway, I just figure it's best to leave the worrying to the dang churches. In the meantime I'm gonna do my best to live the way a man ought to live. If there is a god, what more could he ask? I've got this little personal philosophy about sinning: if a man believes something to be wrong, but does it anyway, I think that's sinning. Pure and simple."

Now that Frog-lips warmed up to the subject, the momentum carried him forward.

"Well, I'm not afraid to take a chance. We were obviously given a free will to choose. Hell, why should I let my natural feelings be crimped by a dopey religion and make myself miserable and hypocritical, when I can thoroughly enjoy myself without one? I can't in all honesty believe in something which *all* of my senses tell me doesn't exist."

"You got something there," said Nelsen. All through Frog-lips excited tirade, he had sat silently and nodded his head in full agreement. It's a wonderful feeling to find somebody else whose brain waves ran along the same convolutions as your own. It's as arousing as reading some secret idea of yours in a book and finding out that you're not alone in your thoughts. At least if he went to hell for it, he'd have a buddy there to keep him company and help beat the heat. It was small comfort.

Nelsen stared at the brightening eastern sky with renewed amazement. Rays of pink and orange shot through tiered clouds of pastel blue, while all this splendid color was amplified and reflected across the ocean waves.

The sun didn't rise properly in that part of the world. Instead of gradually rising out of the sea and growing in intensity like a normal sun, it almost leaped over the eastern horizon. Then the terminator, the line separating the light and dark areas of our planet, went racing away to the west at over a thousand miles per hour. A peculiar sensation of happiness and well-being swept over Nelsen. Dawn induced euphoria in him, it always had.

"It'll be morning soon," he observed.

Frog-lips punctuated this observation with a magnificent yawn that lasted a full thirty seconds. He rose and added a joint-cracking muscular stretch to the yawn.

He rubbed his nose vigorously for a moment before he said wearily, "Well, I had better try and catch at least an hour's snooze before reveille. Man wasn't made to sleep on his feet."

"Christ, how can you sleep in your rack when it's so rough out?" asked Nelsen, puzzled.

"Easy," explained Frog-lips. "I don't sleep in my rack when it's like this. I sleep in the forward hold."

Nelsen laughed at that; the forward hold was a favorite hiding place of his, too. The overweight officers didn't usually care to expend the time or energy required to crawl down into the hold and root out the goldbricks.

"How about waking me up about ten minutes before quarters go down?" requested Frog-lips. "I'll be sleeping on some life preservers behind the old paint raft."

"Roger."

Frog-lips stumbled off sleepily towards the bow. Nelsen slowly rubbed the grit under his eyelids just a bit deeper into his tired eyes. He'd just have to catch up on his sleep the next night, if he could.

It wasn't so bad now that the sun was nearly peeping over the clouds in wonder of what Man had done while it was away. During the night they had come a 100 miles closer to port, steaming along at a dizzy nine knots.

Yes, maybe things would work out after all. He knew he shouldn't let anyone or anything bend him out of shape...especially some fickle female. It just wasn't no big thing. Briefly he contemplated opening the whiskey he had hidden in his locker; but it was a court-martial offense to drink on a Navy ship...if you were caught.

The rest of the crew would be getting up soon. At the insistent loudspeaker they would roll slowly out of their bunks and stand wobbling as the ship pitched. They would then pour gallons of hot, steaming coffee into themselves in an effort to wake up and gird themselves for the day.

Nelsen carefully unsnapped his dog-tag chain, removed a slender silver ring engraved with entwining hearts, and held it up to encircle the sun. And then, after a moment's hesitation, he let it slip through his fingers into the black depths of the ocean. He knew her ring would tumble for hours as it sank to the bottom of the seven-mile-deep Mariana Trench. No human being would ever lay eyes on it again.

Then he smiled confidently and stalked off towards the galley, suddenly hungry, following the wonderful aroma of buttermilk pancakes and frying sausage on the morning air.

January 25, 1971, Monday

Land ho! After entering the San Bernadino Straits, we spotted Romblon, the first outlying island of the Philippines. Shortly afterwards, we entered an area called "Iron Bottom Bay," so named for the 220,300 tons of enemy steel that lies below on the ocean floor. It was there one night that was fought the last surface battle of World War II. The mighty battleships that had been sunk in Pearl Harbor were raised and refitted to deliver a crushing blow to the Japanese fleet right there. How many sailors slept underneath us?

The Philippine Islands are some of the prettiest islands that I've ever seen. They're so rough-looking that it isn't hard to imagine the terrific volcanic activity that thrust them above the ocean's surface.

As soon as we got alee of Luzon Island, the waves lay down and it was smooth sailing ahead. We were riding so calm that you'd swear we were already alongside the pier! For a change, we slept at night without getting pitched out of our racks.

There were countless islands around us then as we swung around the southern tip towards Subic Bay. A lot of the smaller islands are just barren slabs of rock and uninhabited, but some of the others tower dramatically high into the sky, and white chapels can sometimes be seen gleaming on the steep, jungled slopes.

There were many small barrios along the beaches, and several times we saw the banca boats put about. Every now and then we would catch a smell of land. It really felt good to be back!

Doc gathered us all together and delivered a medical lecture today that was scary enough to make us want to take cold showers instead of make whoopee. Olongapo City has the highest VD rate of any port in the world, and this year he says it was unusually high. He made it sound like we should walk down Magsaysay Drive already wearing a condom and juiced to the gills with penicillin!

January 26, 1971, Tuesday

I'm beginning to believe that it is Navy policy to leave everything that needs to be done until the very last minute. There must be some kind of perverse psychology in Navy Regulations that explains why those who masquerade as officers wait until the last day to tell their men what work has to be accomplished before they can hit the beach in port. Do they think this engenders respect for them? I thought that we would never finish the mountain of work that they had for us to do! And there wasn't any logical reason why they couldn't have given us the assignments a few at a time during the cruise when we had more than enough spare time to do them. Oh hell no!

SUBIC BAY, PHILIPPINES
January 31, 1971

Dear Family,

You'll remember that I told you I would be behindhand in writing whenever I got down here in the P.I. Wild horses can't drag us liberty hounds out of Olongapo City! It's good to be back here once again and see the old familiar places.

I found three of my buddies off my old tugboat, but the YTM-182 isn't around anymore – they already put her in moth balls...*sniff*. After all that money we spent on her last overhaul, too! Ridiculous.

I've been doing a lot of spending myself on stereo equipment since I got down here – everyone has!

Cassette player with AM/FM tuner	$125
Headphones	$18
Phonograph	$66
Amplifier	$154
Reverberator	$48
Two 12-inch speakers	$132
TOTAL	$543

Music is such an enjoyment to me that I'm willing to invest all that money in stereo gear. Just imagine what that same Sansui equipment would cost back in the States! I'll be shipping it home piece by piece for Gramma to store for me in her attic.

They caught two Sound and Security watch-standers last week with their pants down – figuratively speaking, of course. During each four-hour watch we are required to hourly test each void and liquid-cargo tank for the depth of water, oil, etc. This is done by using a sounding tape; that is, dropping a brass weight attached to a metal tape-measure down a sounding tube into the void. By comparing hourly readings, the watch is alerted if a void suddenly develops a leak and begins filling up with water.

Well, these two clever fellows had been radioing (fabricating readings from the previous hour) the soundings into the logs out of sheer laziness. One of the first-class shipfitter petty officers, who suspected this was happening, put a piece of paper in each sounding tube which read, "When you find this please notify Washburn, SF1."

And when the two guys went through their entire watches without finding any of the notes, the shipfitter had them dead to rights. They went before the mast while we were yet out to sea and the Old Man took their crows away and stripped them down to Firemen. All for sheer laziness. Not to mention endangering the lives of their shipmates by not doing their jobs properly. I thought the note trick was pretty clever myself.

February 15, 1971

Dear Family,

Here it is the 15th of February already and I planned to have all my valentines in the mail by now. That just goes to show you how little planning ahead amounts to on this ship; you never really know when you're going to have time to do anything.

Boy, I am bone weary tonight! I'm on duty-electrician today and they have been running my butt off! I got up early this morning and finished painting out the deck in the engine room. After that I watered and charged the batteries in the whale-boats. I guess it was about that time when weird stuff started happening.

The rectifier on the pier that we were hooked up to tripped off and we lost shore power. I had to go down into the engine room (in the dark with a battle lantern) and strip the switchboard down, which is no small job. Then we had to call Shop 99, who is in charge of electrical power on this pier, to get some dang yard-bird to come out here and turn our power back on.

We sat dead in the water for an hour before he finally showed up; all the compartments had grown unbearably hot since the air-conditioning was off; all the reefers got dangerously warm because the cooling compressors were off; and the all-important radio gear was non-functional.

After the yard-bird energized the rectifier again I had to go down into the Hole and gradually put all of the ship's circuits back on the line. This particular sequence of events occurred a grand total of SEVEN times today! I began to think I was dreaming all of this.

I found a zero ground in one of the circuits in the switchboard, so I secured that one, and everybody thought that was the end of our problems. Five minutes later the lights went out again and there we sat in the dark, cursing like…uh, sailors.

We finally found out what the real problem was: we were carrying a 700-amp load – and the rectifier tripped out at exactly 700 amps. But the yard-birds couldn't fix us up with a larger rectifier without a lot of hassle, so we seemed doomed to be dropping the load repeatedly. Somehow I just couldn't see going through this rigmarole endlessly all night long.

The solution was to light off one of our ship's generators and go on our own power, but we didn't quite have enough air pressure built up to start one of the big engines. You see, every time the power went off the air compressors would stop and we just couldn't keep any pressure in the tanks to start the engines. Finally we got up just barely enough air pressure to start one of the engines, and from then on it was a cinch to go on our own power and unhook from shore.

BUT, there was only one set-back with that little scheme: having the generator running made it necessary to have three more guys standing watch in shifts down in the Hole throughout the night – including good old Stanger. They never told me about this monkey business when I enlisted. Just another of the million-and-one fine reasons for being a civilian.

I just finished reading "Love Story" by Erich Segal and, like the rest of the people who read it, I cried at the end. I was really surprised to find that I still *could* cry, let alone at a story book! It was such a well-written book that I went ahead and ordered a hard-bound edition to keep in my personal library. Have you read it yet?

The next night I showed the crew a movie called "John and Mary," starring Dustin Hoffman and Mia Farrow. It was a very tender love story, too, and surprisingly the crew really liked it. It must have reminded them of home or something.

Some sailor got stabbed by his girlfriend out in town last weekend; the blade nicked the femoral artery in one of his legs and they just couldn't get him to stop bleeding up at Cubi Hospital. A call went out for blood donors and there were about five guys off our ship who had the right stuff.

But after they gave him over thirty pints of blood they ran out of donors on the entire base. They were desperate to save his life then and started calling out for blood of any type. I didn't think they could do that, but Doc says that they changed the guy's whole blood system…twice! I gave a pint, along with a whole lot of other guys, but we never did hear any more about what eventually happened to him. I hope he pulled through. No way is good to die – least of all being stabbed by a bar hog in Subic.

I took my best buddy, Parker, out to my favorite club in Olongapo City: the Can Can Club. I mentioned to you a long time ago that I liked it because it was a good drinking and talking place. They have a quiet combo there that plays good slow-dance music, and the girls are capable of holding up their end of a conversation.

Naturally, the rest of my buddies think it's a real morgue, so they shuffle off to their loud psychedelic joints that are just stinky with marijuana. Half the crew is high on something, grass or speed or bennies, most of the time, and I am curious just how long this phase will last for them. I mean, do they grow out of it, or do they become junkies for the rest of their lives, and finally go on to harder stuff? Imagine having a daddy or a gran'pap who's a doper. Tsk tsk. There must be something better in life.

Well, I guess that's about all the news from this corner of the world for now. I am looking forward to going to bed in an hour. I used to be quite a night owl in my day, but now I run out of steam earlier and earlier. Is this what they call "over the hill"?

EN ROUTE FROM PHILIPPINES TO HONG KONG

February 17, 1971

Dear Darlene,

Thanks a bunch for the long newsy letter I received from you! Correspondence from the people back home has been practically nil since I arrived in the Philippines. I didn't have time – as I told you I wouldn't – to write much while we were in Subic Bay; it is such a groovy liberty port. So I will probably post this in Hong Kong.

We left Subic yesterday and stopped at Sangley Point, where we off-loaded our whole liquid cargo of JP-5 aviation fuel. We stayed one night at Sangley Point. It used to be a big naval station, but now they're closing it down on account of everybody pulling out of the Vietnam War.

On the way out, we passed Corregidor along the way; it sure didn't look like much of an island to fight over. We also saw several land battleships in Manila Bay. During World War II they took a small piece of rock that was sticking out of the water, poured concrete all over it and built a bunker, complete with twin 14-inch guns. Very small, but very effective.

We left Sangley this noon and are presently on our merry way to Hong Kong. This will be my first time there and I am really looking forward to doing a lot of sightseeing. It is strictly a British-controlled port, though, and so us Yanks will have to wear our dress blue uniforms all the time. What a drag.

We will be in Hong Kong until March 9th, when we will come back to Subic until April. After that we haven't been informed of our schedule. Scuttlebutt has it that they are trying to line us up with a short trip to Bangkok for some R&R. Last week the Old Man sent in a request for us to go back to Vietnam (so we heard), and everybody is pretty sure it will be approved. I could really go for that! Almost everybody on board wants to go back to Nam, some for the extra eighty-five dollars a month, and some for more altruistic reasons. Peace brother, but keep that combat pay a'coming!

Again, this may all be pure scuttlebutt. Some people on the ship, with nothing better to do, will intentionally start a piece of scuttlebutt circulating just to see how long it takes the rumors to get back to them, and see how much the original rumor has been transformed in transit.

Every guy needs a girl, don't you agree? I don't mean a girl like the kind in Subic or Tijuana, but a girl that a guy can talk to, pamper, spend money on, show off, and cuddle up to. Did I leave out love? That most of all.

Well, I've been hung-up on Suzie for about seven years now and I'm nearly ready to lose my mind. But she hasn't answered any of my letters since my last leave. I have come to the conclusion that either her mother is faithfully protecting her daughter, or else I'm simply writing directly to a waste-paper basket. I sure don't know what to do next. Girls drive me crazy…maybe that's why they're so neat.

Since I have been in Subic this time I have found three of my old tugboat buddies; one guy I knew at Mare Island in Vallejo, California; seven guys from South Dakota; and even one guy who used to be on my last ship, the *USS Iredell County*. The Navy is a small world, and they say that if you drop anchor long enough in Subic Bay you will meet half the people you know in the world.

I have mixed feelings about the place, though; being stationed there 18 months can do that to you. There are familiar things that I hate and others that I'm rather fond of. I don't like to be away from home any more than the next guy, but sometimes I really like Subic. And then I can't stand it…until I leave it, and then I miss it. That's dumb, isn't it?

Well, I guess I had better wrap up the Late News here and go off the air till next time. Pardon my scrawl, but I just couldn't drag the typewriter down here in the engine room with me. The ship is starting to rock quite a bit as we are getting farther out to sea, but it's only a three-day cruise to Hong Kong anyway. This sure is a hot corner of the world this time of year, though. How goes it for you landlubbers? I'll try to send some postcards from Hong Kong. Meanwhile I'll be looking for your letters.

As always, more or less,

Steve

HONG KONG

February 24, 1971

Dear Family,

I'm writing this between rounds. It was a rough trip from the P.I. to Hong Kong; the trip was even rougher than the trip from Guam to the P.I. – and we thought *that* was bad! This last trip was so rough that we ruptured some frames about the ship and started taking on water in several spaces.

We took on seawater in our berthing compartment. Every day we'd clean it up, and every night it'd seep back in while we slept. We had about four inches of water slopping back and forth with each roll of the ship. Just like the tide was coming right into your bedroom. Very disconcerting! It was hard to sleep with all this wave action going on right under your bunk. The ship was rocking so bad that we had to hang onto the stanchions of the rack while we slept, just to keep from being thrown out into the water on the deck.

The bunks are called Northampton racks, and are perfectly flat with a metal bottom. That's just fine if you're sleeping in an unmoving barracks or something, but not on a steaming ship. Our old racks were all saggy and had a pit in the center of the mattress where we nested, so we didn't have to worry about flying out.

One day before we pulled into Hong Kong it turned very cold outside. It got cloudy, misty and gray, and we haven't seen the sun since.

Hong Kong is really a beautiful city! I climbed out of the Hole after Sea and Anchor Detail was secured, just to look around the harbor – and I was simply awestruck. You just never know what sort of vista is going to await you when you pull into a new port and are eventually allowed to come topside for your first look around, and it is usually never a dis-appointment.

Upon entering Hong Kong harbor, you can see the rock cliffs painted white, which causes them to gleam through the sea fog and darkness so ships hopefully won't hit them. There were hills on either side of us, with skyscrapers running all the way up and down the steep hills. I think Hong Kong is even prettier than Frisco, and that's really saying something.

Visiting Hong Kong, BCC.

The more money you exchange, the better exchange rate they'll extend you. It's funny because when you go out in town shopping, you can spend either Hong Kong dollars or American dollars. I've found that wherever I go in the world, everybody accepts American money. You couldn't take a Hong Kong dollar or Japanese yen or Filipino peso back to the States and spend it. You wouldn't get very far.

The shopping here is terrific! We've already gone over on the Kowloon side where all the traditional tea-drinking British live. It's a pretty swanky area, and not nearly as cheap as the Hong Kong side. There are so many more nice things to buy there, though. I've seen awesome coffee tables and hand-carved cedar chests that would be exciting to take home. A cedar chest hand-carved with oriental figures only costs forty dollars.

I bought a stone carving of piggy with litter. It's the Year of the Pig here in Hong Kong. They want all their crops and livestock to be real fat and prosperous, and their fish harvest, too. Thus the pig symbol.

There are over 2,000 tailors in Hong Kong. You can walk down one block in Hong Kong and pass fifty tailor shops, and that's just on one side of the street. They cater to a lot of British sailors, too, because it is primarily a British seaport. All the tailor shops serve free beer and whiskey while you are being fitted. (You get more relaxed with the liquor and tend to buy more, I suppose.) I had several shirts created by tailors for me, from a design I insisted they copy, and it was dirt-cheap.

Transportation is very convenient. No matter where or when you want to go, there is some form of transportation waiting anxiously to take you there. Ferries go back and forth across the bay constantly; buses and taxi cabs, water taxis, tramway, streetcars, and rickshaws all operate around the clock. They drive on the wrong side of the street, however…the left side.

All the motor vehicles have the steering wheel on the rider's side of the car. It's really confusing. When you come to a crosswalk, you have to stop and figure out which way to look for oncoming traffic before you cross. No traffic signs, either; you take your life in your own hands when crossing the streets of Hong Kong. At any rate, bicycles should be classified as dangerous weapons, as they don't seem to operate under any laws whatsoever.

We took the cable car funicular from downtown Hong Kong to the top of Victoria Peak. We rose hundreds of feet in 15 minutes. The cable car has a gradient of 1:2, meaning that for every two feet you travel horizontally you rise one foot in height. Or roughly, about a 45-degree angle. Not for the faint-hearted. I kept looking back down the incline and wondering where we would end up if the contraption ever let loose.

A lot of Chinese use the cable cars to commute up and down the Peak. Many of them live at the top, or on the other side of the Peak, or even in Aberdeen, but they work downtown.

At present they are building an underwater tunnel to connect Hong Kong with Kowloon across the bay. It is called the Cross Harbour Tunnel. Huge sections of prefabricated tunnel are floated into position on the surface, then sunk, and attached together on the bottom of the bay by divers. The underwater tunnel will eventually be covered with earth, also.

You can really spot the strong British influence here in Hong Kong, especially with the imported European cars. The names of the streets are predominantly British in origin (i.e., Princess Margaret Boulevard, Prince Phillip Avenue, Edinburgh Street, Harcourt Street, Salisbury Road, Wellington Street, etc.)

The British sailors in town are very nice and quite friendly for the most part. They're good steamers. I just love their accent; they don't think they have an accent, though. I still don't know how they can keep their money system straight with their bob, quid, tuppence, sixpence, sterling, pounds, etc.

We are "station ship" here in Hong Kong, having relieved the *USS Tom Green County* (LST-1159). Being station ship is a lot of work, so they only give it to a ship for four weeks at a time.

Duties include handling all the movies for both the American and British fleets in port. We've got hundreds of movies on board at present, and every day sailors show up alongside and we swap movies with them. If we ever get ahold of any brand-new movies that we'd like to see first, we kind of scoot them out of sight for ourselves. Just one of the perquisites of being station ship.

We also handle tons of mail for all the American and British sailors. Every day we muster a twenty-man working party and carry mail bags from the walla-wallas up to our ship, where we sort it. Then the mailmen from each individual ship come to pick up their own mail.

There are very few United States ships in port at this time. All the businesses downtown will really cater to the station ship, and bend over backwards to give them a good deal. All over downtown they have signs saying "Welcome USS Elkhorn," and then they'll post a list of the crew members who have patronized their store or bar.

"Are you friends of Steve Stanga?" the doorman asks passing sailors. "Well, c'mon in. This is his favorite club!" I see my name is up in front of Suzie Wong's and also the Candlelight Club, being touted as a loyal customer. We'll be station ship here in Hong Kong two more times in the near future, for a total of three months.

I may have to stand Shore Patrol duty next time we're in port, although I've never had it before, nor am I particularly burly or surly. You get an extra thirty dollars a day, just for walking around softly with a big stick…sightseeing, basically… trying to avoid trouble of any sort. For providing this service they put you up in the Hong Kong Hilton, too.

There are a lot of Red Chinese stores downtown, and we've been told how we can spot them and avoid them easily enough. It's really not hard to spot them. They have blood-red curtains and red wallpaper, and cute little pictures of Chairman Mao on the walls, and usually out in their front display windows they have atrocity pictures of Americans burning villages in Vietnam. The Red Chinese propaganda caters mostly to the uneducated populace.

I love to try the local cuisine when we eat out, while my spineless buddies quite often stick with cheeseburgers and ground round. Half the time I can't even identify the type of food that I am eating, nor am I especially eager to find out, but it's usually delicious! One particular vegetable looks like mangled crabgrass, but tastes like tender string beans.

A sign in town read: "For absolutely the best steak in Hong Kong and goodies like pizza, onion rings, imported American beer, etc. Bring your appetite to the Diamond Horseshoe Restaurant, corner of O'Brien and Gloucester Roads."

So many boats in this busy harbor! Taxis, junks, boats that collect garbage, ferries, cargo ships, and even some junks flying the hammer-and-sickle Communist flag. We see the flags of many nations here. Once I even saw a ship from Switzerland – and that's a landlocked country! Now come on!

Each ship that passes us will dip their flag to about half-mast, and then run it back up after we have returned the honor. This is simple maritime courtesy from one country to another, sort of a salute. I think that's fairly civilized of folks. When two United States ships pass by each other, every sailor topside on deck will pop tall and salute the other ship in unison.

Pidgin English is really hard to understand for some people, especially when spoken by the Chinese. It's usually necessary for us to keep asking them to repeat things until we understand, although my long stay in the P.I. helps me understand oriental speech much better than my comrades do. Thus, I am usually the translator for the group.

Filipinos speak much better English than most other Orientals, as they are taught it in school beginning at kindergarten, along with their native language of Tagalog. The Chinese language sounds like they're always choking on something, like they've got a fish bone caught in their throat. It is strident and rough on the ear.

It actually hurts my jaw to try to repeat some of their strange words; I think English is a much more civilized tongue.

A bunch of Chinese workers from Hong Kong came out to our ship to work recently. The gang was called Mary Sue, or most likely it was Mary Soo. The work party is made up of females of all ages, and they are called Mary Soo due to the type of work they do. They perform all of the odd jobs around the ship that we would normally have to do.

For example, where it usually takes the deckapes three to four days to paint out the hull of the ship, the Mary Soo workers did the entire job in just one day! They paint from rafts with long-handled paint rollers, moving quickly around the hull. They will even shinny up and chip out the masts if we secure the radar first. They also painted the stack and some of the engine room spaces for us.

All they ask in return is American cigarettes and old brass. Just about everybody on the ship has a small stash of old brass (i.e., valves, spigots, bolts, valve wheels, fire nozzles, and engine parts that we no longer use). We save old brass the way you save your loose change in a jar, against the day when we'd arrive in Hong Kong and can do us some bartering.

Altogether, we gave them about a thousand pounds of brass. They probably sell it to the Red Chinese, which eventually ends up in Vietnam, made into weapons or ammunition for the Viet Cong. Doesn't make much sense, does it? It's not legal, but everybody in the Navy does it. The officers are the ones who horde the most brass!

Once in a while, a small junk will sneak up under our fantail and try to sell our sailors American whiskey, good Mexican marijuana, and other drugs. Then the officers will order someone to turn the fire hose on those people, and eventually they get the hint and leave...their spirits much dampened. Usually, the Chinese harbor patrol will come zooming right up in their cute little police boats and run them off.

Another boat comes out regularly to pick up our trash. We can't dump

See you next time, sailor!

our junk in the harbor, even though all the Orientals seem to do it. These people pick up our trash and then stand off a ways from us and pick through our junk trying to find something worthwhile to salvage. They even sort through our galley garbage. It's depressing to see them have to live like that.

Well, I guess it's time to make my rounds again.

February 25, 1971

Dear Family,

How about that? Filipino stationery, Hawaiian envelope, pictures of Hong Kong enclosed, all mailed in a British post office overseas – how international can you get?

All we've done so far is go sightseeing and shopping all over the city. Subic Bay is the place for carousing; Hong Kong is a place to see exotic things. And now that I'm out of money until next payday, I shall remain dry until then, too.

You know, it has been good to be able to hit my rack at 2100 and get a good night's sleep, and then wake up without a hangover. I really do enjoy sleeping. They sell San Miguel beer here, and I have been sorely tempted, but I have resisted thus far.

Saturday is our final day to go sightseeing before the last one of us idiots is totally broke; then we are going to be picture-taking fools after that for entertainment. We've still got two weeks left here before we leave for the Philippines once again. Life is good.

We had a little incident happen earlier today. Two Chinese junks, both flying the red Communist flag, pulled up alongside of us (while we were anchored in the middle of the bay) and tied up to us. We told them that they couldn't stay there, and they never even said what they wanted. "No speakee Engleesh!" they jabbered at us.

We aren't supposed to let them get anywhere near us. If they don't firsthand dip their flag in recognition to our country, then we must stand by to repel them. We broke out the .45s and called harbor patrol on the horn. About a half hour later they left us with the two junks in tow. There are many, many junks here that fly the Communist flag. We're surrounded by Commies – yikes!

I have the duty tonight. It's almost 1900 now and I must go to the messdecks and set up the projector for the evening movie. I am showing a Dracula melodrama tonight – "The Fearless Vampire Killers," starring Sharon Tate – and it proves to be an evening of many laughs. We always get such a kick out of vampire movies.

Parker and I have been given free rein in picking out the movies for the crew over at the base movie exchange. They like comedies the best, followed by westerns and mysteries. Girlie flicks draw a lot of hollering and whistling and crude sailor talk. Musical movies are generally despised by one and all, so we hardly ever pick up one of them unless it has already been a proven hit back stateside… like "Woodstock."

Before each feature movie I always show an episode of one popular TV series or another: "Star Trek" (their all-time favorite), "Mission: Impossible," "Mannix," or "High Chaparral." There was loose talk from the officers about paying us electricians one dollar each evening for showing the flick. But I've never seen a dime come my way.

Half of the crew is away tonight at a basketball game that some of the crewmembers play in. They are playing a game against some local Chinese school. We will probably get our butts handed to us in a bamboo basket.

We also play softball games in Subic Bay against other fleet ships about three times a week when we are in port. We always go and scream our lungs out and hassle the other teams who usually have practically no rooting section at all. You'd be surprised how much a little cheering and boosting does to help a team to victory.

Parker and I are the official team hecklers. Our job is to get the other team's players so rattled that they can't concentrate and start playing wild. We shred them with some of our best zingers: "Hey pitcher, whaddya doing out there – bowling?" and "I've seen better heads on a mug of beer!" and "Did your mother have any kids that lived?" and "Oh come on, you throw like a girl!"

Many is the time that Parker and I have had to quickly disappear after a game to escape an irate defeated crew from another ship who are coincidentally carrying baseball bats by that point. But at the games there is free beer, hamburgers and hot dogs, and everyone always has a good time, rain or shine, win or lose.

HONG KONG, B.C.C.

Leaning lazily against the freshly whitewashed lifelines of my ship, I gazed enraptured at what was repudiated to be the most beautiful natural harbor in the world. The mellow, golden sun headed for final pasture behind towering Victoria Peak.

Molten sunshine lay across the water and lapped quietly against the cold, gray hull of the ship. A peculiar haze hung over the city proper like a shroud, trailing

Hong Kong harbor.

ethereal wisps in-between the foursquare phalanx of skyscrapers which rose in ranks up the side of the mountainous island.

Hong Kong is located in the heart of the most uncomfortable climatic zone on earth, and places without air-conditioning are just barely fit for human habitation. In addition, it is directly in the path of every typhoon that wheels across the Pacific.

The expansive bay was teaming with a myriad of water craft, each one apparently unconcerned and oblivious of the other's course. Small, bobbing walla-wallas shuttled back and forth between the piers and the distant ships that lay at anchor.

Lumbering and awkward Chinese junks ploughed through the water, their decks swarming with motley crews of grizzled fishermen, skinny yellow dogs, pregnant women, and small bright-eyed children with safety ropes tied about their waists.

Overcrowded, triple-decked ferries rushed back and forth. Depending on which direction they were traveling, either end of the ferry served as the bow, like some Janus-faced sea vessel.

Rusting and riding low in the water with cargo, merchant ships steamed constantly in and out of the bay. Each one flew a different ensign, and their sailors pledged allegiance to many different lands, and the unreadable characters that were scrawled across the sterns hinted at mysterious, faraway places.

In the far-off mouth of the harbor loomed the ominous and massive, ashen bulk of the *USS Iwo Jima* (LPH-2). Its acres of weather deck were clustered with squatting helicopters like a swarm of dragonflies, their wings folded up at rest. The huge ship was a prime recovery vessel of the Apollo space capsules.

With the occasional, comfortably-warm breeze came a curious mixture of odors. There wafted to the nostrils exciting traces of steaming rice, mouth-watering smells of frying squid, fragrant Chinese tea, trembling scents of exotic vegetable dishes, 100-year-old eggs, the balmy bouquet of almond-curried chicken, the homely fragrance of tender bubbling noodles and fresh scallions, and the arousing aroma of smoked hake – all served with that fabulous hot sake!

San Miguel was the most popular beer in Hong Kong, just as it is in the Philippines. It tastes best ice-cold. In fact, we often asked for a glass of chipped ice to pour the beer over.

Through these hungering odors permeated the unpleasant reek of thousands of vehicles burning natural gas in their engines, and the odious stench of a litter-laden harbor, used as a gigantic sewer by millions of Orientals. The travel posters forget to tell you about that.

The best way to travel around the city is on foot; you can see, hear, feel, and smell more…and it's way cheaper. By wandering up and down those crooked little back streets, I ran across many of the tiny shanty factories where much of our cheap "made in Hong Kong" toys originated. The raggedy Orientals sat around on the floor of these shacks amongst baskets of spare parts, chattering away, assembling toy cars, artificial flowers, squirt guns, etc., and then boxing them up for shipment around the world.

I bought a green jade fish while in Hong Kong, which had been allegedly blessed by a Buddhist monk, and I had it put on a necklace. Jade is reputed to bring good luck to the wearer, and a jade fish is supposedly a strong talisman against drowning. I figured that might come in handy someday.

Small, remote craft tooted gaily and businesslike, while the deep-throated horns of the larger ships came rolling mournfully across the water. They were not comfortable in the confines of the harbor and longed to be at sea.

Along the crowded piers of the vast Wanchai waterfront was pressed a crushing throng of houseboats which comprised Hong Kong's second city. They huddled together like buddies at a bar, shoulder to shoulder, gunwale to gunwale.

SASEBO, JAPAN

March 29, 1971, Sunday – midnight

Dear Family,

Time has been flying by so quickly that I did not even realize it had been a whole month since I last wrote! I decided to sit up here on the messdecks where it is warmer, instead of in our chilly electric shop. The weather has turned much cooler recently. There are a few other dutiful souls sitting here, also, writing wives, girlfriends, buddies or whoever. And with a fresh cup of Constant Comment tea, I'll start my letter to you.

I am saddened to hear about Aunt Lujeanne's deteriorating condition in every letter I receive from the family. It is very hard to believe that this terrible thing is actually happening. I don't know much about diabetic complications, and hope I never have to find out firsthand.

You cannot imagine what a helpless and hopeless feeling it is to be so far away during this family emergency. I know that my being there wouldn't help a darn bit, but it sure would make me feel better. I certainly don't want to receive a Red Cross telegram or anything like that with bad news. As long as she is still alive, I am not going to stop hoping. She is such a good person and I really don't understand why this dreadful thing has to happen to her.

Even if the worse comes true, I wouldn't be able to come home for the funeral. They only allow you to take emergency leave if someone passes away in your immediate family. How can the doctors just give up on her like that? But I suppose they know what they're doing. I wish Lujeanne wouldn't give up either; most likely that is out of her hands, though, too. Hopefully, your next letter will report that she has improved.

While we were yet in Hong Kong, we visited a place called the Tiger Balm Gardens. It was named after Tiger Balm, a marvelous ointment which a certain Mister Aw Boon Haw once produced while he was alive. It is still manufactured by his descendents. The Gardens are the family's personal residences, and the Haw-Par mansion is absolutely beautiful! The whole place is filled with flowers, mosaics, and wild Oriental statuary.

There is a tall, ornate structure on the grounds called the Tiger Pagoda, which is supposed to house the souls of the departed married couples of the family. The spirits reside on the particular floor of the seven-story white pagoda which best reflects their type of marriage during real life – the uppermost level representing the purest forms of love.

In Hong Kong, we were tied up alongside the *USS Sailfish* (SS-572), one of our older submarines. It was originally built as a radar-picket sub, carrying 96 men and 12 torpedoes. I got to tour the boat, and was quite surprised at how much stuff they could cram inside one of those things. I think I would have enjoyed sub duty, but that ship has sailed.

The few days we spent in Subic were packed with shipboard work and various activities in the evenings. We did a bit of skin diving at Grande Island in Subic Bay. I'll bet we swam twenty miles that day, besides getting sunburned good and proper.

It was such a hassle wading across the sharp coral of the shallows to reach the primo diving areas off Chiquita Island that we decided to swim all the way around the island instead. It was really an experience swimming in two-foot-deep water with razor-sharp coral

The Tiger Pagoda, Hong Kong.

just inches below our bellies – especially with the strong buffeting currents that were present. But we made it with only minor slashes and punctures.

I chased a pod of baby squid into deep water; it was neat how they shot themselves through the water. There was also a terrific amount of jellyfish around. One time I came up to breathe right in the middle of them. I got a couple tangled in my beard and got stung around the lips and the shoulders. It hurt terribly at the time, but nothing ever came of it other than numb lips for awhile.

You ask what I am doing here in Japan, of all places, and well might you ask. You probably know more about it than we do, ha ha, since the noble crew of the *Elkhorn* is always the last to know where or why we're steaming. Nobody on the ship really wanted to come here (it's a 14-day roundtrip), and for days previous to our departure from Subic our Old Man was on the radio trying to get us out of the trip.

But much to everyone's regret, we pulled out of Subic Bay Saturday at 1300 in the afternoon and steamed towards Sasebo (pronounced "SASS-ah-boe") at 13 knots. Some dillweed in the Pentagon wanted us to go to Sasebo via the Taiwan Straits, but there was a storm brewing there, so we went east of Taiwan instead.

The Taiwan Straits are infamous for their sudden sea storms. As it turned out, it was the smoothest, most pleasant cruise we've ever made!

Actually, the truth of the matter is that we came here to Sasebo to pick up a liquid cargo of some brand-new diesel fuel that the Navy will be testing in the bigger ships. I had been to Yokosuka (pronounced "yo-KOOSH-kuh"), Japan, once but I didn't care much for the place.

We heard scuttlebutt on the way over that it was snowing here in Sasebo, and we were all looking forward to that. But it was just a vicious rumor after all, and it was not even all that cold when we got here. As a matter of fact, it's much like a spring day back in South Dakota.

To our surprise, we discovered that Sasebo is a very nice place, with a picturesque harbor tucked between steep hills, so we're all glad that we came now. There's nobody here – that's another reason why it's so nice. We're the only American ship in port and the place is really deserted. But after the big and marvelous places we've seen and all the exciting things we've done, it's nice to slow down the pace a little bit. I've got to have some peace and quiet every now and then. Now I kind of wish we were staying here a little longer than eight days.

They have quite an exciting schedule lined up ahead of us in the next few months. It will make the time fly by quickly and I am grateful for that. We will be getting a lot of sea time in this cruise. I'd really like to know how many thousand miles I have traveled, by air and sea and bus and train, since I joined the Navy!

They are still trying to line us up with short stays in Bangkok, Thailand, and Singapore, Malaysia. I feel very fortunate to be able to see all these exotic places, as most people never get to leave their home state.

If we go to Singapore, they are threatening to swing south about twenty miles so we can all cross the equator. That way they can initiate us "polliwogs" into the Realm of Neptune – those of us who haven't yet crossed the equator.

They say the initiation is something terrible to behold, and even worse to experience; you can end up bloody, black and blue, and bald – they don't fool around! I may have to barricade myself up in the electric shop so they can't get to me. I'm too darn short in the Navy to have all my bodily hair removed!

But I am very anxious to see the city of Singapore, though, as they say it is exceptionally beautiful. By July we should be back in Pearl Harbor, and sometime around the middle of August I should be getting discharged. I may have as little as 134 days left in this chicken outfit!

A fellow on board wanted to lose twenty pounds, but he didn't want to give up the habit of eating three squares a day, which was very enjoyable to him (as it is to me). So he devised a plan where he could eat to his heart's content, but still lose weight: after every meal he went directly to the head and stuck his finger down his throat and made himself vomit. *Voila!*

But he unconsciously conditioned his own reflexes like a Pavlov dog, and to-day he still pays the price of his folly, even though he's no longer dieting. Sure, he's lost a lot of weight and is actually too thin for his health …but he has also gotten ulcers and a painful esophagus. And after some meals he automatically throws up now from time to time, whether he wants to or not.

I have rigged a contraption onto my tape recorder where I can listen to music from my rack. Parker did the same to his bunk, too. I ran a cable all the way from the electric shop in the forward part of the ship (where my tape recorder is) clear back to my rack in the after part of the ship. This involved a lengthy run of cable going through many different compartments along the way, but nobody ever questioned what in the heck we were doing. The ways of the electrician mate are many and mysterious. In the electric shop I installed an on/off box and headphones jack. On my rack I installed an on/off switch and headphones plug.

Now I can put on my headphones and listen to music in my rack, and turn the music on and off from there, but of course I cannot change cassette tapes from my rack. It will be nice to have music in my bunk while we're out to sea, when it's too rough to be up in the shop. Ah, the wonderfulness of being an electrician! You tax payers paid for this service – many thanks!

My income-tax refund checks caught up with me whilst in Hong Kong. They were more or less what I had expected to get back. They went into buying more stereo gear. A fool and his money are soon parted.

I was surprised to hear that you got a monkey, but then you've been doing a lot of surprising things since I left home. I imagine that the kids really enjoy the monkey, huh, being a bunch of little monkeys themselves.

I didn't especially care for the news that you got a job, Mom. But if you need the money at home, then I suppose it's all for the best. But just for the record, no wife of mine is going to work outside the home, though!

And now, after countless cups of tea, I'm starting to get a little water-logged. And all of this abnormal handwriting (instead of typing) has given me a dandy cramp. I hope this long letter has made up a little bit for not writing for so long. Write when you find time between all your craziness.

OFFICIAL QUARTERLY MARKS
April 1, 1971
(Still assigned to the *USS Elkhorn*)

"EM3 Stanga stands electrical propulsion control watches while underway, duty electrician while in port. He also stands sound-and-security watches in port. EM3 Stanga is a very capable electrician. He handles assigned tasks enthusiastically and efficiently, and can be depended upon to do a thorough and complete job every time. He is very well-liked and respected by his contemporaries, not only for his professional skill, but for his personal habits and talents as well."

HONG KONG

April 8, 1971

Dear Family,

While crossing the South China Sea from Sasebo back to Hong Kong, I got the Red Cross wire about Aunt Lujeanne passing away on March 28th. They had it on the ship for two whole days before the Executive Officer called me into his stateroom and gave it to me! At first I figured I had committed some hanging offense or something, although for the life of me I couldn't think what it might be. It was the first time in seven months that he was halfway civil with me, the little snot.

Although I was anticipating the worst to happen at any time for Lujeanne, it still came when I least expected it. More than anything else, I really hated getting that sort of news from the likes of him, though. Until now I just haven't been able to make myself sit down and write to anyone at home.

I have been very sad since then and I don't really suppose it's fair to my buddies when they can't figure out what's wrong with me. In some ways, I'm kind of glad I wasn't there when it happened; the whole thing about being terminally ill in the hospital is so depressing and hard on everybody anyway. I hope everyone is holding up as best as possible, though. I suspect that I may have it much easier than the rest of you, as I am so far away from the grief and kept busy most of the time. I am thankful for that.

I hope it wasn't too rough for you all. However will Uncle Swede manage with the boys now? Is Gramma taking it alright? It's not going to be too easy for anyone from here on out.

It would be nice to know that Aunt Lujeanne was bright and without pain right up until the end, but I know that probably wasn't the case at all. It usually never is.

The diabetic coma, the uncontrolled swelling of her body, her blindness – all are too terrible to even imagine.

I can't write any more…I don't know what else there is to say. Please spare me the details of the funeral and burial. It is enough to know that it's over and Lujeanne is gone, her suffering over with, and that I'm really going to miss her for a long, long time.

April 20, 1971

Dear Family,

I feel it's way past time that I should be writing; I was kind of waiting to get back into the letter-writing mood after our recent loss in the family. But I know that it will be quite a long time until things at home will be back to normal…if they ever will.

Life is no bed of roses by a long shot, but why do these things have to happen to nice people like Lujeanne? I've been thinking about that a lot lately. Why is it that misfortune always seems to land squarely on those who are usually not strong enough to bear the trials and burdens – and who do not deserve them in the first place – while the mean and worthless rotters go merrily on their way? But doesn't it happen just that way every time?

Today is Buddha's birthday here in Hong Kong. There is a lot of noise-making involved, and a few parades downtown. All the junks in the harbor are decked out with huge patches of gaily-colored cloths by the dozens. I'll bet there are going to be quite a lot of drunken Chinamen out there tonight!

Tomorrow, then, is Queen Elizabeth's 45th birthday, and since we are here in the British Crown Colony of Hong Kong, and do not wish to dishonor Her Majesty, it is holiday routine for us as well! Early tomorrow morning we are holding a ceremony on the fantail, consisting of raising the British colors and Union Jack. The whole ship will be dressed out in our colors all day. Tomorrow evening there will be a softball game for our team, followed by a ship's party. All in all, it really plans to be quite a regal birthday celebration. God save the Queen!

Sasebo was very peaceful, serene, quiet and – in a word – relaxing. I went down to "sailor town" once or twice with the guys, just to see what it was like, and I didn't care much for it. That area of Sasebo operates along the lines of Tijuana, really just another black hole to suck in poor innocent sailors.

But the Japanese countryside is just what you would imagine if you were to sit down and close your eyes and think of a mystical, terraced, enchanting fog-enshrouded oriental land of mystery. It is very beautiful, and the weather there was perfect the whole time.

We took a bus tour down to Nagasaki, where we had dropped the second atomic bomb on August 9, 1945. We saw many fine sights along the way: colorful junks on the swift rivers, rice-paddy terraces, islands poking up out of the fog, shrines to various gods, pearl farms, peasants harvesting sea cucumbers, and the many interesting types of architecture that they have everywhere.

We crossed Saikai Bridge, which is the largest span bridge in the entire Orient. In Nagasaki itself, we visited a shop where they made things of tortoise shell… everything from a hair comb to a detailed model of a British schooner. We visited a Chinese temple to Confucius, where we witnessed the famed Dragon Dance. We also stopped at the Halfway House, which was once a fort back in the bad old days when the Dutch and Portuguese ran Japan.

We ate dinner at the Grand Hotel, where once again I was the only one of my group to try some of the local cuisine. I even tried some sake, the fermented rice wine that the Japanese drink hot. It seemed rather potent to me that way and it went straight to my head, but at least I got to try some of the real McCoy. The other jokers had fried chicken, cheeseburgers, spaghetti and Budweiser. Oh wow. Be still my heart.

We stopped at *Heiwa* [Peace] Park and took many fine pictures of the Peace Statue there. Long ago I had seen pictures of this Peace Statue in a book, but I certainly had no idea that we were going to see it that day. It was a very nice surprise. The sign next to the statue read, "The people of Nagasaki built this statue to symbolize and appeal everlasting world peace in August of 1955, the tenth anniversary of the atomic bombing which caused the people of Nagasaki to experience unbelievable tragedy and lose great numbers of people. This ten-meter-high bronze statue was completed by sculptor Seibo Kitamura. The right hand pointing to the sky tells the atomic bomb's threat; the left hand stretching out horizontally shows tranquil peace; its solid-built body is the dignity of God; the gentle face is the symbol of divine love; the fast-closed eyes pray for the repose of the war victim's souls; while the folded right leg shows meditation or quiescence; and bent left leg shows help or movement."

Heiwa Statue, Japan.

Nagasaki does not look at all like a city that was once completely leveled to the ground by a nuclear blast, as it is all built back up and very modern in most places. The cherry blossoms were in full bloom, and it was really quite pretty there.

We visited ground zero where the atomic bomb was dropped. There is a black obelisk marking the spot below which the bomb exploded. They exploded it in the air for maximum death and destruction, as the city is spread over many hills and valleys. The sign next to the epicenter marker read, "At 11:02 AM on August 9, 1945, the atomic bomb dropped from the B-52 exploded about 1,600 feet in the air above this black stone pillar. By the blast and thermal rays exceeding 300,000 degrees Centigrade and radioactivity. As a result of this, about one-third of the city area was destroyed and the casualties numbered about 150,000. This area, at one time said to remain barren for 75 years, is now appealing strongly to the world for peace. A number of people have later died of the so-called Atomic Disease."

At ground zero there were the remains of a Catholic Church; all that was left standing was a stone column topped with a statue of Christ and one apostle. Strange… Some would attach an unnecessary importance to that random oddity, and some do. They had also preserved an iron water tower that was literally tied in knots by the 400-mph winds at ground zero. It was really ominous.

But the high point of the whole tour had to be our visit to the Atomic Bomb Memorial Museum in Nagasaki, where they had relics and photos of the disaster. The pictures were terrible to behold. No amount of words from me can describe the lump in my throat that came from looking at those larger-than-life photographs that were taken in the vicinity of where we stood. One display showed a picket fence with an apparent shadow of a human being on it; it was all that remained of a person who was vaporized instantly by the bomb.

After an hour, we left completely speechless. We were genuinely ashamed of something that we had never even had a hand in! And to think that the United States did this to people – not just once, but twice – even though history has shown that this bombing was an absolute necessity which saved thousands of lives; we still felt bad. Never before in my whole life have I felt like such a low-down dirty dog. It was a real eye-opener, and just the sort of thing that a person needs to wake him up to the ugly reality of war.

On the way back to Sasebo on the bus, a young Japanese girl, cute as a button, told us local legends and sang folk songs to us in her native tongue. That was a nice touch which raised our spirits once more.

Sasebo is a city of about 250,000 and its main industry is shipbuilding. I could hardly believe how huge some of their tankers are! Our ship is positively dwarfed beside them! We're going to have to keep our eyes on those inscrutable Nipponese. (I am enclosing a 100-yen bill for your inspection).

Did I tell you that I finally passed my second-class petty officer test?! It was the first opportunity that I even had to take it. I had no hope of passing it at all, as I didn't study one bit, and I took the exam with a terrific hangover. (Maybe that's a prerequisite?) But I was overjoyed to find out that I had passed! This is the highest rank that a guy can reach in a four-year hitch. Now I learn they are not going to give me my extra stripe, however, as I do not have over a year left to serve – which is a requirement for making second-class grade. But it's nice to know that I can pass the test anyway.

We are having a Captain's Personnel Inspection once a week now, and is it ever a royal hassle! I've not had any trouble whatsoever passing inspections since I got out of boot camp, though, but it costs so much money to have our whites washed and pressed every few days, a haircut once a week, shoes shined, etc. Does anybody even need a haircut once a week? We are not made of money, you know.

And during mealtime now they are passing out critique sheets along with the chow trays. I have been telling them like it is, too, as lately all the Stewburners seem to be trying to outdo each other and see how vile they can make the food taste. Do you know what a lousy feeling it is when you reach the bottom of your bowl of oatmeal and find several meal bugs lying there belly up? Hard to have a good day after that. I say we've got good reason to gripe.

In Hong Kong, I bought four Asahi Pentax Spotmatic 35mm cameras for myself, Larry Larson, Ron Wipf, and Larry Goldammer, along with multiplier lenses, telephoto lenses, fish-eye lenses, wide-angle lenses, and polarizing filters for one and all of us. They had sent me the money beforehand. Purchased in Hong Kong where they are made, they ran only about a $100 each, but back in the States they sell for around $425 apiece! I felt pretty vulnerable carrying all that expensive camera gear back to the ship through the mean streets of Hong Kong!

I cannot mail their camera equipment home from here, however; I have to wait until I pass through US Customs back in Hawaii, and then pay duty on the dang stuff. But I've got over $300 for mad money in my division officer's safe, and about 100 days left in this chicken outfit. I can hardly think of little else. It's such a good feeling and certainly something exciting to look forward to.

April 22, 1971

Dear Mary,

We're here in Hong Kong again. I show two movies every night right here on the ship. It is the highlight of our day. Sometimes a Chinese boat comes out to our ship in the middle of the harbor which sells homemade potato chips and the most delicious hot dogs ever! Have you ever seen a floating restaurant? They have lots of them here, too. I wonder if you will like my beard when I get home? Then you'll tell me that I've really got the nubs!

April 22, 1971

Dear Tim,

Just time for a postcard, bro'. These ships are called Chinese junks. There are hundreds of them always sailing around here in Hong Kong harbor. The Chinese people live on them all the time, and sometimes go very far out on the ocean to fish. They say that the Chinese junk is the most seaworthy vessel afloat on earth. They remind me of a bunch of different-colored butterflies, don't they?

April 22, 1971

Dear Julie,

We had another softball game yesterday. We played against some Chinese guys and they are supposed to be the best team here in Hong Kong. One of our guys twisted his ankle right away in the first inning. After that, every time he batted someone else had to run the bases for him. I kept score for both teams. It was very hot and dusty out there on the ball diamond. But we beat them 10 to 9.

They are putting wood paneling up in our messdecks, so we have to eat outside on the fantail temporarily. It's not so groovy when it's raining, though. Nobody likes rain in his mashed potatoes, does he? It's just like a real picnic, but the ants haven't showed up yet. (Only the roaches.)

April 22, 1971

Dear Jennifer,

Last night we had our ship's party at the Candlelight Club in town. The Chinese cooks made us steak, shrimp, baked beans, hot dogs, French fries, and a whole bunch of other good stuff to eat, most of which I didn't even know the name of.

About ten o'clock they had a fun program put on by a boy and girl from Thailand. They juggled and rode unicycles and did balancing tricks. But the best part of the show was when the guy spun some plates on top of long sticks. He only dropped one of them. At the end he had eight plates spinning at the same time! He was really good and we all just loved the show.

EN ROUTE FROM HONG KONG TO SUBIC BAY

April 28, 1971

Dear Family,

How is everyone this week? Aside from the after effects of too much celebrating last night, I am fine as always. I forget what we were even celebrating. We got underway for Subic Bay this morning at 0830, and we should be there by Friday afternoon. That's probably what we were celebrating. This will be our last visit to Subic. *sniff*

The *USS Dennis J. Buckley* (DD-808), a destroyer, relieved us as station ship in Hong Kong, and we will not return there again until early June. Right now it is very smooth sailing, although a typhoon is supposed to intercept us before we arrive in the P.I.

I am enclosing a few pictures that I just got developed. Isn't the ocean pretty in them? The pictures can never do it full justice, though. The Pacific Ocean has as many faces as Carter has liver pills. That's why I love it so much.

The *USS Point Defiance* (LSD-31) was in Hong Kong for a little R&R. The LSD sink the stern of their ship so they can launch small attack boats out the back end directly into the water. The *USS Iwo Jima* (LPH-2) was also there. The *Iwo Jima* was the first amphibious assault ship to be built from the keel up strictly for helicopter use; she cost a mere $40 million new.

You've heard me say this before: the Navy is a small world. Last week I met several old friends; two that I knew personally, and two more that I had something in common with. First I met Joe Hammond, who is a dental technician off the *USS Jason* (AR-8), a repair tender; I used to go to high school with him! Secondly, I met Mike Morelli, who is now a shipfitter on the *Jason,* also; he was on the *Iredell County* with me – an old steaming buddy back in Nam.

Next I met a guy from Sioux Falls, and another guy from Spearfish. I did not know either one of them, but still it's always nice to find someone else from good old South Dakota so far from home. All those chance meetings happened within the space of one hour at four different places in downtown Hong Kong – talk about Old Home Day! The Navy is a small world – really!

One of my best buddies here on the ship, John Doe (his real name!), is getting married...to a bar hostess from the Candlelight Club. He met her in Hong Kong the first time we were there and took her to a hotel. Prostitution is technically against the law in Hong Kong, and we all have a real good laugh about that now and then. He is going to marry her when we go back there in June. He has already obtained the necessary written permission. It was quite a whirlwind romance, and took us all by surprise.

You never know if you should try to talk a guy out of something like that or not, whether they would appreciate the effort or resent it. I can't understand why some guys do half the things they do overseas – myself included. But I do know that a bar is the last place I'd go looking for a bride to take home to mama. I met her, though, at their engagement party and she does seem like a very nice person. He must love her a lot to be willing to forget what she did for a living. And vice versa.

I'm glad that you think I'm so reasonably settled and pretty much decided what I want to do in life – as I sure ain't! You cannot know how close I came just three days ago to signing up for two more years in the Navy! It is really frightening. Only time will tell if I made the right decision or not.

I had been thinking very seriously of returning to Vietnam because of personal convictions which I feel very strongly about. I have been trying to make up my mind for the past three months.

I figured there were three avenues open to me:

(1) I could ship over for two more years in the Navy and receive my second-class stripe,

(2) I could transfer straight across the board to the Army and get ground duty like I wanted,

(3) I could return to civilian life and my senses, and start making something of myself in the real world; get on with my so-called life.

The offers in favor of two more years in the Navy were very tempting. They promised me three things:

(1) Electronics school in Chicago,

(2) riverine action in Nam,

(3) $4,000 cash on the line for my signature.

It was all a package deal. The re-enlistment papers were in front of me...the pen was in my shaking hand...but in the end I said "no thank you" to all of it. My personal freedom was much too precious to sacrifice. I hope I don't regret that decision later.

Maybe if I didn't have a family back home waiting for me, things would have turned out much differently. I just couldn't see going through this rigmarole all over again. I decided once and for all to try life as a college student for a while.

I got my quarterly marks back the other day, and I was genuinely surprised! In the five fields that I was graded upon, I got four "excellents" and a "perfect."

- Extremely effective and reliable. Works well on his own. (Excellent)
- Always acts in the highest traditions of the Navy. (Excellent)
- Impressive. Wears Naval uniform with great pride. (Excellent)
- Gets along exceptionally well. Promotes good morale. (Excellent)
- Handles men very effectively. (Perfect)

These were the highest marks I've received in my four-year Navy career, and they were higher than every other electrician on board. I'll get a fat head.

We had chest X-rays taken of us in Sasebo, and just recently got the results back. I can tell you that I am presently free of any creeping internal disorders, although sometimes I feel my body is surely being eaten away with cancer. It's just a suspicion.

Did I tell you that I have the dubious distinction of having the oldest beard on the ship? All the other inconsistent dummies have shaved theirs off and grown them back several times now. They can't seem to make up their minds if they would rather be *au naturel* or scrape their skin off in layers every day. I find that if I don't shampoo my beard regularly, it will soon begin to itch like the devil and really drive me crazy, though.

I am presently down here in the Hole on watch, and it is beastly hot; my skin just prickles from the heat. It is 94 degrees in the Philippines right now, so it will really be a scorcher there, too. It is almost midnight now; I get off watch then, and I'm going up to the galley to see what they have fixed for mid-rats.

SUBIC BAY

May 9, 1971

Dear Mom,

Happy Mother's Day! Well, I've shipped all of my stereo equipment home in separate boxes now; I sure hope they make it in one piece. I'm sorry that you think I'm blowing so much money on stereo equipment. If I didn't have my music to keep me going, I'd be a pretty miserable fellow. The equipment should last me many, many years.

Friday we had yet another Captain's Personnel Inspection on the pier. It was really a scorcher and we were sweating like butchers before it even got started. As usual, I didn't get gigged on anything; most of the guys who got hit were gigged for haircuts and lengthy sideburns.

They had a short ceremony afterwards where our old XO turned over all his duties, paperwork, whoopee cushions, etc. to the new XO. This new fella is from West Point, and he looks like one of those born rich and snooty. But compared to our old XO, Alfred E. Neuman would have been an improvement. Good riddance.

Yesterday was another ship's party out at Dungaree Beach. We played volleyball (my forte!), swam, water-skied, ate and drank, and had a slow-pitch softball game between the officers and us enlisted guys.

Poor old Doc is completely bald, so he got a bad sunburn on top of his head – it turned a violent purple! I got a little sunburned myself, but not near as bad as some of the Operations guys who never leave the ship much or see the light of

On liberty in the Sierra Club, Olongapo City.

day; they're always hunched over a scope in some dark compartment. I got my fingers slammed in a car door – not once, but twice – and lost my prescription sunglasses before the night was over. There was no fist-fighting between crew-members at all, so it was deemed to be a pretty good party.

The next item on the agenda concerns my upcoming "early out." In a few weeks I will receive a paper that will ask me if I desire a two-month early out or not. If I don't sign it, then I won't get out until my full enlistment is up on October 9th. Otherwise, I could be getting out in mid-August.

There are many reasons why I might want to refuse my two-month cut:

(1) I could get all of my dental work done before I get out of the service,

(2) I could spend some extra time in Honolulu with this one new guy on board named G.R. Morton, whom we all like very much and is great fun to be with,

(3) the extra two months would enable me to save another $400 to start civilian life with.

I figure that if I have already made it this long, I can make it another two months. But on the other hand, I wouldn't mind getting out in August because then,

(1) I could go camping with the family before summer was over with,

(2) I could maybe go on a wilderness canoe trip with Wilt before he has to go to the Army,

(3) I really want to get out of this outfit ASAP, because after four years it is really getting on my nerves!

Some of my buddies think I would really be stupid to turn down the cut, while some others would really like me to hang around another two months before I have to leave the ship permanently – for auld lang syne, y'know. Decisions, decisions, pros and cons.

I got a care package from Darlene Horst up in Berlin, Wisconsin, which really surprised the heck out of me! She is always doing nice unexpected things like that for me; she is really a neat person. You remember that I used to work with her at the Town House Café.

I am really looking forward to seeing Kaohsiung (pronounced "cow-SHUNG"), Taiwan, as the old salts say that it is really a nice liberty port. One of my prime interests, besides girls, is the ridiculous prices they ask for things in the exchanges and out in town. Doc says that you can buy hardbound books for less than a dollar in Kaohsiung, and prerecorded cassette tapes for a like amount. I should be able to get some nice stuff and still save scads of money there.

I am just taking it easy today (as my sunburn demands), reading, writing letters, and listening to music. I showed "Airport" and "A Man Called Horse" this afternoon on the messdecks, which were received fantastically by one and all. After I wrap up this letter I am going down to the Spanish Gate café and get a filet mignon or a New York cut for a late steak supper. It's been yesterday since I last ate, and I feel like something rich.

KAOHSIUNG, TAIWAN

May 18, 1971

Dear Family,

I hadn't really planned to post a letter from Taiwan, but we have one more liberty day here, and I thought you just might like to know where I am now. It's darn hard to make myself stay on the ship and write letters, when I could be out exploring around in a foreign country. We have been in Taiwan for a week. It is a quiet little place, really, seemingly unaware of the rest of the world.

Regardless, Kaohsiung is kind of interesting, I guess. I would have much rather seen Singapore instead, but they forgot to consult me when the Navy changed our plans. The weather here is perfect; it only rained one evening and cooled things down quite nicely.

I have never seen so many ships in such a small harbor before! They use the bay for sewage disposal (just like in Hong Kong) and so it smells now and then when the wind is just right. Or just wrong.

All the ships that belong to the Taiwan Navy are ex-Navy ships from the United States Just looking at the ships here in this one harbor of this one nation, I'd say we have given away quite a number of ships to different countries! Some of the original names can still be seen beneath the haze gray paint, clearly marked by the original weld beads. Most of the ships that we have given to Taiwan are destroyer escorts and harbor service craft.

The taxi drivers here try to rook you every chance they get, though. They are really terrible, and you have to practically threaten them with bodily harm to get where you want to go. All of them have relatives that run nightclubs or restaurants or hotels somewhere, so they try to steer you there instead.

I went to two nightclubs out in town, just to assure myself that sailor town here was no different than anywhere else. And it wasn't, so I spent the remainder of the day at the Naval club, playing table shuffleboard and talking with the merchant marines there.

We had to get a cholera booster shot before we pulled in here, and we were instructed not to eat any food or drink cocktails out in town. (Who are they kidding, anyway?) The town itself was reasonably clean, compared to Olongapo City or Hong Kong. It is a shame that we are not going to be here long enough to do some serious touring of the island.

I will say one thing, though; the most beautiful girls in the world have got to be right here in Taiwan! I must have fallen in love a hundred times just on the first day alone. All the oriental girls in sailor town have had their eyes surgically fixed to resemble round-eyed American girls. You add that attractive attribute to glossy black hair and café au lait skin, and that combination of features is almost too much for any normal sailor to resist.

(And speaking of falling in love, I met a nice girl on my last night in the Philippines that I absolutely adored! Now why did I have to meet her on my last night there? Sheesh – I'll probably never see Carmelita ever again. *sigh* Life can be so cruel sometimes.)

I have enclosed a new Taiwanese ten-dollar bill; it is worth exactly twenty-five cents. The building on the back of the bill is the presidential palace of Chiang Kai-shek. The man on the front of the bill was the president before Kai-shek, whoever that was. The other picture is one of the Eypinjinwang Bridge, which is the longest in the Orient.

The thing I really hate about foreign currency is that you are not always sure of the equivalent American value, so you tend to spend it like Monopoly money, and you can blow a small fortune in a matter of minutes and not even realize it.

Taiwan does not recognize international copyright laws, so they reproduce records and books *en masse* without consent from the different musicians and authors and illustrators, nor do they advance them any royalties whatsoever. That is why they can sell them so cheap. Record albums cost about twenty-five cents apiece! The trouble is that after you play them about ten times they sound very scratchy. So what everybody does is record them onto cassette tape the very first time they play them, and then use the record albums for target practice off the fantail.

Of course, I really packed in the hardbound books in Taiwan. But they are illegal to mail into the States, so I will have to wait until I am in Hawaii to send them home. I paid $3.50 for a 2,100-page unabridged Random House dictionary! (Just about everybody on board bought one of these.) My buddy, Parker, borrowed $100 from somebody and spent it all on pirated books. I wish I had had more money at the time, myself.

Some Taiwanese orphans are coming on board tomorrow to tour our ship, and some of us have to present certain spaces and explain particular pieces of gear to them. I gave my last five dollars to the orphanage relief program when they asked for contributions this morning, and Parker commented on my particularly bad timing. He figured I should have given right away on payday when I had all kinds of money. But I asked him what he thought was more of a sacrifice: giving a small bit when I had plenty, or giving everything I had when I was shorthanded? He couldn't argue with that logic. I was not concerned with how much I gave; I gave because they asked me to, and I found I had five dollars left in my wallet that I would probably just blow anyway. I am always a sucker for a good cause.

Two of my shipmates have gotten themselves married on this South Pacific cruise. John Doe got hitched to that girl from the Candlelight Club in Hong Kong, and "Bilge-Pump" Barney married a girl from the Rocket Room in Olongapo City. I had really thought that they both had more sense than to marry a hostess out of a club, but I do not think ill of them for doing it, and I certainly hope that everything will work out for them in the end. They are reasonably nice girls, smart, good-looking, and well-mannered. They're not the usual run-of-the-mill bar hogs. Just as long as their ulterior motive is not to get a free passport back to the States – and then ditch the poor guys.

So we had a bachelor's party in Sasebo for the two fellas getting married. It was a huge, gala affair complete with chow, free tater juice, taped music, and two strippers later on, naturally. It was a surprise party, and the two guys were really amazed that they had so many friends. Almost the whole ship turned out, even some of the officers. A lot of gag gifts were presented, and some fine words spoken. It was one of the better parties that we've had on this cruise, and everyone had a terrific Akadama wine hangover the next day.

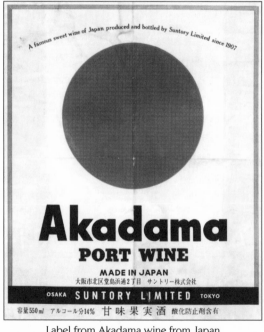

Label from Akadama wine from Japan.

We had a very outstanding meal today, which is a great rarity anymore. It was the best Yankee pot roast I've ever had, with steamed potatoes, rich beef gravy, tangy Harvard beets, cauliflower with melted Cheddar cheese over it, Greek salad, homemade bread, delicious green onions, and banana splits for dessert! We must live right or something. Wow.

Why is it that when we were little kids we hated vegetables and stuffing and homemade soup and other good stuff like that? Were we retarded or something? It's a wonder you didn't smack us in the mouth every mealtime just for general purpose whenever we started whining. Kids are the craziest people.

Well, the mail closes out tomorrow and I want to get at least a postcard from Taiwan off to everybody that I write. A novelty for them, I guess. We have not received any mail since we left the Philippines; heaven only knows where it's bottled up and gathering mold. I hope the big mail logjam gets broken somewhere and letters start pouring in while we are in Sasebo, Japan.

A monthly synopsis of our ship's activities was mailed out to all our families by the yeoman just in case the errant swabbies weren't keeping up their end of the correspondence. But often the Family-Grams distorted the truth so badly that I began printing "the story behind the story" on an underground mimeograph machine and distributing them to the crew, who got a big kick out of them and sometimes even forwarded them to their families as well:

MAY FAMILY–GRAM 1971

Dear *Elkhorn* Family Member:

The visiting kids from the naval orphanage at Tsoying, Taiwan, were between the ages of six and twelve. All hands enjoyed taking pictures of the tykes, who are natural hams. The children generally ran amuck about the ship, sitting on the guns, playing with the engine-order telegraph, climbing ladders, running screaming down passageways, talking over the sound-powered phones, and looking through binoculars. The day was completed with a cookies and ice cream free-for-all on the messdecks, followed by a Charlie Chaplin movie. Our little friends departed then, each bearing an 8x10 glossy color photo of the *Elkhorn* – which were denied even to her own crewmembers.

We had an upkeep period in Sasebo, working long, exasperating hours alongside exasperating non-English-speaking Japanese.

While in Sasebo, we were visited by Rear Admiral P.P. Stackpole. Stackpole spent all of ten minutes aboard examining our various spaces and compartments, which had taken the crew one solid week to prepare for.

In Subic, we had a ship's party at Dungaree Beach featuring steak, hot dogs, and 33 cases of beer. The crowning event was a softball game between the "lifers"(i.e., officers, chiefs, and first-class petty officers) and the regular, sane, enlisted men. Because the fair and impartial umpire failed to call the Old Man "out" a number of times at the plate, the lifers went on to defeat the crew by two points, once more proving their natural superiority.

SASEBO, JAPAN

May 29, 1971

Dear Family,

This is a long holiday weekend, so I am catching up on my letter-writing. We will be here in Sasebo for another two weeks and then we will head back to Hong Kong for the last time. After that, we should be homeward bound for good old Pearl Harbor.

It has rained all the time since we arrived here, and that can get kind of depressing after a while. We limped into port about a week ago on just three engines. Typhoon Carla chased us all the way from Kaohsiung, Taiwan, up the Formosa Straits to here. She was traveling about ten knots faster than we were and the storm followed us right into port.

The typhoon was right on our tail the whole time, so we had a very wet and rough cruise. We were shipping twenty-foot seas over the tank deck. The ship would bury herself right up to the gunwales in every wave. There were a lot of seasick sailors then! There were even a few days when we had holiday routine because it was simply too rough to work! Otherwise, we've had unusually calm weather during the majority of this deployment.

A couple weeks ago we had a flu epidemic on board and it pretty well messed up the crew for a few days, myself included. While I was still weak and punky from this illness I caught a real bad cold and sore throat, too. That was another bug that was going around. I suspect the culprit to be our many Asian ports of call. I am okay at this writing, though. Don't you worry about ol' Steve.

What is the "POD," you ask? (That stands for "Plan Of the Day.") The POD includes: mandated uniform of the day, work uniform, liberty uniform, watch and duty assignments, special ship routines, emergency phone numbers, who is the

Command Duty Officer (CDO) for the day and who is Officer On Deck (OOD.) The plan of the day shall not be removed from the ship!

I sent home another big box from Japan that contains one Pachinko machine. What it amounts to is the Japanese equivalent of a slot machine combined with a pinball machine, and they are everywhere over here. Don't open the thing, for pete's sake, or the kids will have the 500 steel balls lost before I even get home!

I didn't think to ask the postal clerk if it was legal to mail gaming devices from one country to another before I shipped it, and nobody asked me what was in the package at the post office. Oh well. They were selling them for five dollars apiece at the Navy Exchange here, and it sounded like a steal. Visiting a Pachinko parlor here is a real experience, with hundreds of those machines going at the same time. What a racket!

Parker and I have invested fifty dollars in a brand-new half-reefer, one of those tiny two-cubic-feet refrigerators. We have installed it here in the electric shop inside a personnel locker so the officers can't even get to it. We also bought about 25 cases of assorted sodas (which we store under lock and key), and keep the reefer well-stocked with ice-cold pop.

We sell the soda for twenty-five cents a can, which is the going rate here on the ship. And since we only paid ten cents per can of pop in the first place, the icebox has already paid for itself, and we are making a healthy profit to boot. And everybody's happy! It's going to be a long cruise back to Hawaii and we are going to make a killing in the soft-drink business. We also sell hard sucking candy, chocolate candy bars, and buttered popcorn during the movies on board. It provides us with a little extra spending money between paydays.

Our electric shop looks like a darn toy store right now. Every one of us electricians has been over to the Hobby Shop on base and spent a small fortune on models. There are three working Army tanks, one Honda motorcycle, one Formula I sports car, one dune buggy, one operating shipyard crane, and a six-foot model of the Japanese battleship *Yamamoto.*

You would not believe the intricate details and the way these models actually operate; these darn Japanese are really clever little stinkers! With my Russian tank model you have to put together every piece of the treads, and with my Honda motorcycle you have to construct the drive chain link by link!

I am spending tomorrow painting my tank model as realistically as possible, and then take a few pictures of it. We are planning to buy a few more models here before we leave. Most of us will be spending a lot of time on the ship in Hong Kong, and we would like something constructive to do then. The models sell for 300% less than they do back in the States. They are really beautiful things, too!

It should come as no surprise to hear that I decided to accept my early out. I was going to stay in the Navy until October, but it'll be so much more pleasant to get out of the Navy in the summertime. I never did have any will power. Weak as water! I don't know the exact date yet, but I will let you know as soon as I find out.

This could mean that I have as little as 65 days and a wake-up left in this outfit! Every time I think about it I get so excited! I have even dreamed about it at night, and how great it's going to feel to be a free man back in the real world. Oh wow!

I still plan to start school in the spring semester at the University of Wyoming. But if that timetable doesn't pan out, I will start next fall. I am as enthused about starting my Wildlife schooling as ever – maybe more! But first I want to get settled down in a job, find an apartment, buy some form of transportation, and get to know my way around Laramie.

The transition back to civilian life is not going to be an easy one, I suspect. I know I will probably have many difficulties at first. I am very anxious to get back in the routine of a steady job, and quit farting around with this electrician nonsense.

How about hanging onto some of that homemade rhubarb wine until I get home? Will it keep? That sounds like it might be a real treat. On our garbage boat in the Philippines we used to make "jack" out of fermenting apples, raisins, oranges, grapes, and grapefruit. It was pretty tasty, and reasonably potent, but quite illegal.

HONG KONG

June 18, 1971

Hi Dad!

This letter will probably be late for Father's Day, but I just wanted you to know that I was thinking of you just the same. For the love of Pete, I swear I could not find a single Father's Day card anywhere in this town! No reason they should celebrate Father's Day in this country, too, I guess. By now I trust you have received the hamburger cookbook that I sent as a gift.

I'm down in the Hole now and have the throttle watch from midnight until 0400. Normally, we don't stand any kind of engine room watches while we're in port like this, but tonight we just happen to be riding out Typhoon Frieda. We're just standing by down here with the propulsion engines idling to keep us in one place in case we start to drag anchor in this god-awful wind.

Already the wind outside is at least fifty knots (Force 9, Strong Gale), and it's supposed to get up to 70 to 100 knots at the peak of the storm. I'd sure hate to be in those exposed houses on top of Victoria Peak right now. Wow! They've got no shelter whatsoever. The last typhoon through here caused a huge landslide down the side of Victoria Peak, taking many shacks with it and burying dozens of people in mud and debris.

The wind has already ripped away our signal flags and the national ensign. The full force of the typhoon is supposed to hit sometime tomorrow. Most of the big cargo ships from the various countries have moved out of the harbor to deeper anchorage. Our liberty – and mail service – has been secured for three days until the storm passes over. After being stationed in the Philippines for 18 months, I am an old hand at this typhoon business.

And to compound things, we were awakened last night at 0200 in the morning by someone yelling over the 1-MC, "Fire! Fire! Fire in the dry stores! All hands roll out! Now fire! Fire!"

Most of us figured some dang drunk had come back from liberty and was playing with the loudspeakers and there would be hell to pay. But we jumped into our dungarees just the same and ran up forward to the dry-stores hold (where we keep flour, weevily cereal, oatmeal, canned goods, catsup, etc.).

The first thing we do in a fire situation is to secure all electrical power for that particular space (i.e., vents, motors, lighting), but even in the semi-darkness we could see and smell a great deal of smoke. The primary fire monitors, who went into the hold with OBAs on, could not locate the source of the fire, though.

So it was up to us electricians to find it. We noticed that there was a telltale smell of electrical-related smoke, which narrowed down our search considerably. And sure enough, we located it inside a vent motor. (Great! Now we've got to pull the heavy thing out and repair it one of these next few days.) So we restowed all fire-fighting gear, had some hot chocolate and Spam sandwiches which the Stew-burners had whipped up, and went back to bed. All in all, it was a good lesson in organized chaos.

Two days ago the International Red Cross put out an urgent call for A-positive blood and the *Elkhorn* responded vigorously. There were about twenty of us with that blood type and we all gave a pint of blood…except one fellow, a Jewish boy named Dimock from Pennsylvania. He says, "When my dad was in the hospital, nobody gave blood for him! So I'm not gonna give any!" Well, that's real good logic, ain't it? I'm sure glad everybody doesn't think that way.

The blood was used for an old Chinese gentleman. They are having the very first open-heart surgery here in Hong Kong, and they have flown in specialists from the States. We are the primary donors; the first blood he receives during surgery will be ours. That's kind of groovy, huh? They are going to keep us informed about his progress. Giving blood is very easy and generally painless, and it does so much good, both to the receiver and to the donor, that I think I'll make it a regular practice after I get out of the service.

At the same time we got a call from the Hong Kong General Hospital. They had a three-year-old Chinese girl with a hereditary liver disease who was dying. They were going to operate and they needed some blood plasma – and they couldn't locate any in all of Hong Kong! Can you imagine?! So Doc gave them all the blood plasma we had on board, and that little girl is alive today.

These Chinese doctors have made some pretty new and startling innovations in the medical world. They don't even use an anesthetic in half of their operations! Instead, they insert thin metal pins into the patient's nerve centers and block all pain that might be caused by the surgery. The patient is conscious during the whole operation and is not aware of any pain. They call this "acupuncture." On the Chinese mainland they did an open-heart surgery on a woman – took her heart right out of her chest and let her look at it! That's really something, isn't it?

We received some pretty bad news over the radio this afternoon. The *USS Tombigbee* (AOG-11), which was to be our relief ship here in Hong Kong, is still sitting in Pearl Harbor where she is homeported. She suffered an accident which flooded her engine room and ruined most of the machinery down there! All four of her main engines were damaged; they will have to be torn down and rebuilt. The yards in Pearl say that the engines are not even going to be put back together until July 24th.

The *Tombigbee* was supposed to get underway for Hong Kong on July 5th in order to relieve us on time, so we could be back in Pearl by the first week of August. So it is highly possible that nobody, but nobody, is going to get their early discharges off this ship. But there is still hope for us yet. Hope dies last. The Old Man sent in a request that we return to Pearl on schedule anyway – without a relief if necessary. I certainly hope so!

While we were yet in Sasebo, I picked up some oil paints, canvas, easel, pallet, brushes, and the other usual oil-painting paraphernalia. Since I am low on cash I plan to stay on the ship a lot while we are here in Hong Kong and do some painting to amuse myself. I am presently painting a desert scene from the *Arizona Highways* magazine. And yes, I've still got the golden touch.

They were going to have a personnel inspection tomorrow morning, but I hope they have the common sense to call the dumb thing off due to the typhoon. I just went up and stuck my nose outside, and it's howling like a prairie blizzard out there! I hope tomorrow isn't going to be a normal working day either – you've got to be kidding me! In this weather?!

June 23, 1971

Dear Family,

I was very glad to get your letter yesterday, as it had seemed like an awfully long time since I last heard from you. And it struck me, too, that it was a very happy letter, all things considered. As I was pretty homesick at the time, it did a lot by way of cheering me up. The weather here is muggy and unpredictable, and tornado warnings would be quite apropos for this place, too.

Wilt told me a sad tale about a guy who I've known since my Longfellow grade school days. He served several years in the Army in Vietnam, got out, and in the space of one month he got a job, got married, and started college. I guess it was all too much of a change for him to handle, because he went a little nutty – he went *a lot* nutty, actually – and is now receiving psychiatric help in the state mental hospital down in Yankton. I sure hate to hear such things about my old buddies.

Well, we survived Typhoon Freida, and it is just now letting up on the rain and returning to sunshine again. All during the storm, the big harbor was devoid of activity of any kind, and for such a busy international port as this it looked absolutely eerie.

Of course, there were buildings damaged by the high winds, and many streets at the bottom of Victoria Peak were blocked by mudslides. And naturally, during any period of disorder and strife, the crime rate rose like a berserk pop-bottle rocket. By the time they finally secured the storm warnings, we were all more than ready for a little loosen-up liberty out in town.

We have a high-security prisoner on board at present. Other than trying to do away with himself repeatedly, I don't know what his big crime against society was. They're keeping it all pretty hush-hush. Last week he escaped from the brig at the peak of the typhoon, was recaptured and brought out here to the *Elkhorn* in the middle of the harbor (since we are the station ship for all American Navy personnel in port).

That same day he jumped over the side and tried to swim to Kowloon, but was picked up by some of our boys in the Old Man's gig and brought back on board. They locked him in sick bay – which was a totally asinine thing to do – where he promptly tried to swallow some drugs. Since then he has settled down and is acting like anybody else on the ship. (A scary thought.) They shaved his head, and every night he sleeps with his leg chained to the bunk. It is a sad sight.

We were told not even to talk to the guy at all, but he looks pretty miserable, and most of us treat him like a shipmate. Who knows, maybe he had a good reason for trying to put himself under the clover. I don't know if any reason is good enough for killing yourself, I'm sure there are some, but I'm not going to treat the guy like a leper just because I am ordered to. It seems to me that he's got enough troubles already.

For a change of pace, and to get off the ship for a while, Parker, G.R. Morton, Lord Calvert, and I rented a hotel room in downtown Hong Kong. The room was on the twelfth floor and had a nice balcony with a great view. We commenced to drinking and shooting the bull. Late in the evening, we flew huge paper airplanes off the balcony, made of full sheets of newsprint, trying without success to land them on balconies opposite us across the avenue. Most of them landed on the street far below, to be flattened instantly by traffic.

Before retiring, we medicated ourselves heavily with Lord Calvert, but I watched a little TV yet. Sometime long after midnight I drew a scalding hot bath and fell asleep in the tub. I woke up a couple hours later, freezing to death. Parker and G.R. were hogging all the blankets and both the beds, so I took down the balcony door drapes, rolled up in them, and slept on the floor of the closet.

Morning came much too quickly, and I lay there in the dark closet knowing that I had acquired the second-worst hangover in my life – second only to that dreadful day on Makaha Beach in Hawaii. The boys discovered the open balcony door and the missing curtains, and wrongfully concluded I had made a running jump off the balcony sometime during the night. I staggered out of the closet at this point like a hung-over Lazarus. We had a good laugh about it later when we had all recuperated sufficiently and our brains functioned again.

I hope that you will soon begin to receive some of my stereo gear that I mailed home ever so long ago, as I do not relish the thought of them floating around in reach of those nuts in the postal service! I worked in the post office in Subic for a week once, and I've seen how those maniacs handle packages marked "Fragile." And I repeat: don't you dare set up any of my stereo equipment! With all the little mechanical wizards in our house, I don't think it would survive too darn long.

My oil painting is coming along just fine so far. I do believe that it is going to be one of my better ones. I was surprised to find out that I had not forgotten my color wheel, or any of the little tricks of perspective and shading and utilizing natural light sources.

Just today I walked into the IC room, where I have my painting under lock and key out of everybody's reach, and I found a whole bunch of blue uniforms piled carelessly on top of it! I just about went berserk and wanted to throw them over the side! Luckily, it didn't smear the oil at all, but I'll wring the idiot's neck if I ever find out who did it. I'm pretty sure it will be dry enough to mail home by the time we reach Pearl.

I've been doing a lot of reading lately; much more than I normally do. I like to read at least a few chapters before I go to bed each night, as it helps me sleep and sweetens my dreams. I particularly enjoy courtroom dramas (you thought I was going to say science fiction, didn't you?) and have fallen in love with Perry Mason novels. I emptied the ship's library of them and read them all in a batch. But right now I am in the middle of "Peony" by Pearl S. Buck, which is about a little Chinese girl. (A strange thing to read in Hong Kong, you say? On the contrary.) She is an excellent writer! I only wish I had half the talent that she has.

Me and Norton, one of our electrician strikers from Texas, sat up here in the electric shop the other night until about 0230, drinking some Akadama wine we had smuggled on board in Japan and batting the breeze. On the outside, Norton is an easy-going guy and an awfully hard worker. But as the night progressed and the wine did its work, he brought out things about his background that one would never suspect.

His family life is really shot to hell; his dad a drunk and his mother in a mental hospital, his brother in the pen. He has to support his sisters who are not old enough to work yet, and he has debts of his own to deal with as well. He's carrying a pretty big load for being such a young person. I look at him in a whole new light now. I guess you just never really know what anybody else's life is like until you walk a mile in their shoes, huh?

Well, I've got to go on watch here in 15 minutes and I'd like to grab a quick shower first. The officers have all lost their minds and are only making us work half a day tomorrow (Thursday). We suspect something horrible is coming down the pike in the near future that they are going to spring upon us. They have totally lost their credibility with us a long time ago.

EN ROUTE FROM GUAM TO PEARL HARBOR

July 15, 1971

Dear Family,

Like Mark Twain used to say, the reports of my death have been greatly exaggerated. If any of the relatives at home want to know why I haven't written lately, you can tell them from me that I have been terribly sick for a long time. I don't sleep well at night, and I'm about ready to drop over from exhaustion. My throat is so sore that I can hardly stand to eat anything, and so I get weaker yet.

Doc says I've got acute tonsillitis and am verging on strep throat. Nor am I the only one sick right now. He says it's the climate down here that does it, and if I stayed overseas a few more months the tonsils would eventually have to come out.

This is the fourth time in the last year that I've gotten this awful sore throat, but this is the first time he has diagnosed it as tonsillitis. He has shot me so full of penicillin that I feel like I've been doped for the last week. It's not helping, either, and I'm getting groggier and weaker and sorer. I sure don't look forward to making the rest of the cruise in this sorry condition. How unfair.

And I don't like the way the Navy shoots you full of penicillin for every little thing. Your body will build up immunity to it after so long, and then it may not be able to help you fight off a more serious disease later on. He's got me taking 24 pills a day and gargling with some foul stuff. If Doc would just give me a "no duty" chit so I could fight off this thing for a few days in bed, I might be better rather soon. But there I go again, veering off on a logical tangent!

Here we are on the last leg of the homeward-bound journey. For many of us, this will be our last time at sea for who knows how long. It is pretty rough outside right now, but it's supposed to calm down in the next 100 miles and remain smooth sailing for the final 3,200 miles of our trip home.

Using the shaft rpm's of the screws, my calculations tell me that we're doing a mad 12 knots or about 14 mph. Of course, that's not figuring in wind and cross-currents and following seas, so there's no way of telling how fast we're really moving. But it seems pretty damn slow.

Fortunately, our stay in Guam was very short. Most everyone was broke (we haven't been paid in over a month!), so we didn't do much of anything there. We stocked up on sodas for the long trip back to Pearl; all the copycat soda dealers on the ship have agreed to raise their prices from twenty-five to thirty-five cents a can for the duration of the voyage. It's the old concept of supply and demand, I guess.

We had another ship's party at Gab-Gab Beach in Guam, and the swimming and diving was most excellent there. It rained, but we were already thoroughly wet inside and out anyway. It still didn't stop us from getting sunburned, though.

Six of us got our separation physical exams in Guam. It was a lot less hassle than boot camp where we had to wait in line for everything, follow the stupid colored arrows on the floor all over the place, and stand around naked for hours on end.

I've lost partial hearing in both ears at high frequencies, especially in my left ear, which I am told is due to the noise in the engine rooms of the various ships that I've served on. I suspected that. But the corpsman says the frequency loss is not low enough to worry about or even inconvenience me.

In Dental I found out that I have a low-grade gum infection (they even showed me the nasty little critters under the microscope), so now I am brushing my teeth religiously three times a day.

Technically, I went over four years in the Navy last month already, as I entered the Navy on the 120-day delayed-entry program. This means another pay increase for me, and that I can ship all my personal belongings home for free in August. I'll have 16 days of leave accumulated on the books when I get out of the service, and I should get paid about $130 for them. What could be sweeter?

July 18, 1971

I feel a lot better today than before. My throat still hurts a lot, but at least my fever broke and I don't feel dopey anymore. Well, you know what I mean. I don't eat enough to keep a bird alive, but I manage to keep myself full on fluids, jello, soup, fruit juices, etc. That's about the only things I can bear to swallow.

The white patches of infection in my throat are starting to diminish; gargling with warm salt water seems to have done that. Doc says that if they aren't all gone by the end of this week, he is going to give me a triple-dose injection of penicillin. And if they haven't returned to normal by the time we pull into Pearl, I'm going to pop into Tripler Hospital and have my tonsils taken out. I'll do anything for some relief.

Right now it looks as if I may have already stood my last underway engine room watch. They are trying something new with us electricians now: three of us will only stand throttle watches in the engine room and have no outside work to do, while three of us will do all the electrical work required from our department and have to stand no watches in the Hole.

This system is working out real good because there are three of us who hated to work, and three of us who hated to stand watches. Parker, Norton, and I are now the three electrician mates that are carrying the electrical work load of the ship, while the other three Sparkies do nothing but stand watches in the Hole, four hours on and eight hours off. I wonder why we didn't think of this before? Now we can sleep straight through every single night. Ah bliss!

We have been lectured over and over again about how thoroughly the goon squad from Customs is going to pick over this ship when we arrive in Pearl. But a lot of us believe they are just trying to throw a scare into the dope fiends so they will heave their product over the side before we get there. Indeed, it will go bad for everyone if some contraband is found on board – then the Custom's men will really start tearing stuff apart!

They may also confiscate our illegal Taiwan books if they find them in their mad search for drugs, too. I don't think there is a person on this ship who didn't buy some books in Taiwan, and you should have seen the guys roaming all over the ship lately, just looking for little nooks and crannies and cubbyholes to hide a few books. It felt like "Fahrenheit 451"!

Some guys have wrapped their books and placed them inside running machinery; some have put them in ventilation ducts; and still others have put them in ammo boxes with live ammo. Some have gone to great lengths to hide their books; they have wrapped them in waterproof plastic bags and sank them to the bottom of voids and then painted the access lids shut to throw off the Custom's men. Some have actually welded them between bulkheads, and one fella has even put his inside the smoke stack.

As for myself, I have put my books inside boxes of commercial food, put tin banding around them and buried them with the hundreds of other boxes in the dry-stores hold. Sounds like the Spanish Inquisition, doesn't it? I will be very pissed off if they get my books, but I suppose these Custom's guys are no rank amateurs. Like I said earlier, I still figure that they are basically just looking for drugs anyway.

We put new linoleum tile down on the deck of the engineering berthing compartment, and I had no idea that I had such a hidden talent for tiling. And there's many a clever little trick to cutting pieces for weird-shaped angles and corners. We put down two-tone brown tile, painted the bunks a rich chocolate brown, and the bulkheads a pleasant beige. The compartment looks pretty sharp now!

A compartment cleaner goes in there every day to clean up and buff the deck, but we don't have one in there over the weekend. That's when the animals let it all hang out. When Monday morning rolls around it really looks like a pigsty. And the smell of cigarette smoke in everything is absolutely sickening! What a zoo.

Yes, I am forced to live with certain types of people on this ship, and work with some really stupid cretins who have no honest claim to even be walking around upright. But at least I can pick my own friends when it comes to hitting the beach.

As far as anybody can tell, we are not bothered with homosexuals on the *Elkhorn*. There is only one guy that we even remotely suspect of being sort of gay-ish, and he never blatantly approached anybody that we are aware of. It was just little things that led to rumors about him: he likes to sleep naked, he wears a lot of jewelry when he goes on the beach, he lisps just a trifle too much, and he has an overly fine-featured face for a man. But he is a good shipmate and a fun drinking buddy, though, and I have nothing against the guy whatsoever.

I have been put in charge of the six of us who are getting out of the service all together. I wish they wouldn't keep dumping responsibility on me like that; I'd just as soon let someone else do all the bungling and catch the hell when stuff goes wrong. But petty officers are always the designated baby-sitters. Our flight leaves Hickam AFB in Honolulu at 1230 on August 2nd and a few hours later we should be in Travis.

We will probably start our separation procedures on the 3rd at Treasure Island in San Francisco. One of the Dirty Half-Dozen has a brother who works in the Separation Center at T.I. and he is going to try to hustle us through ASAP. Still, the paperwork may take a couple of days.

While we are there, a few of us have been invited to one of the guy's home for all the Italian food and Coors beer that we can gag down. He lives about a half hour from T.I. and it'll give us a chance to unwind. I have been provided cost-free transportation clear back to "...my home of record." One way or another, they are going to get me back to Mitchell, South Dakota. I only expected the government to get me as far as Omaha.

I wrote Aunt Amy and Uncle John concerning when I was arriving, but I don't even know if they will be home or not. I can always stay at the YMCA in Omaha, I guess; I put poor Amy and John through so much rigmarole every time I pass through town. I really appreciate their hospitality!

This is a very beautiful Sunday and most everybody is working on his tan. They couldn't get anybody up for church services, so they had to cancel them. Bunch of unrepentant heathen! Right now they are shooting small arms off the fantail at a target we're towing behind us, and it sounds like a full-scale war is going on back there.

For supper tonight we are being treated to an outdoor chicken barbecue! After that I get to show a Bob Hope and Jackie Gleason comedy "How to Commit Marriage" on the messdecks. The seas have flattened out and it is smooth sailing from here to Hawaii. If I didn't know any better, one would think this was a dang cruise ship in the Caribbean or something.

July 23, 1971

Dear Family,

A few more days go by and we'll be totally out of sodas already! People grumbled about paying thirty-five cents for a soda, but they paid. They paid. Let's see, that's 250% profit on every can. Aren't we awful?

We passed the International Date Line yesterday and so we had two Thursdays in a row. By all rights, the Old Man could have made our extra day any day of the week he wanted, and we were all sort of hoping it would be a Sunday – as we don't have to work on Sundays, you know. But no such luck.

When we were going over to WesPac and lost a day, they took away a Sunday; so it went from Saturday straight into Monday then, and we didn't even get our one measly day of rest. Thus we were hoping that this time around they would take away one of our work days, to be fair, but apparently that would be too inconvenient for them. Anyway, we pull into Pearl bright and early on Monday morning. We will spend the remainder of the cruise reading and catching some gamma rays up on the boat deck.

In the meantime, I have returned back to normal health again, thank Allah! The pockets of infection in my throat have gone away and my tonsils have shrunk back down to their proper size. With all that penicillin in me, something was bound to happen eventually. I was really a grouch during my illness, and I was entitled to be grumpy. A lot of people got pretty exasperated with me, though. And along with my extremely apathetic short-timer's attitude, I was probably not the easiest guy in the world to get along with. I sure wouldn't have won any Mister Congeniality awards, I know.

I had to knock off brushing my teeth for a few days, as I had brushed my gums raw and cracked open the corners of my mouth in the process. I should have known that I couldn't begin "…a conscientiously-applied program of oral hygiene and regular professional care" so strenuously and not expect something amiss to happen.

In the past three days us electricians have been painting fools. We are going to be inspected by the Commodore as soon as we pull into Pearl (presumably after we get shaken down by the Custom's goons) and so we had to paint out all the spaces which we are responsible for – which is not just a few in number. So this is why the officers were being so nice to us lately.

With one guy using the roller and the rest of us cutting in around the edges, the job doesn't take very long for each individual compartment. Our biggest chore was doing the entire throttle flats, which took us two full days to complete. (Up until this time, we weren't even aware that the throttle flats belonged to us!) We could only paint half of it at one time, as we had to be able to move around on it while we're underway. It's going to be walked on until we get to Pearl anyway.

Our goofy division officer wants us to stay up all night Sunday and paint the throttle flats one final time before we get into port. Well, us electricians have a newsflash for him: if Bozo wants the throttle flats painted out a second time he's going to be down there doing it all by himself. I can't see busting ass doing totally unnecessary work – especially for that dim-witted clown.

We have anchor pools for every port we've pulled into while we were over-seas, drawing lots to see who comes closest to the exact time we officially moor. I have never won, but I came as close as second place one time. The anchor pool for arriving in Pearl Harbor is the biggest ever, with the chances costing five dol-lars apiece, and the total pot worth $250! I sure hope I'm lucky this time, as I could really use the money to start civilian life on.

Since tomorrow is holiday routine, maybe I'll show a double feature tonight. We've got an old Audie Murphy war picture on the marquee for this evening. Movie-watching has been a pure pleasure since we got our new Bell and Howell projector. The old derelicts that the Navy issues for use are real bummers and routinely crap out about three times a night, requiring on-the-spot repairs during much jeering and heckling. Besides that, they sound like a hay baler in operation.

I don't think that you'll hear from me again before I'll be home. I can't wait to see you all!

VII.
TREASURE ISLAND
3 AUGUST 1971 — 17 AUGUST 1971

Rather than be billeted in a dumpy military barracks on Treasure Island in the middle of San Francisco Bay, we sought other sleeping arrangements. One of my *Elkhorn* shipmates, Joseph B. Marchetti, invited me to stay at his parent's residence with him while we were being processed. They lived in Pleasant Hill, California, about a half-hour drive east of Frisco. We were given permission to stay off base for the few short days that we had left in the Navy, but had to report to T.I. every morning for work details.

Life on Treasure Island was less than ideal. Our three days stretched into seven; one week dragged into two. And still we hadn't received our termination papers yet. Every day we drove back and forth through Oakland over the beautiful Bay Bridge, hoping each trip would be our last as enlisted men.

The days at T.I. were particularly frustrating because we had to work in Administration, helping to process other men out of the Navy who had arrived there after we did! That was a bitter pill to swallow. The evenings were spent relaxing in the warm Marchetti household, usually after a delicious Italian meal, watching TV and sipping Crown Royal whiskey that I had bought overseas, and entertaining the family with sea stories.

Joey B had a clock radio in the bedroom where we slept. I had never seen one in operation before. What a pleasant change of pace to wake up to quiet, soothing music rather than a rude, clanging alarm bell, or someone yelling at you over a loudspeaker. There lay the primary difference between military and civilian life. I vowed to get myself a clock radio just as soon as I got home. What a nice way to start the day!

On the weekend, Joey B took me camping at Lake Tahoe. It was a jewel of an alpine lake in the Sierra Nevada Mountains, with fabulous resorts for the wealthy, and luxury dream homes along the lakeshore, but much too commercialized to suit me.

On the way back home one day, crossing the infamous Donner's Pass, we saw a highway accident occur directly in front of us, in which a pickup truck towing a VW microbus on a flatbed trailer suddenly veered off the road and disappeared completely over a small cliff. A bunch of us quickly pulled over to assist. But the occupants were all so drunk that nobody was even injured. They crawled out through the broken windshield of their upside-down pickup in the bottom of a ravine…laughing! And one youth wailed between the hysterics, "My dad's gonna kill me, man!"

One evening we even drove over to Stateline, Nevada, to do some gambling. I watched in a state of shock while people frittered away 100-dollar chips like they were only plastic poker chips after all! I was aghast at the amount of money changing hands all around me every minute. I just played the lowly nickel slots, quitting while I was ahead, and managed to come away sixty dollars richer. I got two consecutive jackpots on one particular slot machine before they threw a tablecloth over the top of it and diagnosed it "Out of Order."

Finally, after two incredibly long weeks, it was our turn to be processed and get the hell out of Dodge. The actual paperwork that day took no time whatsoever. (It certainly could have been done two weeks previously, we figured.)

Joey B drove me out to Travis AFB himself, where we said our final goodbyes. We knew we were never going to lay eyes on each other again, in spite of exchanging addresses in all sincerity, but such is life when you're in the service. Friends come and friends go, and life marches on.

On August 17, 1971, I caught a commercial jet back to South Dakota, and the green, green grass of home.

Back to the real world.

AFTERWORD

I've heard that most men consider their experience in the military to be the undisputed highlight of their lives. They will often say with a heavy sigh that they "...should have stayed in the service" (myself included), back where they were among men who were the real movers and shakers of the world.

The military demands effort and excellence from its people, and forces a young man or woman to grow up rapidly, a maturing process which might otherwise take half a lifetime to reach fruition.

Having served in the armed forces colors the way you look at things for the remainder of your life, giving you a view-point that most civilians are not privy to.

There's something unexplainable about memory in that it seems to function all by itself in retaining only pleasant memories while filtering out the worst. Thank goodness for that selective relief valve, I guess.

One thing is very clear, however: a person tends to lose his perspective while involved with the military. This is their intention from the get-go, and is necessary and quite understandable. Also, I distinctly remember being fatigued and tired the whole four years I was in the Navy. Total exhaustion. That's why the military is only for young bucks. The work would kill most ordinary civilians.

All of my old ships have passed into history now, as most ships eventually do. Like I said earlier, the YG-52 was towed across the South China Sea from the Philippines and given to the South Vietnamese in the latter stages of the war.

The USS Mawkaw (YTM-182) tug was disposed of on July 1, 1972 – a mere three years after that costly overhaul – sold by Defense Reutilization and Marketing Service (DRMS) for scrapping. So I can't even dream fondly that my poor old tugboat is pulling light duty somewhere in a sleepy South Pacific backwater. No, it has been made into razor blades and crescent wrenches.

The USS Iredell County (LST-839) served our country well from 1944 until July of 1970 when she was decommissioned and transferred (loaned) under terms of the Security Assistance Program to Indonesia. Renamed Teluk Bone, the ship was struck from the Naval Vessel Register and sold outright to Indonesia in February of 1979. Her final fate is unknown.

The USS Elkhorn (AOG-7) was sold to Taiwan under the same Security Assistance Program on May 1, 1972, and was renamed Hsing Lung (AOG-515) when turned over to Taiwan. She was decommissioned on July 1, 1972 and struck from the Naval Register on April 15, 1976. Final disposition: fate unknown. But I'd be willing to bet that she is still afloat somewhere, possibly in that mothball swamp of foreign ships in Kaohsiung harbor, and they're probably raising pigs and chickens in the engineering berthing compartment even as we speak.

I still use the stereo equipment and the camera gear that I purchased overseas, so that was a good investment after all. Ain't no denying I got my money's worth there.

If it weren't for my parents having the common sense to keep all of the letters that I wrote home while serving in the US Navy, and further efforts on my own part to keep a fairly detailed personal journal and preserve these few incidents, most of my experiences in the Navy would have been blurred, inaccurate recollections at best. And many of them would have been lost completely.

So I created a permanent, written-down memory to help me relive those four strange years from time to time. And part of every watch I stood in the service was spent scribbling in one of those faded green military log books, writing down the anecdotes of my day and recording the incidents that marked off the minutes of my life for four years. These letters and log-book entries form the backbone of this book, as they are rife with particulars I would have otherwise forgotten long ago.

I lost the girl next door, as she broke up with me while I was overseas and we never reconciled; the fault was entirely my own. Thank goodness it was not an ugly breakup; I could not have coped well with that; you never forget your first love. Suzie and I remain friends and today she lives in Maryland (married to a neurosurgeon in Columbia), and we still keep in regular contact by email.

Some things persist and never seem to be lost, though. I have not forgotten my military service number to this day, and I seriously doubt if I ever will. I can remember B617389 easier than I can recall my Social Security number or even my 911 rural addressing.

I still check to see if I have had my pocket picked after walking through a large crowd. I still lapse into nautical jargon when I least expect it. I still have a fondness for San Miguel beer and a weakness for oriental girls. I still feel a deep affinity for the sea, and truly wonder why I find myself living in the center of the continent, as far from any ocean as is possible. And only 38 years later am I beginning to feel relaxed about having pockets on my shirts unbuttoned without fear of reprisal.

Steven Carl Stanga
November 6, 2008

Now taps, taps.
Lights out.
The smoking lamp is extinguished.
All hands turn into your own bunks.
Maintain silence about the deck.
Taps.

APPENDIX

TIME IN SERVICE

Total service = 4 years, 2 months, 10 days
Total active service = 3 years, 10 months, 8 days
Foreign and/or sea duty = 3 years, 1 month, 3 days
Other service = 4 months, 2 days

SERVICE DETAILS AT A GLANCE

Boot camp......................9 October 1967.......to.. 19 December 1967
Leave..........................19 December 1967.......to.........2 January 1968
Electrician school............2 January 1968.......to...........14 June 1968
Leave.................................. 14 June 1968.......to............ 15 July 1968
Philippines........................... 15 July 1968.......to....... 13 January 1970
Leave............................. 13 January 1970.......to..... 12 February 1970
Mare Island.................. 12 February 1970.......to......... 13 March 1970
Vietnam ....13 March 1970.......to............. 15 July 1970
Leave.................................. 15 July 1970.......to........ 14 August 1970
Elkhorn .... 14 August 1970.......to.........3 August 1971
Treasure Island................. 3 August 1971.......to........ 17 August 1971
Discharged .... 17 August 1971
Termination of reserve duty 6 June 1973

GLOSSARY

AA: Anti-Aircraft

AC (Alternating Current): the movement of electric charge periodically reverses direction.

AD: Auxiliary Destroyer Tender, vessel

ADIOS: goodbye *(Spanish)*.

ADRIFT: loose from moorings; something out of place.

AFB: Air Force Base

AFDM: Auxiliary Floating Dry Dock, Medium

AFL-CIO (American Federation of Labor - Congress of Industrial Union): a national trade union center

AH: Auxiliary Hospital, vessel

AO DAIS: the national dress for Vietnamese women *(Vietnamese)*.

AOE (Auxiliary Oilers and Explosives): a fast combat support ship

AOG: Auxiliary Oiler Gasoline, vessel

AR: Auxiliary Repair, vessel

AGS: Auxiliary Hydrographic Survey ship

APB: Auxiliary Self-Propelled Barracks, vessel

ARD: Auxiliary Repair Dry Dock

ARL: Auxiliary Landing-Craft Repair ship

ARMORED CABLE: an electrical cable that is protected on the outside by a flexible sheath of knit aluminum.

ASAP: As Soon As Possible

ASW: Anti-Submarine Warfare

ATHWARTSHIP: from side to side of a ship; crosswise of a ship.

AWOL: Absent Without Leave

BB: Battleship

B.HP: brake horsepower

BAGUIO: typhoon *(Filipino)*.

BARRIO: district or neighborhood *(Spanish)*.

BALLAST: heavy weight in the hold of a vessel to maintain proper stability.

BALUTS: cooked eggs with baby ducks still inside of them.

BANCA BOAT: a dug out canoe used for transportation of produce and other materials.

BASO: drinking glass *(Filipino)*.

BASTUSIN: to act or speak indecently *(Filipino)*.

BAYANIHAN: a cooperative endeavor *(Filipino)*.

BEAM SEA: waves rolling directly against a ship's side, at or nearly at a right angle to its keel.

BEAUCOUP: a lot, a great deal, much, many *(French)*.

BELOW: short for below decks.

BENNIES (Benzedrine): an amphetamine.

BENNY BOYS: transvestites; boys dressed up like girls.

BILGES: the lower part of a vessel, underneath the deckplates, where waste water, oil, and seepage collect.

BILLET: allotted sleeping space; a man's position in a ship's organization.

BIRD FARM: an aircraft carrier.

BITAWAN: the place where cockfights are held *(Filipino)*.

BITAY: capital punishment; death *(Filipino)*.

BITS: a strong iron post on a ship's deck for working or fastening lines, almost invariably found in pairs.

BLACK GANG: slang for the engine room crew.

BM: Boatswain's Mate

BOOD: Barracks Officer Of the Day

BOONDOCKERS: a pair of leather work boots.

BOSTUSIN: rude and crude *(Filipino)*.

BOW: the forward section of a vessel.

BROW: a large gangplank leading from a ship to a pier or wharf, usually equipped with rollers on the bottom and hand rails on either side.

BROWNFOOT: slang for a Filipino.

BS: Bull Shit

BULKHEAD: on a ship this corresponds to the wall of a building on land.

BUSHIPS: the Navy organization responsible for designing, providing, and repairing ships and boats; and for all US Naval Shipyards and ship repair facilities.

C-RATS (C-ration): an individual canned, pre-cooked wet ration intended to be issued to US Military land forces when fresh or packaged unprepared food was not available.

CA: Armored Cruiser

CENTAVOS: the currency of Philippines (100 Centavo = 1 Peso)

CDO: Commanding Duty Officer

CGN: Guided Missile Cruiser Nuclear

CHEESE ROYALE: a man-friendly dish I created at the Town House Café. An open-face cheeseburger sandwich on toasted buns, topped with chili, topped with chopped onion and diced green peppers, all topped with grated cheddar cheese.

CHIT: a small, signed note giving authorization for a special request.

CIA: Central Intelligence Agency

CINC: Commander In Chief

CINCPACFLT: Commander In Chief of the Pacific Fleet

CINDERELLA LIBERTY: authorized absence only until midnight.

CIVVIES: civilian clothes.

CLEAT: a small deck fitting of metal with horns, used for securing lines.

CNO: Chief of Naval Operations

CO: Commanding Officer

COC: Change Of Command

COLORS: our national ensign; the US Flag. Also, the ceremonies performed on a naval installation when colors are hoisted at eight o'clock in the morning and hauled down at sunset.

COMMISSARY: a store handling food and personal supplies.

COMPRENDE: understand *(Spanish).*

CPO: Chief Petty Officer

CROW: the eagle symbol found on petty officer's badges and insignia.

CUBE: a cubical, or small compartment within a barracks to house 2 to 4 men.

CV or CVA: Aircraft Carrier

CVAN: Attack Aircraft Carrier Nuclear

DAVY JONES' LOCKER: the bottom of the sea.

DC: Douglas Commercial, airplane

DC (Direct Current): is the unidirectional flow of electric charge and is produced by such sources as batteries or thermocouples.

D: Australian designation for Destroyer

DD: Dishonorable Discharge or Destroyer

DE: Destroyer Escort

DEAD-PLANT: the engines shut off.

DECK: on a ship this corresponds to the floor of a building on land.

DECKAPE: slang for a seaman of the ship's company who work in the deck department.

DECKPLATES: steel plates of various sizes and shapes which comprise the deck of the engineering spaces, below which are the bilges.

DEEP SIX: to dispose of by throwing over the side into the ocean.

DESRON: Destroyer Squadron

DISPENSARY: a place on a military installation where medicines, medical care, and medical advice are given out.

DIYABLO LOSYON: Devil's Lotion *(Filipino).*

DMZ: Demilitarized Zone

DOD: Department Of Defense

DOG TAG: a metal identification disk used by servicemen, worn around the neck on a chain, and containing such information as service number, blood type, and religious preference if applicable.

DOLLAR: the currency of Hong Kong (1 Dollar = $0.18 US).

DREAM SHEET: the request of preferences for a duty station.

DRMS: Defense Reutilization and Marketing Service

EM: Electrician's Mate

EOD: Explosives, Ordnance, and Demolition

ESCAPE TRUNK: a long vertical shaft with a ladder in it, for connecting the lower levels of the ship to the main deck; an emergency escape route.

ESE: East South East

EXCHANGE: a place on a naval facility where department-store goods are sold to servicemen.

FANTAIL: the main deck section in the after part of a ship; the stern.

FATHOM: a six-foot unit of depth.

FBI: Federal Bureau of Investigation

FIELD DAY: a general cleaning period aboard ship or base, usually the day before an inspection.

FLICK: a movie.

FN: Fireman

FORECASTLE: (pronounced "foke-sull;" abbrev. fo'c'sle') the upper deck in the forward part of a ship.

FREEBOARD: the vertical distance, or the side of the hull, between the water line and the main deck or gunwale.

FUBAR: Fucked Up Beyond All Recognition

GALLEY: the ship's kitchen.

GEDUNK BAR: a small snack bar for junk food.

GI: any member of the United States Armed Forces, literally means Government Issue.

GIG: one of the ship's boats designated for commanding officer's use.

GM: General Motors

GOONEY BIRD: a common name for the Albatross bird.

GQ: General Quarters

GRAB-ASSING: all kinds of general horseplay.

GRINDER: the parade ground.

GUIDON: a small flag or streamer carried as a guide by the military; a small pennant representing a company or regiment.

GUNWALE: (pronounced "gunnel") the upper edge or rail of a ship or boat's side.

GUT NACHT (Gute nacht): good night or good evening *(German)*.

HAUOLI MAKAHIKI HU: Happy New Year *(Hawaiian)*.

HAWSER: heavy-duty line, five-inches or more in circumference, used for heavy work such as towing or mooring.

HEAD: a compartment on the ship having toilet facilities.

HEIWA: peace *(Japanese)*.

HOLE: slang for the engine room of a ship.

HOLIDAY ROUTINE: leisure routine followed aboard ship on Sundays and authorized holidays.

HMS: His Majesty's Ship

HUSQVARNA: a brand of motorcycle made in Sweden.

IC: Interior Communication

ICBB: Inter-Contental Ballistic Bite

JARHEAD: any member of the Marine Corps; not a derogatory term.

JEEPNEY: a reconverted US Army jeep, made into a covered taxi, which you enter and exit from the rear.

JP: a singularly disagreeable type of aviation fuel that is highly volatile and very unstable.

JODIE: a march ditty

KNOT: one nautical mile per hour. Never say "knots per hour;" this would be the same as saying "miles per hour per hour." (1 Knot = 1.15 mph).

KP: Kitchen Patrol

LAPU-LAPU: a grouper fish *(Filipino)*.

LASING: drunk *(Filipino)*.

LASINGERO: a drunkard *(Filipino)*.

LAZARETTE: a place on some ships, near the stern, in which supplies are kept.

LIMEYS: slang for British sailors.

LIBERTY: authorized absence of less than 48 hours.

LIFER: a military career officer.

LLAMADA: the favorite in a cockfight contest *(Filipino)*.

LPH: Landing Personnel Helicopter, vessel

LSD: Landing Ship Dock, vessel; a semi-synthetic psychedelic drug with unusual psychological effects, which include visuals of colored and crawling geometric patterns, and a sense of time distortion have made it one of the most widely known psychedelic drugs.

LST: Landing Ship Tank

LUMPIYA (Lumpia): a kind of shrimp, meat, and vegetable treat, rolled in thin flour wrappers and deep-fried crisp, then dipped in a sweet-and-sour sauce. *(Filipino)*.

MAA (Masters at Arms): a petty officer on a ship who keeps order and takes charge of any prisoners.

MABAHO: stinky *(Filipino)*.

MABUHAY: "long live!" *(Filipino)*.

MABUTI: better than average; good *(Filipino)*.

MAGANDA: beautiful *(Filipino)*.

MAHIYAIN: bashful *(Filipino)*.

MALAKI: large, big *(Filipino)*.

MALIGAYANG PASKOAT MANIGONG TAON: Merry Christmas and Happy New Year *(Tagalog)*.

MASARAP: delicious *(Filipino)*.

MECHANICAL FOAM: a combination of soybean oil, crushed animal blood, and other inert chemicals, used to smother fires quickly.

MELE KALIKIMAKA: Merry Christmas *(Hawaiian)*

MESSDECKS: the compartment aboard ship where the crew eats together.

MI: Military Intelligence

MID-RATS (Midnight Rations): food prepared for the watch-standers just beginning or ending security watches around midnight.

MIDWATCH: the 0000 to 0400 watch (midnight until 4:00 AM).

MISSILE HAZARDS: any loose or unsecured object which could potentially become a deadly moving hazard during the normal rolling of a ship at sea.

MP: Military Police

MPC: Military Payment Certificate

MPO: Motion Picture Operator

MONKEY FIST: a heavy ball of lead that's encased in a knot of rope.

MRF: Mobile Riverine Force

NAV REGS (Navy Regulations): the "Bible" of Naval procedures and rules.

NEST: two or more vessels moored alongside one another.

NON COMPOS MENTIS: not of sound mind *(Latin)*.

NOONER: a nap.

NTC: Naval Training Center

OBA: Oxygen Breathing Apparatus

OD: Officer of the Day

OJ: Orange Juice

OLD MAN: affectionate seamen's term for the captain of a ship.

OOC: Out Of Commission

OOD: Officer Of the Deck

ORI: Operation Readiness Inspection

OVERHEAD: on a ship this corresponds to the ceiling of a building on land.

PANSIT: noodle dishes *(Filipino)*.

PARADE REST: the formal position of rest with the feet 12 inches apart and, when unarmed, hand clasped behind the back; when armed, the left hand is behind the back and the right hand holds the rifle upright with its butt rest on the ground.

PBR (Patrol Boat Rapid): any of the small, agile, armed, swift patrol boats used for riverine duty in Vietnam.

PESO: the currency of the Philippines. (1 Peso = $0.25 US).

P.I.: Philippine Islands

PIASTER: an old currency of the Vietnamese (1 Piaster = $0.01 US).

PLANKTON: tiny sea plants and animals.

PM: Preventative Maintenance

PNS: Philippine News Service

PO: a term used to express respect *(Filipino)*.

POD (Plan of the Day): a comprehensive schedule of the days activities in work, training, recreation, etc.

POL: Petroleum-Oil-Lubricant pier

PORT: the left side of a ship when facing forward; originally called "larboard," which was often audibly confused with "starboard."

PUNJI: a booby trap set by a single stake placed upright in the ground.

PYROMETER: a gauge used for measuring the high temperatures found inside the cylinders of a diesel engine.

QUARTERDECK: that part of the main deck reserved for honors and ceremonies, and as the station of the Officer Of the Deck while in port.

QUOPPO: handsome *(Filipino)*.

RAT-GUARD: a wide disk of sheet metal fitted around a mooring line to prevent rats from boarding a vessel while tied to a dock in port.

REEFER: a refrigerator; or any refrigerator vessel used for carrying chilled and
    frozen foodstuffs. Also, a marijuana cigarette.

REF-TRA: Refresher Training

REVEILLE: the wake-up call for soldiers and sailors in the morning.

R&O: Receiving and Outfitting

R&R (Rest and Relaxation): a short holiday away from duties; leave.

RIOT GUNS: sawed off shot guns that fired tiny metal arrowheads.

ROACH COACH: a mobile snack canteen which usually services the sailors from
    the piers.

SALAMAT: thank you *(Filipino)*

SALAMAT PO: thank you very much *(Filipino)*.

SARI-SARI: convenience store *(Tagalog)*.

SCOPE DOPE: a radarman.

SCULLERY: the compartment for washing and sterilizing eating utensils and trays.

SCUPPER: opening in the side of the ship to carry off water from the deck.

SCUTTLE: a small opening through a hatch cover, deck, or bulkhead to provide
    access to a compartment; to attempt to sink by opening holes in a ship's
    hull.

SCUTTLEBUTT: a drinking fountain; also, a rumor, usually of local importance.

SDS (Students for a Democratic Society): a radical political organization in the
    United States during the 1960's. Most of its members were college students
    or young people. They opposed United States participation in the Vietnam
    War, and what they called the hypocrisy of American society.

SEA PRINTS: movie reels taken along on voyages, then turned back in to the
    Movie Exchange at different bases or even traded with other ships.

SERVPAC: the service fleet in the Pacific, usually smaller auxiliary vessels used to
    service the larger, more important combat ships.

SF: Special Forces

SHITCAN: to throw away; a garbage can.

SIGE: to leave *(Filipino)*.

SK: Storekeeper

SKATE: to goof off, to shirk work, to have a light work load.

SKIVVIES: underwear.

SKYLARKING: general horsing around instead of working; originally to run up and
    down the rigging of a ship in sport; new Navy word for goofing off.

SNAFU: Situation Normal All Fucked Up

SNIPE: slang for members of the engineering department on a ship. Includes enginemen, electricians, boiler technicians, machinist mates, damage controlmen, etc.

SOB: Sonuvabitch

S.O.S. (Save Our Ship): a call for help at sea; also, shit-on-a-shingle, a type of creamed chipped beef served over toast, generally for breakfast, universally despised.

SP: Shore Patrol

SPACE: a compartment.

SPARKY: a term of endearment for an electrician.

SQUARED AWAY: settled down and all in order.

SQUID: any member of the US Navy.

SRF: Ship Repair Facility

SS (Submersible Ship): a submarine.

STARBOARD: the right side of a ship when facing forward.

STATESIDE: back in the United States.

STERN: the after part of a ship.

STEWBURNER: slang terminology for cooks and their assistants aboard ships.

SURVEY: to throw away, or toss over the side.

TAPS: the bugle call for lights out at night.

TDE: Training Destroyer Escort

TENDER: an auxiliary vessel with many different types of shops aboard that repair ships and aircraft.

TGIF: Thank God It's Friday

T.I.: Treasure Island

TIN CAN: a destroyer or destroyer escort.

TURN TO: an order to begin work.

ULAN: rain *(Filipino)*.

USAFI: United States Armed Forces Institute

USN: United States Navy

USO: United Service Organization

VD: Venereal Disease

VOID: an empty space inside the armored hull of the ship, used for protection or control of list and trim.

VOILA: a term to express sucess or satisfaction *(French)*.

WALLA-WALLAS: delightful little motorized water taxis which transport you any time of the day or night, generally for just one Hong Kong dollar (18 cents).

WATER KING: the petty officer in charge of fresh water storage and transfer.

WAVES (Women Appointed for Voluntary Emergency Service): female members of the US Navy.

WEATHER DECK: that portion of the main, forecastle, poop, and upper deck exposed to the weather.

WESPAC: the Western Pacific region.

WSW: West South West

XO (Executive Officer): the second-in-command below the captain on a ship.

YD: Yard Derrick, vessel

YELO: ice *(Filipino)*.

YEN: the currency of the Japanese (100 Yen = $0.36 US).

YG: Yard Garbage, vessel

YO: Yard Oiler, vessel

YTM (literally, Yard Tug Medium): a medium harbor tugboat.

YW: (Yard Waterer, vessel): a small boat that takes fresh water out to the bigger ships in the harbor.

Z-GRAM: far-reaching Navy directives which further improve the lot of the common sailor.

ZIPPO: Vietnam military slang for bits of branches or debris floating down a river, under which are sometimes lurking Viet Cong soldiers attempting to attach mines to ships.